READINGS IN THE CONCEPT AND MEASUREMENT OF INCOME

READINGS IN THE CONCEPT AND MEASUREMENT OF INCOME

Edited with an introduction by

R.H.PARKER

Associate Professor of Finance
European Institute of Business Administration
Fontainebleau

and

G.C.HARCOURT

Professor of Economics
University of Adelaide
Sometime Fellow of
Trinity Hall, Cambridge

CAMBRIDGE at the University Press

1969

Published by the Syndics of the Cambridge University Press
Bentley House, 200 Euston Road, London N.W.1
American Branch: 32 East 57th Street, New York, N.Y. 10022

This selection and Introduction © Cambridge University Press 1969

Library of Congress Catalogue Card Number: 75–87137
Standard Book Numbers:
521 09591 3 paperback
521 07463 0 clothbound

Printed in Great Britain
at the University Printing House, Cambridge
(Brooke Crutchley, University Printer)

328065

Contents

Contents

Contents

Acknowledgements

We are greatly indebted to all the authors, editors and publishers who have so kindly allowed us to reprint the papers included in this book and to Mr D. M. Nuti, of King's College Cambridge, for the information contained in the editorial footnote on page 370. A number of our academic colleagues (notably Professor W. T. Baxter of the London School of Economics, Mr P. A. Bird of the University of Kent at Canterbury, Mr W. Birkett of the University of Sydney and Professor D. Solomons of the Wharton School of Finance and Commerce, University of Pennsylvania) read drafts of the introduction and gave us good advice, but we are, of course, solely responsible for the final result.

Throughout these *Readings*, references in square brackets refer to the reprint in this book, not to the original.

Introduction

'A man will turn over half a library to make one book.'
Samuel Johnson as reported in Boswell's *Life*, 6 April 1775.

PLAN OF THE BOOK

The purpose of this book of readings is to bring together under one cover some important writings in economic and accounting literature on the concept and measurement of income. It is hoped that the book will be of interest to both economists and accountants. The papers chosen for reprinting (but not this introduction) reflect a bias towards economics rather than accounting, partly because accountants are already blessed with at least three excellent books of readings* with which we are in no way trying to compete.

We have divided the book into six sections. In the first section various concepts of income are discussed by Fisher, Lindahl, Simons, Hicks, Frankel and Solomons. Most economists (with the notable exception of Fisher) have included the 'maintenance of capital intact' as part of their definition of income. In the second section we reprint from the pages of *Economica* a discussion by Pigou, Hayek and Hicks of the meaning of this concept. In the third section we reprint two surveys of the economic literature on income. Wueller surveys the little-known nineteenth-century German contribution to concepts of taxable income and Kaldor discusses the contributions of such economists as Fisher, Lindahl and Hicks.

The fourth section is concerned with the measurement of business income. Bell summarizes the influential ideas put forward by Edwards and himself in their book *The Theory and Measurement of Business Income.* Paish and Mathews and Grant express differing ideas on the effects of changing price levels on the measurement of business income. Baxter discusses the possible contribution to the trade cycle of conventional methods of measuring business income; Edey traces the effect of accounting practice on taxable income; and Parker discusses the origins of the lower of cost and market rule of inventory valuation.

* W. T. Baxter and S. Davidson (eds.), *Studies in Accounting Theory* (London, 1962); S. Davidson, D. Green, Jr, C. T. Horngren and G. Sorter (eds.), *An Income Approach to Accounting Theory* (Englewood Cliffs, N.J., 1964); S. A. Zeff and T. F. Keller (eds.), *Financial Accounting Theory* (New York, 1964).

I

Introduction

The fifth section includes four papers on the vexed problem of depreciation. Hotelling and Wright concern themselves with general theories of depreciation; A. R. Prest discusses replacement cost depreciation; and Harcourt analyses the discrepancies between the economist's and the accountant's measures of the rate of profit which arise from their different methods of measuring depreciation and valuing capital.

The sixth and final section contains three articles on national income accounting. In an historically important paper Meade and Stone discuss the construction of tables of national income, expenditure, savings and investment. The problem of measuring economic growth is analysed in an excerpt from the Australian *Report of the Committee of Economic Enquiry*. The national accounting conventions used in Eastern Europe and the Soviet Union, which still differ widely from those currently used in the West, are surveyed in a note of the *Secretariat of the Economic Commission for Europe*.

Choosing articles for inclusion in a book of readings is an exercise of some delicacy and difficulty. How was it done in this case? Our first criterion was merit: we hope it will be agreed that all the items included make a contribution to our understanding of the concepts and measurement of income. But so, we hasten to admit, do many articles not included in this volume. Limitations of space and time have forced us to adopt certain constraints. No attempt has been made to include translations of papers in languages other than English. Other things being equal, short papers have been preferred to long ones. We have excluded some important papers because they are readily available elsewhere, e.g. Sidney S. Alexander (revised David Solomons), 'Income Measurement in a Dynamic Economy' and Ronald S. Edwards, 'The Nature and Measurement of Income' both of which are reprinted in Baxter and Davidson's *Studies in Accounting Theory*. On the other hand, their relative inaccessibility encouraged us to include Lindahl's 'The Concept of Income' (from *Essays in Honour of Gustav Cassel*) and an extract from the Australian *Report of the Committee of Economic Enquiry*. We have purposely not limited ourselves to one or two journals. Reprints are included from *Abacus, Accounting Research, The Accounting Review, British Tax Review, Economica, The Economic Journal, Journal of Accounting Research, Journal of the American Statistical Association, Oxford Economic Papers, Political Science Quarterly*, and the *U.N. Economic Bulletin for Europe*. No previously unpublished papers are included.

We have not consciously chosen articles just because we agree with the opinions of the author and we have tried hard to represent various points of view, but the fact that so many of the papers in this book were written by present or former members of the University of Cambridge, the London

School of Economics and the University of Adelaide is due no doubt not only to the excellence of those institutions but also to the academic background and prejudice of the editors.

PLAN OF THE INTRODUCTION

In the remainder of this introduction we discuss some of the problems of defining and measuring income and the solutions suggested by the authors represented in this book. We have not hesitated to make clear our own views or, occasionally, to bring in the views of some authors not represented in this book whose writings are readily available.

We first of all discuss whether income measurement is useful. Having decided that it is, we look in some detail at a number of *ex post* concepts of *business* income and conclude that the concept relevant to most situations is what we call 'real income' which is divided into 'current operating profit' and 'real holding gains'. We then consider the problem of valuing non-monetary assets and some of the practical problems of measuring the concepts we find most relevant. Finally we discuss briefly the use of current operating profit and real holding gains as tax bases.

IS INCOME MEASUREMENT USEFUL?

Why measure income? Hicks suggests that 'income', like 'saving', 'depreciation' and 'investment', is a rough approximation used by the businessman to steer himself through the bewildering changes of situation which confront him and that the purpose of income calculations in practical affairs is to give people an indication of the amount which they can consume without impoverishing themselves [p. 75]. Income is, as Solomons points out [pp. 107–8], currently used as a measure of taxable capacity, as a determinant of corporate dividend policy, as a guide to investment policy, and as a measure of the success of the management of business enterprise. He would no doubt have added, if he had been writing for a different audience, that income is also used as a measure of the success of the management of an economy.

All these uses can be criticized. Kaldor's criticism of income as a measure of taxable capacity is well known;* Solomons suggests that command over capital resources is a fairer guide to ability to pay taxes and thinks that a system of direct taxation could get along quite well, and perhaps better, with no concept of income at all. In defence of income tax one might reply, first that the major industrial nations show no signs of abandoning the taxation of income (this retort carries much practical weight

* *An Expenditure Tax* (London, 1955).

3

but is not very convincing conceptually); secondly, that arguments in favour of taxing expenditure or capital are not necessarily arguments against taxing income as well; and thirdly, that the concepts of income and capital are so intertwined that one cannot escape the difficulties of defining income by trying to define capital instead.

Solomons rightly points out that using periodic income as a guide to corporate dividend policy may be inadequate if the losses of previous periods or the need for short-term solvency are ignored. But this does not necessrily mean that we should abandon our measure of income, although it may be that we need a better concept or a more precise measure of the concept. We must also recognize clearly that income may only be one of a number of measures which need to be considered.

It must be admitted that income as a guide to investment policy or as a measure of business or national economic success may suffer from being overmuch concerned with the past rather than the future. It is nevertheless true that the past can be of some help in forecasting the future and that shareholders and citizens need a report of stewardship from their company or government.

SOME INCOME CONCEPTS

There is no reason to suppose that there is only one useful concept of income. Even a cursory glance at the contributions to this book suggests that there are many possible concepts. Economists, mindful of Jevons's remark that 'bygones are forever bygones', have tended to define income in terms of expectations. The best-known definition is that of Hicks in *Value and Capital*, the maximum value which [a man] can consume during a week, and still *expect* to be as *well off* at the end of the week as he was at the beginning (italics added). The difficulties of attaching any precise meaning to this definition are well known and are explained at some length by Hicks himself [pp. 75–82]. Kaldor argues that if we define income in terms of expectations neither income *ex ante* nor income *ex post* can be objectively measured. For if K_1 and K_2 are the 'actual' value of assets at the beginning and end of an accounting period; K_2' is the value which the assets are expected to have at the end of the period; and K_1' is the revised value of the assets at the beginning of the period as estimated at the end of the period; then

$$\text{income } \textit{ex ante} \text{ is } K_2' - K_1$$
$$\text{income } \textit{ex post} \text{ is } K_2 - K_1'$$

and both of these concepts depend on a hypothetical value (K_2' or K_1') [pp. 168–9].

4

One could, however, following Hicks, define income *ex post* as $K_2 - K_1$, whilst retaining income *ex ante* as $K_2' - K_1$. We shall discuss later some of the problems of measuring $K_2 - K_1$, but it is worth noting that these definitions are not too far away from contemporary accounting practice and are useful both for planning and control and for stewardship reporting. At the beginning of a period an individual or firm has a known set of assets, K_1, and plans to have, based on his or its expectations of the future, a set K_2' at the end of the period. By measurement at the end of the period he finds that he has, in fact, K_2. The extent to which the plans and expectations are not realized, $K_2 - K_2'$, will show up as a 'variance' (in the cost accounting sense of that word) which can be used as a guide to corrective action. For reporting to shareholders and as a base for income tax $K_2 - K_1$ is (subject to the discussion below) the relevant concept.

As Hicks has shown it is possible to construct a number of *ex post* $(K_2 - K_1)$ concepts of income. The one which he considers to be the most objective is, for an individual, 'the value of the individual's consumption *plus* the increment in the money value of his prospect which has accrued during the week' [p. 81]. This, claims Hicks, is not subjective but is almost completely objective since the capital values of the individual's property both at the beginning and end of the week are assessable quantities. It follows that the income of all individuals can be aggregated without difficulty and the same definition of income applied to the community as a whole. This concept we shall call *money income*:

a man's money income in any period is equal to the money value of his consumption plus the increase in the money value of his capital assets. For the sum of these two is the amount which he could have spent on consumption *while maintaining the money value of his capital stock intact.* [Meade and Stone, p. 332.]

A similar concept is put forward by Simons [p. 68]:

Personal income connotes, broadly, the exercise of control over the use of society's scarce resources. It has to do not with sensations, services, or goods but rather with rights which command prices (or to which prices may be imputed). Its calculation implies estimate (*a*) of the amount by which the value of a person's store of property rights would have increased, as between the beginning and end of the period, if he had consumed (destroyed) nothing, or (*b*) of the value of rights which he might have exercised in consumption without altering the value of his store of rights. In other words, it implies estimate of consumption and accumulation.

We shall discuss in more detail later the meaning of such phrases as 'money value of his capital assets' and 'the value of a person's store of property rights'.

For a business enterprise we can, following the work of Edwards and Bell,*

---

* E. O. Edwards and P. W. Bell, *The Theory and Measurement of Business Income* (Berkeley & Los Angeles, 1961). Our debt to their book is obvious.

divide money income into (*a*) *current operating profit* (or 'current income' as Mathews and Grant, pp. 201–14 below, call it); and (*b*) *holding gains*. Current operating profit is defined as 'the excess over a period of the current value of output sold over the current cost of the related inputs' [Bell, p. 187]. A holding gain arises whenever the current market value of an asset exceeds its historical cost [p. 186].

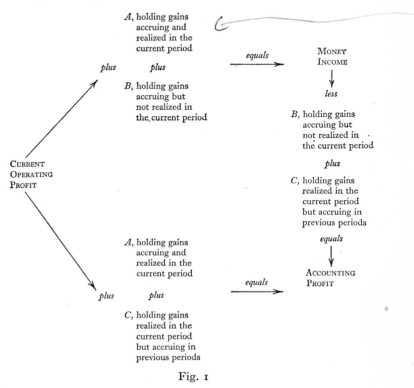

Fig. 1

Neither money income nor current operating profit is equivalent to *accounting profit* as found in business practice. This is usually defined as the difference between the historical costs of the net assets at the beginning and end of an accounting period (net of depreciation of fixed assets based on historical cost) after adjusting for new capital introduced and for dividends or other distributions to proprietors. The most important exception to this rule—the valuation of inventories at market value—is only applied when the effect is to reduce accounting profit. Ignoring this, the difference between money income and accounting profit will be made up of: (i) holding gains which have accrued during the current accounting period but have

6

not yet been 'realized'; (ii) *less* holding gains which accrued in previous accounting periods and have been 'realized' in the current period. There is clearly one other kind of holding gain: (iii) those holding gains which have both accrued and been 'realized' during the current accounting period.

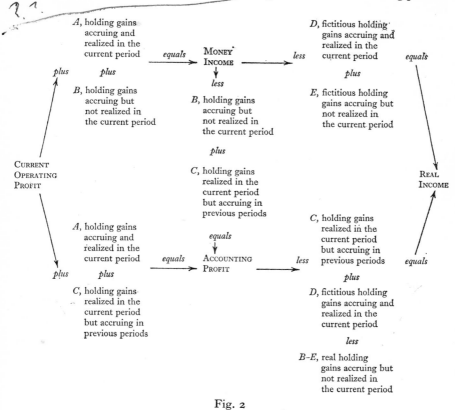

Fig. 2

A holding gain may be 'realized' either directly by sale of the asset concerned (a building, for example) or indirectly when the asset concerned (e.g. raw materials) is converted and sold in the form of finished goods.

The relationship between money income, current operating profit and accounting profit is shown in Fig. 1.

Neither money income nor accounting profit makes any allowance for changes in the general price level, both real gains resulting from changes in relative prices and fictitious gains resulting from the effects of a rise in the general price level being regarded as income. There is clearly room for a concept of *real income*. For a man this is 'the value of his expenditure

7

on consumption plus the value of any increase in the real amount of his capital assets' [Meade and Stone, p. 332]. For a business enterprise, real income can be obtained by separating holding gains into their real and fictitious elements. Figure 2 shows the relationship between current operating profit, accounting profit, money income and real income.

It could be argued that holding gains and losses should be regarded not as part of income but as changes in capital. This is really a matter of definition. Fisher, for example,* defined income to exclude savings but, as Kaldor points out:

If we defined income as consumption we should still require another term to denote as potential income the consumption that would obtain if net savings were zero. Hence apart from the trivial question of which is the right use of words, it is evident that income and consumption (as ordinarily understood) do not refer to the same thing, but to two different things; and if we reserved the term income for consumption we should still need another term for what would otherwise be called income; and we should still be left with the problem of how to define the latter [p. 164].

Similarly, if one *defines* income as resulting only from operations then holding gains can clearly not be included but one still needs a name to describe that increase in real wealth which we have called 'real income'.

Holding gains (or losses) can arise on both monetary and non-monetary assets.† Consider a firm which during an accounting period has no transactions and holds the same quantities of net monetary assets (e.g. cash *plus* debtors *minus* creditors) and non-monetary assets (e.g. land, machinery, inventories) at the beginning and end of the period. The net assets at the beginning can be written as

$$M_0 + N_0 \tag{1}$$

where M_0 = net monetary assets, N_0 = non-monetary assets.

If during the period the general price level rises by a rate p, and the specific price level of non-monetary assets by a rate r, then at the end of the period the net assets in end-of-period market prices will be

$$M_0 + N_0(1 + r). \tag{2}$$

M_0 has not changed because the monetary value of cash, debtors and creditors has not changed.

To discover the 'real income' of the period we must subtract expression (1) from expression (2) *after* allowing for the change in the general price level. Thus although 'money income' would be

$$M_0 + N_0(1 + r) - (M_0 + N_0) = N_0 r, \tag{3}$$

---

* I. Fisher, *The Nature of Capital and Income* (New York, 1906).
† The next few paragraphs owe much to R. J. Chambers, *Accounting, Evaluation and Economic Behavior* (Englewood Cliffs, N.J., 1966), ch. 10.

real income will be

$$M_0 + N_0(1+r) - (M_0+N_0)(1+p) = N_0(r-p) - M_0 p. \tag{4}$$

By not changing the quantities of the assets, current operating profit has been assumed to be zero, so it follows that equation (4) represents the real holding gains (or losses) accruing during the period (realized and unrealized). These arise both from the effect on non-monetary assets of the differential movement of specific and general prices, and from holding monetary assets through a change in the general price level.

Dropping the assumption that M_0 and N_0 are constant in quantity throughout the accounting period, let M_1 and N_1 be the values of net monetary assets and non-monetary assets at end-of-period prices. This means that real income will be

$$(M_1+N_1) - (M_0+N_0)(1+p). \tag{5}$$

Subtracting the holding gain element, current operating profit will be

$$(M_1+N_1) - (M_0+N_0)(1+p) - [N_0(r-p) - M_{0p}]$$
$$= (M_1+N_1) - [M_0+N_0(1+r)], \tag{6}$$

i.e. current operating profit is equal to the difference between the current values of the net assets at the end of the period and the end-of-period values of the opening net assets.

Current operating profit is not, however, measured in practice by the comparison of two balance sheets but by the recording of revenues and expenses. Expression (5) and equation (6) need to be rewritten accordingly. Assume that non-monetary assets are divided into fixed assets (F) and inventories (I), that their values increase at a rate r during the accounting period, and that all transactions take place on the last day of the period. This ignores the problem, which we shall discuss later, of holding gains on assets acquired during an accounting period. In summary a typical period's transactions might be as follows:

(a) Bought goods costing P, thus increasing inventories and decreasing monetary assets.

(b) Sold goods whose current cost was Q, receiving in exchange monetary assets of S.

(c) Fixed assets depreciated (in current values) by D.

(d) Used monetary assets of E to pay other expenses.

From the above:
$$M_1 - M_0 = S - P - E$$
$$N_1 - N_0 = (F+I)r + P - Q - D.$$

9

Introduction

Equation (6) can now be rewritten as

$$S - Q - D - E, \tag{7}$$

i.e. current operating profit = sales *less* current cost of goods sold, depreciation at current cost and other expenses.

Similarly expression (5) can be rewritten as

$$S - Q - D - E + (F + I)(r - p) - M_0 p, \tag{8}$$

i.e. real income = current operating profit + real holding gains accruing.

We have so far distinguished three *ex post* concepts of income: accounting profit, money income and real income. A fourth concept, which we shall call adjusted accounting profit (or adjusted historical cost), has been supported by a number of economists and accountants. With this concept changes in relative price levels are ignored but a general price index is used to adjust for changes in the general price level. Thus, during an accounting period in which there are changes in relative and general prices but no change in the quantities of assets held, adjusted accounting profit will be

$$M_0 + N_0(1 + p) - (M_0 + N_0)(1 + p) = - M_0 p,$$

compared with an unadjusted accounting profit of zero, money income of $N_0 r$ and real income of $N_0(r - p) - M_0 p$.

ARITHMETICAL ILLUSTRATION OF FOUR INCOME CONCEPTS

As a simple arithmetical illustration of the four income concepts of accounting profit, real income, adjusted accounting profit and current operating profit (current income) consider the following example which is an adaptation of one given recently by Professor Baxter.* A firm starts with a capital of £1,300 in cash and uses £1,000 of this to buy goods for resale. Three-quarters of the goods are sold at retail for £1,500 at a time when the wholesale replacement cost of all the goods bought is £1,560 (i.e. the special index has increased from 100 to 156). During the same period, the general index has increased from 100 to only 120.

Balance sheets drawn up under four different income concepts are shown below for

(*a*) the start of the period;

(*b*) immediately after the increases in the assets' replacement cost and in the general index but before the sale; and

(*c*) immediately after the sale.

---

* W. T. Baxter, 'General or Special Index?—Capital maintenance under changing prices', *Journal UEC*, no. 3 (July 1967). Professor Baxter does not necessarily agree with our conclusions.

BALANCE SHEETS

Price Change (handwritten)

	(1) Start £	(2) Before sale £	(3) After sale £
I *Accounting profit*			
Assets			
Cash	1,300	300	1,800
Inventory at historical cost	.	1,000	250
	£1,300	£1,300	£2,050
Proprietorship			
Capital	1,300	1,300	1,300
Profit	.	.	750
	£1,300	£1,300	£2,050
II *Real income*			
Assets			
Cash	1,300	300	1,800
Inventory at current value	.	1,560	390 (a)
	£1,300	£1,860	£2,190
Proprietorship			
Capital			
historical	1,300	1,300	1,300
inflation adjustment	.	260 (b)	260 (b)
Real holding gain on inventory			
unrealized	.	360 (c)	90 (c)
realized	.	.	270 (c)
Loss on holding money	.	−60 (c)	−60 (c)
Current operating profit	.	.	330 (d)
	£1,300	£1,860	£2,190
III *Adjusted accounting profit*			
Assets			
Cash	1,300	300	1,800
Inventory at adjusted historical cost	.	1,200 (e)	300 (e)
	£1,300	£1,500	£2,100
Proprietorship			
Capital			
historical	1,300	{1,300	{1,300
inflation adjustment	.	{260 (b)	{260 (b)
Loss on holding money	.	−60 (f)	−60 (f)
Profit	.	.	600
	£1,300	£1,500	£2,100

Handwritten annotations:
75% Sold

II
Sales 1500
Cos (1200 × 75%) 900
600

	(1) Start £	(2) Before sale £	(3) After sale £
IV *Current operating profit*			
Assets			
Cash	1,300	300	1,800
Inventory at current value	.	1,560	390 (a)
	£1,300	£1,860	£2,190
Proprietorship			
Capital			
historical	1,300	1,300	1,300
inventory revaluation reserve	.	560 (g)	560 (g)
Current operating profit	.	.	330 (d)
	£1,300	£1,860	£2,190

The income statements resulting from the various methods are given below.

INCOME STATEMENTS

	(1) Accounting profit £	(2) Real income £	(3) Adjusted accounting profit £	(4) Current operating profit £
Sales	1,500	1,500	1,500	1,500
Cost of goods sold:				
Historical	−750	.	−750	.
Inflation adjustment	.	.	−150	.
Adjusted historical	.	.	−900	.
Current	.	−1,170	.	−1,170
Current operating profit	.	330	.	330
Real holding gain (net)	.	300 (c)	.	.
Loss on holding money	.	.	−60	.
Income	£750	£630	£540	£330

Notes

(a) The current value of the goods remaining in stock, i.e. $\frac{1}{4} \times £1,560$.

(b) The inflation adjustment is derived by multiplying the opening capital by the rate of change in the *general* price level.

(c) The unrealized holding gain on inventory is £1,000 $(0.56−0.20) = £360$ before sale, and $\frac{1}{4} \times £360 = £90$ after sale. The realized holding gain is $\frac{3}{4} \times £360 = £270$. The loss on holding money is $£300 \times 0.2 = £60$.

(d) The current operating profit can be derived either from a comparision of balace sheets (second and third columns),

$$(M_1 + N_1) − [M_0 + N_0(1 + r)] = £(1,800 + 390) − £(300 + 1,560) = £2,190 − £1,860 = £330,$$

or by deducting current cost of goods sold from sales, $£1,500 − £1,170 = £330$.

(e) The inventory at adjusted historical cost is derived by multiplying the purchase price of the goods by the change in the *general* price index.

(f) The loss on holding money is Mp, i.e. £300 × 0·2 = £60.

(g) The inventory revaluation reserve represents the difference between the historical and current costs of inventory purchased; it is the equivalent on the credit side of revaluing the asset on the debit side.

Income concept I, accounting profit, represents conventional practice but is clearly unsatisfactory in that it completely ignores market values and changing price levels. Income concept III, adjusted accounting profit or the use of a general price index only, is an improvement but it still ignores market values and it still reflects the unwillingness of accountants to abandon historical cost. There is no real violation of the 'historical cost convention' but merely a recognition that the unit of account is elastic. For this reason it may be that this is the only method which has any chance of acceptance in practice. Certainly half a loaf is better than no bread, but it is important to recognize that a second-best solution will have been adopted. The results reflect the change in the general price level, and once agreement has been reached on the index to be used the method can be objectively applied. On the other hand, an historical cost remains an historical cost even when it has been adjusted by a general price index. It does not represent a current valuation. It is possible for the prices of particular goods to differ quite markedly from the change in the general price level. For example, Whitehead and Cockburn in their study of prices and productivity in 39 Australian manufacturing industries for the period 1954–8 point out that whilst during this period the consumer price index rose from 101·4 (September quarter 1954) to 114·8 (June quarter 1958) and the wholesale price index from 322 to 339, 14 of the industries showed overall reductions in 1954–5, 11 in 1955–6, 6 in 1956–7 and 12 in 1957–8.*

Income concepts II and IV, real income and current operating profit, are the only ones which bring current market values into the balance sheet and in fact the assets side of their balance sheets is identical. The two concepts differ only in their handling of holding gains. The latter concept ignores changes in the general price level and excludes real holding gains from income.

A possible compromise might be to produce financial statements that disclosed more than one concept of business income. It would not be difficult to combine income concepts I, II and IV (accounting profit, real

* D. H. Whitehead, 'Price-Cutting and Wage Policy', *Economic Record*, XXXIX (June 1963), 189. For some British data see W. A. H. Godley and C. Gillion, 'Pricing Behaviour in the Engineering Industry', *National Institute Economic Review*, no. 28 (May 1964), pp. 50–2.

income and current operating profit). The income statement would be as follows:

Sales
less historical cost of goods sold
historical depreciation
other expenses
equals Accounting profit
less holding gains *realized* (whether accruing or
not) in the current period
equals Current operating profit
plus real holding gains *accruing* (but not necessarily
realized) in the current period
equals Real income

This statement is equivalent to a clockwise movement around Fig. 2 [p. 7 above] starting at Accounting profit and going from Current operating profit to Real income in one jump instead of two.

Using our existing arithmetical illustration gives:

COMBINED INCOME STATEMENT

	£
Sales	1,500
Historical cost of goods sold	750
Accounting profit	750
Excess of current over historical cost of goods sold	420
Current operating profit	330
Real holding gain (net)	300
Real income	630

BALANCE SHEET

	(1) Start £	(2) Before sale £	(3) After sale £
Assets			
Cash	1,300	300	1,800
Inventory			
historical cost	.	1,000	250
excess of current over historical cost	.	560	140
current cost	.	1,560	390
	£1,300	£1,860	£2,190

14

	(1) Start £	(2) Before sale £	(3) After sale £
Proprietorship			
Capital			
historical	1,300	1,300	1,300
inflation adjustment	.	260	260
Accounting profit	.	.	750
Excess of current over historical cost of goods sold	.	.	−420
Current operating profit	.	.	330
Real holding gain (net)	.	300	300
	£1,300	£1,860	£2,190

THE VALUATION OF NON-MONETARY ASSETS

It is worth pausing at this point to remind ourselves that the 'accounting profit' which we regard as the least useful of the concepts discussed is, however, the dominant one in accounting practice. Why have accountants been so reluctant to adopt another concept? There are at least four possible reasons.

(i) Accountants are 'practical' men and like most practical men they tend to 'repeat the mistakes of their forefathers' and to avoid solving theoretical problems. One certainly gets the impression that the leading professional accounting bodies in Britain and the United States have hoped that if they waited long enough the problems of accounting for changing price levels would fade away.

For example, the Council of the Institute of Chartered Accountants in England and Wales accepts that the significance of accounts prepared on the basis of historical costs is subject to limitations and that the results shown by such accounts are (*a*) not a measure of increase or decrease in wealth in terms of purchasing power, or of the amount which can prudently be regarded as available for distribution; (*b*) not necessarily suitable for purposes such as price fixing, wage negotiations and taxation. In spite of this, the Council has been unable to find a practicable and generally acceptable alternative. It has recommended that fixed assets should not, in general, be written up, 'especially in the absence of monetary stability'.*

Similarly, the American Institute of Certified Public Accountants has stated that 'accounting and financial reporting for general use will best serve their purposes by adhering to the generally accepted concept of

---

* Institute of Chartered Accountants in England and Wales, *Recommendation on Accounting Principles*, no. 15, 'Accounting in Relation to Changes in the Purchasing Power of Money' (issued 30 May 1952), paragraphs 28 and 30.

depreciation on [historical] cost, at least until the dollar is stabilized at some level'. In 1961, however, the Institute's Accounting Principles Board agreed that 'the assumption in accounting that fluctuations in the value of the dollar may be ignored is unrealistic'. As a result the authors of an accounting research study published by the Institute in 1963 concluded that 'recognition of price-level changes in financial statements is practical, and not misleading or dangerous' and recommended that the effects of such change should be disclosed as a supplement to the conventional statements. A single index of the general price level should be used,* i.e. the concept of 'adjusted accounting profit' should be adopted.

(ii) In most countries historical cost is used for taxation purposes. Historical cost is unlikely to be abandoned for income measurement so long as its use is compulsory for the measurement of taxable income.

(iii) The practising accountant can legitimately complain that the critics of historical cost have failed to agree among themselves as to the alternative which should be adopted.

(iv) But what makes most practising accountants (and some academic accountants also) cling to historical cost is the fear that although published financial statements might gain in relevance they would lose their present objectivity. We can be sympathetic to this plea for objectivity without accepting that historical cost is necessarily more objective than market value. It is well known that even depreciation based on historical cost is an estimate. It is perhaps not so well known that the so-called historical cost of a manufactured article depends on a number of rather arbitrary decisions about which overheads are 'inventoriable' (a useful but horrible word) and how they should be allocated between jobs or processes. On the other hand, many, though admittedly not all, assets have easily verifiable market values.

Many assets have market values which differ according to whether one is a buyer or a seller. Edwards and Bell† call these 'entry' and 'exit' values respectively. Clearly, we can subdivide our concepts of money income and real income according to whether we use entry values only, exit values only or some combination of the two. This is illustrated in the table below.

	Money income	Real income
Entry values only	'Business profit'	'Real business profit'
Exit values only	'Realizable profit'	'Real realizable profit'

* American Institute of Certified Public Accountants, Accounting Research Study no. 6, *Reporting the Financial Effects of Price-Level Changes* (New York, 1963), p. xi. The sources of the earlier quotations can be found in ch. 9 of Accounting Research Study no. 7, *Inventory of Generally Accepted Accounting Principles for Business Enterprises* (New York, 1965), by Paul Grady.
† *Business Income*, p. 75.

The titles in quotation marks are taken from Edwards and Bell. They regard all four concepts as useful but develop their arguments mainly in terms of 'business profit'.

There is, however, a strong argument for a concept of income which uses both entry and exit prices.* An upper limit to the value of an asset to a firm is set by its current replacement cost (RC), for the loss which the firm suffers from being deprived of the asset cannot exceed the cost of restoring it to its former position. Other possible values are net realizable value (NRV), the present value (PV) of the expected net cash receipts from the asset where this differs from RC and NRV, and the present value of the best alternative use of the funds locked up in the asset. We define NRV to be the larger of net realizable value and (in a capital-rationing situation) the present value of the best alternative investment. The six possible relationships between RC, NRV and PV can be set out as follows:

1	NRV > PV > RC	4	PV > NRV > RC
2	NRV > RC > PV	5	RC > PV > NRV
3	PV > RC > NRV	6	RC > NRV > PV

The relevant value to the firm in each case can be worked out in the following manner:

(a) Divide the cases into two groups according to whether the asset should be held for use or resale. This is roughly but not exactly the same as the accountant's distinction between fixed and current assets. An asset should be held for use only where PV > NRV. Thus we have:

Use		Resale	
3	PV > RC > NRV	1	NRV > PV > RC
4	PV > NRV > RC	2	NRV > RC > PV
5	RC > PV > NRV	6	RC > NRV > PV

(b) If we now delete all NRVs from the 'use' group as irrelevant and all PVs from the 'resale' group as irrelevant and also remember that the upper limit of value to the firm is current replacement cost, the six cases can be rewritten as follows:

Use		Resale	
3	RC	1	RC
4	RC	2	RC
5	RC > PV	6	RC > NRV

---

* The next few paragraphs owe much to D. Solomons, 'Economic and Accounting Concepts of Cost and Value' in M. Backer (ed.), *Modern Accounting Theory* (Englewood Cliffs, N.J., 1966). See also J. C. Bonbright, *The Valuation of Property* (Charlottesville, Va., 1965), 1, ch. IV (first published in 1937).

Introduction

That is to say, value to the firm is current replacement cost in all cases except 5 and 6. Case 5 is the situation where it would not be worth buying the asset were it not already held. The value to the firm is therefore, we suggest, the present value of the expected net cash receipts from the asset. Case 6 is the situation where an asset which the firm intends to sell is not worth replacing. Value to the firm is therefore net realizable value.

We are now in a position to suggest the following general rule of asset valuation:

The 'value to the firm' (VF) of an asset is its current replacement cost, with two exceptions:

(i) where the asset is held for use (i.e. PV > NRV) it should be valued at the present value of the expected net cash receipts if this is lower than current replacement cost;

(ii) where the asset is held for resale (i.e. NRV > PV) it should be valued at net realizable value if this is lower than current replacement cost.

The rule can be expressed even more briefly as follows: Value to the firm = RC, except where RC > PV or RC > NRV, when VF = PV or NRV, whichever is the greater.

How helpful is this rule as a guide to valuations in practice? There is little difficulty in the case of stocks of raw materials, work in progress and finished goods. Both raw materials and finished goods will usually have reasonably easily ascertainable replacement costs and net realizable values. The present value of expected net cash receipts can be regarded for all practical purposes as equal to net realizable value.

Work in progress as such will usually have a very low net realizable value, but the present value of the expected net cash receipts calculated on the usual incremental basis (see next paragraph) may be both large and difficult to calculate. Perhaps the best practical solution is to assume, except where it is expected that the RC of the *finished product* will be greater than its NRV, the work in progress to be at least equal in value to its current replacement cost as measured by the firm's standard costing system (see next section). Value to the firm will then usually be replacement cost.

Fixed assets are by definition acquired for use rather than resale. It is rather curiously argued by some accountants that this being so we need to know only the asset's historical cost. If one of a manager's aims is to maximize the wealth of his firm this is clearly wrong. He needs to know when to scrap the asset and this point must come when NRV as defined above becomes greater than the present value of the expected net cash receipts. The relevant net receipts are those which would not be receivable by the firm if it did not own the asset. Such a figure may, of course, be very large indeed: in the limiting case *all* the receipts of the firm might cease if it did not own the asset. Happily we can escape from the rather frightening prospect of the whole firm being valued at several times the sum of its parts by falling back on our rule that an upper limit is provided by an asset's current replacement cost. But this also could be a suspiciously high figure for a machine which could only be replaced by another one specially made for the firm. It is essential therefore to interpret current replacement cost not as the cost of replacing the actual physical asset used by the firm but as the cost of currently acquiring the *services* provided by the asset.* It is even more difficult to arrive at an objective estimate of an asset's PV. Fortunately this is only relevant to income measurement when both PV and NRV are less than current replacement cost. In most cases current replacement cost will be the relevant measure of value to the firm and the remaining sections of this introduction have been written mainly on this assumption.

A. R. Prest has put forward a number of persuasive but not, we think, entirely convincing arguments against the use of replacement cost depreciation [pp. 290–309].† First, while he does not dispute that replacement cost is appropriate in the measurement of the national income he is doubtful of its relevance to business income, principally on the grounds that he cannot agree that '"the" correct *motif* of action for the individual firm is to aim at preserving intact its stock of physical assets' ([p. 296]. This argument, however, seems to confuse income with distributable income. The supporter of replacement cost depreciation does not have to argue that a firm *must* maintain its physical assets intact, but merely that any distribution of real capital should be recognized as such and not regarded as a distribution of income.

Secondly, Prest rightly attacks loose arguments about depreciation providing funds for replacement: 'after all, if depreciation charges on a replacement-cost basis were not earned then it would be possible to have no liquid resources available for replacement despite the most conscientious accounting' [p. 300]. One must be careful of assuming, however, that replacement cost depreciation for income measurement purposes has any connexion with the *replacement requirements* of a firm. No method of income measurement can by itself provide funds or replace assets.

Thirdly, Prest does not believe that historical cost depreciation tends to exaggerate the trade cycle: 'the profitability of new investment must depend *inter alia* on the current costs of purchasing equipment; simple extrapolation of current profits reckoned on the basis of *past* capital costs

* For the contrary view see Edwards and Bell, *op. cit.* p. 186n.
† See also his *Public Finance in Theory and Practice* (London, 3rd ed. 1967), ch. 16.

Introduction

is a path which surely few would follow [p. 302]. We shall not pursue this argument here; reference should be made to the paper by Baxter reproduced on pp. 215–29 below.

THE MEASUREMENT OF CURRENT OPERATING PROFIT AND REAL HOLDING GAINS

If, as we believe, current operating profit and real holding gains are elements of business income of great practical significance to both managers and shareholders it is important to tackle the problem of how to measure them. A concept of income which cannot be measured reasonably objectively is not likely to have much impact in practice.

From the point of view of management accounting it is highly desirable that changes in specific prices be integrated with a company's routine standard costing system. That this is possible in practice is shown by the experience of Philips Electrical Industries.*

Many items in a company's income statement are automatically recorded in current terms, e.g. sales and purchases of goods. The two exceptions are the stock element in cost of goods sold and the depreciation of fixed assets.

One of the incidental advantages of a system of standard costing is that the detailed stock records can be kept in quantities only. We suggest that standard costs should be calculated for each item of stock in the usual way but that price indexes should also be prepared for groups of related articles. A significant movement in an index should be followed by a revaluation. (In practice Philips do not usually revise standard prices more than once a year.) At a revaluation, adjustments are made *in total* by writing up the value of stock in hand, recognizing the existence of a Real holding gain (or loss) to the extent that the specific price rise is greater than or less than the rise in the general price level, and transferring the difference to an Inflation adjustment account.

If, as in the arithmetical illustration on p. 10 above, the original value of the stock was £1,000, the specific price level had risen by 56 per cent, and the general price level by 20 per cent, then the following entry needs to be made:

		£
Stock	Dr.	560
Real holding gain	Cr.	360
Inflation adjustment	Cr.	200

* See A. Goudeket, 'An Application of Replacement Value Theory', *Journal of Accountancy* (July 1960), pp. 37–47; also R. S. Gynther, *Accounting for Price-Level Changes: Theory and Procedures* (Oxford, 1966), pp. 223–40.

A purchase of raw materials after such a revaluation would be recorded by debiting Stock account with the revised standard cost, crediting Trade creditors with the actual amount payable and debiting or crediting a Materials price variance account in the usual way with the difference if any between the revised standard cost and the actual amount payable. Materials would be issued to production at the revised standard cost so that the values placed on work in progress and finished goods stock would take into account significant changes in the price of raw materials.*

If the above suggestions are regarded as impracticable by some companies, end-of-year adjustments could be used instead. The usual historical figures are recorded during the year and accounting profit is calculated in the normal fashion. From this a figure for stock appreciation is then deducted. There are a number of ways in which this adjustment could be calculated:

(i) If stock accumulation *during* the year is ignored then the stock appreciation adjustment is simply the difference between the opening stocks valued at end-of-year prices and the same stocks valued at beginning-of-the-year prices.

(ii) Stock appreciation can be calculated as the difference between the historical cost of sales and the quantity sold during the year multiplied by the weighted average purchase price of the year.

(iii) A third method is based upon a suggestion made by Paish [see p. 198 below]. The adjustment is calculated as the average of the appreciation on opening and closing stocks, i.e.

$$S = \tfrac{1}{2}[(O_o^c - O) + (C - C_c^o)],$$

where S = stock appreciation, O = opening stocks at beginning-of-the-year prices, C = closing stocks at end-of-year prices, o = beginning-of-the-year prices, c = end-of-year prices. Changes in the physical levels of stocks are thus taken into account.

A simple example will show the relative effect of these methods. At the beginning of a year a company's stocks consisted of 1,000 units valued at £10 each. During the year it bought 3,800 units at £10·2 each and 1,200 units at £10·3 each (in that order). It sold 4,500 units at £20 each and had a closing stock of 1,500 units at which time the purchase price was still £10·3 per unit. Using the conventional first-in, first-out assumption the closing stock

---

* Readers who are not accountants are reminded that expenses and increases in assets are debits (Dr.) and that gains and increases in liabilities and proprietorship are credits (Cr.). For details of accounting and costing procedures see R. Mathews, *Accounting for Economists* (Melbourne, 2nd ed. 1965).

would be valued at £15,420 (i.e 1,200 × £10·3 + 300 × £10·2) and accounting profit can be calculated as

		£
Sales		90,000
Cost of goods sold	£	
Opening stock	10,000	
Purchases	51,120	
	61,120	
less Closing stock	15,420	
		45,700
Accounting Profit (gross)		£44,300

The various stock appreciation estimates (£) will be

(i) $1,000 \times (10\cdot3 - 10\cdot0) = 300$,

(ii) $(4,500 \times [51,120/5,000]) - 45,700 = 308$,

(iii) $\frac{1}{2}\{[(10,000 \times 10\cdot3/10\cdot0) - 10,000]$
$$+ [15,450 - (15,450 \times 10\cdot0/10\cdot3)]\} = 375.$$

To the extent that stock prices have risen more rapidly than prices in general the stock appreciation estimate will include a real holding gain. If for example there has been a 2 per cent rise in the general price level during the year, then the real holding gain element calculated on opening stocks only would be £100.

Practical problems also arise in the measurement of current cost depreciation.* There is little difficulty in obtaining current replacement costs for those fixed assets which are marketed continually and which are subject to little technical change. Where no market exists for new fixed assets of the type used by the firm, resort must be had either to appraisal or specific price indexes (such as those prepared in the United Kingdom by the Economist Intelligence Unit).

One way of handling the necessary calculations is to incorporate them in the normal monthly entry recording depreciation expense and the increase in the accumulated depreciation of the fixed asset. So long as there are no significant changes in price the entry will be based on historical cost. If a significant change occurs the fixed asset should be written up (debited) accordingly and the Inflation adjustment and Real holding gains accounts credited.

* The argument of this section ignores those questions whoch arise from viewing depreciation as the change over time in the value of an asset, on the one hand, and as an arbitrary allocation of past expenditure, on the other. For a discussion of these aspects, see the papers in section v below and also H. R. Hudson and Russell Mathews, 'An Aspect of Depreciation', *Economic Record*, xxxix, no. 86 (June 1963), pp. 232–6, and J. W. Bennett, J. McB. Grant and R. H. Parker, *Topics in Business Finance and Accounting* (Melbourne, 1964), pp. 91–4.

As an example, assume that a company bought a machine on 1 January for £12,000. Only one significant price change occurred during the year: an increase of £600 (5 per cent of £12,000) on 1 June. Assuming straight-line depreciation and an estimated life of ten years (120 months) the historical depreciation will be £100 per month. Suppose also that the general price level had risen by 3 per cent over the first five months of the year. The entry to record the increase in the purchase price of the machine will be

		£
Machine	Dr.	600
Inflation adjustment	Cr.	345
Real holding gain	Cr.	230
Accumulated depreciation	Cr.	25

The real holding gain is £12,000 $(0.05 - 0.03) \times 115/120 = £230$. The written-down value of the machine at 1 June should be £12,600 less the accumulated depreciation based on the new purchase price, i.e.

$$5/120 \times £12,600 = £525.$$

Since only £500 has so far been credited to Accumulated depreciation account it is necessary to place there another £25. The credit to the Inflation adjustment account represents the fictitious element in the *net* monetary increase in the asset's market value, i.e.

$$0.03/0.05 \times £600 \times 115/120 = £345.$$

By the end of the year the balance in the Machine account will be £12,600 (its current replacement cost) and in the Accumulated depreciation account £1,260 (i.e. £500 credited in the first five months, plus the £25 credited on 1 June, plus £105 per month for seven months). The machine would thus be shown in the year-end balance sheet at its written-down current replacement cost of £11,340. The total depreciation expense of the year, however, will not be £1,260 but £1,235 (i.e. five months of £100, plus seven months of £105) representing the *average* current depreciation expense of the year. The balance of the Inflation adjustment account would remain at £345 and would be shown in the proprietorship section of the balance sheet. It is important to realize that it is merely an inflation adjustment and not in any way a source of funds for replacing the machine.

Some companies may prefer to make year-end adjustments only. These are inevitably more approximate. Current cost depreciation could for example be calculated as

$$\text{Accounting depreciation} \times \frac{\text{Average current replacement cost during the year}}{\text{Purchase price of asset}}.$$

Introduction

If average current replacement cost is interpreted as simply the arithmetic mean of the current replacement cost at the beginning and end of the year, then current cost depreciation in our example would be

$$\pounds 1,200 \times \frac{\frac{1}{2}(12,600+12,000)}{12,000} = \pounds 1,230.$$

The only item of real income whose measurement in practice remains to be discussed is the holding gain or loss on monetary assets. If prices are rising this item will usually be negative. It is useful to distinguish between monetary assets with a market value, which we shall call *marketable securities*, and those without a market value which we shall call *net monetary claims*.*

Examples of marketable securities are quoted investments held by the firm. Each marketable security can be treated as if it were a fixed asset. A significant change in market value should be followed by a revaluation and appropriate transfers to the Inflation adjustment and Real holding gains (or losses) accounts.

Assume, for example, that on 1 March a company owns investments quoted on the stock exchange at £10,000. During the month this value rises to £10,500 (an increase of 5 per cent) and the general price level increases by 1 per cent. The following entry should be made:

		£
Investments	Dr.	500
Real holding gain	Cr.	400
Inflation adjustment	Cr.	100

The explanation of this entry is that the investments are written up to their new market value; a real holding gain of £400 is recorded; and a 'fictitious holding gain' of £100 is transferred to the Inflation adjustment account.

Net Monetary Claims Example

	General index	Unadjusted amount	Multiplier	Adjusted amount
Opening balance	120	£10,000	140/120	£11,667
Net change (+ or −)	130[a]	+2,000	140/130	2,154
Closing balance	140	£12,000		13,821
				12,000
				Loss £1,821

[a] The average for the period, assumed to $(120+140)/2$.

Net monetary claims are those whose value apparently remains constant, e.g. cash, debtors and creditors. The loss or gain from holding these through

* Net of current liabilities such as trade creditors. We do not recommend the recognition of price-change gains or losses on *long-term* liabilities. See Gynther, *op. cit.* ch. 11.

a rise or fall in the general price level can be calculated (from a managerial point of view, preferably monthly) as in the example above. The loss would be debited to a Loss on holding net monetary claims account and credited to Inflation adjustment account.

CURRENT OPERATING PROFIT AS TAX BASE

We have argued in the preceding sections that current operating profit is a more useful concept than accounting profit for reporting to managers shareholders. Is it also more suitable as a tax base?

It is a basic principle of the tax system of the United Kingdom (and we shall confine ourselves to the U.K. in the discussion that follows) that tax-payers should be taxed in accordance with their 'ability to pay'. The income of the taxpayers is regarded as the most objective measure of this ability. In order to achieve this the income of different classes of taxpayers should, as far as is practicable, be measured in a similar way. The taxable incomes of wage and salary earners, and of companies in insurance, banking and finance, are measured in current terms, but when accounting profit is the tax base and the prices of fixed assets and stocks are changing the taxable incomes of manufacturing companies and farmers are not so measured. On the grounds of comparability, therefore, current operating profit is more suitable than accounting profit as a tax base. The income of all classes of taxpayer would be measured in a similar way and the tax-able incomes of manufacturing firms of the same technical nature and the same replacement costs would be the same. The present use of accounting profit as the base tends to favour new firms, firms which bought plant in periods of high prices and firms which spend more on repairs than replacement.

Because companies are not persons, we have deliberately argued below in terms of comparability rather than in terms of equity, which can only apply to persons—even though it is true that what is being taxed are incomes which are attributable to the owners of companies. Prior to the recent (1965) change to a corporation tax there was no capital gains tax in the United Kingdom, and distributed company profits were taxed for the period 1947–58 at a different rate from undistributed profits. The latest changes, however, include the introduction of a capital gains tax, a corpora-tion tax on companies' incomes as such and taxation at the standard rate on distributed company incomes. Any consideration of equity, therefore, must concern the sizes of the rates of these various taxes as they apply to individuals, not the company tax base itself, which is the concern of the present discussion.

Introduction

What are the possible objections to current operating profit as tax base? If tax rates remained unchanged there would be a fall in the total amount of revenue collected which would have to be dealt with by an increase in the rate. The relative burden of tax on different companies would, of course, change. The conditions most favourable to a company paying *less* tax than previously are moderate increases in the prices of fixed assets and moderate stock appreciation in the country as a whole, combined with severe increases in the prices of fixed assets and severe stock appreciation for the company itself. In these circumstances the difference between taxable income before and after the change will be great and the increase in the rate of tax will be small. On the other hand, severe stock appreciation and severe increases in the prices of fixed assets generally, combined with moderate stock appreciation and moderate increases in the prices of fixed assets (or, worse still, stock *depreciation* and price falls) for the particular company would lead to considerably heavier tax payments than previously.*

A second possible objection is that firms lack the necessary data to adjust for the changing prices of fixed assets and stocks and that such adjustments would increase the scope for tax evasion. We have already discussed the practicality of adjustments in the previous section. It may be objected that more objective methods should be used for tax purposes. This could be achieved if official indexes of specific categories of fixed assets and stocks were published. A company would then receive normal statutory capital allowances based on original purchase costs as at present and additional allowances (which could be negative) for changes in the prices of specific assets since the dates when they were acquired. In effect, the company would be allowed on each fixed asset an historical cost capital allowance multiplied by an 'inflation factor' P_c/P_a where P_c is the current replacement cost of the asset and P_a the purchase price at the date of acquisition. In practice, these allowances might have to be restricted to assets acquired during the post-war period. The rates of capital allowances already exist; the indexes of prices of fixed assets probably exist also, as the Central Statistical Office publishes figures of annual capital consumption valued at current replacement cost which are presumably based on an index of this sort.† (Indexes for specific categories of fixed assets are also compiled by, and available from, the Economist Intelligence Unit.) The taxpayer and the Board of Inland Revenue could decide between them the categories to which fixed assets of the taxpayer belonged, and taxpayers could be re-

---

* The order of magnitude of these changes for the years 1950 and 1951 will be found in G. C. Harcourt, 'The quantitative effect of basing company taxation on replacement costs', *Accounting Research*, IX, no. 1 (January 1968), pp. 1–16.

† See, for example, *National Income and Expenditure* (1967).

quired to use the official indexes when calculating their allowances for changes in the prices of their fixed assets.

A third possible objection to the use of current operating profit as the tax base is that it would mean a departure from the consistent application of generally accepted accounting principles and involve the use of arbitrary and individual judgments. This objection is implied in the rejection of revaluation schemes by the Millard Tucker Committee and the Royal Commission on the Taxation of Profits and Income.* Current operating profit, however, differs from accounting profit only by the amount of the stock and depreciation adjustments already discussed and these can be calculated in an objective manner. The construction of the price indexes would require individual judgments, but not by taxpayers.

A fourth possible objection is that it would be impossible to make retro-spective tax refunds or payments when the change in the tax base was introduced.† This is true, but it is irrelevant to considerations of equity and comparability between different classes of taxpayers in the future.

The Millard Tucker Committee objected to this and similar changes in the tax base because they would give preferential treatment to taxpayers who had to replace fixed assets and stocks. But a tax base of current operating profit would, on the contrary, restore comparability to these tax-payers. The same committee argued (by implication) that a tax base of current operating profit would not encourage firms which were, or could become, of importance to the national interest, e.g. new or expanding firms.‡ (A tax base of accounting profit does encourage these firms, relative to old-established ones, in that they pay relatively less tax.) This objection could be overcome by having a tax base of current operating profit and making cash investment grants at different rates to particular firms and for expenditure on particular types of assets. (This is, of course, the current government policy in the United Kingdom.)

It is of great interest to note that in most years since 1953—and especially since 1954 when investment allowances were first introduced—the aggregate taxable incomes of companies have been *less* than their total current operating profits. In Table 1, total allowances, both investment and other, to companies by the taxation authorities are compared with the total of stock appreciation and current-cost capital consumption for the period 1953–66. The table shows that stock appreciation has often been greater than the shortfall of historical-cost depreciation allowances compared with

---

* See *Report of the Committee on the Taxation of Trading Profits*, Cmd. 8189 (London, 1951), para. 115 and Cmd. 9474, para. 354.
† Cmd. 8189, para. 105; Cmd. 9474, para. 361.
‡ Cmd. 8189, para. 132.

TABLE 1. *U.K. Companies 1953–66*

£m.

	1953	1954	1955	1956	1957	1958	1959	1960	1961	1962	1963	1964	1965	1966
Initial and investment allowances	104	157	205	227	269	347	400	476	539	544	652	778	764	318
Other allowances	303	364	420	500	569	625	675	737	813	907	1,104	1,298	1,390	1,252
(1) Total	407	521	625	727	838	972	1,075	1,213	1,352	1,451	1,756	2,076	2,154	1,570
Current-cost capital consumption	429	459	516	581	637	680	706	747	813	868	914	985	1,073	1,179
Stock appreciation	−44	53	119	159	141	−18	66	89	115	100	163	271	282	273
(2) Total	385	512	635	740	778	662	772	836	928	968	1,077	1,256	1,355	1,452
(1)−(2)	22	9	−10	−13	60	310	303	377	424	483	679	820	799	118

Source: National Income and Expenditure (1967), Tables 62, 71, p. 124 for 1956–66. Earlier editions for 1953–5.

TABLE 2. *U.K. Companies 1958–66*

Difference between Taxable income and Current operating profit as percentage of Current operating profit								
1958	1959	1960	1961	1962	1963	1964	1965	1966
12	10	11	13	15	19	21	20	3

Taxable income: company income arising in the United Kingdom, less interest payments, initial, investment and other allowances.

Current operating profit: company income arising in the United Kingdom, less interest payments, stock appreciation and current-cost capital consumption.

Source: *National Income and Expenditure* (1967). Tables 30, 62, 71; p. 124.

current-cost capital consumption. For many companies, for example woollen and worsted manufacturers whose stocks form a large proportion of their total assets, it must be even more important.

It can be seen from the table that, with the exception of 1955 and 1956, total allowances exceeded stock appreciation and current-cost capital consumption combined. From 1958 to 1965 the allowances were, in fact, considerably greater; the annual average excess for 1958–65 is £524m. Since 1960 the aggregate historical-cost depreciation allowances have been greater than current-cost capital consumption. This is explained by the fact that depreciation allowances given by the Inland Revenue are mainly on a reducing-balance basis, while those in the estimates of current-cost capital consumption are on a straight-line basis adjusted by an inflation factor. If a capital stock is growing, historical-cost reducing-balance allowances exceed straight-line ones. Evidently the rate of growth of fixed assets in the company sector in the United Kingdom has been great enough to offset, through the reducing-balance effect, the effects of the mild rates of inflation of recent years.

The degree to which the aggregate current operating profits of U.K. companies have exceeded their aggregate taxable incomes is quite surprisingly large. The difference between the two as a percentage of current operating profit is shown for the years 1958–66 in Table 2. The astonishing figures of 19 per cent, 21 per cent and 20 per cent for the years 1963–5 reflect two changes in the 1963 Budget. The first is the increase in investment allowances on certain assets to 30 per cent; the second is the increase in annual allowances on plant and machinery to 15, 20 and 25 per cent, and on industrial buildings to 4 per cent. In the development areas up to 100 per cent write-offs were allowed in the first year for the period 4 April 1963 to 17 June 1966.

Introduction

A NOTE ON THE TAXATION OF REAL HOLDING GAINS

We have argued in preceding sections that real income consists of current operating profit plus real holding gains accruing and that the former is a suitable base for taxation. Should real holding gains accruing also be taxed? It would seem that if we consider them part of income and think that comparability demands that the tax laws take account of changing price levels then they ought to be taxed. We do indeed think this but doubt whether the taxation of such gains as they *accrue* is administratively and politically practicable. To avoid taxing fictitious holding gains we suggest that a suitable *general* index published by the government be applied to the historical cost of the asset being taxed and that capital gains tax be charged only on the selling price less the adjusted historical cost. In other words (using our previous notation) the gain subject to tax would not be $N(1+r) - N = Nr$, but $N(1+r) - N(1+p) = N(r-p)$, where $N(1+r)$ is a *realized* market value. A system similar to this is in force in Belgium.*

* Confederation of British Industry, *Taxation in Western Europe* (London, 1967), pp. 47–8.

PART I

CONCEPTS OF INCOME

1 Income and capital[1]

by Irving Fisher[*]

I. SUBJECTIVE, OR ENJOYMENT, INCOME

Income is a series of events.[2]

According to the modern theory of relativity the elementary reality is not matter, electricity, space, time, life or mind, but events.

For each individual only those events which come within the purview of his experience are of direct concern. It is these events—the psychic experiences of the individual mind—which constitute ultimate income for that individual. The outside events have significance for that individual only in so far as they are the means to these inner events of the mind. The human nervous system is, like a radio, a great receiving instrument. Our brains serve to transform into the stream of our psychic life those outside events which happen to us and stimulate our nervous system.

But the human body is not ordinarily regarded as an owned object, and only those events in consciousness traceable to owned objects other than the human body are generally admitted to be psychic income. However, the human machine still plays a rôle in so far as, through its purposeful

[1] *The Nature of Capital and Income* (first published in 1906) was primarily intended to serve as a foundation for *The Rate of Interest* which immediately followed it. It was my expectation that the student would read the former before reading the latter.

But now, for the convenience of those who do not wish to take the time to read *The Nature of Capital and Income*, I have written this first chapter summarizing it. I have availed myself of this opportunity to redistribute the emphasis and to make those amendments in statement which further study has indicated to be desirable.

A friendly critic, Professor John B. Canning, suggests that *The Nature of Capital and Income* should have been called 'The Nature of Income and Capital' and that the subject matter should have been presented in reverse order, inasmuch as income is the basis of the concept of capital value and is, in fact, the most fundamental concept in economic science.

While it might not be practicable to employ the reverse order in such a complete presentation as I aimed to make in *The Nature of Capital and Income*, I have, in this chapter, where brevity may justify some dogmatism, adopted Professor Canning's suggestions. This radical change in mode of presentation may induce some who have already read that book to review it now in the reverse order employed in this chapter. I hope also that some who have not read it may be moved, after reading this chapter, to read *The Nature of Capital and Income* in full. I have tried, in this chapter, to confine myself merely to those conclusions most essential as a preliminary for proceeding to the consideration of the origins, nature and determinants of the rate of interest.

[2] The first writer to employ the concept of events as fundamental in interest theory appears to have been John Rae, whose book, originally published in 1834, is commented on elsewhere.

[*] Professor of Political Economy, Yale University, 1898–1935.

activities, it produces or helps produce other owned objects which are material sources of desirable events—food, houses, tools, and other goods, which in their turn set in motion a chain of operations whose ultimate effect is registered in our stream of consciousness. The important consideration from this point of view is that human beings are ever striving to control the stream of their psychic life by appropriating and utilizing the materials and forces of Nature.

In Man's early history he had little command over his environment. He was largely at the mercy of natural forces—wind and lightning, rain and snow, heat and cold. But today Man protects himself from these by means of those contrivances called houses, clothing, and furnaces. He diverts the lightning by means of lightning rods. He increases his food supply by means of appropriated land, farm buildings, ploughs, and other implements. He then refashions the food by means of mills, grinding machinery, cooking stoves and other agencies, and by the labour of human bodies, including his own.

Neither these intermediate processes of creation and alteration nor the money transactions following them are of significance except as they are the necessary or helpful preliminaries to psychic income—human enjoyment. We must be careful lest, in fixing our eyes on such preliminaries, expecially money transactions, we overlook the much more important enjoyment which it is their business to yield.

Directors and managers providing income for thousands of people sometimes think of their corporation merely as a great money-making machine. In their eyes its one purpose is to earn money dividends for the stockholders, money interest for the bondholders, money wages and money salaries for the employees. What happens after these payments are made seems too private a matter to concern them. Yet that is the nub of the whole arrangement. It is only what we carry out of the market place into our homes and private lives which really counts. Money is of no use to us until it is spent. The ultimate wages are not paid in terms of money but in the enjoyments it buys. The dividend cheque becomes income in the ultimate sense only when we eat the food, wear the clothes, or ride in the automobile which are bought with the cheque.

2. OBJECTIVE, OR REAL, INCOME (OUR 'LIVING')

Enjoyment income is a psychological entity and cannot be measured directly. We can approximate it indirectly, however, by going one step behind it to what is called real income. Real wages, and indeed real income in general, consist of those final physical events in the *outer* world which give us our *inner* enjoyments.

This real income includes the shelter of a house, the music of a victrola or radio, the use of clothes, the eating of food, the reading of the newspaper and all those other innumerable events by which we make the world about us contribute to our enjoyments. Metaphorically we sometimes refer to this, our real income, as our 'bread and butter'.

These finals in the stream of outer events are what we call our 'living', as implied in the phrases 'cost of living' and 'earning a living'. The final outer events and the inner events which they entail run closely parallel or, rather, the inner events generally follow closely in time on the outer. The enjoyment of music is felt almost instantaneously as the piano or singer produces it. The enjoyment of food is experienced with the eating or soon after the eating.

These outer events, such as the use of food or clothes, etc., are like the resultant inner events in not being very easily measured. They occur largely in the privacy of the home; they are often difficult to express in any standard units. They have no common denominator. Even the individual who experiences them cannot weigh and measure them directly. All he can do is to measure the money he paid to get them.

3. COST OF LIVING, A MEASURE OF REAL INCOME

So, just as we went behind an individual's enjoyment income to his real income, we now go behind his real income, or his living, to his *cost* of living, the money measure of real income. You cannot measure in dollars either the inner event of your enjoyment while eating your dinner or the outer event of eating it, but you can find out definitely how much money that dinner cost you. In the same way, you cannot measure your enjoyment at the cinema, but you do know what you paid for your ticket; you cannot measure exactly what your house shelter is really worth to you, but you can tell how much you pay for your rent, or what is a fair equivalent for your rent if you happen to live in your own house. You cannot measure what it is worth to wear an evening suit, but you can find out what it costs to hire one, or a fair equivalent of its hire if, perchance, the suit belongs to you. Deducing such equivalents is an accountant's job.

The total cost of living, in the sense of money payments, is a negative item, being outgo rather than income; but it is our best practical measure of the positive items of real income for which those payments are made. For from this total valuation of positive real income may be subtracted the total valuation of the person's labour pain during the same period, if we wish to compare a labourer's income with that of a man who does no labour but lives on his income from capital (other than himself), a *rentier*.

Irving Fisher

Enjoyment income, real income, and the cost of living are merely three different stages of income. All three run closely parallel to each other, although they are not exactly synchronous in time. These discrepancies, as has been intimated, are negligible as between real and enjoyment income. So also the time elapsing between the cost of living and the living is usually brief. There is a little delay between the spending of money at the box office and the seeing of the entertainment, or between paying board or rent and making use of the food or housing facilities. In many cases, the money payment follows rather than precedes the enjoyment.

4. COST OF AN ARTICLE *v.* COST OF ITS USE

The only time discrepancy worth careful noting is that which occurs when the money spent is not simply for the temporary use of some object but for the whole object, which means merely for all its possible future uses. If a house is not rented but bought, we do not count the purchase price as all spent for this year's shelter. We expect from it many more years of use. Hence out of the entire purchase price, we try to compute a fair portion of the purchase price to be charged up to this year's use. In like manner, the statisticians of cost of living should distribute by periods the cost of using a person's house furnishings, clothing, musical instruments, automobiles and other durable goods, and not charge the entire cost against the income of the year of purchase. To any given year should be charged only that year's upkeep and replacement, which measures, at least roughly, the services rendered by the goods in question during that particular year. The true real annual income from such goods is the equivalent approximately of the cost of the services given off by those goods each year.

Strictly speaking, then, in making up our income statistics, we should always calculate the value of *services*, and never the value of the objects rendering those services. It is true that, in the case of short-lived objects like food, we do not ordinarily need, in practice, to go to the trouble of distinguishing their total cost from the cost of their use. A loaf of bread is worth ten cents because its use is worth ten cents. We cannot rent food; we can only buy it outright. Yet there is some discrepancy in time in the case of foods that keep, such as flour, preserved foods and canned goods. These we may buy in one year but not use until a later year, and in such cases the money given for the food might almost be said to be invested rather than spent, like the money given for a house. A man who buys a basket of fruit and eats it within an hour is certainly spending his money for the enjoyment of eating the fruit. But, if he buys a barrel of apples in the fall to be eaten during the winter, is he spending his money or is he investing it for a deferred enjoyment? Theoretically, the barrel of apples is an investment comparable to a house or any other durable good. Practically it is classed as expenditure, although it is a border-line case.

Spending and investing differ only in degree, depending on the length of time elapsing between the expenditure and the enjoyment. To spend is to pay money for enjoyments which come very soon. To invest is to pay money for enjoyments which are deferred to a later time. We spend money for our daily bread and butter or for a seat at the theatre, but we invest money in the purchase of bonds, farms, dwellings, or automobiles, or even of suits of clothes.

5. MEASURING AT THE DOMESTIC THRESHOLD

In practice, we can estimate with fair accuracy in all ordinary cases how much of what we pay is for this year's use. That is to say, we can find out pretty nearly our cost of living for the year. We need only reckon what is spent on personal articles and services—on everything which enters our dwellings (or enters us), food, drink, clothes, furniture, household rent, fuel and light, amusements, and so on, our 'bread and butter'—exclusive of what is left over for future years, such as what we pay for securities, machinery, or real estate, or what we put into the savings bank. The domestic threshold is, in general, a pretty good line of division. The cost of almost every object which crosses it measures a portion of our real income, and few other expenditures do.

Thus, at the end of production economics, or business economics, we find home economics. It is the housekeeper, the woman who spends, who takes the final steps through the cost of living toward getting the real income of the family, so that the family's enjoyment income may follow.

6. MONEY INCOME

We have just been dealing with money payments for consumption goods, or money *outgo*. We may now go back one further step to money received by the individual spender, or money income. Money income includes all money *received* which is not obviously, and in the nature of the case, to be devoted to reinvestment—or, as the expression is, 'earmarked' for reinvestment. In other words, all money received and readily available and intended to be used for spending is money income. It sometimes differs from real income considerably. For instance, if you more than 'earn your living' of $6,000 with a salary of $10,000, you voluntarily put by the $4,000 remaining as savings. This part of your money income is saved from being turned immediately into real income. That is, instead of

37

spending all your salary for this year's living you invest $4,000 of it to help toward the cost of living of future years. And so, the $4,000 is not only credited as income but debited as outgo. With it you buy durable objects such as land or buildings, or part rights in these, such as stocks or bonds. Your money income is in this case your salary (or it may be dividends, rent, interest, or profits) and it exceeds real income by the amount of your savings. On the other hand, you may be living beyond your (money) income. This means, expressed in terms of the concepts here used, that your real income for the year is greater than your money income.

That all one spends on his living measures real income, even when he 'lives byond his income' (beyond his *money* income), may be a hard saying to some who have never attempted to work out consistent definitions of economic concepts which will not only satisfy the requirements of economic theory but which will also bring these economic concepts into conformity with the theory and practice of accountancy. But a definition of income which satisfies both theory and practice, in both economics and accountancy, *must* reckon as income in the most basic sense all those uses, services, or living for which the cost of living is expended even though such expenditure may exceed the money income.

Thus we have a picture of three successive stages, or aspects, of a man's income:

Enjoyment or psychic income, consisting of agreeable sensations and experiences;

Real income *measured* by the cost of living;

Money income, consisting of the money received by a man for meeting his costs of living;

The last—money income—is most commonly called income; and the first—enjoyment income—is the most fundamental. But for accounting purposes real income, as measured by the cost of living, is the most practical.[1]

To recapitulate, we have seen that the enjoyment income is a psychological matter, and hence cannot be measured directly. So we look to real income instead; but even real income is a heterogeneous jumble. It includes quarts of milk, visits to the cinema, etc., and in that form cannot be measured easily or as a whole. Here is where the cost of living comes in. It is the practical, homogeneous[2] measure of real income. As the cost of living is expressed in

---

[1] Later in this chapter we shall see that these three sorts of income are all of a piece, parts of the entire economic fabric of services and disservices. Which of the three comes out of our accounting depends merely on which groups of these services and disservices are included in our summation.

[2] Even this is not homogeneous as a measure of subjective enjoyment; for a dollar to the poor and a dollar to the rich are not subjectively equal. See my 'A Statistical Method for Measuring "Marginal Utility" and Testing the Justice of a Progressive Income Tax', *Economic Essays contributed in honor of John Bates Clark*, pp. 157–93.

terms of dollars it may, therefore, be taken as our best measure of income *in place of* enjoyment income, or real income. Between it and real income there are no important discrepancies as there are between money income and real income. Money income practically never conforms exactly to real income because either savings raise money income above real income, or deficits push money income below real income.

7. CAPITAL VALUE

Savings bring us to the nature of capital. Capital, in the sense of capital *value*, is simply future income discounted or, in other words, capitalized. The value of any property, or rights to wealth, is its value *as a source of income* and is found by discounting that expected income. We may, if we so choose, for logical convenience, include as property the ownership in ourselves, or we may, conformably to custom, regard human beings as in a separate category.

I define wealth as consisting of material objects owned by human beings (including, if you please, human beings themselves). The ownership may be divided and parcelled out among different individuals in the form of partnership rights, shares of stock, bonds, mortgages, and other forms of property rights. In whatever ways the ownership be distributed and symbolized in documents, the entire group of property rights are merely means to an end—income. Income is the alpha and omega of economics.

8. THE RATE OF INTEREST

The bridge or link between income and capital is the *rate of interest*. We may define the *rate of interest as the per cent of premium* paid on money at one date in terms of money to be in hand one year later. Theoretically, of course, we may substitute for money in this statement wheat or any other sort of goods. But practically, it is only money which is traded as between present and future. Hence, the rate of interest is sometimes called the price of money; and the market in which present and future money are traded for that price, or premium, is called the money market. If $100 today will exchange for $105 to be received one year hence, the premium on present money in terms of future money is $5 and this, as a percentage of the $100, or the rate of interest, is five per cent. That is to say, the price of today's money in terms of next year's money is five per cent above par. It should always be remembered *that interest and the rate of interest are not identical*. Interest is computed by multiplying capital value by the rate of interest.

Irving Fisher

The aim of this book is to show how the *rate* of interest is caused or determined. Some writers have chosen, for purposes of exposition, to postulate two questions involved in the theory of the rate of interest, namely (1) why any rate of interest exists and (2) how the rate of interest is determined. This second question, however, embraces also the first, since to explain how the rate of interest is determined involves the question of whether the rate can or cannot be zero, i.e. whether a positive rate of interest must necessarily exist.

9. DISCOUNTING IS FUNDAMENTAL

But although the rate of interest may be used either way—for computing from present to future values, or from future to present values—the latter process (discounting) is by far the more important of the two. Accountants, of course, are constantly computing in both directions; for they have to deal with both sets of problems. But the basic problem of time valuation which Nature sets us is always that of translating the future into the present, that is, the problem of ascertaining the capital value of future income. The value of capital must be computed from the value of its estimated future net income, not vice versa.

This statement may at first seem puzzling, for we usually think of causes and effects as running forward not backward in time. It would seem then that income must be derived from capital; and, in a sense, this is true. Income *is* derived from capital *goods*. But the *value* of the income is not derived from the *value* of the capital goods. On the contrary, the value of the capital is derived from the value of the income. Valuation is a human process in which foresight enters. Coming events cast their shadows before. Our valuations are always anticipations.

These relations are shown in the following scheme in which the arrows represent the order of sequence—(1) from capital goods to their future services, that is, income; (2) from these services to their value; and (3) from their value back to capital value:

Capital goods ⟶ Flow of services (income)

                                                     ↓

Capital value ⟵ Income value

Not until we know how much income an item of capital will probably bring us can we set any valuation on that capital at all. It is true that the wheat crop depends on the land which yields it. But the value of the crop does not depend on the value of the land. On the contrary, the value of the land depends on the expected value of its crops.

The present worth of any article is what buyers are willing to give for it and sellers are ready to take for it. In order that each man may logically decide what he is willing to give or take, he must have: (1) some idea of the value of the future benefits which that article will yield, and (2) some idea of the rate of interest by which these future values may be translated into present values by discounting.

10. COSTS, OR NEGATIVE INCOME

Cost of production of durable agents or capital goods has its influence included in the preceding formulation, since any cost is simply a negative item of income. Future negative items are to be discounted exactly as future positive items. It is to be remembered that at the given point of time when the value is being computed only *future* costs can enter into the valuation of any good. Past costs have no *direct* influence on value. Only indirectly do they enter to the extent that they have determined the existing supply of goods and have thus either raised or lowered the value of the services of these goods.

In this indirect way, past costs can determine present values temporarily and until the prices of goods available are brought into conformity with the present costs of production through the operation of supply and demand. For example, the cost of producing woollen cloth declined very sharply after the close of the [First] World War, but the price did not decline for many months because the new cloth made at less expense was not sufficient to meet the demand, hence the price remained above the new costs of production for a time. Again, the cost of making shoes advanced rapidly during the early years of the twentieth century, but the price of shoes did not advance *pari passu* with increased costs, because the supply of more cheaply made shoes was still large and for a time controlled the market price. In the same indirect way, many other influences affect the value of the services of any good, especially any alternative to those services. But none of these considerations affects the principle that the value of the good itself is the discounted value of the value (however determined) of its future services.

11. THE DISCOUNT PRINCIPLE APPLIED

The principles which have been explained for obtaining the present value of a future sum apply very definitely to many commercial transactions, such as to the valuation of bank assets, which indeed exist largely in the form of discount paper, or short time loans of some other kinds. The value of a note is always the discounted value of the future payment to which it entitles the holder.

Elaborate mathematical tables have been calculated and are used by brokers for informing their customers what price should be paid for a five per cent bond in order that the purchaser may realize 5 per cent, 4 per cent, or any other rate of interest on the prices to be paid. The price of the bond is calculated from two items, the rate of interest to be realized and the series of sums or other benefits which the bond is going to return to the investor. Aside from risk, there can never be any other factors in the calculation except these two. Of course, an investor may refuse to buy a bond at the market price because he has, as an alternative, the opportunity to buy another bond cheaper so that he can realize a higher rate on his purchase price. But that fact does not alter the principle that market prices represent discounted benefits. The only market effect of this man's refusal will be a slight tendency to lower the market price of the first bond and raise that of its rival, that is, to alter the rate of interest realized. Later we shall study more fully the effects of such alternative opportunities. Here we are concerned only to note that the price of the bond is dependent solely on two factors: (1) its benefits and (2) the interest rate by which these are discounted.

The principle is, of course, not confined to bonds. It applies in any market to all property and wealth—stocks, land (which has a discounted capital value just as truly as any other capital), buildings, machinery, or anything whatsoever. Risk aside, each has a market value dependent solely on the same two factors, the benefits,[1] or returns, expected by the investor and the market rate of interest by which those benefits are discounted.

The income which he expects may be a perpetual income (flowing uniformly or in recurring cycles) or it may be any one of innumerable other types. If we assume that five per cent is the rate of interest, any one of the following income streams will have a present value of $1,000: a perpetual annuity of $50 per year; or an annuity of $50 a year for ten

---

[1] Including, of course, all benefits or services whatever from the possession of the wealth such as the option to subscribe to stock, now often attached to bonds, or the privilege attaching to certain bonds which permits National Banks to use the bonds for the security of National Bank notes. Some of these benefits may be very indirect and related to whole groups. A man seeking voting control as a benefit who already possesses 49 per cent may pay a specially high price for a few more shares of stock for the benefit of raising his holdings to 51 per cent. Or, a man may include in the benefits of his wealth the fun of running the business, or the social standing he thinks it gives him, or political or other power and influence, or the mere miserly sense of possession or the satisfaction in the mere process of further accumulation. However indirect, unusual, or bizarre the benefit, the principle still holds that the value of any capital good or goods is derived solely from the prospect of future benefits.

years, together with $1,000 at the end of the period; or $100 a year for fourteen years, after which nothing at all; of $25 a year for ten years, followed by $187.50 a year for ten years, after which nothing at all.

12. DOUBLE-ENTRY BOOKKEEPING

We began this chapter with the enjoyment income received by a person and then travelled back, by way of real income, cost of living, and money income to capital value, which simply embodies the capitalization or anticipation of income. This was going upstream, as it were, from the enjoyer of income to its source. We may now reverse our point of view and look downstream. We then think of the income stream not so much as flowing *to* its enjoyers as flowing *from* its various sources.[1]

Capital value is income capitalized and nothing else. Income flows from, or is produced by, capital goods and human beings, so that the capital value is also the value of capital goods. The income is credited to (and outgo or cost debited to) these goods and (or including) human beings.

As every bookkeeper knows, most of the items of income (positive or negative) take the form of *money payments*. (These are not a *stock* of money, which is always capital, but a *flow* of money.) Some are operations paid for—events in the productive process, such as grinding, spinning, weaving, hoisting, hauling, ploughing; others are events of consumption, such as eating food, wearing clothes, hearing music, or seeing a play at the theatre; while still others are within the human mind, such as enjoyments or their opposite, labour effort or discomfort.

It might seem that in sorting and combining such a miscellany of income items we could never avoid confusion and double counting and that the sum total would far exceed the true psychic or enjoyment income. But the fact is that almost as many negative items as positive items are included here and that, *in fact, except for enjoyment income and labour pain,*

---

[1] Possibly it would help to adjust our mental attitudes to this changed point of view if we could change the name of income to outcome, or output. Income suggests coming *toward us* while outcome suggests coming *from the source*. Thus the outcome from a farm is the net value of its crops; the outcome from a railway company is its dividends, etc.

Under this new procedure, we credit each item of income as outcome from its source and debit every negative item. Negative items of income are outgo. If we could change this name also, we would call it ingo, or input.

It is a mere clerical matter of bookkeeping thus to credit to its source every service rendered as so much outcome (or income) and debit it with every disservice rendered, as so much ingo (or outgo).

Having suggested these new terms, however, so that the student may mentally, or literally by lead pencil, substitute them for the old, I shall hereafter, for simplicity, adhere uniformly to the original terminology, using the term income even when we are thinking merely of its coming *from its capital source* while the recipient is forgotten.

every positive item is also negative, according to its relation to the capital source. Thus when Smith pays Jones $100 (no matter where it came from), Jones receives an item of income of $100 while Smith suffers an item of outgo of the same amount; and when a coupon of $100 is cut from a bond and deposited, the bond is credited with yielding $100 and the bank account is debited with the same sum. The same principle is applicable to the final big coupon called the principal of the bond. The same item is thus entered twice, once on one side of somebody's books and the other time on the other side of somebody's books.

The bookkeeping implications of such couples of items were discovered by accountants long ago and are the basis of their double-entry book-keeping, though its economic significance has been largely overlooked. One important significance is that this double entry prevents double counting; when we take the sum total of all income items for society, including psychic as well as physical items, this double entry results in cancelling out everything except the psychic items of enjoyment and labour pain.

Every operation of production, transportation, exchange, or consumption—every process, in fact, except final enjoyment—is double faced, or two items in one. I have called such an operation an 'interaction' because it is income to be credited to the capital which yields it, while it is outgo to be debited to the capital which receives it. Thus, in any complete bookkeeping, $100 worth of ploughing, on the one hand, is credited jointly to the plough, the ploughman, and the team, or motor, which do the ploughing; that is, which yield or bestow the service. On the other hand, it is debited to the land which is ploughed, that is, which receives the service.

If the plough is owned by one person and the land by another, the latter paying $100 to the former, then the service of ploughing, though a self-cancelling interaction for the two persons taken together, evidently cannot be ignored by either separately. If $100 is paid for this service of ploughing, the $100 item is an expense to the landowner to be subtracted from his gross income. It is no concern of his that this selfsame service of ploughing is counted as income by the plough-owner. So this item of $100 worth of ploughing affects our accounts quite differently according to the point of view. It may be a plus item from the point of view of one person and a minus item from that of another. When, however, the two accounts are combined and the plus and minus items are added, their algebraic sum is zero. For society as a whole, therefore, no postitive income results from ploughing until the land has yielded its crop and the crop has been finally consumed.

Thus, simply by the mechanical, clerical processes of making book-keepers' entries, we reach again, in the opposite order, the various stages originally described in the opening pages of this chapter. That is, the sum total of income flowing from a group of capital sources is naturally different according to which capital sources are included. There are certain cancellations within any group of capital goods which have an uncancelled fringe, and this may itself in turn disappear by cancellation if the group is enlarged by including other capital items with interactions between the new and old members. Henry Ford's mines yield a net income, the difference between certain credits and debits. If we include the railway which transports the product to the factory, certain credits to the mines from turning their product over to the railroad now disappear, being debits to the railway. If the circle be still further enlarged, say to include the Ford factories, other items likewise disappear as parts of interactions within the enlarged circle, and so on.

We must of course, include all services as income. A dwelling renders income to the owner who dwells in it himself just as truly as when he lets it to another. In the first case, his income is shelter; in the second, his income is rent payments in money. All wealth existing at any moment is capital and yields income in some form. As a business man said to me, his pleasure yacht is capital and gives him dividends every Saturday afternoon.

13. SIMPLICITY UNDERLYING COMPLICATIONS

In our present-day complicated economic life we are likely to be confused by the many industrial operations and money transactions. But net income still remains exactly what it was to primitive Robinson Crusoe on his island—the enjoyment from eating the berries we pick, so to speak, less the discomfort or the labour of picking them. The only difference is that today the picking is not so entirely hand-to-mouth, but is done by means of complicated apparatus and after the frequent exchange of money; that is, a long chain of middlemen, capital, and money transactions intervenes between the labour of picking at the start and the satisfaction of eating at the end. To continue the literal example of berry picking, we find today huckleberries picked by hired labourers on the Pocono Mountains, sorted, graded, shipped by rail and motor to New York City wholesalers, resold to retailers who sell and deliver them to the housewife in whose kitchen they are again sorted and prepared for their ultimate mission of giving enjoyment. The individual's total income when elaborately worked out, after cancelling, in pairs or couples, all such credits and debits, whether of money payments or the money value of services—in production or exchange—coincides necessarily with his enjoyment income, less the labour pain suffered in the same period, from which sort of income we started our discussion in this chapter. This coincidence occurs necessarily and automatically, by virtue of these mathematical cancellations.

It is interesting to observe that a corporation as such can have no net income. Since a corporation is a fictitious, not a real, person, each of its items without exception is doubly entered. Its stockholders may get income from it, but the corporation itself, considered as a separate person apart from these stockholders, receives none.

The *total income* of a real person is his *enjoyment income* only provided we include the credits and debits of his own body. The physical music, or vibrations which pass from his piano to his ear are, strictly speaking, only interactions to be credited to his piano and debited to his bodily ear. The music in his consciousness comes at the other, or brain, end of the auditory nerve. The piano plays to his ear, his ear to his brain, and his brain to his consciousness. His whole body mechanism is a transmitter from the outer world to his inner life, through ear, eye, and its other sense organs.

Or if the body mechanism, with its debits and credits, be omitted the total result is not his enjoyment income, subjectively considered, but the real income as above set forth. If we measure this, his real income, in money units, we find it equal to the total valuation of his cost of living less the total valuation of his own labour pain.

How to place a money valuation on a labour pain is a difficult question. This question is important in accounting theory, especially in its relation to the problems of measuring human welfare. But fortunately for us the difficulties of this valuation do not disturb the theory of the rate of interest, since this theory is actually concerned only with *differences* in the income stream at different times, not in a meticulous measurement of the *total*. Moreover, practically the only point in interest theory where labour pain enters is the case of a worker who suffers present labour pain in order to secure future satisfactions for himself or his family. This case is that of a labourer's savings; and all we need do here is to take the labourer's own valuation. Presumably, if the rate of interest is 5 per cent, the labour he will exert this year for the sake of $100 next year has a valuation in his mind of about $95.

But a labourer's savings are practically a negligible element in determining the rate of interest. To others than labourers the only important way labour enters is through the payment of wages and salaries, and these are money expenses incurred for the sake of future money returns. A labourer building a railway does not work for the future dividends from the railway. He is paid for immediate living by his employer in expectation of those future dividends. Thus wages are a sort of measure of labour pain to the employer of labour, whether or not they be so regarded by the labourer.[1]

If we exclude labour pain and further exclude from the labourer's book-keeping the income items, positive and negative, flowing from his household effects—the use of furniture, clothing, food, and so on—the total income then turns out to be not his real income *but his money income*—assuming that, as is ordinarily true, all his income flows in through money payments and none in kind.

14. CAPITAL GAIN NOT INCOME

The most interesting and valuable result of applying these bookkeeping principles is that thereby we automatically separate capital from income, two things which are so often confused and in so many ways. It is not uncommon for economic students to make the mistake of including capital gains as income. Capital gains, as already implied, are merely capitalization of future income. They are never present income. Therefore, a true meticulous accounting, item by item, of the income, or of the services and disservices, rendered by any specified group of capital items will infallibly grind out this truth. It will never confuse capital gain in that capital group with income realized from that group. This is true whether our capital group and its income are so extended as to include enjoyment income (positive and negative) as the final net income, or whether our specific group is so restricted as to leave ploughing or money payments as the uncancelled fringe.[2] We shall always find that only the income actually detached from, or given off for enjoyment by, that group, as in cutting coupons from a bond, will result from the summation of the accountant, who will never record as income the increase or decrease in the capital itself.

A bond price, for example, will grow with accrued interest *between* two coupon cuttings. That growth in its value is not income but increase of capital. Only when the coupon is detached does the bond render, or give off, a service, and so yield income. The income consists in the event of such off-giving, the yielding or separation, to use the language of the United States Supreme Court. If the coupon thus given off is reinvested in another bond, that event is outgo, and offsets the simultaneous income realized from the first bond. There is then *no* net income from the group but only growth of capital. If the final large payment of the principal is commonly

---

[1] They may be so regarded in cases where labour is paid by the piece and the labourer is free to stop work at any point.

[2] See *The Nature of Capital and Income*, chapters VII–X.

thought of not as income (which it is if not reinvested) but as capital it is because it is usually and normally so reinvested.

Likewise, if my savings bank account gains by compound interest, there is no income but only an accretion of capital. If we adopt the fiction that the bank teller hands over that accretion at any moment to me through his window, we must also adopt the fiction that it is simultaneously handed back by me through the same window. If the first event is income, the second is outgo. If it passes both ways, or does not pass at all, there can be no net income resulting. This is good bookkeeping and sound economics. There is no escape from such mathematical conclusions. By no hocus pocus can we have our cake and eat it too. This is as impossible as perpetual motion, and fundamentally as absurd. The absurdity is especially evident when the cause of an increase or decrease in the capital value of a bond or investment is not due to any change in the expected income at all but comes through a change in the *rate of interest*. Consols and *rentes* fluctuate in value every day with every change in the money market. Yet the income they actually yield flows on at the same rate. Merely the capital value is found sometimes on a 3 per cent basis and sometimes on a 4 per cent basis. A rise in the market is a capital gain, but it is not income. Income may be *invested* and thus transformed into capital; or capital may be *spent* and so transformed into income. In the first case, as we have seen, capital accumulates; in the second case, capital is diminished. In the first case the man is living inside his money income; in the second case he is living beyond his money income.

If Henry Ford receives $100,000,000 in dividends but reinvests all but $50,000, then his real income is only $50,000,[1] even if his money income is $100,000,000. And if, during the year of rebuilding his factories to make his new car, he received no dividends and yet spent $40,000 in that year for living expenses and all other satisfactions, then his *real* income was this $40,000 even if his money income that year was zero.

Thus, the income enjoyed in any year is radically different from the ups and downs of one's capital value in that year—whether this is caused by savings or the opposite, or by changes in the rate of interest or by so-called chance.

We may in our bookkeeping add our savings to our real income and call the sum total gain. For my part, I prefer not to call it income. For the two parts of this total—enjoyed income and accumulation of capital or capitalized future enjoyments—are unlike. The only argument for adding

---

[1] Except as already stated in a previous footnote, he derives in addition to this obvious income other less tangible and more subtle income from the sense of possession, prestige, power, etc., which go with great wealth.

them together is that the recipient *could* use the savings as income and still keep his capital unchanged. Yes, he *could*, but he didn't, otherwise there would be no savings! One part is income, and the other is capital gain.

This distinction between the real income, actually enjoyed, and the accretion or accrual of capital value, that is, the capitalization of future enjoyments, is not only in general vital, but vital to the understanding of this book.[1]

We cannot understand the theory of interest so long as we play fast and loose with the concepts of capital and income. And enjoyment income, which plays the central rôle in interest theory, is never savings or increase of capital.

15. CAPITAL-INCOME RELATIONS

In conclusion we may say that the chief relations between capital and income are:

(1) Capital value is income capitalized or discounted.

(2) If the rate of interest falls, the capital value (capitalized value of expected income) rises, and vice versa.

(3) This rise or fall in capital value is relatively great for durable goods like land, and relatively small for transitory goods like clothes.

(4) Capital value is increased by savings, the income being decreased by the same amount that the capital is increased.

(5) These savings thus diverted from income and turned back into capital will, except for mischance, be the basis for real income later.

16. APPLICATION TO THE RATE OF INTEREST

The problem of the rate of interest is entirely a problem of spending and investing, of deciding between various possible enjoyments constituting income, especially between relatively small but immediate enjoyments and relatively large but deferred enjoyments. There is an eternal conflict between the impulse to spend and the impulse to invest. The impulse of a man to spend is caused by his impatience to get enjoyments without delay, and his impulse to invest is caused by the opportunities to obtain by delay relatively more enjoyment either for himself or others.

For the study of interest from this point of view we need as our chief

---

[1] For fuller treatment of this subject the reader is referred to: 'The Nature of Capital and Income; Are Savings Income?', *Journal of American Economic Association*, third series, IX, no. I, 1–27; *The Income Concept in the Light of Experience*, privately printed as English translation of article in vol. III of the Wieser Festschrift, *Die Wirtschaftstheorie der Gegenwart* (Vienna, 1927), 29 pp.

subject matter a picture of a person's income stream. We may get this most clearly by plotting day by day, month by month, or year by year, the closest statistical measure of one's real income, namely, one's cost of living.

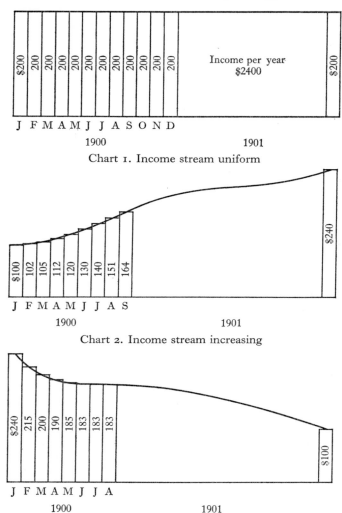

Chart 1. Income stream uniform

Chart 2. Income stream increasing

Chart 3. Income stream decreasing

If this income flows at a constant rate of $200 a month or $2400 a year, the picture of the income stream is as shown in Chart 1.

If the income stream flows at an increasing rate, the picture is as shown in Chart 2.

If it flows at a decreasing rate, the picture is as in Chart 3.[1]

Of course, these particular forms are only special types; numerous other types might be given.

In interest theory the incomes with which we deal are not statistical records of the past but those of the expected future. What is to be one's future income stream, chosen from among several income streams available, becomes of supreme importance.

17. CONFUSIONS TO BE AVOIDED

The very first effort of the beginner in this subject should be to rid his mind of all prepossessions as to the nature of income and capital. My grandchild of six recently asked the cashier of a savings bank, 'Show me the money I am going to get when I grow up'. The cashier gravely took him into a back room and held up a bag of coins. The vision of that bagful will doubtless persist into adult life as a picture of a savings bank account, even after he has learned in college that the total deposits of a bank far exceed the cash on hand, and that the depositor's capital is not actual cash but the right, measured in terms of cash, to the services or benefits flowing from the bank's assets, real estate, mortgages on real estate, stocks and bonds, and all the rest of its resources. Both capital and income *seem* to be simply money. We can always show a money sample, as did the cashier, and where one's capital is liquid so that it may readily be turned from one form to another via money—or rather credit—it is most simply and lazily pictured to the mind's eye as being itself money.

The student should also try to forget all former notions concerning the so-called supply and demand of capital as the causes of interest. Since capital is merely the translation of future expected income into present cash value, whatever supply and demand we have to deal with are rather the supply and demand of future income.

It will further help the student if he will, from the outset, divest himself of any preconception he may have acquired as to the rôle of the rate of interest in the distribution of income. It may be well here to point out that interest is not, as traditional doctrine would have it, a separate branch of income in addition to rent, wages and profits.

[1] In all three examples, each month's income is represented by a rectangular column or bar. In the last two cases, the resultant row of bars makes a series of flat tops or steps. But by taking days instead of months, we come nearer to a sloping curve which is a better and simpler ideal picture. Hereafter we shall use such continuous curves. But they may always be thought of as made up approximately of a series of columns or bars. For fuller discussion of such charts, see *The Nature of Capital and Income*, pp. 204 ff.

Irving Fisher

The income stream is the most fundamental fact of economic life. It is the joint product of many agencies which may be classified under many heads, such as human beings, land, and (other) capital. The hire of human beings is wages; the hire of land is land rent. What, then, is the hire of (other) capital—houses, pianos, typewriters, and so forth? Is it interest? Certainly not. Their hire is obviously house rent, piano rent, typewriter rent, and so forth, just as the man in the street calls them. Rent is the ratio of the payment to the physical object—land, houses, pianos, typewriters, and so forth—so many dollars per piano, per acre, per room. Interest, on the other hand, is the ratio of payment to the money *value* of these things—so many dollars per hundred dollars (or per cent). It is, in each case, the ratio of the net rent to the capitalized value of that rent. It applies to all the categories—to land quite as truly as to houses, pianos, typewriters. The income from land is thus both rent and interest just as truly as the income from a typewriter or a bond. We can and do capitalize land rent just as truly as we do house rent. For example, land worth '20 years purchase' yields 5 per cent interest. All this is true quite irrespective of the question of distinctions between land rent, on the one hand, and house rent, piano rent, typewriter rent, and so forth on the other.[1] It is a question of that sort of price which links one point of time with another point of time in the markets of the world. And it is a question concerning every branch of economic theory in which the time element enters. The rate of interest is the most pervasive price in the whole price structure.

As to profits, I believe the most fruitful concept is also that of the man in the street. When risk attaches to any one of the aforementioned forms of capital—human beings, land, houses, pianos, typewriters and so forth—the man in the street calls the net income profits. And profits, likewise, may be measured either (as rent) in relation to the physical units producing them, or (as interest) in relation to the values of these profits; that is, either as dollars per acre, per room, per piano and so forth; or dollars per $100 worth of land (houses, pianos, and so forth); or as dollars per share of ownership in any of these; or dollars per $100 worth of such shares. To pretend that either interest or profits is the income solely from capital goods other than land and that these two concepts are inapplicable to land—to pretend, in short, that wages, rent, interest and profits are four mutually *exclusive* divisions of the income stream of society is to treat different classifications of one thing as if they were themselves different

---

[1] See Frank A. Fetter, 'Interest Theories Old and New', *American Economic Review* (March 1914), pp. 76 and 77; Fetter, *Principles of Economics*, pp. 122–7; H. J. Davenport 'Interest Theory and Theories', *American Economic Review* (December 1927), pp. 636, 639.

things. It is as if we should speak of a certain total space as consisting partly of acres of land, partly of tons of soil, and partly of bushels of ore. Or again, it is like classifying a pack of cards into aces, clubs and red suits and pretending that these three classes are mutually exclusive.

The simple fact is that any or all income may be capitalized, including that credited to human beings, thus giving the resultant economic value of a man. William Farr, J. Shield Nicholson, Louis I. Dublin and others have made such computations.[1] However, we so seldom capitalize wages that we have no practical need to call wages or any portion of them interest. Nor where risk is a dominant factor, as in profits, is there real need to call the income interest. For instance, hoped-for dividends, according as the hope varies, are daily and automatically capitalized in the stock market and need not themselves be called interest. Much less would it be worth while to call enterpriser's profits interest. No one ever attempted to capitalize them. But in meticulous theory, all may be capitalized and so become interest.

18. A WORKING CONCEPT OF THE RATE OF INTEREST

While any exact and practical definition of a pure rate of interest is impossible, we may say roughly that the pure rate is the rate on loans which are practically devoid of chance. In particular, there are two chances which should thus be eliminated. One tends to raise the rate, namely, the chance of default. The other tends to lower it, namely, the chance to use the security as a substitute for ready cash. In short, we thus rule out, on the one hand, all risky loans and, on the other, all bank deposits subject to withdrawal on demand, even if accorded some interest. We have left, safe securities of fixed terms not likely to be transferred or transferred often before maturity. Such securities give us the nearest approach to pure interest both for short and long periods according to the time to maturity.

I shall usually confine the concept of the rate of interest to the rate in a (humanly speaking) safe loan, or other contract implying specific sums payable at one date or set of dates in consideration of repayment at another date or set of dates. The essentials in this concept are (1) definite and assured payments, and (2) definite and assured repayments, and (3) definite dates. The concept includes the concept of the rate realized on a safe security such as a bond purchased in the market. It is this that concerns us. We are not primarily concerned with *total* interest, but with the *rate* of interest.

[1] For instance, Dr Dublin computes the total value of the 'human capital' of the United States to be 1,500 billion dollars, or about five times the value of all other capital.

2   The concept of income

by Erik Lindahl

The main essentials of the concept of income have perhaps been most clearly laid down by Irving Fisher in his well-known definitions: 'A *stock of wealth* existing at a given *instant* of time is called *capital*; *a flow of benefits* from wealth through a *period* of time is called *income*.'[1] According to this, income consists of certain benefits accruing during a definite period of time, and further, these benefits arise from the employment of wealth; legacies, gifts, and the like are considered as falling outside the concept of income.

In order to give expression in one comprehensive measure to the size of these benefits, they are best considered as *amounts of exchange value*. It is simplest to base these calculations on the market prices during the period to which the estimation of income refers and subsequently to allow for changes in monetary purchasing power. Thus income is regarded as a concept of value; this applies also to the term 'real income', by which is simply meant income expressed in some unchanging monetary unit.

The following is designed to show that, starting from these premises, it is possible to arrive at alternative definitions of scientific importance which should be kept quite separate.

I. INCOME AS CONSUMPTION

This is Irving Fisher's own concept which he expounds in the following way. The benefits which constitute income consist of the *services* obtained from capital goods during a certain period, services from human beings included under this head. The problem of how to avoid double counting, when adding up those services which result in new capital goods and those services which flow from these goods, is solved in this manner: the capital-producing services are credited to the capital goods that deliver them, but at the same time they are debited to the resulting new capital goods; they are therefore excluded from the net income obtained from the total capital stock. The net income consists only of the services for the said period which are debited to various persons as consumers, that is to say, which enter into their consumption and thereby lead to the satisfaction of wants.

[1] Irving Fisher, *Elementary Principles of Economics* (New York, 1919), p. 38. See his earlier fundamental work, *The Nature of Capital and Income* (New York, 1906).

54

Irving Fisher's analysis is carried out in masterly fashion, but all his attempts to demonstrate that his concept of income is the usual one and that it is the only logical one must be considered unsatisfactory. In neither popular nor scientific terminology are income and consumption equated; on the contrary, income is generally taken to include saving (either positive or negative), and the crux of the matter is to decide just what this term saving may be taken to cover. It should also be possible to construct quite logically a concept of income to include saving, starting from the same premises as Irving Fisher.

In that case, however, it is best to distinguish between *anticipated income*, which refers to a certain period forward, and *income obtained*, which is reckoned after the termination of the period in question. The first of the following concepts is of the former type, the two others of the latter.

2. INCOME AS INTEREST

This concept, reduced to theoretical simplicity, may be taken as referring to the continuous *appreciation* of capital goods owing to the time-factor, that is to say, the current interest on the capital value which the goods represent. Income in this sense stands in quite a different relation to the concept of capital as against income regarded as a stream of services. The expected future services of the capital goods are the basic factor in the estimation of capital value, for the latter can be considered equal to the sum of the anticipated value of these services, discounted at the current rate of interest, due reduction also having been made for the risk factor. Capital value must again be the starting-point for the estimation of income as interest, that is to say, as the appreciation which arises when the discounted future services come nearer and nearer—an increase in value which for a given period forward can be regarded as the product of the capital value and the rate of interest applying to the period. We thus arrive at a quite different and in a certain sense secondary concept of income. But the term income in this case is quite as justifiable as in the former, for the continuous appreciation due to the time-factor can fairly be regarded as a 'flow of benefits from wealth through a period of time'.[1]

---

[1] The above-given deduction of the concept of income from Fisher's own premises, Fisher himself has chosen to disregard. He lays it down emphatically that the term income should be reserved for the stream of services on which the estimation of capital value is based, and should not, therefore, be taken to cover the appreciation of capital goods: 'Clearly, then, increase of capital is not income in the sense that it can be discounted in addition to other items of income. If it is income at all, it is income in a peculiar sense, and nothing but confusion can result from having to consider two kinds of income so widely divergent that whereas one is discounted to obtain capital-value, the other is not' (*The Nature of Capital and Income*, p. 249). He thus lays himself open

Erik Lindahl

If services created by one group of capital goods are invested in another, a certain amount of value is thereby transferred. The total value of the capital stocks is not necessarily affected by such a procedure. If, on the other hand, the services created pass directly into personal consumption, a corresponding diminishing effect on the total capital value may be expected. During a given period of time, this reduction in value through consumption may be less or greater than the contemporaneous appreciation due to the time-factor. These differences between interest and consumption anticipated for a certain period can be regarded as the *saving*, positive or negative as the case may be, which takes place during the period. But it should be pointed out that the net increase in capital values, in which saving expresses itself, need not correspond to the actual change in value during the period for, through more or less unforeseen circumstances, the capital values may at the same time undergo other more discontinuous changes in the shape of gains or losses (see below).

Income as interest can thus be said to correspond to the total *sum of the consumption and the saving* expected to take place during a certain period, the element of saving being expressed in the increase in value of the capital, exclusive of gains and losses.

Here it is assumed that the concept of income as interest is to apply generally, that is to say, not only as regards produced capital instruments, but also as regards land and labour, analogically with the comprehensive concept of capital developed with such success by Fisher, Fetter, and others. Interest can, then, no longer be regarded as a special income-category side by side with rent and wages: on the contrary, all forms of income are to be taken as current interests on the corresponding capital values. If, in accordance with the traditional definitions, rent and wages are taken as the value of services supplied during a certain period, an addition should consequently be made for any increases in value which these factors of production have undergone by reason of a surplus of accumulated interest, and alternatively, deductions should be made for any decreases in value that may have arisen as a result of the value of the services supplied exceeding the interest.

to the charge of inconsistency in making the term capital include all increase of capital, even such increases as arise through the accumulation of interest: 'Daraus folgt, daß Ersparnisse und Wertvermehrung immer Kapital und nicht Einkommen sind' (*Der Einkommensbegriff im Lichte der Erfahrung*, in *Wirtschaftstheorie der Gegenwart*, III, Wien, 1928, p. 28). This obviously runs contrary to his fundamental postulate, according to which capital consists of value at a given *instant* of time. The interest which applies to a *period* of time is in the nature of a time stream and cannot, from this point of view, be dragged into the concept of capital; it is clearly income. It is, moreover, significant that Fisher himself employs the terms 'earned income' and 'standard income' for this concept, which he contrasts with his own concept of income, 'the realized income'. The conflict is to be solved in this way: that we clearly distinguish two different categories of income—income as a 'flow of services' and income as a 'flow of capital value'.

If it is considered desirable to adhere more closely to the conventional concepts, the most satisfactory compromise would be wholly to disregard changes in the capital value of labour. By way of justification, it may readily be urged that since the abolition of slavery it has not been necessary to set a capital value on human labour-power, except in the way one estimates the solvency of an individual when advancing him credit. In this case the total income emerges as the sum of the current interest on all capital, exclusive of human capital, and the value of the labour-services during the period. But from this sum a deduction must be made for expenses incurred in bringing the workers up to the requisite standard of efficiency (provided that these expenses do not at the same time conduce to personal satisfactions). Otherwise double counting will arise, as in the calculation of wages no deduction corresponding to the amortization of these expenses is made. Consequently the saving included in the calculation of income only corresponds to external capital goods; capital in a personal form is left out of account.

It does not matter so much which of these constructions one chooses, provided only that it is carried to its logical conclusion. In both cases a concept of income emerges of great value from the point of view of theoretical analysis; for, referring to a certain period forward, it allows a quite consistent determination of the much debated concept of saving as one of the price-determining factors for the said period. For statistical purposes, on the other hand, this concept of income is less useful, as it is based to such a great extent on subjective factors, not statistically computable.[1]

The question arises, therefore, how may we widen the usefulness of the concept of income for statistical purposes, without too big a sacrifice of its theoretical preciseness.

[1] It should be understood that this calculation of interest is undertaken by the owners of the capital and is, accordingly, based upon their own individual anticipation of yields and their own judgment and valuation of the risk factor. Also the rates of interest at which the estimated yields of future periods are discounted, and the rate at which the current interest on capital is estimated, are not the same for all persons, as the conditions of making and receiving loans are fixed in different ways. Further, it should be borne in mind that both the capital values and the rates of interest may change as time goes on; so that the total current interest for so long a period of time as a year should be calculated as a sum of the interests during the shorter periods of time during which the capital value, no less than the rate of interest, can be assumed to remain unchanged. (As regards the calculation of current income from work, this presents no difficulties as far as it is contractual in character. A calculation of other kinds of income from work must again be based upon an anticipation of unascertained items, that is to say, upon subjective factors as in the case just considered.)

Erik Lindahl

3. INCOME AS EARNINGS

The simplest procedure would perhaps be to add together income as interest and the gains and losses which arise during the period to which the calculation of income applies. Income in this very wide sense would thus be calculated as the sum of the actual consumption and the increase of capital value which has taken place during a certain period. Both these items could be treated statistically, especially if human beings are excluded from capital stock. For this concept of income, the term used in this paper is 'earnings'.

The concept 'earnings', understood in this sense, has the great merit that its compass can be determined in a quite obvious way. It has therefore proved of great use in business economics, and in certain cases it has been used (though in a somewhat modified form) as a basis for assessing the taxation of income, e.g. in the case of the federal income tax of the United States of America. It is, accordingly, of interest to investigate the theoretical significance of the points of divergence between this concept of income and the one discussed just above, i.e. the nature of the before-mentioned gains and losses.

If the future could be completely foreseen, so that future streams of services and the rates of interest at which they should be capitalized were known beforehand, the total value of the capital stock could only be changed by the element of saving as defined above, that is to say, the difference between the interest income and the consumption. On this supposition, income as earnings (actual consumption plus appreciation of capital stock) would correspond to income as interest (anticipated consumption plus saving).

Actually, however, as the future is only anticipated as a series of more or less probable alternatives, the determination of capital values becomes dependent on a number of factors which change as time goes on. Thus the expectations of future services clearly change their character the nearer the time comes for these services to fall due. At the same time the estimation of the risk factor will undergo modification. The result of this will not necessarily be a change in capital value, as these changes in effect may neutralize each other. But, as a general rule, it may be assumed that changes in the factors of capitalization will be accompanied by greater or smaller changes in the capital values themselves. These discontinuous changes in the value of capital stock, dependent as they are on the fact that individuals, through unforeseen circumstances, find themselves obliged to modify their capitalizations, are what have here been termed 'gains and losses'.[1]

---

[1] See Gunnar Myrdal, *Prisbildningsproblemet och föränderligheten* [The Pricing Problem and the Change Factor] (Uppsala, 1927), where the distinction between incomes and costs on the one side and gains and losses on the other is considered fundamental in the treatment of the problem of profits.

From the above it follows that, for the reasons given, the classification of gains and losses as positive or negative items of income for the period in which they occur is hardly satisfactory. For here it is not a question of a flow of benefits through a *period* of time, but of changes which occur at certain *instants* of time (that is to say, when the owner of capital goods changes his estimation of its value) and thus, strictly speaking, have no time dimension. Consequently these instantaneous changes should not be reckoned in with the saving which occurs during a certain period either, as the term saving should really be kept for the refraining to consume income. Instead, we may assert that the gains and losses constitute *adjustments* of the estimation of savings which have been realized during *preceding* periods, because the anticipation of the future, upon which every attempt to estimate the savings must be based, changes in nature with the passing of time. These adjustments of the existing capital values have of course a quite different economic meaning from an increase or reduction in capital value through an excess or deficit of current interest in relation to consumption.

The conclusion must be, then, that the concept 'earnings', understood in the above-determined sense, is inclusive of elements which must be kept separate in a theoretical analysis. This concept, therefore, hardly provides an ideal solution of the problem of how to arrive at a concept of income that will be both tenable theoretically and practically useful at the same time.

4. INCOME AS PRODUCE

In this case, income is defined analogously to the concept of production. Net income becomes identifiable with the net value which the owners of the factors of production receive as remuneration for their contributions to the productive process. This net value is usually defined as the difference between the value of the product realized during the period and certain items which have been reckoned as products of previous periods and therefore must be deducted to avoid double counting.

In the majority of cases, income in the practical sense is understood in this way. In business economics and tax law this concept of income, the 'income produced', is more favoured than the concept of income we have just discussed, the earned income. It lies at the base of most computations of the national income, and corresponds roughly to what, in the language of daily life, usually goes under the name of income.

It is to be regretted, therefore, that this concept of income cannot be defined in such unambiguous terms as the concepts which have already been dealt with. In determining the plus and minus items which are included in the income calculation for a certain period, different principles are often applied, so that the content of the concept is apt to vary within rather wide limits. These variations can be brought into line with each one of the three concepts of income dealt with above: in determining the positive items the choice lies between the consumption concept on the one hand and the interest and earnings concepts on the other; as far as the negative items are concerned, one has to choose between the two latter concepts.

As regards the calculating of the positive items, an approach is made to the first alternative—income as *consumption*—according as to whether we insist that only finished products should be reckoned in the value of production. The more it is insisted that the reckoned products should be considered as marking the climax of the productive process, the more will the income calculus for these products tend to be postponed to the consumption period. The agreement between income as consumption and income as produce would clearly be complete if only the products consumed were reckoned as positive items, in which case there would of course be no negative items.

If, again, the positive items are not limited to finished products in the technical or economic sense, but are taken to cover all services rendered during the period, the net value of the production will be equal to the whole increase in value of the capital stock, which results from the productive process. In this case we come nearer the two other concepts of income (interest and earnings).

The minus items are, in the produce concept of income, calculated in a different way from that of Fisher. He, as mentioned above, subtracts all capital-producing services during the period when they are furnished. Here, on the contrary, they are not deducted until the periods during which the capital goods concerned are utilized. Thus income as produce will cover not only consumption but also the amount by which the production of capital goods exceeds the capital consumed. The capital consumed can, however, be calculated in different ways. Approach may be made in this connexion either to the concept of income as earnings or to the concept of income as interest.

The concept of *earnings* we approach, according as the deductions for raw materials and the depreciation of capital instruments are based on the original costs of production. If (owing to unforeseen circumstances) the value of these goods subsequently rises or falls, the gain or loss which this change in value implies is, by this method of calculating, partly reckoned in with the net income. The gains and losses, however, cannot be so fully accounted for as in the concept earnings as above defined. In the first place, as regards the durable capital instruments, the gains and losses are not reckoned in the income for the period during which they take place. They are, on the contrary, spread out over all the periods during which the capital is used, since the amounts written off, which have been determined by the original costs, are too high or too low in relation to the later values. It is to be noted, further, that gains and losses referring to land and capital instruments which are not being used up and for which, therefore, no deduction is made, do not enter into the calculation of income at all.

In so far as these deductions, on the other hand, are calculated according to the prices for the current period and are thus based not on the original but on the actual cost of production, income as produce will tend to correspond to income as *interest*. In this case capital gains and losses will not be included in the income: the income will correspond to the net value earned during the period, due deduction having been made for the actual diminution in value of the capital instruments caused by the productive process. This diminution can, for a durable capital instrument, be defined as the amount by which the value of the services rendered exceeds the accumulated interest on the capital value during the same period. If this amount is written off, that is to say, deducted from the positive item, i.e. the value of the services rendered, the accumulated interest emerges as the net income.

Even so, this correspondence to the income as interest concept can never be regarded as complete. Firstly, all appreciation due to the time-factor is not counted as produce. In so far as this appreciation does not apply to the product but to the factors of production, it can only be included in a somewhat incomplete way by fixing the deductions for the using up of capital. Further, the calculation of income as produce is made after the termination of the period concerned, whilst income as interest applies to a certain period forward. Consequently gains and losses referring to the interest realized during a certain period (not the capital proper) are included in the latter but not in the former concept.

For various practical purposes it is perhaps possible to defend different variants of the produced income concept. But from the point of view of theoretical analysis there can be no doubt as to which of the variants is most satisfactory. An approach to the consumption or the earning concept leads to mere compromise which should be abandoned in favour of the fundamental concepts, consumption and earnings. These concepts, moreover, could be turned to good statistical use. An approach to the interest concept—which implies that all services rendered during the period are reckoned as positive items and that the negative items, referring to services furnished during previous periods, are reckoned according to, not the original, but the actual costs of production—has, on the other hand, a more definite theoretical content: that the produced income is the interest which is realized during a given period.

The result of this investigation is, then, that for a certain period forward the anticipated interest, and for a period reckoned backward the produce in the sense of realized interest, is the most adequate expression of the income idea. According to this, saving can be defined as the difference between the anticipations of interest and those of consumption, and realized savings as the difference between realized interest and actual consumption during a given period.

3 The definition of income

by H. C. Simons*

The development of income taxes may be viewed as a response to increasingly insistent and articulate demand for a more equitable apportionment of tax burdens.[1] These taxes are the outstanding contribution of popular government and liberal political philosophy to modern fiscal practice. Thus they may properly be studied in the light of considerations raised in the preceding chapter [not reproduced here]. Income taxation is broadly an instrument of economic control, a means of mitigating economic inequality. In what follows we shall assume that moderation of inequality is an important objective of policy and proceed to consider income taxes as devices for effecting it. We shall be concerned, that is to say, largely with problems centring around that elusive something which we call 'discrimination'. Income taxes, in general, may seem peculiarly equitable; but serious problems arise when one proceeds to the task of describing, delimiting, and defining closely the actual tax base. Here, too, the problems may be dealt with largely in the light of considerations of justice.

We must face now the task of defining 'income'. Many writers have undertaken to formulate definitions, and with the most curious results. Whereas the word is widely used in discussions of justice in taxation and without evident confusion, the greatest variety and dissimilarity appear, as to both content and phraseology, in the actual definitions proposed by particular writers. The consistent recourse to definition in terms which are themselves undefinable (or undefined or equally ambiguous) testifies eloquently to the underlying confusion.

The fact that the term is widely used without serious misunderstanding in certain ranges of discourse, however, is significant. Since it is widely agreed that income is a good tax base, its meaning may be sought by inquiring what definition would provide the basis for most nearly equitable levies. At the same time we may seek to point out conflicts and contradictions in established usage and to discover the connotations of income which are essential and relevant for present purposes. Thus we may find those

---

[1] For stimulating development of this thesis see W. Moll, *Über Steuern* (Berlin, 1911), pp. 3–46. See also Bruno Moll, *Probleme der Finanzwissenschaft* (Leipzig, 1924), *passim*. The latter writer remarks (p. 99): 'Vermögens- und Einkommensbegriff entspringen der gleichen Wurzel, dem Begriff des wirtschaftlichen Könnens, dem Vermögensbegriff im weitesten Sinne.'

* Formerly Professor of Economics in the University of Chicago Law School.

denotations which may best be accepted, to avoid ambiguity, and to minimize disturbance of terminological tradition.

What is requisite to satisfactory definition of income will appear clearly only as we come to grips with various problems. It may help, however, to indicate some general requirements—if only because their neglect has been responsible for so much careless writing in the past. Income must be conceived as something quantitative and objective. It must be measurable; indeed, definition must indicate or clearly imply an actual procedure of measuring.[1] Moreover, the arbitrary distinctions implicit in one's definition must be reduced to a minimum. That it should be possible to delimit the concept precisely in every direction is hardly to be expected.[2] The task rather is that of making the best of available materials; for no very useful conception in 'social science' or in 'welfare economics' will entirely satisfy the tough-minded; nor can available materials so be put together as to provide an ideal tax base. But one devises tools of analysis which are useful, if crude; and a tax base may be defined in such manner as to minimize obvious inequities and ambiguities. Such at least is the present task.

The noun 'income' denotes, broadly, that which comes in. Thus, it may be used with almost any referent.[3] Even in the current usage of economics and business the term is commonly used in different contexts to denote several different things. It will suffice here to note three or four distinct senses in which the term is employed.

There is, first, and most common in economic theory, the conception of what may be called *income from things*.[4] In this sense, income may be conceived in terms of services derived from things or, quantitatively, in terms of the market value of uses. Thus, we speak commonly of income from land, from produced instruments, or from consumers' capital. When

---

1 The importance of this requirement may be suggested by the following definition: 'Net individual income is the flow of commodities and services accruing to an individual through a period of time and available for disposition after deducting the necessary costs of acquisition' (W. W. Hewett, *The Definition of Income*, Philadelphia, 1925, pp. 22–3). The author never undertakes to specify how this conception might be reduced to quantitative expression; he simply leaves the reader to guess how 'the necessary costs of acquisition' might be deducted from 'the flow of commodities and services accruing', or how either of these 'quantities' might be arrived at separately.

2 Kleinwächter, notably, endeavours to discredit the whole concept of income by pointing out that some arbitrary delimitations are unavoidable (*Das Einkommen und seine Verteilung*, Leipzig, 1896, pp. 1–16). He confounds himself and his reader with interesting conundrums having to do mainly with income in kind.

3 For discussion of the development of the income concept see Kleinwächter, *op. cit.* introduction; also Bruno Moll, *op. cit.* esp. chapter XII; also Bücher, *Zwei mittelalterische Steuerordnungen* (*Fests. z. Leipziger Hist.* 1894), pp. 138–9 (cited in B. Moll, *op. cit.* p. 96).

4 This is nicely covered by the German *Ertrag*—which most writers distinguish (some, carefully and consistently) from *Einkommen*. The *Ertrag* conception is that commonly employed (e.g. by Irving Fisher) in analysis of the discounting process.

used in this way, the term may have a merely acquisitive implication; for any property right, any mortgage against the community, has its yield.

The term is also frequently used to denote, second, *gain from transactions* or trading profit. If a share of stock is purchased for $100 and later sold for $150, it is customary to say that the venture has yielded an income of $50. The distinguishing feature of this conception is that it presupposes no allocation of income to assigned periods of time—that it does not raise the often crucial question as to when 'income' accrues.[1] The period is merely the time between the first and last transactions in a complete and mutually related series. 'Income' is imputed neither to preassigned time intervals nor to persons but merely to certain ventures, certain market operations.

There is, third, the familiar conception of *social or national income*—which appears frequently in the literature and is often defined after a fashion.[2] Social income denotes, broadly, a measure of the net results of economic activity in a community during a specified period of time. This, of course, is no definition; indeed, it is perhaps impossible to do more than indicate some roughly synonymous, and equally ambiguous, expressions. While commonly employed as though it denoted something quantitative, social income cannot be defined to any advantage in strictly quantitative terms. Economics deals with economy; economy implies valuation; and valuation is peculiarly and essentially relative. The prices with which rigorous economics deals are pure relations; and relatives cannot be summated into meaningful totals. Market prices afford only the most meagre clues (or none at all) to the 'value' of *all* goods produced and services rendered.

The concept of production, moreover, has itself a strong ethical or welfare flavour. The social income might be conceived in terms either of the value of goods and services produced or of the value of the productive services utilized during the period (after deduction for depreciation and depletion).[3] On neither basis, however, is it possible to avoid the question as to whether all economic (acquisitive) activity may be deemed productive. The use of resources to establish monopoly control can hardly be thought of as adding to the income of the community as a whole; nor is it easy

[1] Actually, it is always misleading to talk about the accrual of income.

[2] 'The aggregate money income of a country...must equal the aggregate money value of all goods produced and services rendered during the year' (R. T. Ely, *Outlines of Economics*, 4th ed. New York, 1923, pp. 100 and 105). One may remark upon the failure to introduce depreciation or depletion into the calculation. The necessity of such deduction is recognized in Alfred Marshall, *Principles of Economics* (8th ed.), p. 81; but Marshall's conception of social income is nowhere made explicit.

[3] This view is developed especially in Cassel, *The Theory of Social Economy*, trans. Barron (New York, 1932), chapters I and II. See also the same author's *Fundamental Thoughts on Economics* (New York, 1925).

to include the cost of the more egregious frauds perpetrated upon consumers. The tough-minded economist may argue that advertising is merely a service demanded by consumers—that an advertised product is simply a different commodity from a physically identical article with no distinctive label on the container; and this may solve the difficulty for one interested in the mechanics of the pricing process. But even a person of such interests will hesitate to maintain that all selling devices, truthful, false, and ludicrous, contribute to the social income. Large amounts of resources are employed to conceal issues in elections and to secure favour with actual and prospective government officials. But the point need not be laboured. Surely it is impossible to distinguish sharply between uses of resources which involve production, predation, and mere waste. Such distinctions, however, are implicit in the idea of social income.

In short, social income is merely a welfare conception. To say that it has increased is to say that things which must be economized are more abundant (or, perhaps, are utilized with greater 'efficiency'). This manifests an ethical or aesthetic judgment. Increase in the social income suggests progress toward 'the good life', toward a world better in its economic aspect, whatever that may be; and it is precisely as definite and measurable as is such progress.

If it be true that social income belongs far outside the realm of rigorous, quantitative concepts, the conclusion is important for the definition of *personal income*—a fourth sense in which the term is commonly used. Many writers imply or assert explicitly that personal income is merely a derivative, subordinate concept in the hierarchy of economic terminology. The view that personal income is merely a share in the total income of society is to be found in almost every treatise on economics; and some writers, forgetting even the distinction between a real and a personal tax (and that between *base* and *source*), insist that income taxes must bear—presumably by definition!—only on the net social income as it accrues to individuals.[1] On this view, gifts, capital gains, and other items must be excluded from the base of a personal tax because such items cannot be counted in the income of society as a whole!

Such notions derive, perhaps, from the central emphasis placed upon national income by Adam Smith and the mercantilists and from the central place of so-called distribution theory in classical economics. Economists have discussed the influence of trade policy upon the size of the national income; they have broken up that income curiously into functional elements; indeed, they have done almost everything with the income concept except to give it such definition as would make it eligible to a place among our

[1] E.g. Walther Lotz, *Finanzwissenschaft* (1st ed. Tübingen, 1917), pp. 444–50.

analytical tools. As a matter of fact, traditional theory is concerned primarily not with *Einkommen* but with *Ertrag*—with the pricing of goods and productive services. Its acquaintance with *Einkommen* is tenuous, implicit, and largely incidental.[1] Social income is neither an indispensable analytical tool for relative-price theory nor a concept whose content must be specified implicitly by a sound system of theory. At all events no writer, to our knowledge, has succeeded in giving any real meaning to the idea that personal income is merely a share in some undistributed whole. The essential point has been most happily phrased by Schmoller, who says in an early work, 'Nach unserer Ansicht gehört der Einkommensbegriff aber überhaupt streng genommen nur der Einzelwirtschaft an, der Volkswirtschaft nur in bildlich analoger Ausdehnung'.[2] Certainly much should be gained by cutting loose from a terminology ambiguous at best and inherited from the discussion of problems largely, even totally, irrelevant to those with which we are here concerned.[3]

Although personal income is not amenable to precise definition, it has, by comparison with the concept of social income, a much smaller degree of ambiguity. Its measurement implies estimating merely the *relative* results of individual economic activity during a period of time. Moreover, there arises no question of distinction between production and predation. Social income implies valuation of a total product of goods and services; while personal income is a purely acquisitive concept having to do with the possession and exercise of rights.

[1] For discussion of this point see A. Ammon, 'Die Begriffe "Volkseinkommen" und "Volksvermögen" und ihre Bedeutung für die Volkswirtschaftslehre', *Schr. d. Verein für Sozialpolitik*, CLXXIII, 19–26.

[2] G. Schmoller, 'Die Lehre vom Einkommen...', *Zeitschrift für die gesamte Staatswissenschaft*, XIX (1863), 78. Schmoller himself actually defines national income as the sum of all individual incomes (*ibid.* p. 20) but in such context that one may hardly charge inconsistency.

[3] Most of the innumerable German discussions of the meaning of income start with, and pretend to lean upon, Hermann, who was concerned primarily with the concept of social income, and who certainly did not write from the point of view of taxation (as do his 'followers'). See Hermann, *Staatswissenschaftliche Untersuchungen* (2nd (posthumous) ed., München, 1870), esp. chapter IX.

In Germany the 'correction' of Adam Smith's overemphasis upon the 'accounting' conception of social income ('ausschliesslich in dem von Standpunkte des capitalistischen Unternehmers berechneten Überschusse das reine Einkommen zu erblicken', is Robert Meyer's characterization of Smith's 'narrow' conception (*Das Wesen des Einkommens*, Berlin, 1887, p. 3) is regarded as a major contribution of German economics. Schmoller and most writers after him give credit to Hermann for this contribution. Meyer (*ibid.* chapter I) insists, however, that Schmoller has found in Hermann the opposite emphasis from what is really there and that credit for the contribution belongs really to Schmoller (and to Rodbertus). The controversy is hardly important for present purposes in any event, for the present writer's position implies, so far as concerns the definition of personal income, that Schmoller to some extent, and his followers especially, erred simply in getting away from Smith.

H. C. Simons

Personal income connotes, broadly, the exercise of control over the use of society's scarce resources. It has to do not with sensations, services, or goods but rather with rights which command prices (or to which prices may be imputed). Its calculation implies estimate (*a*) of the amount by which the value of a person's store of property rights would have increased, as between the beginning and end of the period, if he had consumed (destroyed) nothing, or (*b*) of the value of rights which he might have exercised in consumption without altering the value of his store of rights. In other words, it implies estimate of consumption and accumulation. Consumption as a quantity denotes the value of rights exercised in a certain way (in destruction of economic goods); accumulation denotes the the change in ownership of valuable rights as between the beginning and end of a period.

The relation of the income concept to the specified time interval is fundamental—and neglect of this crucial relation has been responsible for much confusion in the relevant literature. The measurement of income implies allocation of consumption and accumulation to specified periods. In a sense, it implies the possibility of measuring the results of individual participation in economic relations *for an assigned interval* and without regard for anything which happened before the beginning of that (before the end of the previous) interval or for what may happen in subsequent periods. All data for the measurement would be found, ideally, within the period analysed.

Personal income may be defined as the algebraic sum of (1) the market value of rights exercised in consumption and (2) the change in the value of the store of property rights between the beginning and end of the period in question. In other words, it is merely the result obtained by adding consumption during the period to 'wealth' at the end of the period and then subtracting 'wealth' at the beginning. The *sine qua non* of income is *gain*, as our courts have recognized in their more lucid moments—and gain *to* someone during a specified time interval. Moreover, this gain may be measured and defined most easily by positing a dual objective or purpose, consumption and accumulation, each of which may be estimated in a common unit by appeal to market prices.

This position, if tenable, must suggest the folly of describing income as a flow and, more emphatically, of regarding it as a quantity of goods, services, receipts, fruits, etc. As Schäffle has said so pointedly, 'Das Einkommen hat nur buchhalterische Existenz'.[1] It is indeed merely an arithmetic answer and exists only as the end result of appropriate calculations. To conceive of income in terms of things is to invite all the confusion

[1] Quoted by Schmoller (*op. cit.* p. 54) from Schäffle, 'Mensch und Gut in der Volkswirtschaft', *Deutsche Vierteljahrschrift* (1861).

of the elementary student in accounting who insists upon identifying 'surplus' and 'cash'.[1] If one views society as a kind of giant partnership, one may conceive of a person's income as the sum of his withdrawals (consumption) and the change in the value of his equity or interest in the enterprise. The essential connotation of income, to repeat, is *gain*—gain *to* someone during a specified period and measured according to objective market standards. Let us now note some of the more obvious limitations and ambiguities of this conception of income.

In the first place, it raises the unanswerable question as to where or how a line may be drawn between what is and what is not economic activity. If a man raises vegetables in his garden, it seems clearly appropriate to include the value of the product in measuring his income. If he raises flowers and shrubs, the case is less clear. If he shaves himself, it is difficult to argue that the value of the shaves must also be accounted for. Most economists recognize housewives' services as an important item of income. So they are, perhaps; but what becomes of this view as one proceeds to extreme cases? Do families have larger incomes because parents give competent instruction to children instead of paying for institutional training? Does a doctor or an apothecary have relatively large income in years when his family requires and receives an extraordinary amount of his own professional services? Kleinwächter suggests[2] that the poorest families might be shown to have substantial incomes if one went far in accounting for instruction, nursing, cooking, maid service, and other things which the upper classes obtain by purchase.

A little reflection along these lines suggests that leisure is itself a major item of consumption; that income per hour of leisure, beyond a certain minimum, might well be imputed to persons according to what they might earn per hour if otherwise engaged. Of course, it is one thing to note that such procedure is appropriate in principle and quite another to propose that it be applied. Such considerations do suggest, however, that the neglect of 'earned income in kind' may be substantially offset, for comparative purposes (for measurement of relative incomes), if leisure income is also neglected. For income taxation it is important that these elements of income vary with considerable regularity, from one income class to the next, along the income scale.

[1] This point, with all its triteness, can hardly be overemphasized, for it implies a decisive criticism of most of the extant definitions of income. Professor Hewett, e.g., asserts and implies consistently that income is merely a collection of goods and services which may, so to speak, be thrown off into a separate pile and then measured in terms of money. He and others too, no doubt, know better; but, when one undertakes the task of definition, one may expect to be held accountable for what one literally says.

[2] *Das Einkommen und seine Verteilung*, Introduction. We have drawn heavily, in this and other passages, on Kleinwächter's conundrums.

H. C. Simons

A similar difficulty arises with reference to receipts in the form of compensation in kind. Let us consider here another of Kleinwächter's conundrums. We are asked to measure the relative incomes of an ordinary officer serving with his troops and a *Flügeladjutant* to the sovereign. Both receive the same nominal pay; but the latter receives quarters in the palace, food at the royal table, servants, and horses for sport. He accompanies the prince to theatre and opera and, in general, lives royally at no expense to himself and is able to save generously from his salary. But suppose, as one possible complication, that the *Flügeladjutant* detests opera and hunting.

The problem is clearly hopeless. To neglect all compensation in kind is obviously inappropriate. On the other hand, to include the perquisites as a major addition to the salary implies that all income should be measured with regard for the relative pleasurableness of different activities—which would be the negation of measurement. There is hardly more reason for imputing additional income to the *Flügeladjutant* on account of his luxurious wardrobe than for bringing into account the prestige and social distinction of a (German) university professor. Fortunately, however, such difficulties in satisfactory measurement of relative incomes do not bulk large in modern times; and, again, these elements of unmeasurable psychic income may be presumed to vary in a somewhat continuous manner along the income scale.

If difficulties arise in determining what positive items shall be included in calculations of income (in measuring consumption), they are hardly less serious than those involved in determining and defining appropriate deductions. At the outset there appears the necessity of distinguishing between consumption and expense; and here one finds inescapable the unwelcome criterion of intention. A thoroughly precise and objective distinction is inconceivable. Given items will represent business expense in one instance and merely consumption in another, and often the motives will be quite mixed. A commercial artist buys paints and brushes to use in making his living. Another person may buy the same articles as playthings for his children, or to cultivate a hobby of his own. Even the professional artist may use some of his materials for things he intends or hopes to sell, and some on work done purely for his own pleasure. In another instance, moreover, the same items may represent investment in training for earning activity later on.

The latter instance suggests that there is something quite arbitrary even about the distinction between consumption and accumulation. On the face of it, this is not important for the definition of income; but it must be remembered that accumulation or investment provides a basis for expense deductions in the future, while consumption does not. The distinction in question can be made somewhat definite if one adopts the drastic expedient of treating all outlays for augmenting personal earning capacity as consumption. This expedient has little more than empty, formal, legalistic justification. On the other hand, one does well to accept, here as elsewhere, a loss of relevance or adequacy as the necessary cost of an essential definiteness. It would require some temerity to propose recognition of depreciation or depletion in the measurement of personal-service incomes—if only because the determination of the base, upon which to apply depreciation rates, presents a simply fantastic problem. It is better simply to recognize the limitations of measurable personal income for purposes of certain comparisons (e.g. by granting special credits to personal-service incomes under income taxes).

Our definition of income may also be criticized on the ground that it ignores the patent instability of the monetary *numéraire*;[1] and it may also be maintained that there is no rigorous, objective method either of measuring or of allowing for this instability. No serious difficulty is involved here for the measurement of consumption—which presumably must be measured in terms of prices at the time goods and services are actually acquired or consumed.[2] In periods of changing price levels, comparisons of incomes would be partially vitiated as between persons who distributed consumption outlays differently over the year. Such difficulties are neglible, however, as against those involved in the measurement of accumulation. This element of annual income would be grossly misrepresented if the price level changed markedly during the year. These limitations of the income concept are real and inescapable; but it must suffice here merely to point them out.

Another difficulty with the income concept has to do with the whole problem of valuation. The precise, objective measurement of income implies the existence of perfect markets from which one, after ascertaining quantities, may obtain the prices necessary for routine valuation of all possible inventories of commodities, services, and property rights. In actuality there are few approximately perfect markets and few collections of goods or properties which can be valued accurately by recourse to market prices. Thus, every calculation of income depends upon 'constructive valuation', i.e. upon highly conjectural estimates made, at best, by persons of wide information and sound judgment; and the results of such calculations have objective validity only in so far as the meagre

---

[1] See Jacob Viner, 'Taxation and Changes in Price Levels', *Journal of Political Economy*, XXXI (1923), esp. pp. 494–504.

[2] In a sense relevant to income measurement, two persons' consumption of, say, strawberries might be very unequal for a period, though the physical quantities involved were identical, provided one consumed them largely in season and the other largely out of season.

objective market data provide limits beyond which errors of estimate are palpable. One touches here upon familiar problems of accounting and, with reference to actual estimates of income, especially upon problems centring around the 'realization criterion'.

Our definition of income perhaps does violence to traditional usage in specifying impliedly a calculation which would include gratuitous receipts. To exclude gifts, inheritances, and bequests, however, would be to introduce additional arbitrary distinctions;[1] it would be necessary to distinguish among an individual's receipts according to the intentions of second parties. Gratuities denote transfers not in the form of exchange—receipts not in the form of 'consideration' for something 'paid' by the recipient. Here, again, no objective test would be available; and, if the distinctions may be avoided, the income concept will thus be left more precise and more definite.[2]

It has been argued that the inclusion of gratuities introduces an objectionable sort of double counting. The practice of giving seems a perhaps too simple means for increasing average personal income in the community. But philosophers have long discoursed upon the blessings of social consciousness and upon the possibilities of improving society by transforming narrow, acquisitive desires into desire for the welfare of our fellows. If it is not more pleasant to give than to receive, one may still hesitate to assert that giving is not a form of consumption for the giver. The proposition that everyone tries to allocate his consumption expenditure among different goods in such manner as to equalize the utility of dollars-worths may not be highly illuminating; but there is no apparent reason for treating gifts as an exception. And certainly it is difficult to see why gifts should not be regarded as income to the recipient.

The very notion of double counting implies, indeed, the familiar and disastrous misconception that personal income is merely a share in some

---

[1] The greater part of the enormous German literature on *Einkommensbegriff* may be regarded as the product of effort to manipulate verbal symbols into some arrangement which would capture the essential connotations of *Einkommen* (as something distinct from *Ertrag, Einnahme, Einkünfte*, etc.), provide a not too arbitrarily delimited conception, and yet decisively exclude gifts and bequests. It is as though an army of scholars had joined together in the search for a definition which, perfected and established in usage, would provide a sort of 'linguistic-constitutional' prohibition of an (to them) objectionable tax practice. For summary of this literature see Bauckner, *Der privatwirtschaftliche Einkommensbegriff* (München, 1921).

Of course, we must avoid the implication that our definition establishes any decisive presumption regarding policy in income taxation. The case for or against taxation of gratuitous receipts as income ought not to be hidden in a definition.

[2] The force of the foregoing argument is perhaps diminished when one remembers that the distinction creeps in unavoidably on the other side of the transaction—i.e. in the distinction between consumption and expense in the case of the donor. But there remains a presumption against introducing the distinction twice over if once will do.

undistributed, separately measurable whole.[1] Certainly it is a curious presumption that a good method for measuring the relative incomes of individuals must yield quantitites which, summated, will in turn afford a satisfactory measure of that ambiguous something which we call social income. This double-counting criticism, in the case of some writers (notably Irving Fisher), carries with it the implied contention that all possible referents of the word 'income', in different usages, must be definable or expressible in terms of one another. We have pointed out several different usages of the term in order to show that they represent distinct, and relatively unrelated, conceptions—conceptions which only poverty of language and vocabulary justifies calling by the same name.

[1] Some writers explicitly avoid the implication that social income should be definable in terms of individual incomes or vice versa: Held, *Die Einkommensteuer* (Bonn, 1872), chapter IV, esp. pp. 92 ff.; F. J. Neumann, *Grundlagen der Volkswirtschaft* (Tübingen, 1899), pp. 220–1; Schmoller, *op. cit.* p. 78; Ammon, *op. cit.* pp. 21–6; Meyer, *op. cit.* chapter XII.

4 Income

by J. R. Hicks*

We have now concluded our discussion of interest; and, by so doing, we have also concluded all that it is absolutely necessary to say about the foundations of dynamic economics. If we chose, we could thus proceed at once to analyse the working of the dynamic system, proceeding on parallel lines to those on which we analysed the working of a static system in Part II [not reproduced here]. That is what we shall do, ultimately; but meanwhile the reader has the right to raise an objection. Nothing has been said in the foregoing about any of a series of concepts which have usually been regarded in the past as fundamental for dynamic theory. Nothing has been said about Income, about Saving, about Depreciation, or about Investment (with a capital I). These are the terms in which one has been used to think; how do they fit here?

My decision to abstain from using these concepts in the last five chapters was, of course, quite deliberate. In spite of their familiarity, I do not believe that they are suitable tools for any analysis which aims at logical precision. There is far too much equivocation in their meaning, equivocation which cannot be removed by the most painstaking effort. At bottom, they are not logical categories at all; they are rough approximations, used by the business man to steer himself through the bewildering changes of situation which confront him. For this purpose, strict logical categories are not what is needed; something rougher is actually better. But if we try to work with terms of this sort in the investigations we are here concerned with, we are putting upon them a weight of refinement they, cannot bear.

I do not think that anyone who has followed the theoretical controversies of recent years will be very surprised at my putting foward this view. We have seen eminent authorities confusing each other and even themselves by adopting different definitions of saving and income, none quite consistent, none quite satisfactory. When this sort of thing happens, there is usually some reason for the confusion; and that reason needs to be brought out before any further progress can be made.

---

* Drummond Professor of Political Economy, University of Oxford, 1952–65. Fellow of All Souls.

2

Although we have refrained from using the term income in our dynamic theory, the reader will remember that we had no such inhibition when we were concerned with statics. In statics the difficulty about income does not arise. A person's income can be taken without qualification as equal to his receipts (earnings of labour, or rent from property). Sleeping dogs can be left to lie. The same is true in the economics of the stationary state, a branch of dynamic economics, but one which (as we have seen) blacks out some of the most important of dynamic problems. If a person expects no change in economic conditions, and expects to receive a constant flow of receipts, the same amount in every future week as he receives this week, it is reasonable to say that that amount is his income. But suppose he expects to receive a smaller amount in future weeks than this week (this week's receipts may include wages for several weeks' work, or perhaps a bonus on shares), then we should not regard the whole of his current receipts as income; some part would be reckoned to capital account. Similarly, if it so happened that he was entirely dependent on a salary paid every fourth week, and the present week was one in which his salary was not paid, we should not regard his income this week as being zero. How much would it be? We cannot give an exact answer without having a clear idea about the nature of income in general.

The purpose of income calculations in practical affairs is to give people an indication of the amount which they can consume without impoverishing themselves. Following out this idea, it would seem that we ought to define a man's income as the maximum value which he can consume during a week, and still expect to be as well off at the end of the week as he was at the beginning. Thus, when a person saves, he plans to be better off in the future; when he lives beyond his income, he plans to be worse off. Remembering that the practical purpose of income is to serve as a guide for prudent conduct, I think it is fairly clear that this is what the central meaning must be.

However, business men and economists alike are usually content to employ one or other of a series of approximations to the central meaning. Let us consider some of these approximations in turn.

3

The first approximation would make everything depend on the capitalized money value of the individual's prospective receipts. Suppose that the stream of receipts expected by an individual at the beginning of the week is the same as that which would be yielded by investing in securities a sum of £M. Then, if he spends nothing in the current week, reinvesting any receipts which he gets, and leaving to accumulate those that have not yet fallen due, he can expect that the stream which will be in prospect at the end of the week will be £M plus a week's interest on £M. But if he spends something, the expected value of his prospect at the end of the week will be less than this. There will be a certain particular amount of expenditure which will reduce the expected value of his prospect to exactly £M. On this interpretation, that amount is his income.

This definition is obviously sensible in the case when receipts are derived entirely from property—securities, land, buildings, and so on. Suppose that at the beginning of the week our individual possesses property worth £10,010, and no other source of income. Then if the rate of interest were $\frac{1}{10}$ per cent per week, income would be £10 for the week. For if £10 were spent, £10,000 would be left to be reinvested; and in one week this would have accumulated to £10,010—the original sum.

In the case of incomes from work, the definition is less obviously sensible, but it is still quite consistent with ordinary practice. Not having to do with a slave market, we are not in the habit of capitalizing incomes from work; but in the sorts of cases which generally arise this makes no difference. Fluctuations in receipts from work are not usually easy to foresee in advance; and any one who expects a constant stream of receipts (and does not expect any change in interest rates) will reckon that constant amount as his income, on this definition. If fluctuations are foreseen, they are nearly always so near ahead that interest on the variations is negligible. With interest neglected, calculation by capitalization reduces to mere arithmetical division over time. £20 per month of four weeks can be taken as equivalent to £5 per week.

Income No. 1 is thus the maximum amount which can be spent during a period if there is to be an expectation of maintaining intact the capital value of prospective receipts (in money terms). This is probably the definition which most people do implicitly use in their private affairs; but it is far from being in all circumstances a good approximation to the central concept.

4

For consider what happens, first, if interest rates are expected to change. If the rate of interest for a week's loan which is expected to rule in one future week is not the same as that which is expected to rule in another future week, then a definition based upon constancy of money capital becomes unsatisfactory. For (reverting to the numerical example we used above), suppose that the rate of interest per week for a loan of one week is $\frac{1}{10}$ per cent, but that the corresponding rate expected to rule in the second week from now is $\frac{1}{5}$ per cent, and that this higher rate is expected to continue indefinitely afterwards. Then the individual is bound to spend no more than £10 in the current week, if he is to expect to have £10,010 again at his disposal at the end of the week; but if he desires to have the same sum available at the end of the second week, he will be able to spend nearly £20 in the second week, not £10 only. The same sum (£10,010) available at the beginning of the first week makes possible a stream of expenditures

$$£10, £20, £20, £20, \ldots,$$

while if it is available at the beginning of the second week it makes possible a stream

$$£20, £20, £20, £20, \ldots$$

It will ordinarily be reasonable to say that a person with the latter prospect is better off than one with the former.

This leads us to the definition of Income No. 2. We now define income as the maximum amount the individual can spend this week, and still expect to be able to spend the same amount in each ensuing week. So long as the rate of interest is not expected to change, this definition comes to the same thing as the first; but when the rate of interest is expected to change, they cease to be identical. Income No. 2 is then a closer approximation to the central concept than Income No. 1 is.

5

Now what happens if prices are expected to change? The correction which must be introduced suggests itself almost immediately. Income No. 3 must be defined as the maximum amount of money which the individual can spend this week, and still expect to be able to spend the same amount *in real terms* in each ensuing week. If prices are expected to rise, then an individual who plans to spend £10 in the present and each ensuing week must expect to be less well off at the end of the week than he is at the beginning. At each date he can look forward to the opportunity of spending £10 in each future week; but at the first date one of the £10s will be spent in a week when prices are relatively low. An opportunity of spending on favourable terms is present in the first case, but absent in the second.

Thus, if £10 is to be his income for this week, according to definition No. 3 he will have to expect to be able to spend in each future week not £10, but a sum greater or less than £10 by the extent to which prices have risen or fallen in that week above or below their level in the first week.

Some correction of this sort is obviously desirable. But what do we mean by 'in real terms'? What is the appropriate index-number of prices to take? To this question there is, I believe, no completely satisfactory answer.

J. R. Hicks

Even when prices are expected to change there is, indeed, still available a very laborious criterion which would enable us to say, for any given set of planned expenditures, whether it is such that the planner is living within his income or not.[1] If the application of this test were to show that the individual's expenditure equalled his income, then of course it would determine his income; but in all other cases it does not suffice to show by how much he is living within his income, that is to say, exactly how much his income is.

Income No. 3 is thus already subject to some indeterminateness; but that is not the end of the difficulty. For Income No. 3 is still only an approximation to the central meaning of the concept of income; it is not that central meaning itself. One point is still left out of consideration; by its failure to consider this even Income No. 3 falls short of being a perfect definition.

This is the matter of durable consumption goods. Strictly speaking, saving is not the difference between income and expenditure, it is the difference between income and consumption. Income is not the maximum amount the individual can *spend* while expecting to be as well off as before at the end of the week; it is the maximum amount he can *consume*. If some part of his expenditure goes on durable consumption goods, that will tend to make his expenditure exceed his consumption; if some part of his consumption is consumption of durable consumption goods, already bought in the past, that tends to make consumption exceed expenditure. It is only if these two things match, if the acquisition of new consumption goods just matches the using up of old ones, that we can equate consumption to spending and proceed as before.

But what is to be done if these things do not match? And worse, how are we to tell if they do match? If there is a perfect secondhand market for the goods in question, so that a market value can be assessed for them with precision, corresponding to each particular degree of wear, then the value-loss due to consumption can be exactly measured; but if not there is

---

[1] If his is living within his income he must be able to plan for the second Monday the same stream of purchases as for the first, and still have something left over. Suppose he plans to purchase of commodity X quantities X_0, X_1, X_2,... in successive weeks; of commodity Y quantities Y_0, Y_1, Y_2,...; and so on. The condition for him to live within his income in the first week is that the stream of purchases actually planned for later weeks,
$$X_1 Y_1 Z_1 ..., \qquad X_2 Y_2 Z_2 ..., \qquad X_3 Y_3 Z_3 ...,$$
valued at the prices at which each is actually expected to be made (those of the 2nd, 3rd, 4th,...weeks respectively), should have a greater value than the original stream
$$X_0 Y_0 Z_0 ..., \qquad X_1 Y_1 Z_1 ..., \qquad X_2 Y_2 Z_2 ...,$$
valued, not at the first but at the second Monday, and valued at the same prices as that of the other stream (those of the 2nd, 3rd, 4th weeks, &c.), that is to say, valued at prices expected to rule one week later in each case than the dates at which these purchases are expected to be made in fact.

nothing for it but to revert to the central concept itself. If the individual is using up his existing stock of durable consumption goods, and not acquiring new ones, he will be worse off at the end of the week if he can then only plan the same stream of purchases as he could at the beginning. If he is to live within his income, he must in this case take steps to be able to plan a larger stream at the end of the week; but how much larger can be told from nothing else but the central criterion itself.

6

We are thus forced back on the central criterion, that a person's income is what he can consume during the week and still expect to be as well off at the end of the week as he was at the beginning. By considering the approximations to this criterion, we have come to see how very complex it is, how unattractive it looks when subjected to detailed analysis. We may now allow a doubt to escape us whether it does, in the last resort, stand up to analysis at all, whether we have not been chasing a will-o'-the-wisp.

At the beginning of the week the individual possesses a stock of consumption goods, and expects a stream of receipts which will enable him to acquire in the future other consumption goods, perishable or durable. Call this Prospect I. At the end of the week he knows that one week out of that prospect will have disappeared; the new prospect which he expects to emerge will have a new first week which is the old second week, a new second week which is the old third week, and so on. Call this Prospect II. Now if Prospect II were available on the first Monday, we may assume that the individual would know whether he preferred I to II at that date; similarly, if Prospect I were available on the second Monday, he would know if he preferred I to II then. But to inquire whether I on the first Monday is preferred to II on the second Monday is a nonsense question; the choice between them could never be actual at all; the terms of comparison are not *in pari materia*.

This point is of course exceedingly academic; yet it has the same sort of significance as the point we made at a much earlier stage of our investigations, about the immeasurability of utility. In order to get clear-cut results in economic theory, we must work with concepts which are directly dependent on the individual's scale of preferences, not on any vaguer properties of his psychology. By eschewing *utility* we were able to sharpen the edge of our conclusions in economic statics; for the same reason, we shall be well advised to eschew *income* and *saving* in economic dynamics. They are bad tools, which break in our hands.

avoid (shun)

J. R. Hicks

7

These considerations are much fortified by another, which emerges when we pass from the consideration of individual income (with which we have been wholly concerned hitherto) to the consideration of social income. Even if we content ourselves with one of the approximations to the concept of individual income (say Income No. 1, which is good enough for most purposes), it remains true that income is a subjective concept, dependent on the particular expectations of the individual in question. Now, as we have seen, there is no reason why the expectations of different individuals should be consistent; one of the main causes of disequilibrium in the economic system is a lack of consistency in expectations and plans. If A's income is based on A's expectations, and B's income upon B's expectations, and these expectations are inconsistent (because they expect different prices for the same commodity at particular future dates, or plan supplies and demands that will not match on the market), then an aggregate of their incomes has little meaning. It has no more to its credit than its obedience to the laws of arithmetic.

This conclusion seems unavoidable, but it is very upsetting, perhaps even more upsetting than our doubts about the ultimate intelligibility of the concept of individual income itself. Social income plays so large a part in modern economics, not only in the dynamic and monetary theory with which we are here concerned but also in the economics of welfare, that it is hard to imagine ourselves doing without it. It is hard to believe that the social income which economists discuss so much can be nothing else but a mere aggregate of possibly inconsistent expectations. But if it is not that, what is it?

In order to answer this question, we must begin by making a further distinction within the field of individual income. All the definitions of income we have hitherto discussed are *ex ante* definitions[1]—they are concerned with what a person can consume during a week and still *expect* to be as well off as he was. Nothing is said about the realization of this expectation. If it is not realized exactly, the value of his prospect at the end of the week will be greater or less than it was expected to be, so that he makes a 'windfall' profit or loss.[2] If we add this windfall gain to any of our preceding definitions of income (or subtract the loss), we get a new set of definitions, definitions of 'income including windfalls' or 'income *ex post*'. There is a definition of income *ex post* corresponding to each of our previous definitions of income *ex ante*; but for most purposes it is that corresponding to Income No. 1 which is the most important. Income

---

[1] To use a term invented by Professor Myrdal, and exported by other Swedish economists.
[2] To use a term of Mr Keynes.

No. 1 *ex post* equals the value of the individual's consumption *plus* the increment in the money value of his prospect which has accrued during the week; it equals consumption *plus* capital accumulation.

This last very special sort of 'income' has one supremely important property. So long as we confine our attention to income from property, and leave out of account any increment or decrement in the value of prospects due to changes in people's own earning power (accumulation or decumulation of 'human capital'), Income No. 1 *ex post* is not a subjective affair, like other kinds of income; it is almost completely objective. The capital value of the individual's property at the beginning of the week is an assessable figure; so is the capital value of his property at the end of the week; thus, if we assume that we can measure his consumption, his income *ex post* can be directly calculated. Since the income *ex post* of any individual is thus an objective magnitude, the incomes *ex post* of all individuals composing the community can be aggregated without difficulty; and the same rule, that Income No. 1 *ex post* equals consumption *plus* capital accumulation, will hold for the community as a whole.

This is a very convenient property, but unfortunately it does not justify an extensive use of the concept in economic theory. *Ex post* calculations of capital accumulation have their place in economic and statistical *history*; they are a useful measuring-rod for economic progress; but they are of no use to theoretical economists, who are trying to find out how the economic system works, because they have no significance for conduct. The income *ex post* of any particular week cannot be calculated until the end of the week, and then it involves a comparison between present values and values which belong wholly to the past. On the general principle of 'bygones are bygones', it can have no relevance to present decisions. The income which is relevant to conduct must always exclude windfall gains; if they occur, they have to be thought of as raising income for future weeks (by the interest on them) rather than as entering into any effective sort of income for the current week. Theoretical confusion between income *ex post* and *ex ante* corresponds to practical confusion between income and capital.

8

It seems to follow that anyone who seeks to make a statistical calculation of social income is confronted with a dilemma. The income he can calculate is not the true income he seeks; the income he seeks cannot be calculated. From this dilemma there is only one way out; it is of course the way that has to be taken in practice. He must take his objective magnitude, the social income *ex post*, and proceed to adjust it, in some way that seems plausible or reasonable, for those changes in capital values which look as if they have had the character of windfalls. This sort of estimation is normal statistical procedure, and on its own ground it is wholly justified. But it can only result in a statistical estimate; by its very nature, it is not the measurement of an economic quantity.[1]

For purposes of welfare economics it is generally the *real* social income which we desire to measure; this means that an estimate has to be made which will correspond to Income No. 3 in the same way as the above estimate corresponds to Income No. 1. Here we have the additional difficulty that it is impossible to get an objective measurement of Income No. 3, even *ex post*; since Income No. 3 always depends upon expectations of prices of consumption goods. But something with the same sort of correspondence can be constructed. Variations in prices can be excluded from the calculation of capital values, in one way or another; one of the best ways theoretically conceivable would be to take the actual capital goods existing at the end of the period, and to value them at the prices which any similar goods would have had at the beginning; any accumulation of capital which survives this test will be an accumulation in *real* terms. By adding the amount of consumption during the period, we get at least one sense of real income *ex post*; by then correcting for windfalls, we get a useful measure of real social income.[2] But it is just the same sort of estimate as the measure of social money income.

I hope that this chapter will have made it clear how it is possible for individual income calculations to have an important influence on individual economic conduct; for calculations of social income to play such an important part in social statistics, and in welfare economics; and yet, at the same time, for the concept of income to be one which the positive theoretical economist only employs in his arguments at his peril. For him, income is a very dangerous term, and it can be avoided; a whole general theory of economic dynamics can be worked out without using it. Or rather, it only becomes necessary to use it at a very late stage in our investigations, when we shall wish to examine the effect of the practical precept of 'living within one's income' upon the course of economic development. For that purpose, it is not necessary to have an exact definition of income; something quite rough, suitable to a rough practical precept, will do quite well.

---

[1] Since the statistician must adopt this line, it is not surprising to find him turning for assistance to those other seekers after objective income—the Commissioners for Inland Revenue. The best thing he can do is to follow the practice of the Income Tax authorities. But it is the business of the theoretical economist to be able to criticize the practice of such authorities; he has no right to be found in their company himself!

[2] The process of correcting for windfalls will usually be less important in this case of real income, since all windfalls due to mere changes in money values have already been excluded; only such things as windfall losses due to natural catastrophes and wars are left to be allowed for.

5 'Psychic' and 'accounting' concepts of income and welfare

by S. Herbert Frankel*

1. INTRODUCTION

In this essay I propose to discuss certain conceptual problems concerning the meaning of income and product in under-developed countries which have confronted investigators endeavouring to compare national income aggregates of advanced societies with similar calculations attempted for so-called under-developed or pre-industrial communities. The same problem arises, as I myself have found in the course of making official estimates of the National Income of South Africa, in trying to arrive at a satisfactory meaning for income aggregates calculated for a society like South Africa which incorporates so greatly differing 'economies' as that of the indigenous peoples of the country on the one hand, and that of the modern economic sector on the other.

At the outset I wish to record the benefit I have received from the work of Professor Simon Kuznets on this question, particularly from his valuable paper on 'National Income and Industrial Structure'.[1] This paper exhibits the impasse which confronts national income calculators when they endeavour to compare income aggregates for developed and under-developed societies—or as Professor Kuznets calls them, 'industrial and pre-industrial' countries; by which he denotes

on the one hand, an economy dominated by business enterprises, using advanced industrial techniques and ordinarily with a large proportion of its population in large cities; and, on the other hand, an economy in which a large part of production is with the family and rural community, a minor share of resources is devoted to advanced industrial production and a minor part of its population lives in cities.

The crux of the difficulty of definition arises from the fact that as between, *and even within*, developed and under-developed societies there are great differences in the range of activities to which a *highly refined accounting concept of income* can be applied.

The difficulty with which I am here concerned arises, not merely as a result of different technical methods of organizing production, for example,

---

[1] Read before the Washington Meeting of the Econometric Society in September 1947; *Econometrica*, XVII, supplement (July, 1949).

* Professor in the Economics of Under-developed Countries, University of Oxford.

in business enterprises and market economies as opposed to authoritarian, family or subsistence economies, but has its origin rather in the different objectives and ideals which consciously or unconsciously dominate the communities whose individual and social economic activities are being compared. In the last resort it is these historical and traditional factors, and not merely the state of technique and organization, which are the basic cause of differences in the nature and form of the 'income' produced by them.

To anyone who has had experience of economically less advanced communities, in which fundamental social factors often reveal themselves more directly and forcefully than they do in more complex societies, it is clear that at all times the attempt by the individual to obtain what we call 'income' is an attempt to achieve a social purpose and is not an isolated activity. It is not merely (and sometimes not at all) an attempt to create a set of individual values or an abstract entity such as 'an individual income stream'. The creation of 'income' is of a piece with social communication—even if the accounting or economic symbolism which we employ in more advanced societies is such as to disguise this fact. What 'income' is, and how it is valued, is determined by the society in which the individual finds himself. The 'creation' of income is not the solo act of a Robinson Crusoe marooned on an island. Even Robinson Crusoe did not act merely according to the dictates of his 'natural' appetites: he brought with him from the society to which he belonged not only a stock of goods but, far more important, a set of values, ideals, and objectives.

Our actions are not solely determined in isolation: they depend also on the influence we wish to exert upon others, and which their activities in turn exert upon us. Just as economic production depends on social co-operation, so the symbolism according to which it is regulated is socially determined.

To take an imaginary example; in a community of absolute pagans, he that wishes to build a temple to the deity would be engaged upon a social act of persuasion, and he could not engage upon it unless his views had gained sufficient acceptance to bring about social co-operation; therefore to pursue an ideal in isolation is to cut oneself off from the community and from social life. The 'satisfaction' derived from an individual's acts or thoughts in complete isolation has no social significance, and there is no way of measuring it.

The paramount influence of social situations is well illustrated by the experience of colonial administrators. Individual Africans, for example, who have attained to a high standard of technical proficiency when trained as agriculturists in a modern environment have, on returning to their own tribal community, 'forgotten' or abstained from applying what they have learnt. They break off contact with the market economy because they are afraid of being isolated from or incurring the ill-will of their fellows should they practise modern methods. They are happier to use again the methods of their forefathers, and to be at one with the objectives of the community in which they again desire to live.

What is the significance of this type of behaviour? Is it not the renunciation by such people of the objectives and ideals which dominate, or are assumed to dominate, advanced societies? Is it not a renunciation of the accounting symbolism on which the European economy in the West is generally based?

This accounting symbolism expresses the system of value coefficients which, as Ragnar Frisch has shown,[1] must be established by 'some sort of convention' which in itself is an axiomatic datum without which the sectional—or national—accounting streams with which we may be concerned have no meaning. As he rightly stresses, all the definitional equations of the ecocirc-system hold good 'whatever the system of value coefficients used, *provided only that the same system is applied throughout*' (my italics). Our problem, however, arises precisely because we are dealing with different value systems and conventions. And thus the concept of abstract welfare has been and is being used as a bridge—but in my opinion an inadequate bridge—between different incomparable welfare systems.

Mr Colin Clark, in criticizing the view of some modern theoretical economists that it is impossible to compare the level of income between two communities,[2] argues that exponents of this view 'do not realize what an intellectual anarchy they will let loose if their theories are adopted'. 'Deprive economics of the concept of welfare,' he writes, 'and what have you left? Nothing: except possibly the theory of the trade cycle, where all values may be capable of expression in money terms without the introduction of the concept of welfare.' He does not hesitate to make 'com-

---

[1] As an example of such a system of value coefficients he writes: 'We may take the market prices of the goods. We may specify the concept of market prices further by saying that it should be prices actually paid by the buyer. With this specification—and with certain supplementary conventions for such items as the product of housewives' work or other products of the household—it will in most actual cases be clearly defined what sums should go into the basic magnitudes. This definition becomes a meaningful one because in order to define the value concept used, we have had recourse to some criterion outside the ecocirc-system itself. We have established the definition by referring to the concrete facts surrounding each individual payment. We may, if we wish, establish the value definition by some other sort of convention, for instance, by an elaborate system of social valuations or socially determined priority figures, etc., but in all cases we must postulate some system of value coefficients before the basic concepts get a meaning.' 'Attempt at Clarification of Certain National Income Concepts', *see* stencilled memorandum 8 October 1949, University Institute of Economics, Oslo.
[2] See Colin Clark, *The Conditions of Economic Progress* (2nd ed.), pp. 16–17.

parisons of economic welfare of different times, places, and groups of people', and writes:

To compare for instance the real value of $0.795 produced per hour worked in U.S.A. in 1929, and 1.28 Rm., or $0.305 at par of exchange, produced per hour worked in Germany in the same year, we must take account of the actual quantities of goods and services produced, or, in other words, what the money will buy. The average American over that period spent his income in a certain way, purchasing certain quantities of goods and services. If he had gone to Germany and had set out to purchase exactly the same goods and services, he would have found that they were 0·9 per cent cheaper in the aggregate than in his own country. The German with his income purchased certain goods and services, by no means in the same proportion as the American. He spent much less of his income on motor cars and rent, and much more on food. The German going to America and purchasing the goods and services which he was accustomed to consume would find that they were 19·8 per cent dearer. In comparing the real value of incomes in the two countries we must therefore allow something between 19·8 and 0·9 per cent for the difference in net purchasing power of money.

He then discusses Fisher's and Pigou's well-known formulae for doing this.

This example, I suggest, exposes the hidden assumption on which Colin Clark is working: that either an American in Germany or a German in America could spend his income *as if* the fact that he was from a different society would not affect the purposes for which he desires or spends income. It may, of course, be argued that the social objectives of Germans and Americans are, on the whole, similar; that a German can adapt himself relatively easily to the American way of life when he goes to America, and vice versa. But when comparing developed and under-developed, or industrial and pre-industrial, societies this argument is quite unreal. An American prepared to live in China as the Chinese do might be able to obtain specific goods and services more cheaply than these could be obtained in America. But if he wishes to live there as an American the position might be quite different. And the real question—which Colin Clark does not face—is: Are we comparing 'income' in terms of the American or the Chinese *way of life* when we make such calculations? For, obviously, the experience of isolated, 'atomized' individuals living in foreign communities is of no comparative interest whatsoever.

Professor Kuznets no doubt had this point in mind when he quoted Colin Clark's figures showing that more than half the population of pre-industrial countries receive a per capita income of less the $40 in international units, and asked: 'Could people live in the United States during 1925–34 for several years on an income substantially below $40 per capita?'

The answer [he thought] would be 'yes', if they were sufficiently wealthy to have lots of possessions to sell, sufficiently lucky to have rich relations or sufficiently bold to rob other people. The one-third to one-half of the pre-industrial population of the world would scarcely be in that position; and if we assume that all they have produced and could consume per capita was less than 40 international units for several years, the conclusion would be that all would be dead by now.

He is led to infer, therefore,

(*a*) either that the estimates, even after the customary adjustments for comparability with industrial countries, are still deficient in omitting many goods produced in pre-industrial countries; or (*b*) in fact the whole complex of goods produced and consumed is so different that we cannot establish any equivalence of the type represented by Mr Clark's international units.[1]

2. THE SYMBOLISM OF ECONOMIC ACTIVITY

These difficulties of comparison, I believe, are in no small measure due to the concept of income which governs what might be called the symbolism of economic activity in economic literature (though not necessarily always in the minds of the economic actors themselves), in the advanced and complex money economies of the modern world.

That symbolism consists in the belief, as I show later in this essay, that the members of such societies are engaged in creating, and strive to increase and indeed to maximize, certain individual, abstract, psychological entities called utilities, or satisfactions which reside in, or take the form of individual states of consciousness. At this point I wish merely to stress that even if this mental symbolism were found to be an accurate portrayal of reality in advanced societies I would argue that it had little or no parallel in the social and economic life of most of the inhabitants of the underdeveloped countries of the world. In the economically backward communities economic activity cannot possibly be regarded as governed by highly refined individual choices or abstract evaluations directed towards increasing individual mental satisfactions. For the most part these peoples

---

[1] Professor Kuznets adds: ' The form in which the question was raised—how it is possible for a large proportion of the population in pre-industrial countries to survive on an income that produced, for several years, less than the equivalent of $40 per year— obviously reflects my bias as a member of an industrial society. Personal experience and observation tell me that such an annual product is well below the starvation level. But were I a member of a pre-industrial society I might well have asked how it is possible for the majority of the population in the United States to dispose of as much as $500 per year, or whatever its equivalent would be in international units of rupees or yuan. Especially, on being told that of this huge income less than 10 per cent is saved for net additions to capital stock, I might well ask how the population manages to consume so much—given the limited amount of food one can eat, clothes one can wear, or houses one can inhabit. And a suspicion similar to that voiced above could be entertained, namely, that these income figures for industrial countries must include many categories of items that are *not* included in income as ordinarily conceived in pre-industrial countries; and that the whole pattern of consumption and living in industrial countries is so different as to explain the ease with which these *huge quantities* of goods are produced and especially consumed.'

are engaged in narrow economic pursuits circumscribed by an environment from which they have, as yet, learned to wring only a precarious existence in accordance with the traditional social and economic precepts to which they still cling. To speak in their case of the creation of income in a monetary, a psychological, or even an individual sense is to apply a foreign symbolism to express, or to account for, activities which are not conducted in terms of such symbolism, and cannot be expressed by it.

By far the greater part of the activities of such societies are directed to the production of goods and services to satisfy the 'concrete' needs of immediate or seasonal consumption and not in any sense to the creation of 'rights' to goods and services or 'values' in the abstract—such as the right to an abstract stream of 'income' in an accounting or proprietary sense. That is why we meet so frequently, in such communities, with the well-known phenomenon that when particular goods or services are traded against money, production is not necessarily stimulated by higher prices for them, or by higher rewards to labour. On the contrary higher prices may result in a falling off both of production and of the supply of labour: what stimulates the people concerned is the achievement of particular limited purposes—purposes which are socially determined by custom and tradition. In such societies money is only one 'good' among other goods, and it has limited uses. What money is, and what role is assigned to it, is always an expression of the institutional arrangements of society as a whole—a truth often forgotten even in 'advanced' societies. The individual accumulation of money, as for example in societies where the possession of it can do little to affect the willingness, or ability, of persons to alter traditional patterns of economic activity (e.g. when it cannot be used to acquire land, or property-rights or other resources, or to employ labour for other than traditionally determined purposes) is of little use to the individual. It does not necessarily even yield him increased security since this also may be determined by social forces which the possession of money cannot necessarily control.

The main point which, I suggest, emerges from an examination of economic activity in most under-developed societies is that it cannot be expressed adequately by highly abstract concepts of individual income in accounting or monetary terms; to attempt to do so is to do violence to their traditional systems of social organization and evaluation: just as one would do violence to the values created in the family if one were to try to express them only in terms of the 'income' yielded to each of its members; or to regard its mutual co-operant activity as based only on the desire to magnify their individual satisfactions.

It is not only the fact that a very limited range of the activities of pre-industrial societies may be covered by accounting symbolisms of any kind that makes comparison with more advanced societies difficult. There is the further important consideration that the pre-industrial societies are, in most cases, undergoing rapid transition. They are in a process of disintegration; rapid changes are occurring in their way of life and in their social value systems; members of the society are becoming attached to modern money economies in which value systems are entirely different. How can one compare the income of 'individuals' or 'groups' at different times when they have been subject to such changes? How can one attempt to assess whether the pre-industrial community is 'better off' when, as in South Africa, for example, it has undergone a rapid process of urbanization, and has been integrated into a modern economy in a quite different social framework?

The income which we record for such groups in their new modern environment portrays only the new objectively recorded relations between them and others. But the accounting records tell us nothing of interest concerning the value of the social system which has been destroyed as compared with the one which has taken its place.

3. AN UNRESOLVED DICHOTOMY

At the root of all these difficulties of definition and comparability there lies, I believe, an unresolved dichotomy in the meaning ascribed to national income aggregates. This is due to the fact that, although the process of measuring the national income is a strictly accounting procedure, the aggregates so obtained are frequently used for purposes which transcend the accounting relations which can alone be expressed by them. It is precisely this extension of the concept of income which belongs to one category of logical thought, to express something such as welfare or 'ecfare'[1] which falls into another category of thought, and cannot be expressed in accounting terms at all, which is responsible for the state of disillusionment with 'welfare economics'.

This dichotomy cannot be avoided by a flight into neutral concepts designed to by-pass the problem, for example by measuring changes in productivity in order to avoid 'value' judgments. Indeed not even the use of such specially manufactured words as 'ecfare' will help us out of the difficulty. This is so not only because the mere calculation of statistical aggregates divorced from social reality and purpose is valueless, and indeed

---

[1] To use a term which Professor Robertson substitutes 'partly for brevity and partly in the hope of craftily dispelling the notion that the phrase "economic welfare" is bulging with ethics and emotiveness', in 'Utility and All That', *Manchester School* (May 1951), p. 130.

dangerous in that it results in the creation of an empty symbolism in place of realistic goals of social action, but because it avoids the fundamental issue—namely, whether the logical principles which lie at the root of the procedure are valid.

It will be the main thesis of this essay that it is a logical fallacy to regard the satisfaction or utility which (it is alleged) is 'yielded' by, or derived from, goods and services as 'income' in any meaningful sense, because the term 'income' is an accounting term and can only meaningfully express an accounting relation. I submit that the assumption that there are comparable abstract private criteria or values embedded in an indivdual's stream of consciousness which represent income as something other than, additional to, or a counterpart of purely accounting relations recorded in objective transactions—'income' which is thought to be the 'stuff' out of which welfare is constructed—is a fiction; and I submit that the belief that the simple comparison of accounting aggregates between different societies indicates something more than the specific accounting relations which such aggregates alone portray is untenable.

In order to develop this thesis I must crave the reader's indulgence for an unavoidable detour along well-worn paths as it is necessary to re-examine some of the basic definitions and analytical procedures of the two pioneers in this field, Pigou and Irving Fisher.

4. LOGICAL LIMITATIONS TO INCOME COMPARISONS

Pigou,[1] in defining economic welfare as 'that *part* of social welfare that can be brought directly or indirectly into relation with the measuring rod of money', was not primarily concerned with measuring 'economic welfare'[2] in order to obtain a barometer or index of total welfare, nor to discover how large total welfare is, but how its magnitude *would be affected* 'by the introduction of causes which it is in the power of statesmen or private persons to call into being'. Indeed, he emphasizes this view by saying that 'though the whole may consist of many varying parts, so that a change in one part never *measures* the change in the whole, yet the change in the part may always *affect* the change in the whole by its full amount'. Thus

it will not, indeed, tell us how total welfare *after the introduction of an economic cause,* will differ from what it was before, but it will tell us how total welfare will differ from what it would have been if that cause had not been introduced.

---

[1] All quotations from Pigou are from *The Economics of Welfare* unless otherwise indicated.
[2] To Pigou the two concepts, economic welfare and the national dividend, are co-ordinate, and 'just as economic welfare is that *part* of total welfare which can be brought directly or indirectly into relation with a money measure, so the national dividend is that part of the objective income of the community...which can be measured in money'.

Moreover, he specifically states:

> It will be sufficient to lay down more or less dogmatically two propositions; first, that the elements of welfare are *states of consciousness* and, perhaps, their relations; secondly, that welfare can be brought under the category of greater or less. (My italics.)[1]

Indeed in his most recent article he writes:

> What do we mean by the economic welfare of an individual? It will be generally agreed that this must be somehow resident in his state of mind or consciousness. When we speak loosely of 'material welfare', in the sense of a man's income or possessions, that is not welfare, as we are thinking of it here. Material welfare may be a *means* to welfare, but it certainly is not identical with or *a part of it*. As it seems to me, welfare must be taken to refer either to the goodness of a man's state of mind or to the satisfactions embodied in it. (Italics in the original.)[2]

Now I suggest that the goods and services which we are, or believe ourselves capable of bringing, directly or indirectly, into relationship with the measuring-rod of money are not one set of data or events, while the welfare which Pigou regards as following from them, directly or indirectly, is another set of data or events. To say that a man has more of certain goods and services and that his welfare will consequently be increased because he has them is to speak of two series of events where there is only one. In accordance with this definition of welfare, i.e. *as expressed in terms of goods and services*, welfare will necessarily be increased or diminished as the amount of goods and services is increased or diminished. *As defined*, they are a part of some larger whole which we can describe as his welfare as a whole—but logically speaking an increase or decrease in the amount of goods and services does not affect his total welfare, except only by the increase or decrease in the amount of those goods and services themselves, i.e. in so far as welfare has been defined in terms of goods and services.

The national dividend represents an arbitrary addition of certain gross of net values arbitrarily ascribed by society, or by the *national income calculator*, to certain events or happenings perceived by human beings. They are usually those events which take the form of goods and services which can more or less readily be so valued or measured. But in adding up such a series of events or happenings and calling the total the national

---

[1] In a note on 'Real Income and Economic Welfare' (*Oxford Economic Papers*, February 1951), Professor Pigou now concludes that it is only in one case out of the three which he discusses that 'inferences about economic welfare are possible', and that in others 'no inferences about changes in economic welfare can be drawn from price quantity statistics'. I am not, however, concerned in this paper with the practical difficulties of interpreting price quantity statistics. My analysis is designed to show that *welfare inferences from them (irrespective of the number of cases) are either logically invalid or necessarily tautologous as when economic welfare has already been defined in terms of the very goods and services which can be measured by price quantity statistics*.

[2] 'Some Aspects of Welfare Economics', *American Economic Review* (June 1951), p. 288.

dividend, we must not imagine that they throw light on yet another series of events or happenings.

It is this manner of looking at the national dividend as a counterpart of something else which, I believe, is responsible for the dichotomy to which I have referred. It is one of those types of mistake which, as Professor Ryle has explained,[1] arise from representing facts 'as if they belonged to one logical type or category...when they actually belong to another'. Among other illustrations he gives the following:

A foreigner visiting Oxford or Cambridge for the first time is shown a number of colleges, libraries, playing fields, museums, scientific departments and administrative offices. He then asks 'But where is the University? I have seen where the members of the Colleges live, where the Registrar works, where the scientists experiment and the rest. But I have not yet seen the University in which reside and work the members of your University.' It has then to be explained to him that the University is not another collaterial institution, some ulterior counterpart to the colleges, laboratories, and offices which he has seen. The University is just the way in which all that he has already seen is organized. When they are seen and when their co-ordination is understood, the University has been seen. His mistake lay in his innocent assumption that it was correct to speak of Christ Church, the Bodleian Library, the Ashmolean Museum, *and* the University, to speak, that is, as if 'the University' stood for an extra member of the class of which these other units are members. He was mistakenly allocating the University to the same category as that to which the other institutions belong.

Now I suggest that when, by using a common unit of account, we add up 'net values' of certain events or happenings (goods and services) we are simply *measuring* certain *parts* of a larger whole, just as if we were describing different parts of the University. It would be as wrong to regard these goods and services as *causing* welfare as it would be to regard the different buildings as *causing* the University. The University is not a *counterpart* to its teachers and buildings; nor is society's welfare a *counterpart* of its goods and services. Similarly, when we say that we have measured the increase in the value of goods and services produced in a society, we cannot then proceed to speak about this increase causing a further increase in the welfare (or 'ecfare') of society. An increase in the amount of goods and services does not affect the total welfare of society, except *by definition* through this very increase or decrease in such goods and services themselves. Pigou is thinking of the national dividend as an objective counterpart of something else, i.e. of subjective experiences. But it is, I submit, logically fallacious to imply that because we can 'measure' some of the former we can thereby imply or measure the latter.

[1] Gilbert Ryle, *The Concept of Mind* (London, 1949), p. 16. I am greatly indebted for permission to quote from this book and to Professor Ryle personally for valuable suggestions.

What I should like to stress particularly at this point is, however, that it is not a change in the national dividend or measurable net money income, as narrowly defined, which *causes* a change in welfare, but that it is a change in what is, by habit, custom, or belief, regarded by the society as constituting welfare which determines the nature, and frequently the amount of the national dividend itself. In terms of Professor Ryle's analogy, it is the idea of what the University is or should be which determines how its constituent parts will grow or be permitted to grow, and not vice versa. It is the ultimate (conscious or unconscious) purpose for which those events we call 'income' are desired that determines the nature and extent of the forms in which income will be incorporated. We cannot, therefore, compare 'income' aggregates for different societies, or even 'evaluate' income in them, without taking into account the social purposes and system which govern the creation of income. A society which glorifies war will have a different 'system or concept of welfare' and hence different concepts of what is 'income' from one which desires peace. It is said of the Bushmen of South Africa that no attempts to bring them to adopt the social life of a modern community were at any time successful. They remained hunters —notwithstanding their high intelligence, capability of practising arable agriculture and of creating other goods and services—because they liked hunting. Hunting was their ideal form of welfare, and therefore 'income' to the Bushmen (if we can use the word in this context at all) was defined in terms of success in the chase and in the sustenance yielded by the chase alone. Such 'income' could not be compared with 'equivalent' goods and services which might have resulted from some other form of activity, or with 'income' in a society of non-hunters.

The income-creating process is itself part and parcel of the income it yields, and the results of the process cannot be abstracted from the process itself. It is inadmissible to 'evaluate' the activity of hunting merely by the number of animals caught, and still more fallacious to compare the figure so obtained with, say, the 'value' of meat obtained by another society from the slaughter of domestic beasts. The activity and the income are inseparable and are both embedded together in the customs and ways of thought which mould the social life of the community as a whole.

In other words, the relation between total welfare and economic welfare or income (Pigou's national income or dividend) is a relationship similar to that between the rules, laws, constitutional arrangements, habits, institutional patterns, and beliefs which govern society and the results of the social activities so regulated. It is a relationship similar to that between the rules according to which a game is played, the playing of the game, and the points in which the score is reckoned. To identify, or seek for, a functional relationship between income and total welfare is as logically fallacious as to identify the points scored in playing a game with the 'value 'of the game to the players.

As I endeavour to show below, when we speak of, for example, 'the maximization of income' we are using a term with strictly limited meaning —one which is meaningful only as an accounting expression, the expression being implicitly subsumed under the accounting 'laws' or rules which we have adopted for that kind of reckoning. It would be absurd to speak of maximizing the rules of the game itself. The game of chess is played in accordance with certain prescribed and generally accepted rules. If we so desire we can measure, evaluate, or account the skill of the player according to an accepted scale of points or awards and penalties. The player, by the exercise of appropriate skill, could thus maximize his points or 'earnings'. But we cannot meaningfully assess the 'welfare' or psychic income, or utility or pleasure flowing from the game of chess to the player by adding up the score.

It is logically as fallacious to speak of maximizing total welfare as it is to speak of maximizing the University. The total welfare of society is not some 'ulterior counterpart' to the production of goods and services which can be measured in money; nor does it consist only of those events which cannot be so measured; nor is it necessary for an understanding of it to postulate states of consciousness, 'psychic' income, and the like.

When we examine the different activities of society, both those which can and those which cannot be expressed or symbolized in accounting terms as income, we are examining aspects of its welfare. Society's total welfare is just the way in which all these activities are organized. When they are perceived and assessed, and when their system of ordering and co-ordination has been described and grasped, the total welfare of society has been, *ipso facto*, assessed also. To speak as if total welfare stood for an extra member of the class of which these other activities are members is mistakenly to allocate total welfare to the same category as that to which the other institutions which govern the activities of society belong.

I submit that this analysis shows how dangerous it is to embark too hastily on international and indeed inter-temporal comparisons between income aggregates.

To endeavour to assess and compare 'welfare' merely by comparing national income aggregates for societies with different laws, rules, conventions, hopes, and ideals is as fallacious as to try to assess the pleasure which a pair of players derive from playing dominoes, and then compare it with that yielded to another pair engaged in playing chess, by comparing the points scored by the players in each game.

Where the system of rules, the social order of preference, or the value system as a whole is different, comparisons of parts of each system are invalid unless those parts are related to some external objective standard of measurement. Thus it is meaningful to compare the average expectation of life in different communities, or the incidence of different diseases, or the number of calories of food, *if we are agreed as to the purpose for which we make such comparisons*; but if our laws, rules, or conventions differ as to the importance of any of these, comparison itself can tell us very little.

I submit that the belief that we can readily compare national income aggregates between greatly differing societies is, in the last resort, to be explained by a peculiar assumption which underlies the concept of income in advanced Western societies, namely, that the individual possesses certain essentially private criteria (or even that welfare *consists in having* certain private units of something) according to which he alone can assess his welfare; criteria which are inaccessible to, and which cannot be objectively assessed by, others; criteria which are to be found in individual states of consciousness and can therefore only be measured indirectly.

On this assumption it is argued that, if we can measure in money terms the goods and services which make up the 'income' of these individuals, we can infer and assess the *private* values of criteria, the inner stream of consciousness, the satisfaction or the utility, which individuals, *irrespective of the society to which they belong*, enjoy. It is implied, then, that international comparisons of income are meaningful precisely because such comparisons refer to this abstract entity—this individual 'income'; 'income', namely, which is dissociated from the specific social context in which it is embedded, and which all individuals 'enjoy' irrespective of the society to which they belong.

5. 'PSYCHIC' AND 'ACCOUNTING' INCOME

What is 'welfare' or 'economic welfare' to Pigou was 'psychic or enjoyment income' to Irving Fisher. This psychic theory of income is by no means of merely historical interest. In my opinion it is, notwithstanding many modern devices to escape from it, still embedded in our ways of thought.[1]

To Fisher 'income' is a series of events,[2] but the events he regards as constituting 'ultimate income' for each individual 'are *only* those events which come within the purview of his individual experience'. It is the

---

[1] See for example, the quotation from Kenneth E. Boulding below, and my subsequent remarks.

[2] *The Theory of Interest*, pp. 1 and 5. [See above, pp. 33, 35.]

abstract 'psychic experience of the individual mind' with which Fisher is concerned. To him ultimate income is nothing if not a *private process of observing* (and privately measuring) these *inner* events of enjoyment: the counterpart of real income—a counterpart located in the 'mind' of the observer. It is as if, while eating my dinner, I am observing, recording, or reporting to myself on the 'agreeable sensation' and experience of eating it; and it is as if I calculate or measure my *net* psychic income by not only continually observing, recording, and reporting on 'agreeable sensations'— if that is possible—but also by observing and reporting on accompanying disagreeable ones (such as those which Fisher calls the 'labour pains' involved in earning income) and deducting the latter from the former.

Herein also lies the source of the belief that somehow the goods and services which an individual receives are the *cause* of welfare—the cause, namely, of something additional to them; something which occurs in the minds of individuals.

I submit that this concept of the relation between measurable 'income' and welfare is simply a para-mechanical hypothesis, the dangers of which Professor Ryle has so trenchantly exposed. It is based on that type of category mistake which he has called 'the category mistake which underlies the dogma of the ghost in the machine'. He states that, in unconscious reliance upon this dogma,[1]

Theorists and laymen alike constantly construe the adjectives by which we characterize performances as ingenious, wise, methodical, careful, witty, etc., as signalizing the occurrence in someone's hidden stream of consciousness of special processes functioning as ghostly harbingers or more specifically as occult causes of the performances so characterized.

But in opposition to this entire dogma he argues that:

in describing the workings of a person's mind we are not describing a second set of shadowy operations. We are describing certain phases of his one career; namely, we are describing the ways in which parts of his conduct are managed...When a person talks sense aloud, ties knots, paints or sculpts...he for a person is bodily active and he is mentally active, but he is not being synchronously active in two different 'places'.

I submit that in defining ultimate income as enjoyment or psychic income and as the 'inner events of the mind' Fisher[2] falls into the type of category mistake which we have been discussing. This psychic income is not an event or happening which 'occurs' somewhere, i.e. in a person's mind, and is 'caused' by another 'external' event or happening, for example by the receipt of goods and services by that person. To ask where and when does the psychic income occur would be like asking, for example, con-

---

[1] *Op. cit.* p. 50.   [2] *Op. cit.* p. 4. [See above, p. 35.]

cerning the meaning of an expression, 'When and where do these meanings occur?'...'The phrase "what such and such an expression means" does not describe a thing or happening at all, and *a fortiori* not an occult thing or happening.'[1] Eating my dinner and enjoying it are not two events but one. 'We do...things because we like doing them, or want to do them, and not because we like or want something accessory to them...The angler would not accept or understand an offer of the pleasures without the activities of angling. It is angling that he enjoys, not something that angling engenders.'[2]

The agreeable sensations which Fisher would have us believe are the stuff of which ultimate psychic income is made are not things or episodes. It is therefore 'nonsense to speak of observing, inspecting, witnessing, or scrutinizing them'; and it is, I submit, equally nonsense to try, as Fisher would have us try, to 'measure' them, however indirectly, 'since the objects proper to such verbs are things and episodes'.

It does not make sense to speak of my observing, scrutinizing, reporting on, being conscious of, inferring, or *measuring* that I am enjoying the eating of my dinner. If it did, then

it would seem to make sense to ask whether, according to the doctrine, I am not also conscious of being conscious of inferring,[3] that is, in a position to say 'Here I am, spotting the fact that here I am deducing such and such from so and so.' And then there would be no stopping place; there would have to be an infinite number of onion-skins of consciousness embedding any mental state or process whatsoever.

Now it is precisely this infinite regression in the thing we are trying to 'measure' which puzzled Fisher and which, I submit, underlies the dichotomy to which I have referred. What we call the 'measurement' or 'calculation' of the national income is nothing more or less than the application of accounting principles to certain types of economic data. Fisher was an early pioneer in this field. To him accounting was 'not a mere makeshift, but a complete, consistent, and logical system'. In critically applying it he aimed, firstly, at making the most rigid logical distinction between the nature of capital and income. He wished to avoid the heterogeneous combination of 'commodities' and 'services'; the first he regarded as concrete wealth and the other as the abstract use of it.[4] His second main objective

---

[1] Gilbert Ryle, *op. cit.* p. 295.   [2] *Ibid.* p. 132.
[3] *Ibid.* p. 163.
[4] 'To bring about homogeneity', he writes, 'we could exclude *uses* altogether and confine "income" to concrete commodites'; or '*we could exclude commodities altogether and restrict the term to uses*'. (My italics.) 'The only true method', he insists, 'is to regard uniformly as income the *service* of a dwelling to its owner (shelter or money rental), the *service* of a piano (music), and the service of food (nourishment); and in the same uniform manner to exclude alike from the category of income the dwelling, the piano,

was to elucidate that what we call the measurement of income is but the drawing up of a system of accounts. The significant feature of any consistent system of accounts is always that in it every receipt of 'income' appearing on the debit side of the account is exactly offset by an equal item of 'outgo' on the credit side. Thus the process of bookkeeping 'amounts to a continued series of snapshots of the train of enterprise moving through time'.[1] Even a profit and loss account covering a period between the dates of two balance-sheets is only a detailed reconstruction of how the capital accounts changed as between the two dates of the balance-sheets.

Unfortunately, however, under double-entry bookkeeping *transactions* only can be recorded, and a transaction involves the passing of money or money's worth. This fact immediately brings us up against Fisher's central difficulty, namely, that 'money receipts', as he says,[2] may be

good makeshifts for *true* income [my italics], but even from a practical point of view they will not always serve, while as a matter of strict theory they are always wrong. They could be right only under the condition that *all* income, *from whatever source* [my italics], flowed through the cash drawer.

If it were true that

the flow out of that drawer consisted exclusively of expenditures for each and every satisfaction as it occurred, then the flow of money through the cash drawer would serve as a true measure of income, and the cash drawer might be called a sort of income *meter*.

But, in fact,

not all income passes through the meter. Some passes around it, as, for instance, the shelter derived from a man's own house or the comforts from his own furniture...[3]

and even the food. These are capital, not income; ...*Their income follows later in the form of piano music and nourishment.*' (My italics.) *The Nature of Capital and Income* (New York and London, 1919) pp. 105–6.

It is this extension of the use of the accounting term 'income' to cover *the process of consumption* which I analyse and criticize in the text above. Fisher's distinction between capital and income in an accounting sense is, however, extremely important and is still frequently overlooked.

[1] W. J. Busschau, *Measure of Gold* (South Africa, 1949), p. 17.

[2] See *The Nature of Capital and Income*, p. 137.

[3] It should again be noted that, to Fisher, 'The income from any instrument is therefore the flow of abstract services rendered by that instrument'—unlike capital which is a fund at an instant of time and consists of concrete wealth. The word 'flow', however, is apt to be very misleading in any case, because in fact in dealing with transactions we do not measure a flow at all in the sense of measuring, say, the flow of water past a certain point over a period of time. What we do is to construct a balance-sheet at different points of time, and the construction of balance-sheets involves evaluation of assets at these different points of time. But evaluation of assets in that sense involves the introduction of an ideal or standard income.

Here we come to the crux of the matter, for in order to overcome the inherent logical distinction between what can and what cannot be expressed in accounting terms—between what takes place in the transactions of the market-place and is recorded in money terms (or its equivalent) and what is never so recorded, i.e. the utility or satisfaction yielded by commodities when finally consumed (which Fisher calls the abstract use of wealth *and which he regards as 'true' income*)—Fisher has to invent a bridge between two logically different and incompatible categories of thought. He has to go beyond the system of accounts of the market-place; for in the case of real persons, i.e. final consumers, the two sides of the account containing only such *recorded* transactions do not finally balance, because the accounts do not, as to be consistent they should, consist solely of double entries. On the contrary, the income and outgo accounts of such 'real persons' contain a residue of items which will not pair, e.g. the shelter of a person's home, use of furniture, use of food, use of clothes, etc. For, of course, those items constitute a kind of 'income' (i.e. the final 'use' of those commodities) which does not appear elsewhere as 'outgo'. There always remains, when applying the accounting system to real persons, 'some *outer fringe* (my italics) of uncancelled income'.[1] All other services are merely preparatory to such services, and pass themselves on from one category of capital to another. Thus the 'income' from investments, being deposited in a bank, is 'outgo' with respect to the bank account; the bank account yields 'income' by paying for stocks and bonds, food, etc., but in each case the same item enters as 'outgo' with respect to these and other categories of capital. In all these cases the individual receives no 'income' which is not at the same time 'outgo'. It is only as he consumes the food, wears the clothes, or uses the furniture that he receives 'income'.

What is significant in Fisher's approach is that to overcome this dichotomy he invents a fiction similar to the one which is usually employed to obtain the symmetry of a double-entry accounting system in connexion with the investment made by the proprietors of a business in that business. This fiction consists in our conventionally regarding such a business or venture as something *apart or dissociated* from its proprietors. So Fisher employs, as a last resort, the fiction that the body as a transforming instrument is something *apart or dissociated* from its 'proprietor', namely, 'the mind' to which the 'body' pays out final (or 'true') income, which final income, he argues, is not received until, as subjective income, it emerges into 'the stream of consciousness of any human being'[2]—a concept which,

---

[1] Which consists of what economists have usually called consumption (Fisher, *The Nature of Capital and Income*, p. 164).
[2] *Ibid.* p. 168.

S. Herbert Frankel

as I have shown, is on all fours with that held by Pigou concerning the ultimate nature of 'welfare'.

Many examples in Fisher's book show how powerfully he was influenced by this attempt to complete the system of accounts of the workaday world by extending it to the realms of the mind; for example

If we include the body as a transforming instrument, while we must *credit* with their respective services all these outside agencies, such as, food, clothing, dwelling, furniture, ornaments and other articles which, as it were, bombard a man's sensory system, we must also at the same time *debit* the body with the same items. In this case the only surviving credit items after these equal debits and credits are cancelled are the resulting final satisfactions in the human mind.[1] (My italics.)

Now it will be immediately apparent that, if we accept this concept of 'ultimate' or 'true' income based on fictional mental accounting, we would have to postulate another 'mind' or skin of consciousness in which the mental accounting is conducted. But then, as Professor Ryle has demonstrated, 'there would be no stopping place in an infinite number of such minds or states of consciousness'.

For clearly the net psychic income (negative or positive) could only be calculated by 'balancing off' the mental accounts at different time-intervals. If, for example, exertion, labour, pain, anxiety, or trouble is expended by a person in obtaining durable goods in period 1, but these only begin to be consumed in period 2, does the person keep a mental 'income' and 'outgo' or a mental 'profit and loss' account? Does he carry in his mind a mental capital account? When he receives a new suit of clothes does he make a mental debit entry, e.g. 'To unconsumed satisfaction', and a mental credit entry to that account whenever he wears the suit? When a person has paid for his education or physical training does he keep a mental capital account showing this investment, and does he credit himself with the 'income' it yields to him in the future? If he does indeed conduct these peculiar operations in his mind it would be most interesting to know when they occur—hourly, daily, weekly, or annually!

6. LIMITS TO MEASUREMENT

I have dealt at length with Fisher's abortive attempt to build an artificial bridge between an accounting and a psychic concept of income, in order to show that such concepts as 'income', 'outgo', 'receipts' and 'expenditure' can only be meaningfully used as accounting concepts and cannot be extended to embrace 'income' in a psychological sense. Until we realize this clearly we cannot hope to rid ourselves of serious current confusions.

[1] *The Nature of Capital and Income*, p. 167.

Even so constructive a thinker as Kenneth Boulding uses the words 'income' and 'outgo' in both an accounting and a psychological sense.[1] The distinction he makes between the pair of terms 'income' and 'outgo' on the one hand, and the pair of terms 'receipts' and 'expenditure' on the other hand, while interesting, does not get him out of this tangle since these are all accounting terms and can only refer to *recorded transactions*, until we come to Fisher's 'residue of items which will not pair', i.e. the 'consumption' of objective goods and services which cannot be expressed in accounting terms, unless we follow Fisher's attempt and postulate that the individual keeps subjective mental accounts with himself. And indeed Boulding ends up just as Fisher did by saying:

When psychic capital is taken into consideration, however, it may be doubted whether there are any really non-durable goods. Even the things usually labelled as services, such as movies, in fact produce psychic capital with a limited rate of depreciation. We go to the movies in order to *produce the mental state* of just having gone to the movies. *This mental state is the commodity* which we purchase with the price of admission: it is a commodity which depreciates like every other commodity. For some individuals it depreciates rapidly, so that it has to be replaced in a week or less: in other individuals the rate of depreciation is slower, so that they do not have to go to another movie for a month or even several months. (My italics.)

Moreover, to say, as Boulding does, that 'a farmer earns income as the value of his crop grows' is to confuse capital and income on the one hand, and to fail to distinguish between 'standard' and 'realized' income on the other.[2] The growing crop does not represent the 'earnings' of 'income'. Such growth can be 'reflected' in a capital account which attempts to assess the value of income *in prospect*, but what *may eventually* be realized as income is not income that has been realized. Realized income is precisely that income which has been detached from capital by being converted into money (or into another recorded asset form) in a recorded transaction. It is the recorded *transaction* which shapes it as income in an *accounting* sense. Our measurement of 'income' can logically refer only to income which has so been 'realized'. For only this income can enter into any form of accounting—which is basically a process of objective social evaluation. That such objective social evaluation, depending on 'market transactions', is never free from subjective hopes and expectations concerning the future, and that over large sectors of the economy transactions may be recorded which are not based on 'market' valuations at all, does not alter the fact that there is a basic logical distinction between such *objective* evaluation

[1] K. Boulding, *A Reconstruction of Economics* (1950), pp. 139–41.
[2] Fisher rightly insisted on the fundamental logical distinction between the ideal (or standard) income and the actual (or realized) income.

and that procedure which I contend is illegitimate, namely, the use of accounting concepts to evaluate subjective processes which allegedly take place within a person's mind or within himself.

The 'income' of which we can take account and 'measure' must, willy-nilly, refer only to *publicly disclosed* evaluations arising out of recorded transactions. If we wish to distinguish between 'consuming' and 'spending', the farthest point to which accounting can take us is to that objective balance-sheet which records the expenditure by a person on durable goods; but the use or consumption of these goods does not 'yield' income. To speak as if it does is to apply accounting concepts to a category of thought which it does not fit. One cannot speak of consumption yielding 'income' in the same sense as a bank account or stocks and shares yield 'income'. We do not, when we consume a piece of bread, speak of the bread yielding 'income', nor do we regard that portion of the bread which remains un-consumed as capital. To speak in this way would involve that process of mental accounting, the fallacious nature of which I have endeavoured to expose.

Private persons may of course keep private accounts which would indicate the change in the values of durable goods in their possession between two periods of time; but if one were to attempt to argue that persons keeping such accounts would thereby be measuring the 'income' they receive from the use of such goods (the fall in their value being taken to represent the income which has 'accrued' to the person in the intervening period), one would again be falling into a fallacious use of the word 'income', which really expresses an accounting *relation* and not something which is the counterpart of the using up of a durable good in the process of consumption.

Moreover, in this connexion one must avoid confusing windfall gains (or losses)—which might accrue to a person if he sold a durable good in the market—with income. Such gains (or losses) are not 'income' but capital appreciation (or depreciation) and are due to the society's valuation of expected future income; income, however, which is expected in the future is but the prospect of income—an ideal or target which may never be realized.

Now it is quite true that persons or fictitious persons can and do buy and sell prospects (and can thus individually realize in a true accounting sense windfall gains or losses made at the expense of other persons) which are changes on capital account; but *for the whole system of social accounts* there can be no windfall gains or losses of this nature. Society as a whole cannot convert its prospects into income until time and good fortune have fulfilled them. Society cannot make a windfall gain or loss except in the sense in which a person can be said to gain where an *unexpected* pleasurable event occurs or lose when an *expected* pleasurable event fails to occur. If society tried to measure such psychological windfalls, it would be keeping a mental account with itself.[1] But no accounts can portray the relationship of a person to himself. Meaningful measurement ceases at the point at which persons acquire objective goods and services; to go beyond is to enter the realm of hope and fancy.[2]

7. CONCLUSION

It might appear that the previous analysis has led us to disconcerting conclusions, but I suggest that this is not the case. Once we cease to be misled by the mirage of fictional mental accounting, and by attempts to portray through very simple accounting aggregates the infinite variety in the value and preference systems of different societies with which we are confronted, we will free the welfare concept from a serious dichotomy of thought, and will realize that the mere calculation of accounting relations cannot in itself answer, and should not be expected to answer, questions the answers to which do not lie in the realm of measurement.

Moreover, we will realize that the accounts (and accounting symbolism) of different societies are not comparable; that we cannot compare separate accounting aggregates for one society with those relating to another with a different social and economic framework, and hence a different system of accounting values. We cannot assume that what appears to be 'income' in one society can be compared with 'income' recorded in another, because since the 'income' which we can grasp is an accounting relation and not a psychic entity what will be so recorded in the two different societies will differ in its significance according to the nature and ideals of the society itself.

Thus one of the main tasks which now confronts economists, statisticians, and sociologists emerges more clearly, namely, to determine which factors constitute the welfare pattern—rather than to stop short at comparing symbols which do not adequately portray it. To say this, of course, raises many more questions than it answers. Perhaps I may be permitted to ask that supremely inconvenient question which has popped up its head

---

[1] Society can, however, like the individual, sell prospects (a capital transaction) to *other* societies. For example, the sale of mineral rights or prospects to foreigners (and the import of other goods in exchange). This illustration precisely indicates the difference between objective accounting transactions to which the terms capital and income can be applied and subjective ones to which they cannot.

[2] As Professor J. R. Hicks has so rightly concluded in his important book *Value and Capital* [p. 82 above]: 'the concept of income' is 'one which the positive theoretical economist only employs in his argument at his peril. For him, income is a very dangerous term...'

throughout this article only to be resolutely suppressed: What do we gain by the complicated symbolism which pictures this mental thing—this alleged counterpart to reality—called utility, satisfaction, welfare, ecfare, or plain Everyman's 'equal capacity to enjoy life' which Scitovsky has now called it in discussing inter-personal comparisons of it?[1] Thirty years after the publication of *The Economics of Welfare*, Pigou is, like so many others, still of the opinion that 'if the satisfaction of different individuals cannot be compared, a large part of that subject (Welfare Economics) is undermined', and he comforts himself with the conclusion that

on the basis of analogy, observation and intercourse, inter-personal comparisons *can* properly be made; and, moreover, unless we have a special reason to believe the contrary, a given amount of stuff may be presumed to yield a similar amount of satisfaction, not indeed as between *any* one man and any other, but as between representative members and groups of individuals, such as the citizens of Birmingham and the citizens of Leeds. This is all we need to allow this branch of Welfare Economics to function. (Italics in the original.)

But why do we need this fictional comparison at all? For the inter-personal comparison which Pigou here apparently succeeds in making rests not on the essential comparability of this abstract 'utility' or 'satisfaction' in the minds of different individuals. The comparison appears to succeed only because 'the given amount of stuff' which according to Pigou 'may be presumed to yield it (utility)' is by implication comparable on the hidden assumption that the citizens of Birmingham and of Leeds have broadly similar tastes and thus demand broadly similar kinds of 'stuff'; just as Marshall took it for granted that 'it would naturally be assumed that a shilling's worth of gratification to one Englishman might be taken as equivalent with a shilling's worth to another...until cause to the contrary was shown'.[2] In other words, the 'welfare' *yielded* by the 'stuff' is assumed to be equal *because* the welfare pattern itself was first assumed to be the same. Thus the utility or satisfaction was found to be apparently comparable in the abstract, precisely and only because it had already been defined *ab initio* as flowing from, yielded by, and dependent on the same 'real' things. That the inter-personal comparison of abstract utility rests on such circular reasoning becomes finally obvious if we take a different case and try to compare the satisfactions of the citizens of Birmingham not with those of Leeds but with the satisfactions yielded by a given amount of 'stuff' peculiar to the customs, say, of an African tribe prone to cannibalism and the like. The abstract satisfactions would not be regarded as comparable—and why not?—precisely because the underlying pattern of stuff was so different.

[1] 'The State of Welfare Economics', *American Economic Review* (June 1951).
[2] Alfred Marshall, *Principles of Economics* (8th ed.), p. 130, referred to by Scitovsky.

There is no harm, as Professor Robbins pointed out long ago[1] (when he warned against the dangers inherent in the use of aggregates to portray social income), in conventional ways of looking at certain things. The danger arises when we forget what is convention and what is reality, and when merely conventional symbolism determines unduly the goals of public policy.

Perhaps after all it is time for some searching questions about the significance of the nature and content of, and variations in, the *real pattern of welfare* in different societies rather than about the mental fictions which are alleged to symbolize it.

[1] *An Essay on the Nature and Significance of Economic Science* (1932).

6 Economic and accounting concepts of income[1]

by David Solomons*

In recent years, discussion of the measurement of income has been largely coloured and dominated by problems created by changes in the value of money. Serious as these problems are, they are really secondary ones, for they presuppose some basic agreement about the nature and measurement of income during a period of stable prices. Between accountants and economists, it need hardly be said, no such agreement exists. My purpose in this paper is first to examine these differences—a task which has been performed, with greater or less thoroughness, many times before—and then to consider the only attempt known to me to work out a concept of income which would, like the accountant's, be capable of practical use and yet would stay close to the fundamental definition of income with which we begin. The attempt at reconciliation to which I refer is Sidney Alexander's concept of variable income, put forward in his monograph, *Income Measurement in a Dynamic Economy*.[2] Alexander's suggestion deserves more discussion than it has received hitherto, whether we finally judge it to be a workable concept or not. It is for that reason that I shall have something to say about it here. My conclusion about the practical utility of the concept, as a matter of fact, will be adverse; and from that disappointing conclusion I am led on to the view that the time has come to develop other and more effective tools to do the jobs which periodic income so signally fails to do in the field of financial planning and control. As I shall suggest, there are signs that the central position which income occupies in accounting is already being usurped.

[1] This paper was presented at the Northeast Regional Meeting of the American Accounting Association at the Massachusetts Institute of Technology on 28–9 October 1960.

[2] Published as the first of *Five Monographs on Business Income* by the Study Group on Business Income, 1950. Alexander's work in a slightly revised version has been re-published in W. T. Baxter and Sidney Davidson (editors), *Studies in Accounting Theory* (London, 1962).

* Professor of Accounting, Wharton School of Finance and Commerce, University of Pennsylvania.

USEFULNESS OF THE INCOME CONCEPT

Any discussion of competing ideas of income ought, I think, to start with the question: 'Do we really need an income concept, and if so, what for?' Only when we have asked and answered this question can we say whether there is anything we need to define, and whether one or more than one concept of income is necessary.

Let us consider income for taxation purposes first. It is really rather remarkable that income has become so universally accepted as a good measure of taxable capacity, for on closer inspection it seems to have grave defects. Command over capital resources would seem to be a much fairer guide to the subject's ability to pay taxes, and also to the demand made by the individual on various governmental services such as defence and law and order. Alternatively, as suggested by Mr Kaldor, it might be more sensible to tax people according to what they spend rather than on what they earn. This is not a plea for the substitution of indirect for direct taxation, of course, but for the use of a computation of expenditure rather then of income as the basis of taxation. It is not necessary to go into this matter here. For my purpose, it is enough to note that our system of direct taxation could get along quite well, and, indeed, perhaps better, if we did not have a concept of income at all.

A second important purpose which the concept of income is said to serve is in the determination of corporate dividend policy. So long as dividends are paid out of income and not otherwise, it is asserted, the rights of creditors will not be prejudiced by the return of capital to stockholders. If this means, as it does in certain jurisdictions, that currently or recently earned net profits may be distributed without making good earlier losses of capital, it is clear that the rights of creditors are being very imperfectly protected. The payment of a legal dividend by no means implies, in such circumstances, that the stockholders' capital is intact. Moreover, a corporation may earn a profit and yet be too short of cash to be able to pay a dividend without endangering its short-term solvency. The existence of current net income, therefore, may tell directors nothing about the dividend policy they ought to follow. It makes much more sense for the law to require, as it sometimes does, either that stockholders' capital should be intact before a dividend is paid out of any excess, or to require some defined margin of assets over and above those necessary to pay creditors' claims, before allowing the payment of dividends to stockholders. Either type of restriction is more effective in protecting the rights of creditors than one based on an income concept, while at the same time being free of the difficulties of defining and measuring net income.

David Solomons

A third major need served, or said to be served by the concept of income, is as a guide to investment policy. Prospective investors seek to maximize their return on investment, and their search will be guided by the income earned on existing investments. This is related to another argument—that income provides the best measure we have of success in the management of business enterprise in a competitive economy. These are important needs, and they both point in the same direction. That investment is most attractive which offers us the greatest present value of future receipts per dollar invested, when discounted at the going rate of interest, and in so far as historical data can help us in the choice of investments, it will be data about the growth in present value of existing investments. Again, that manager is most successful who, during a given period, increases the present value of the enterprise entrusted to him proportionately the most. In both of these cases, it is growth in present value which alone appears to be significant; and since it seems to carry out the function generally attributed to income, growth in present value must be what we had better understand income to mean.

ECONOMIC INCOME

The concept of income to which we have been led corresponds, of course, to Hicks's definition of income. For an individual, he defines income as the maximum amount a man can consume in a period and still be as well off at the end of the period as he was at the beginning. There is no doubt that when, as individual salary-earners and investors, we think of our personal income for a year, we commonly do not think of it in this way, but rather as a stream of prorated receipts, unaffected by any changes in the value of the tangible assets with which we started the year and certainly as having nothing to do with any change in our future prospects—in our 'goodwill', in other words—which may take place during the year. But this does not lead me to concude that 'the income of a person or other entity is what he believes to be his income...'[1] for we can be mistaken about the nature of income just as men were once mistaken about the nature of combustion when they attributed it to phlogiston. Rather, I would say 'Income is as income does.'

If we take Hicks's definition of income as applied even to an individual, it is easy to see, however we define our terms, that income in Hicks's sense and income as the accountant measures it will only by accident ever be the same thing. As Hicks points out, the difficulty about his definition is

---

[1] Myron J. Gordon, 'Scope and method of theory and research in the measurement of income and wealth', *Accounting Review* (October 1960), p. 608.

in saying what we mean by 'being as well off' at one
He offers us three different measures of well-offness wh
together, if we abstract from changes in the value c
changes in the rate of interest, to give us a single meas
command over money capital. If we accept constanc
as representing constancy of well-offness, then incon... in
becomes the amount by which the individual's net worth has increa...
during the period, due allowance being made for the value of what he has
consumed or given away during that time.

To use Hicks's definition for the income of a business entity rather than
for that of an individual, we need only modify it slightly; the income of
the business, whether it is incorporated as a separate legal entity or not,
is the amount by which its net worth has increased during the period, due
allowance being made for any new capital contributed by its owners or
for any distributions made by the business to its owners. This form of
words would also serve to define accounting income, in so far as net
accounting income is the figure which links the net worth of the business
as shown by its balance-sheet at the beginning of the accounting period
with its net worth as shown by its balance-sheet at the end of the period.
The correspondence between the two ideas of increased net worth is, however, a purely verbal one: for Hicksian income demands that in evaluating
net worth we capitalize expected future net receipts, while accounting
income only requires that we evaluate net assets on the basis of their
unexpired cost.

It is hardly open to question that you cannot really assess the well-offness
of an enterprise by aggregating the costs, or the unexpired costs, of its
assets and deducting its liabilities. Any differences between the current
value of its tangible assets and their book value based on cost will be excluded; and any value which the enterprise may have over and above the
value of its tangible assets will also be excluded. We may sum up the
relationship between these two different concepts of increase in net worth,
economic income and accounting income, by starting with accounting income and arriving at economic income thus:

Accounting income

+ Unrealized changes in the value of tangible assets which took place
  during the period, over and above value changes recognized as depreciation of fixed assets and inventory mark-downs,

− Amounts realized this period in respect of value changes in tangible
  assets which took place in previous periods and were not recognized
  in those periods,

changes in the value of intangible assets during the period, hereafter
to be referred to as changes in the value of goodwill

= Economic income.

THE REALIZATION PRINCIPLE

Obviously the main difference between these two income concepts lies in
the accountant's attachment to realization as the test of the emergence of
income. The Study Group on Business Income, in its 1952 report, rather
surprisingly suggested that 'the realization postulate was not accepted prior
to the First World War',[1] and supported this with quotations from both
American and British sources. It seems to me, on the contrary, that the
trend has, for a long time now, been away from, rather than towards,
placing emphasis on the importance of realization. For a long time the
relationship of income to capital was likened to the relation of the fruit
to the tree. Just as there was no difficulty in separating the crop from the
tree, so there need be no difficulty in distinguishing income from the capital
which produced it. It was in line with this thinking that, for the first
thirty-six years after Peel had re-introduced the income tax in Britain in
1842, no relief was given by the British tax code for the using up of fixed
assets in the course of carrying on a business. The introduction of income
tax depreciation allowances in Britain in 1878, and their growth in importance there and here since then, constitute a movement away from the
idea that you can evaluate the fruit without giving thought to the value
of the tree—that realized profits can be measured in disregard of what
have sometimes been called 'mere value changes' in the assets of the
business. Another earlier step away from the pure realization principle was
the 'cost or market-price' rule for valuing inventory. You will not find
this in accounting literature before the mid-nineteenth century, for before
that time consistent valuation at cost seems to have been the rule. The
recognition of unrealized losses on inventory is a clear recognition of 'mere
value changes', if only in one direction, as being relevant to the determination of income. As final evidence of the same tendency, I suppose we might
cite the development of cash accounting into accrual accounting as itself a
de-emphasizing of the importance of realization. For what it is worth, we
can perhaps say that over the years accounting income and economic income have moved a little closer together. Yet of course, when everything
has been said, accounting income is still substantially realized income.

The tableau set out above may make it easier for us to evaluate the two
income concepts in terms of the two qualities which outweigh all others

[1] *Changing Concepts of Business Income* (New York, 1952), p. 23.

in importance, their usefulness and their practicality. It is because the results of this evaluation are what they are that it is natural to hanker after a compromise income concept which has a greater share of these qualities combined than either accounting or economic income has, taken by itself.

THE CASE FOR AND AGAINST ACCOUNTING INCOME AND ECONOMIC INCOME

Whether we use one concept of income or another, or indeed whether we use any concept of income at all, clearly should depend, as I have already said, on the purpose we want to serve and the income concept which will best serve it. In what follows I shall concentrate my attention on one aspect of this matter only, namely, the measurement of business income for the purpose of assessing entrepreneurial success or failure in the profit-making sector of the economy. From this point of view it must be said that accounting income is seriously defective. By focusing attention on the result of current realization of assets and ignoring all other value changes except such as are covered by the 'cost or market' rule, and by depreciation, it can lead to some rather ridiculous results. One such result is that described by Kenneth MacNeal.[1] Two investors each have $1,000 to invest. One buys $1,000 worth of stock A, the other buys $1,000 worth of stock B. By the end of the year both stocks have doubled in price. The first investor sells out just before 31 December, and reinvests the $2,000 he gets from the sale in stock B. The second investor continues to hold his block of stock, which is also worth $2,000 at the end of the year. Thus both start equal, with $1,000 each in cash; they also finish equal, both holding equal quantities of stock B worth $2,000. It is impossible to say that one investor has been more successful than the other. Yet one of them shows an accounting profit of $1,000 as the result of his realization, while the other shows no accounting profit at all.

Another absurd result is cited by Sidney Alexander, that of the manager of a large corporation who is considering a deal which will increase his accounting profit by a million dollars but which will result in the destruction of the firm's goodwill by forcing it out of business. By looking only at changes in tangible equity (and only at a part of that), while ignoring changes in goodwill, accounting income provides us with a very unsatisfactory measure of managerial success. Another way of putting this is to say that if maximizing profit is ever a rational business goal, it is rational only if profit means economic profit, not accounting profit.

[1] In his article 'What's Wrong with Accounting', *The Nation* (7–14 October 1939), and reprinted in *Studies in Accounting*, ed. W. T. Baxter (London, 1950).

David Solomons

It may be said, and with truth, that the differences between accounting income and economic income are only short-run differences, i.e. if we take a sufficiently long period in the life of an enterprise the changes in the value of equity which distinctively enter into economic income will also be reflected in accounting income. Thus MacNeal's second investor will have his wise investment reflected in his profit when eventually he sells his stock in a later period, if by then it has not fallen in value. That over the whole life of an enterprise its total accounting income and economic income must be identical cannot be gainsaid. But this is poor consolation for short-run defects in our measure of income. *All* the problems of income measurement are the result of our desire to attribute income to arbitrarily determined short periods of time. Everything comes right in the end; but by then it is too late to matter.

Having cast some doubt on the effectiveness of accounting income as a gauge of managerial success, we have to recognize that it emerges satisfactorily from the other test, that of practicality. In so far as objectivity is regarded as an indispensable quality of an income concept which is to have any claim to being practical, accounting income is practical enough. But this is of little moment if it does not measure what we want to measure. Objectivity without relevance is not much of a virtue. The question is whether we can retain some or all of the objectivity of accounting income while answering the question which accounting income palpably fails to answer: How much better off has the accounting entity become during the period?

In passing, we might notice a contrary point of view on the relevance of the two income concepts we are comparing in a statement by Professors Hill and Gordon.[1] Rejecting the idea that unrealized profits should be included in income, they argue that 'information as to what management *expects to make* on the things it *has not sold* is no substitute for information as to what management *has made* on the things it *has sold*'. The answer to this is that neither is the second kind of information a substitute for the first, and it is only the second kind which accounting conventionally provides. Both kinds of information are necessary to assess managerial success. As I have already tried to show, to look at realized profits and losses only may be to ignore an important part of the total picture.

In advocating their particular brand of business income, economists have usually argued that the increase in net worth of the enterprise, which constitutes income, must be arrived at by valuing the whole enterprise at the beginning and the end of the period whose income we wish to measure.

[1] T. M. Hill and Myron J. Gordon, *Accounting: a management approach* (2nd ed. 1960, Homewood, Ill.), p. 143.

These valuations, they say, must be made by discounting, at each date, the expected stream of receipts less the expected stream of payments of the enterprise as far into the future as possible, to arrive at the present value of the net stream. Any amounts distributed by the enterprise to its proprietors during the period must, of course, be added back to give the increase in net worth which, in this view, is synonymous with income. Expressed in this way, the concept looks quite unpractical, for it seems to demand a superhuman degree of foresight, not only about the broad sweep of events but also about the details of day-to-day transactions.

I do not think that too much should be made of this difficulty. We do not allow uncertainty about the future entirely to inhibit us from valuing property on the basis of expected net receipts, or at least on the best estimate we can make of them. Moreover, there are simplifying assumptions we could make which would render the valuation process more manageable. Nevertheless, the difficulties are still somewhat formidable.

A second difficulty about the concept of economic income is that in successive discounting of expected future receipts and payments, effect will have to be given not only to real foreseeable changes in the enterprise's future, but also to changes in human expectations about this future. Thus, suppose that at the beginning of the period a large receipt is foreseen as coming in in three years' time. At the end of the period (of, say, a year) the receipt is thought to be much less certain, and in any case probably smaller than was previously expected. The net worth of the enterprise will have apparently shrunk during the year, then, not because of a real change in the future but only because of a change in expectations about the future. Thus economic income will react both to real future changes and to changes in human expectations, and the effects of these two sets of factors will be inextricably combined.

THE CONCEPT OF VARIABLE INCOME

The concept of 'variable income' attempts to eliminate the effect of a change in expectations from our measure of economic income. Alexander, it will be remembered, approaches the problem of measuring business income by considering first the income from a bond, indeed from quite a variety of bonds. He starts with a perpetual bond which pays no interest in the ordinary sense, but whose owner annually receives $10 if, on the toss of a coin, it comes down heads and nothing if it comes down tails. As a matter of fact this example is hardly more bizarre than the British premium savings bonds which have been in issue since 1956 and which, while securing the investor's capital, pay no interest in the ordinary sense but offer the chance, after a qualifying period, of a prize in a monthly lottery. The amount of the prize fund is determined by calculating interest, at the rate prescribed from time to time, on the bonds eligible for the draw. In the case of Alexander's perpetual bond, he argues that, assuming a 5 per cent rate of interest, the bond would maintain a steady value of $100, whatever the results of the tosses from year to year, for an even chance of receiving $10 or nothing is equivalent to an expectation of receiving $5 each year, giving a capital value, at 5 per cent, of $100. As a matter of fact, according to the strength of the gambling instinct in the community in question, the bond might just as easily be worth more or less than $100; but so long as its value is accepted as being unaffected by the results of each toss, it does not matter just what that value is. And of course, since each toss is a separate event, the chances of success next time are unaffected by past results, so there is no reason why the value of the bond should be affected by the incidence of heads or tails. The income from the bond in any year is then equal to its owner's receipts from it, $10 or nothing according to the result of the toss.

We get closer to real life with Alexander's second bond, which is like the first but has a life limited to 20 years. This bond at the outset will have a capital value of $62.70, this being the present value, at 5 per cent, of a 20-year annuity of $5 annually (the expectation of receipts from the bond). A year later, regardless of the outcome of the toss, it should be worth only $60.42, the present value of a 19-year annuity of $5, and each year, as the bond's expectation of life diminishes, its value will continue to fall. In this case the bondholder enjoys an income which is always less than his receipts by the amount of the diminution in the value of his security. The loss of capital value in the first year was $2.28, so that if the coin came down heads his receipts were $10 and his income was $7.72, while if the coin came down tails his receipts were zero and his income was − $2.28. This illustration leads us straight to Alexander's first definition of variable income, at least as it applies to income from securities, which is that variable income is equal to the net receipts from the security plus or minus any change in its value which was, *at the beginning of the period*, expected to take place during the period.

This, it must be noted, is a first approximation to the definition of variable income, for the full definition has to provide for the possibility that the net receipts of the period may themselves cause future expectations of receipts to be modified during the period, as where a particularly large distribution to owners of a security during the present period is made at the expense of distributions to be made in future periods. In such a case, variable income has to be defined as the net receipts from the security plus or minus any change in its value during the period which was expected at the beginning of the period, plus or minus the discounted present value of any consequential change in expected future receipts brought about by the level of current receipts. This modification of the definition to take account of consequential change in the value of the security will be seen to be of some significance when shortly we consider the determination of the variable income of a business enterprise.

Because changes in the value of a security which result from changes in expectations which occur during the period are excluded from the definition of variable income, this does not mean that they must be neglected altogether. What it does mean is that they are considered to be best kept separate from income, to be reported separately as unexpected gains. Here, another of Alexander's illustrations makes the point clear. Suppose, he says, the amount paid on the perpetual bond is suddenly raised from $10 or nothing on the toss of a coin to $12 or nothing. At a 5 per cent rate of interest this announcement will raise the value of the bond from $100 to $120. There is an unexpected gain of $20, quite apart from any variable income there may be during that year.

This is perhaps a suitable point at which to compare the informativeness of the three income concepts we can choose from in this case. Accounting income would be reported as $10 for the year if the coin came down heads. The change in the terms of the bond would not be regarded as having any relevance to the determination of current income. Economic income would be reported as $30, the receipts for the period plus the increase in the value of the bond. Alexander's proposal is that we should report a variable income of $10 and an unexpected gain of $20. There seems to me to be no room for doubt that this last method of reporting is more informative than either of the others, if our purpose is to assess the success of the bondholder's investment policy for the year.

Incidentally, the relationship between economic income and variable income can be expressed symbolically quite simply, if we write V as the value of the asset whose income we are considering, R for the net receipts from it, use the subscripts o and 1 for the beginning and end of period 1, and the further subscripts a and e for actual magnitudes and expected magnitudes respectively. Then:

Economic income = Variable income + unexpected gain

$$V_{1a} - V_{0a} + R_a = (V_{1e} - V_{0a} + R_a) + (V_{1a} - V_{1e})$$

However, it has to be admitted that this formulation is incomplete in so far as it excludes from variable income and leaves in unexpected gain the consequential changes in V_{1a} which have already been referred to.

David Solomons

THE VARIABLE INCOME OF A BUSINESS ENTERPRISE

It is easy enough to separate the receipts of the owner of a security from the security itself. When we turn to a business enterprise, we cannot use the amounts distributed by the enterprise to its proprietors to help us in determining the income of the enterprise; and the net receipts of the enterprise will include the proceeds of converting non-cash assets into cash, which proceeds we obviously cannot reckon as income. What corresponds to R_a, in the case of an enterprise, is the change in net tangible assets during the period, all assets being valued at cost. This is equal to accounting net income before charging depreciation or providing for inventory mark-downs, and it is the first element in enterprise variable income.

The second element, $V_{ie} - V_{0a}$, is the change in the ex-dividend value of the enterprise during the year which can be predicted with more or less certainty at the beginning of the year. This predictable change in value is, I suggest, what we ought to be measuring when we provide for depreciation, that is to say, it is depreciation based more on the expected loss of market value through use or obsolescence of assets rather than on allocations of historical cost.[1] Of course, in a world from which uncertainty had been banished, these two concepts of depreciation would amount to the same thing.

The third and last element in the variable income of a business enterprise, corresponding to the consequential change in the value of a security resulting from the year's distribution to proprietors, could be of major importance. We must include in variable income any change in the value of the enterprise which is the result of managerial activity during the year over and above the predictable change just discussed. Such change may take the form of a change in the value of tangible assets or a change in the value of goodwill. To qualify for inclusion in variable income these value changes must be brought about by the activity of the firm. If they are purely the result of factors extraneous to the firm, such as a change in the law or a change in the market rate of interest, then they are not part of variable income but are unexpected gains.

The distinction which has to be drawn here is between value changes which are merely the result of a change in expectations and value changes which are the result of managerial activity. If variable income is to measure the firm's success in adding to its well-offness, value changes of the latter

---

[1] I must repeat here that I am assuming away changes in the value of money. In so far as these must be reckoned with, some form of stabilization would have to be built into the above scheme.

type must be included in it. In his original formulation of the way in which the variable income of a corporation might be determined, Alexander did not draw a distinction between internally and externally generated changes in the value of goodwill, but suggested that any change in its value might be included in variable income. However, this seems to me to be inconsistent with his earlier definition. The principal difference between variable income and economic income, as I understand it, is that while economic income includes all changes in the value of net worth which have taken place during the period, variable income includes only those changes which inevitably result from the passage of time or are the result of the activities of the period. To implement this idea, we have to try to distinguish changes in the value of goodwill which are the result of managerial activity, those which reflect, that is to say, changes in expectations brought about by the management and changes in the value of goodwill which cannot so be accounted for.

We have, then, these three constituents of variable business income:

1. The change in net tangible assets, valued at cost.

2. As a deduction, the expected loss of market value of assets through use or obsolescence.

3. Internally generated differences between the value of both tangible and intangible assets at the accounting date and their cost at date of acquisition (or their value at the previous accounting date), to the extent that these differences have not already been included in (2) above.

It is this third element, and especially the recognition of certain changes in the value of goodwill as constituting part of the firm's net income, which particularly distinguishes variable income from accounting income.

CAN WE MEASURE VARIABLE INCOME?

Variable income is a valuable idea, I think, in clarifying our thinking about what an income concept should give us and in recognizing the limitations of accounting income. But can we, in practice, hope to make the distinction between those value changes which are to be included in variable income and those which are to be included in unexpected gain?

Regretfully, I do not think that we can. We must remember that we have two problems, one of valuation and one of attribution, if we want to implement the idea of variable income for a business enterprise. Even if we are prepared to ignore any but quite substantial divergences between the depreciated cost and the current value of tangible assets, we should as a minimum have first to revalue goodwill at the end of each accounting period and then to apportion any change in its value between that part which was the result of managerial activity and that part which was the result of good or bad luck. One has only to state this difficulty to see that there can never be any simple solution to it. Even in very simple domestic situations we know that we can rarely separate the results of good luck and good judgment. In a complex business situation, how much less likely are we to be able to do so!

This difficulty, which would confront us even if our accounts were kept in monetary units of constant purchasing power, is exacerbated when we have to allow for price-level changes. When an asset is bought for $1,000 and prices in general rise so that a year later the asset, though then partly worn out, is worth more on the market than when it was first bought, is this value change to be regarded as an 'unexpected gain' or are we to attribute it to the good judgment of management in purchasing the asset in anticipation of a price rise? If the use of the variable income idea requires us to answer questions like this, I conclude that we simply cannot use it, except perhaps in simple non-business situations.

CONCLUSION

Just as Hicks was led to the conclusion that income was not an effective tool of economic analysis, so it seems to me that we are led to the conclusion that periodic income is not an effective tool of financial planning or control. This conclusion seems to accord ill with the fact that income measurement has long been a central theme of accounting and the main preoccupation of the accounting profession. Yet this fact need not impress us. The practice of medicine once consisted largely of blood-letting. It may be that we are already witnessing a decline in the importance of income measurement. Certainly there is a livelier sense of the shortcomings of ascertained profit figures than there once was, for most of the purposes for which such figures have traditionally been used. There is a rather striking confirmation of this in the preamble to Recommendation XV of the Institute of Chartered Accountants in England and Wales. This recommendation is concerned with the price-level problem, and the passage I have in mind (paragraph 312) reads as follows:

The Council cannot emphasize too strongly that the significance of accounts prepared on the basis of historical cost is subject to limitations, not the least of which is that the monetary unit in which the accounts are prepared is not a stable unit of measurement. In consequence the results shown by accounts prepared on the basis of historical cost are not a measure of increase or decrease in wealth in terms of purchasing power; nor do the results necessarily represent the amount which can prudently be regarded as available for distribution, having regard to the financial requirements of the business. Similarly the results shown by such accounts are not necessarily suitable for purposes such as price fixing, wage negotiations and taxation, unless in using them for these purposes due regard is paid to the amount of profit which has been retained in the business for its maintenance.

This seems pretty much to throw away the baby with the bath-water.

The fact is that for several important purposes periodic income, either historical or prospective, has already been or is being superseded. For decision-making purposes the idea of 'contribution' has taken over from net income. In the field of taxation, we depart from income as the tax base every time we introduce special allowances for depletion, or provide for accelerated depreciation, or permit an anomalous treatment of capital gains. Even for reporting to stockholders, just as in the first half of this century we saw the income statement displace the balance-sheet in importance, so we may now be de-emphasizing the income statement in favour of a statement of fund flows or cash flows. Each of us sees the future differently, no doubt. But my own guess is that, so far as the history of accounting is concerned, the next twenty-five years may subsequently be seen to have been the twilight of income measurement.

PART II

INCOME AND THE MAINTENANCE OF CAPITAL INTACT

7 Maintaining capital intact

by A. C. Pigou*

In a rough general way the concept 'maintaining capital intact' is easy to grasp. Capital consists at any given moment of a definite inventory of physical things. What these are depends in part on how the general interplay of demand and supply has worked in the past. But at any given moment they are constituted by an unambiguous physical collection. In order that capital may be kept intact, if any object embraced in this collection becomes worn out or is thrown out (scrapped), it must be replaced by 'equivalent' objects. When we have got hold of this notion we are able to develop a correlative notion, net real income. From the joint work of the whole mass of productive factors there comes an (annual) in-flowing stream of output.[1] This is gross real income. When what is required to maintain capital intact is subtracted from this there is left net real income. This is Marshall's way of approach.

In his book on *The Pure Theory of Capital*[2] Professor Hayek proposes to throw over the concept of maintaining capital intact and—necessarily—with it the concept of net real income, and to use only the concept gross real income. When he speaks of 'the really relevant magnitude, income' (p. 298), it is gross real income that he has in mind. His reasons for this attitude are twofold. On the one hand, except in a stationary state the notion of maintaining capital intact has no 'strict meaning'; on the other hand, it is a concept of which the economist has no need. Thus, whereas I like to set out three identities: (1) net income = net investment plus consumption, (2) net income = gross income minus depreciation, (3) net investment = gross investment minus depreciation, Professor Hayek only cares to set out one, namely gross income = gross investment plus consumption. My identities, of course, imply Professor Hayek's, but his identities do not imply mine. He is satisfied with a part only of what I require. I shall begin with the first of his two reasons.

The gist of it, if I have not misunderstood, is as follows. If capital were perfectly homogeneous, consisting of a single type of article only, the quantity of capital would be something perfectly self-contained and un-

---

[1] There are, of course, depletions of capital other than those due to wear and tear and obsolescence, e.g. capital losses due to earthquake or war, which it is *not* customary to offset before reckoning net income. In what follows these will be ignored. They are discussed in my article on 'Net Income and Capital Depletion' in the *Economic Journal* of June 1935.　　　　[2] London, 1940.

---

* Professor of Political Economy, University of Cambridge, 1908–43.

ambiguous. What this quantity amounted to at any time would, of course, be a consequence of the interplay of demand and supply in the past. But at any given moment it would be a physical datum, independent of, prior to, affecting, not affected by, the equilibrating process. But in actual life capital is not homogeneous; it is heterogeneous, consisting of a great number of different sorts of things. It is still true that at any given moment the quantities of the several items included in it constitute an independent physical datum. But how exactly is an inventory of diverse items to be conceived as a 'physical magnitude'? Clearly it can only be so conceived if we treat the given quantities of its several items as all *equivalent to* so many units of one item; and the only plausible way of doing this is to equate a unit of B to a unit of A when it is *worth* a unit of A. But the relative values of A and B and of all other things, so far from being independent of the equilibrating process, are determined through that process. For example, the relative current values of different types of machines are affected by the rate of interest, those promising a given yield in the distant future being more valuable relatively to those promising the same yield in the near future, the lower is the rate of interest.[1] Hence the quantity of capital expressed in the only way in which it is practicable to express it is not an unambiguous physical datum, as it would be if capital were an homogeneous entity. On the contrary, the quantity expressed in terms of any given component will be different at two times if the relative values of the components have changed, even though the physical constituents of the capital stock are identical at both times. It follows that the maintenance of these physical constituents unaltered need not entail that capital is maintained intact. That concept has no clear or sensible meaning.

The whole of this reasoning apart from the two last sentences I accept. I accept too the view that, if maintaining capital intact has to be defined in such a way that capital need not be maintained intact even though every item in its physical inventory is unaltered, the concept is worthless. But the inference I draw is, not that we should abandon the concept; rather that we should try to define it in such a way that, when the physical inventory of goods in the capital stock is unaltered, capital *is* maintained intact; more generally, in such a way that, not indeed the quantity of capital—which, with heterogeneous items, can only be a conventionalized number—is independent of the equilibrating process, but changes in its quantity are independent of changes in that process. Let us enquire whether and how this can be done.

---

[1] For, if machine A promises a yield x, n years hence and machine B an equal yield m years hence (m being greater than n) the value of B = the value of A multiplied by $(1/1 + r)^{m-n}$ where r is the annual rate of interest.

Suppose that capital consists of two sorts of goods only, A and B, that at date 1 there are 500 units of each, and that one unit of A is worth 2 units of B. Then the stock of capital as a whole is 'equivalent' either to 750 units of A or to 1,500 units of B. At date 2 one unit of A has become worth 4 units of B, so that at that date 500 units of A plus 500 units of B are equivalent to either 625 units of A or to 2,500 units of B. As between the two dates one unit of A has become worn out or has been discarded out of the capital stock (e.g. scrapped on account of obsolescence). How many additional units of B must have been created in order that capital as a whole may have remained intact between the two dates? *Prima facie* it seems that there is nothing to choose between two answers, first, 2 units (in accordance with the valuation of the first date), secondly, 4 units (in accordance with that of the second date). But let us seek guidance from the special case of homogeneous capital. The quantity of this is a physically given magnitude, and nothing that happens either to people's desire attitude towards capital or to the cost (in any sense of cost) of producing new units can affect it in any way. By analogy, with heterogeneous capital also it is proper so to define quantity change that, the physical constituents of the capital stock being given, no such change can be brought about by anything that happens either to desire attitudes or to cost of production. Hence, if between dates 1 and 2 a unit of A disappears, capital will be maintained intact provided that a new unit of A is introduced irrespective of what the relative values of A and B have become and irrespective of the cost of production of A. If it is decided for any reason not to provide a new unit of A, but to provide instead some units of B, the number of units of B required to make up for the loss of the unit of A must then clearly be the number that at date 2 is worth—which is equivalent to saying is expected to yield the same income as—one unit of A.[1]

This way of defining maintenance of capital intact is readily generalized when capital consists, not of two, but of many kinds of goods. Moreover, if we suppose wearing out or discarding on the one side and replacement on the other to be a continuous balanced process, it is unambiguous. In practice, indeed, we have to do with finite time-intervals. That being so, the quantity of B that is deemed equivalent to a given quantity of A over any period may be different if replacement of decayed or discarded capital takes place once a week, once a month, once a quarter or once a year; for the relative values of A and B may undergo frequent variations. Hence the precise meaning of maintaining capital intact is relative to the length of

---

[1] We must not say 'which has the same cost of production as one unit of A would have', for that would give absurd results if A had become impossible to produce, i.e. had come to have infinite cost of production.

the accounting period with which we are accustomed to work. It will be agreed, however, I think, that in normal conditions this is not an important matter. In a rough general way then this definition will serve. It is not necessary to my purpose, nor do I wish, to claim that it is the best possible one. The possibility or, if we will, the high probability, that a better one could be found only strengthens my case.

Turn then to Professor Hayek's second reason for proposing to abandon the concept maintaining capital intact, namely that it is not needed. Against this I have two considerations to offer. First, as we have seen, and as is indeed obvious, to abandon this concept entails abandoning also that of net real income. In spite, however, of Professor Hayek's claim (p. 336) that the distinction between gross and net investment—which is, of course, the same as that between gross and net income—'has no relationship to anything in the real world', it cannot be denied that both business men and the income tax authorities seek after and make practical use of this distinction—or the best approach to it that they can find. It is net income, not gross income, upon which income tax is assessed. If a Chancellor of the Exchequer were to attempt to assess it upon gross income, what an outcry there would be! Surely it is proper for economists to take cognizance of this fact and, while admitting that perfect definitions cannot be found, to try to make them as little imperfect as they can.

Secondly, real income is of interest to economists largely because of its relevance to what Professor Irving Fisher calls psychic income—income of satisfaction or utility. Of course the relationship between these things is highly intricate—a matter not to be discussed here. But gross and net income are not on a par. We can easily imagine two situations in one of which the production of a given gross real income entails the wearing out or using up of a much larger mass of capital elements than it does in the other. Hence net real income is, or at all events may be, a great deal more relevant to psychic income than gross real income. This is, so far as it goes, a second good reason for economists to try to disentangle it.

No doubt, if it could be shown that the disentanglement is, from the nature of the case, utterly and for ever impossible, it would be the part of wisdom to abandon the attempt. We do not want to spend our lives in squaring the circle or inventing perpetual-motion machines. But that is not the situation with which we are faced. We cannot, indeed, in this field evolve concepts which are perfectly clean cut. There are bound to be rough edges. Some of us, myself among the number, have tried our hand at smoothing these down. No doubt we have in some degree failed. But we have not, I suggest, failed so grievously that others, instead of giving our baby another wash, should empty both it and the bath away.

8 Maintaining capital intact: a reply

by F. A. Hayek[*]

Professor Pigou's defence of the conception of 'maintaining capital intact' consists essentially of two parts. The first is a restatement of his own attempt to define its meaning. The second is a plea that, even if this particular attempt should not be regarded as successful, economists ought still to continue to seek for the definite and unique sense which he believes must be behind the admittedly vague meaning that this concept has in practice. I shall try briefly to answer each point in turn.

I

Professor Pigou's answer to the question of what is meant by 'maintaining capital intact' consists in effect of the suggestion that for this purpose we should disregard obsolescence and require merely that such losses of value of the existing stock of capital goods be made good as are due to physical wear and tear. Once this proposition is accepted and the concept is defined so that in all instances 'when the physical inventory of goods in the capital stock is unaltered, capital *is* maintained intact', the rest of his argument necessarily follows. I am unable to accept this basis of his solution.

If Professor Pigou's criterion is to be of any help, it would have to mean that we have to disregard *all* obsolescence, whether it is due to foreseen or foreseeable causes, or whether it is brought about by entirely unpredictable causes, such as the 'acts of God or the King's enemy', which alone he wanted to exclude in an earlier discussion of this problem.[1] Now this seems to me to be neither useful for theoretical purposes nor in conformity with actual practice. The consequences of using this concept of 'maintaining capital intact' can best be shown by considering an imaginary case. Assume three entrepreneurs, *X*, *Y*, and *Z*, to invest at the same time in equipment of different kinds but of the same cost and the same potential physical duration, say ten years. *X* expects to be able to use his machine continuously throughout the period of its physical 'life'. *Y*, who produces some fashion article, knows that at the end of one year his machine will have no more than its scrap value. *Z* undertakes a very risky venture in which the chances

---

[1] See *Economics of Welfare* (4th ed. 1932), p. 46, and my discussion of the various stages in the evolution of Professor Pigou's theory of 'maintaining capital intact' in *Economica* (August 1935), particularly pp. 245–8.

---

[*] Professor of Economics, University of Freiburg i. B.

of employing the machine continuously so long as it lasts and having to scrap it almost as soon as it starts to produce are about even. According to Professor Pigou the three entrepreneurs will have to order their investments in such a way that during the first year they can expect to earn the same gross receipts: since the wear and tear of their respective machines during the first year will be the same, the amount they will have to put aside during the first year to 'maintain their capital intact' will also be the same, and this procedure will therefore lead to their earning during that year the same 'net' income from the same amount of capital.[1] Yet it is clear that the foreseen result of such dispositions would be that at the end of the year X would still possess the original capital, Y one-tenth of it, while Z would have an even chance of either having lost it all or just having preserved it.

I find it difficult to conceive that this procedure could have any practical value or any theoretical significance. That entrepreneur Y, acting in this manner, would to all intents and purposes throw his capital away, i.e. would plan to lose it, hardly needs pointing out. But take the case where a clear concept of net income is most wanted, namely, direct taxation. To treat all receipts except what is required to make good physical wear and tear as net income for income tax purposes would evidently discriminate heavily against industries where the rate of obsolescence is high and reduce investment in these industries below what is desirable. The manufacturer of wireless sets, for example, who expects this year's model to be superseded in a year's time by technical improvements, would certainly have to restrict investment and output so as to keep prices high enough to enable him to write off obsolescing equipment in the course of the year. But if his allowance for obsolescence were treated as income, this would in effect amount to a special capital turnover tax and force him further to reduce his investment. Such a system would therefore discriminate heavily against all industries with rapid technological progress (or new and experimental industries) and thus slow down technological advance.

Analytically the use of this concept of 'maintaining capital intact' would be no less misleading. One of the purposes for which we want a definition of net income is to know what are the long run costs on which an adequate profit must be made in order that investment in that particular industry should appear profitable. It is immediately clear that all foreseeable obsolescence (whether it can be predicted with certainty or only with a certain degree of probability) must here be taken into account. No entrepreneur would regard the three alternatives mentioned before as equally

---

[1] For our present purposes we can disregard any differences in the cost of operating the three machines.

profitable, if the gross returns to be expected were the same—although if he accepted Professor Pigou's conception of 'maintaining capital intact' he would have to do so. But in that case he would not long remain an entrepreneur.

But while I feel that it is impossible simply to disregard obsolescence in this connexion, it is not difficult to see why Professor Pigou is reluctant to admit it among the factors which have to be taken into account in 'maintaining capital intact': because, once one admits it, one is on the path which leads inevitably to complete scepticism concerning the possibility of any objective criterion of what 'maintaining capital intact' means. Most people will agree with Professor Pigou that not *all* obsolescence has to be made good before we can consider any income as being 'net'. To demand that all capital losses due to unforeseen and unforeseeable changes should be made good before any income can be described as net income might mean that not only certain individuals but, in certain circumstances, even whole communities, might have no net income for years on end—although they might be in a position permanently to maintain their consumption at their accustomed level or even to raise it. I entirely agree with Professor Pigou's implied contention that in many such cases the making good of past losses should be regarded as new saving rather than as mere main-tenance of capital. But this applies only to losses due to causes which had not been foreseen. And the real problem of maintaining capital intact arises not after such losses have been made, but when the entrepreneur plans his investment. The question is what allowance for amortization he ought to make in his calculations so that, in view of all the circumstances known to him, he can expect to be able to earn the same income in the future. But the knowledge on the basis of which he has to make this decision will necessarily change as time goes on, and with it will change the provision he has to make in order to achieve his aim. No watching of the 'quantity' of his capital from the outside, that is, without knowing all the information he possesses at different dates, can tell us whether he has done his best to avoid involuntary encroachments upon his sources of income or the opposite. And if we know what information he commands at the different successive dates, the action which we should think most appropriate on his part is not likely to be one which would keep any measurement of his capital constant. In a changing world, where different people, and even the same people at different times, will possess different knowledge, there can be no objective standards by which we can measure whether a person has done as well in this effort as he might have done. In such a world there is no reason to expect that the quantity of capital, in whatever sense this term be meant, will ever be kept constant, even though every individual owner of capital might do all in his power to avoid that involuntary 'splashing' or 'stinting' which capital accounting seeks to prevent. This is a conclusion of some importance, since much of present economic theory is based on the contrary assumption, so well expressed by Professor Pigou when he wrote of 'the concept of capital as an entity capable of maintaining its quantity while altering its form and by its nature always drawn to those forms on which, so to speak, the sun of profit is at the time shining'.[1]

There is one more point in this connexion where I am anxious to correct a wrong impression which seems to have been left by what I said on this question. I hope I nowhere did say, and I certainly ought not to have said, that with the concept of 'maintaining capital intact' the concept of net income should also disappear. All that I meant to argue was that we cannot hope to define the latter by any reference to the 'quantity' of capital and its changes. For an explanation of the alternative procedure I must refer to my *Pure Theory of Capital*, particularly pp. 336 ff.

2

It is unlikely that Professor Pigou would have been led to advocate a solution of the puzzle which is so obviously imperfect if it were not for the fact that among the various solutions yet suggested it seemed to be the least imperfect, and if he had not been convinced that there must be a solution. His argument is that business men and legislators constantly use the concept of maintaining capital intact and seek after a clear distinction, and that the economist ought to help them to approach as closely as possible to the ideal solution which has not yet been found. Nobody denies, of course, that the practices actually followed in this connexion are of the greatest importance for the economist and that he ought to know as much about them as possible. Nor do I want to deny that these practices aim at some purpose and that the economist ought to try to help as much as he can in achieving it. The question is, however, whether this ultimate purpose of the practices ostensibly aiming at 'maintaining capital intact' is adequately described by these words. I personally have come to the conclusion that while the ordinary practice of trying to keep the money value of capital constant is in most circumstances a fairly good approximation to the real purpose of capital accounting, this is not true in all circumstances. I have tried to show that this ultimate purpose has no direct or necessary connexion with changes in the quantity of capital, however measured, and that therefore no policy which aims at maintaining a particular measurement of capital constant can fully achieve that purpose in all circumstances. If this conclusion is essentially negative, it need for that reason be no less

[1] *Economic Journal* (June 1935), p. 239.

useful. If the usefulness of the practices aiming at 'maintaining capital intact' have definite limitations, the important thing is that these limitations be recognized. The fact that practical men try to apply to all cases a formula which has served them well in a great many cases does not prove that in these attempts the formula must necessarily have any meaning at all. The problem which the accountant and the income tax inspector face is not what constitutes in any real sense 'maintaining capital intact' in these cases—although they may have to interpret legal provisions which use such or similar phrases—but what are the most appropriate practices which will achieve the same end, which in the more ordinary situations is adequately achieved by keeping the money value of capital constant.

9 Maintaining capital intact: a further suggestion

by J. R. Hicks*

I

To intrude upon a controversy being waged by such paladins as Professor Pigou and Professor Hayek seems an act bold even unto rashness; but the question of maintaining capital intact just cannot be left where they left it last summer. The present note will have justified itself if it serves to provoke them to another round.

At the point which has now been reached, Professor Pigou has offered us a carefully constructed method of measuring capital; it is based upon a comparison of physical units *in use* at the two dates which are being compared, the different sorts of capital goods being reduced to a common measure by using their relative values at the *latter* of the two dates. This principle of Professor Pigou's stands up very well to most sorts of criticism, but it has (I think) been torpedoed by Professor Hayek. His example of the firm which produces fashion goods, installs machinery which it plans to use for a limited period and then to scrap before the machinery is physically worn out, establishes conclusively that there are instances where the physical maintenance of capital would not suffice to ensure the maintenance of capital in an economic sense. If the second of our two dates was taken just previous to the time when the specialized machinery is discarded, the fact that the equipment would still be there, technically almost as good as new, would not prevent the firm from needing to have set aside amortization allowances for almost the whole original value of the machinery, if it was to have maintained capital intact in any significant sense. A satisfactory definition of maintaining capital intact has got to be able to deal with this case, and it seems clear that Professor Pigou's cannot do so.

Professor Hayek, on the other hand, having demolished the rival construction, fails (in my view) to provide anything solid to put in its place. His definition of net income (constructed so as to avoid the necessity of defining the maintenance of capital *en route* for the definition of net income) contains far too many subjective elements to be usable in practice,

* Drummond Professor of Political Economy, University of Oxford 1952–65. Fellow of All Souls.

and is much more at home in those simplified models beloved of economic theorists than it is when it seeks to put on flesh and blood. As we widen our assumptions to bring them nearer reality, the more tenuous does a definition by 'constant income stream' become. In a world in which ex-pectations were *certain* (by *certain* I do not mean necessarily *correct*) the definition by constant income stream would be eminently reasonable; but when we allow for uncertainty of expectations it soon becomes unrealistic, or rather it has to be metamorphosed into something else.[1]

In what follows I shall try to suggest what that something else is. For certain purposes, at any rate, it turns out to be something not very far removed from Professor Pigou's definition, though it is inevitably not the same as Professor Pigou's definition. But it is near enough for me to have some hope that he may be willing to accept it as a possible modification.

I must emphasize the qualification 'for certain purposes'. I feel rather strongly nowadays that most economic controversies about definition arise from a failure to keep in mind the relation of every definition to the purpose for which it is to be used. We have to be prepared to use different definitions for different purposes; and although we can often save ourselves trouble by adopting compromises, which will do well enough for more than one purpose, we must always remember that compromises have the defects of compromises, and in fine analysis they will need qualification. It is not profitable to embark on the fine analysis of a definition unless we have decided on the purpose for which the definition is wanted.

The purpose I have in mind is the measurement of the net social income. It seems clear that this is the problem which is in Professor Pigou's mind too. I am not sure about Professor Hayek; it may be that he is thinking of a different problem and that the argument is thus proceeding to some extent at cross-purposes. In any case, I shall do no more than suggest a definition which I consider to be appropriate for defining the ideal measure-ment of the net social income; it needs a separate investigation to deter-mine whether it is suitable for other purposes as well.

2

The way in which the problem is conceived by Professor Pigou is (I think) this. His ultimate object is the measurement of the net social income in real terms; all the magnitudes in his fundamental identities are to be taken

[1] When I wrote *Value and Capital*, chapter XIV [reproduced as chapter 4 above], I was myself an adherent of the Hayekian school on this matter, so I can appreciate the qualities of Professor Hayek's definition. I can also appreciate what Professor Hayek must feel about the quite unfounded accusation by Professor Pigou that the definition by constant income stream is a definition of gross income.

in such senses that they can be converted into real terms by a suitable multiplier. When he writes

$$\text{net income} = \text{consumption} + \text{net investment}$$

the various terms in the equation may be measured in terms of money, but we have only got to choose our units properly, and they would be capable of being understood in real terms. The definitions have got to be chosen so as to make this transformation possible. At once we run into the difficulty that if net investment is interpreted as the difference between the value of the capital stock at the beginning and end of the year, the transformation would not be possible. It is only in the special case when the prices of all sorts of capital instruments are the same (if their condition is the same) at the end of the year as at the beginning, that we should be able to measure the money value of real net investment by the increase in the money value of the capital stock. In all probability these prices will have changed during the year, so that we have a kind of index-number problem, parallel to the index-number problem of comparing real income in different years. The characteristics of that other problem are generally appreciated; what is not so generally appreciated is the fact that before we can begin to compare real income in different years, we have to solve a similar problem within the single year—we have to reduce the capital stock at the beginning and end of the year into comparable real terms.

This, I think, is how the problem has appeared to Professor Pigou; Professor Hayek's substantial reply is to deny that the problem of comparing *capital* at different dates is an index-number problem. The comparison of capital values at the beginning and end of the year is not the same kind of thing as the comparison of the prices of consumable goods in different years; for the price of a durable good at one date is related to its price at another date in a way in which the prices of different (albeit similar) consumable goods at different dates are not. The price of a house in January 1941 is largely based upon an estimate of what its price will be in January 1942; but the price of a loaf of bread in one year is influenced by expectations about the price of bread in another year to a usually negligible extent.

The value of a capital good at any particular time is based upon the anticipated quasi-rents which it will earn during its future 'life'. (This 'life', it should be noticed, does not only depend upon the physical durability of the good; it also depends upon the length of time for which it is expected to be useful.) Since it will be implicit in such expectations that the article will have some capital value at each date during its life, we may say that the capital value at the beginning of the year depends upon the quasi-rents the article is expected to earn during the year, and the capital value it is expected to have at the end. In practice, these expectations must be interpreted in a sense which allows for risk; but however we allow for risk, the proposition that capital values at the beginning and end of the year are intimately related magnitudes still holds.

The suggestion I desire to make here is that we can allow for this intimate relationship without sacrificing the general approach which Professor Pigou is naturally determined to preserve. A way of doing so has been indicated by the Swedish economists, particularly Professor Lindahl.[1] In their presentation it has been mixed up with other elements which are perhaps less acceptable. My contention is that we can use Professor Lindahl's solution of this problem without at the same time swallowing more than we like of his *ex ante–ex post* constructions for use in our theory of the trade cycle.

3

The changes which may have taken place in the price-level of capital goods are not the only reason why the difference between the money value of an article at the beginning of the year and its money value at the end will not do as a measure of depreciation; the underlying reason why this measure will not do is that the beginning-value and end-value were arrived at on a different basis of knowledge. When a particular article from the capital stock was valued in January, there was implicit in that valuation an estimate of what the value would be in December; but the December value which is used for calculating the year's depreciation is not an estimate in the same sense—December is now past, so we *know*. If C_0 is the value of the capital stock at the beginning of the year, C_1 the value of these same goods at the end, then to measure depreciation by $C_0 - C_1$, and net income by

$$\text{consumption} + \text{gross investment} + C_1 - C_0$$

is internally inconsistent. The figures for consumption and gross investment will be based upon the actual historical events of the year; the figure for C_1 also takes into account the actual events of the year, though it is still influenced by uncertainty about what will happen when the year is over; but the figure for C_0 was arrived at when the events of the year were still in the future. As far as the events of the year in question are concerned, consumption, gross investment and C_1 all shine in the light of history; but what is history for them is shrouded for C_0 in the mists of futurity. In order to get a true measure for depreciation, hence for net investment, and hence for net income, C_0 must be brought out into the light too.

[1] *Theory of Money and Credit,* part I, 'Algebraic Discussion'.

Let us then define the depreciation of the original stock of capital as the difference between the total value of the goods comprising that original stock as it is at the end of the year (C_1) and the value (C_0') *which would have been put upon the initial stock at the beginning of the year if the events of the year had been correctly foreseen, including among those events the capital value C_1 at the end of the year.*[1] Net income is then

$$\text{consumption} + \text{gross investment} + C_1 - C_0'.$$

This, I think, is the Swedish definition of *ex post* income; unlike their definition of *ex ante* income, which presents difficulties of interpretation in a world of uncertainty, the definition of *ex post* income is no harder to apply in a practical case than any other method which has been suggested for dealing with the problem of depreciation.

The corrected value for the initial capital stock is of course not easy to arrive at; but what we need is not this corrected value, but the consequential figure for depreciation $(C_0' - C_1)$. We can proceed to estimate this by distinguishing, of the various experiences which the initial capital goods will have had during the year, which sorts will cause a divergence between C_0' and C_1. These are the things which will cause true depreciation. By applying the rule to each case as it comes up we ought to be able to discover them.

4

In nearly all the cases where I have been able to try it out, the Swedish definition gives eminently sensible results. They are not always the results which might have been expected beforehand, but they are always intelligible, and they stand looking at from several points of view. Let us check over a few of them.

Normal wear and tear in the course of production is clearly a reason why the value of a capital instrument should be greater at the beginning of a year than at the end, even if the final value was foreseen accurately. Normal wear and tear is therefore an element in true depreciation. So is exceptional wear and tear, due to exceptionally heavy usage; if the exceptionally heavy usage had been foreseen, the gap between the beginning-value and the end-value would have been larger. On the other hand, any deterioration which the machine undergoes outside its utilization does *not* give rise to true depreciation; if such deterioration had been foreseen, the initial capital value would have been written down in consequence; the deterioration is therefore not depreciation, but a capital loss. If a machine remains

---

[1] It should be noticed that this supposed foresight only extends to the events of the year under discussion; later events are still in the dark at the end of the year, so they must be left in the dark when we are constructing our corrected figure for the initial capital.

idle throughout the year, any deterioration which it undergoes is therefore not depreciation, but capital loss; and the use of productive resources to maintain the idle machine in good condition is net investment. This last result may appear surprising at first sight, but it is only reasonable when one thinks it over; the fact that the machine may have produced some output in the past is irrelevant; the 'maintenance' work done in the present is not a contribution to current final output, but to the final output of future years.

Obsolescence of the kind described in Professor Hayek's example is true depreciation on our test; the fashion firm scraps its machinery in accordance with anticipations; it is not failure of foresight which makes the end-value less than the beginning-value. But most problems of obsolescence do arise from imperfect foresight. The allowance for obsolescence which firms reckon among their costs is for the most part a reflection of their uncertainty about the value of their equipment at the end of the year; once this value is assumed known, the necessity for such obsolescence allowances disappears.

5

The definition of net income which I have been describing is, I think, in complete accordance with that proposed by Professor Hayek; in all cases where they can both be employed they would give the same results. There are certain instances, however, where the difference between the consequences of the Swedish definition and those of Professor Pigou's definition become striking. One of these is the obsolescence case, which has been referred to; another is the case of a capital instrument, which is not used during the year, but also suffers no physical deterioration or technical supersession. Professor Pigou would (I think) say that in such a case capital is maintained intact; on the Swedish definition (and also on Professor Hayek's) there is accumulation of capital. For, assuming the end-value to be known, the beginning-value would be the discounted value of the end-value, that is, less than the end-value. Although it remains idle, nevertheless the instrument yields a net income. This looks absurd, particularly in the case of involuntary idleness (if the instrument is deliberately held over, it is more intelligible that it should earn an income by being deliberately devoted to the satisfaction of future wants). The involuntary case becomes a little more intelligible when we notice that it is almost inevitable for involuntary unemployment of a capital instrument to be attended by a capital loss during the year considerably in excess of the income earned. ($C_0' < C_1$ but $C_0 > C_1$.) It is thus not surprising that the business man should pay little attention to such 'income', but it does not follow that the economist should not pay more attention.

J. R. Hicks

I have a strong feeling that the reason why Professor Pigou answers these borderline questions in a different way from that in which they would be answered by Professor Hayek, Professor Lindahl, or myself, is because he is primarily thinking of the measurement of real national income as a means of comparing economic welfare in different periods. As I have shown elsewhere,[1] such comparison is only possible if one is prepared to assume that the wants of the community (their utility or indifference functions) are the same in each of the periods; nor does it seem possible to make much allowance when making these comparisons for the hopes and fears of different future conditions which exist in each or the periods. So long as one sticks to the welfare problem, Professor Pigou's definition of maintaining capital intact will do very well; the borderline cases will not come up. But comparing economic welfare is not the only purpose (nowadays, alas! it is not even the main purpose) of measuring the national income.

[1] 'The Valuation of the Social Income', *Economica* (1940), pp. 107 ff.

138

PART III

SURVEYS OF ECONOMISTS' VIEWS
ON INCOME

10 Concepts of taxable income: the German contribution

by Paul H. Wueller

The absolute load carried by federal and state net income tax bases has increased rapidly since 1929.[1] The rise in income tax rates in the face of adverse economic conditions has inspired numerous protests. Complaints of taxpayers, in conjunction with a few spectacular cases of alleged income tax avoidance[2] and a substantial decline in yields,[3] have elevated the problems surrounding the taxation of net income to issues of national importance.

One of the many problems involved is concerned with the formulation of concepts of income adequate for purposes of public policy. The formulation of such concepts is not the exclusive responsibility of students of economics. Professional economists, by virtue of their preoccupation with a limited sector of the social universe, can be expected only to clarify some of the issues involved and to outline some of the alternatives available to the legislator.

Unfortunately, the contributions which American and foreign students of economics have made toward the formulation of concepts of taxable income have never been brought together.[4] This study represents an attempt to present to the American reader a critical examination of the principal concepts of income advanced by German, Italian and American economists. It may serve not only to correct the impression that economic literature in this field is limited to a few casual remarks but also to challenge the dogmatism of some of the proponents of the various concepts. In any case,

[1] This article has been made possible by a grant from the Council for Research in the Social Sciences. The task was undertaken under the direction of Robert Murray Haig and Carl Shoup of Columbia University, to whom the present writer is indebted for generous aid and counsel.

[2] *New York Times*, 26 May 1933, p. 1; 7 June 1933, p. 1; 10 June 1933, p. 7; 13 June 1933, p. 40; 16 June 1933, p. 18; 13 March 1934, p. 2; 5 May 1934, p. 9.

[3] *Annual Reports of the Secretary of the Treasury* for the fiscal year ended: 30 June 1929, p. 173; 30 June 1930, p. 202; 30 June 1932, p. 159.

[4] Legal students of income taxation seem to labour under the impression that economists have failed to give extensive thought or study to the subject in hand. In 1931, for example, Messrs. Miller, Hendricks and Everett, attorneys-at-law, observed: '...most economists have confined their discussions of income to a few passages in textbooks on economics and articles in learned journals'. R. N. Miller, H. Hendricks, E. Everett, *Re-organizations and Other Exchanges in Federal Income Taxation* (New York, 1931), p. 9.

Paul H. Wueller

it will certainly demonstrate that no 'general agreement' exists among economists regarding the content of 'the' concept of income.[1]

The selection of the economists has been determined by two considerations. In the first place it was decided that to be eligible for selection a student would have to be a member of a culture group whose economic and fiscal institutions roughly approximated our own. On this basis American, British, French, German and Italian students qualified. In the second place it was considered advisable to confine detailed consideration to those groups of investigators whose contributions did not represent a mere collection of casual comments. This latter principle eliminated treatment of the contributions of British and French scholars.

A survey of the French literature indicated that, in the absence of a net income tax in the French fiscal system until recently, few Frenchmen had given evidence of more than a passing interest in the subject and they had largely confined themselves to a simple restatement of the contributions of their German predecessors.[2]

The British, though they look back upon a century and a half of income tax experience,[3] apparently have never undertaken—in a continuous and systematic way—to develop general concepts of income. No evidence has been discovered which would lead one to suspect that the Inland Revenue definition of income has ever been seriously questioned by British students.[4]

[1] For a brief exposition of this point of view, *see* H. L. Lutz, 'Should Capital Gains Be Taxed As Income?', *Bulletin of the National Tax Association*, XXII, no. 5 (February 1937).

[2] See G. Koenig, *Un Nouvel impôt sur le revenu* (Paris, 1883); Y. Guyot, *L'Impôt sur le revenu* (Paris, 1887); A. Raynand, *Les Réformes fiscales...*(Paris, 1888); J. Roche, *Contre l'impôt sur le revenu* (Paris, 1896); E. Lauriot, *Étude sur l'impôt sur le revenu* (Paris, 1898); E. Villey, 'De l'exagération des critiques adressées à notre système d'impôts', *Revue d'Economie Politique* (Juillet–Août 1896); H. Meyer, *Die Einkommensteuerprojekte in Frankreich bis 1887* (Berlin, 1905); J. Caillaux, *Les Réformes fiscales* (Paris, 1905); A. E. Gauthier, *La Réforme fiscale par l'impôt sur le revenu* (Paris, 1908); C. de Mouquet, *La Réforme des impôts sur les valeurs mobilières* (Lille, 1908); L. Petiot, *Projet d'impôt global et progressif sur le revenu* (Paris, 1908); E. H. Vogel, 'Die direkten Steuern Frankreichs und ihre Reform', *Finanz-Archiv*, XXXI (1914), 497; R. Pupin, *Richesse privée et finances françaises de l'avant-guerre à l'après-guerre* (Paris, 1919); F. Rompe, *Die ideengeschichtliche Entwicklung des Einkommensteuerproblems in Frankreich* (Leipzig, 1930).

[3] R. Magill, L. H. Parker, E. P. King, *A Summary of the British Tax System with Special Reference to Its Administration* (Washington, 1934), p. 2.

[4] The acquiescence of British economists may be explained in terms of their favoured type of analysis. Early nineteenth-century economists were preoccupied with analysis which ran in terms of factorial distribution. See J. M. Clark, 'The Socializing of Theoretical Economics', in *The Trend of Economics*, ed. R. G. Tugwell (New York, 1924), pp. 73 ff. In the same volume, see F. H. Knight, 'The Limitations of Scientific Methods in Economics', pp. 229 ff.; T. Veblen, 'The Preconceptions of Economic Science', in *The Place of Science in Modern Civilization* (New York, 1919), p. 82. Also J. M. Keynes, *The General Theory of Employment, Interest and Money* (New York, 1936), chapter II. As will subsequently appear, those students who have contributed substantially to the concept of income literature have placed considerable emphasis upon 'personal' rather than functional distribution.

Alfred Marshall accepted it[1] and Pigou did not quarrel with it.[2] Even the Royal Commission on the Income Tax (1920), which made a comprehensive study of income taxation in Great Britain, did not attempt the formulation of a general concept of income. By way of introductory remark, the Commissioners observed: '...the plan adopted has been not to attempt a general covering definition of income, but to define income that falls under each of these [referring to schedules A, B, C, D, E] divisions'.[3]

Though the British did not make a contribution to the literature of the concept of income which is as significant as that of American, German and Italian students, some British economists have thrown penetrating light upon germane problems. They will be introduced in connexion with the presentation of the contributions of their 'foreign' colleagues whenever possible.

In the discussion of the American, German and Italian theories, the order has been determined by conceptual affinity. The exposition of the contribution of the German economists precedes the discussion of the concepts of American and Italian students. Techniques and definitions of the Italian investigators, in turn, are more meaningful after perusal of the concepts of American scholars. This choice suggests itself, because as a matter of chronological sequence the basic contributions in the different countries were made in the order indicated. In fact, at times there was conscious, duly accredited 'borrowing' of the basic approaches and tools from antecedent 'foreign' writers. By way of preliminary caution, however, it is urged that the order of presentation is not to suggest an evolutionary sequence. If a general orientation may be suggested, it would seem more appropriate to think of the different national contributions, though related, as distinct by virtue of focus and emphasis.

In Germany, the major contributions to the literature of the concept of income were made in the period from 1832 to 1892. The economist Hermann (1832)[4] was the first to attempt a concise formulation of a concept of income and the economist-administrator Schanz[5] closed the formal discussion in 1892. During this period, interesting and significant developments occurred in Germany's political, economic and fiscal institutions.

A loose union of political principalities[6] prior to 1871, Germany under Bismarck became a closely knit federation of states. Much earlier than is

---

[1] A. Marshall, *A Memorandum on Imperial Taxes* (London, 1899), p. 112.
[2] A. C. Pigou, *A Study in Public Finance* (London, 1928), p. 98.
[3] *Report of the Royal Commission on the Income Tax* (London, 1920), p. 4.
[4] F. B. W. Hermann, *Staatswirtschaftliche Untersuchungen* (Munich, 1874), *passim*. (This work was first published in 1832.)
[5] G. v. Schanz, 'Der Einkommensbegriff und die Einkommensteuergesetze', *Finanz-Archiv* (1896), p. 1.
[6] F. Nauman, *Central Europe* (London, 1917), pp. 296 ff.

Paul H. Wueller

commonly realized Germany enjoyed a rapid industrial growth.[1] The forms of its economic organization, those of private, laissez-faire capitalism, closely resembled our own [in the U.S.] of the late nineteenth century. But the German development though somewhat more complex because of social legislation[2] was not deflected by anti-trust agitation and regulation.[3] The absence of imperialistic ventures of consequence during this period suggests that the relatively heavy load carried by Germany's fiscal machine at the time when her economists developed their concepts of income was primarily a result of internal industrial expansion. However, it must be noted that the expansion in question took place under a governmental policy which insisted that a relatively large percentage of the non-entrepreneurial costs of production be borne by the state rather than the individual upon whom they happened to fall in the first instance.[4]

In her fiscal mechanism and procedure Germany differed markedly from the United States. In this country, faculty and income taxes were virtually nonexistent throughout the nineteenth century.[5] In Germany, on the other hand, net income taxes were continuously relied upon.[6]

Though the income tax movement was not uniformly successful[7] during the first half of the nineteenth century, it regained considerable momentum upon the termination (1871) of the Franco-Prussian War. Between 1870 and 1910 some nineteen jurisdictions of the Reich, including such economically and politically important states as Prussia and Saxony, incorporated net income taxes in their fiscal systems.[8]

Together with the enactment of net income tax statutes, German

[1] W. H. Dawson, *The Development of Modern Germany* (London, 1909), *passim.*

[2] A. Epstein, *Insecurity: a Challenge to America* (New York, 1933), pp. xi ff. and Part I.

[3] H. von Beckerath, *Modern Industrial Organization: an Economic Interpretation* (New York, 1933), *passim.* Also R. Leifmann, *Cartels, Concerns and Trusts* (London, 1932), pp. 21 ff.

[4] See J. M. Clark, *Studies in the Economics of Overhead Costs* (Chicago, 1933, 5th impression), pp. 1–16, 27–30, 33, 361, 376 ff. Also *idem, Social Control of Business* (Chicago, 1926), pp. 106–10, 451, 465 ff.

[5] E. R. A. Seligman, *The Income Tax* (New York, 1914), pp. 367 ff.

[6] R. Grabower, *Preussen's Steuern vor und nach den Befreiungskriegen* (Berlin, 1932), pp. 230 ff. Also, B. Moll, *Lehrbuch der Finanzwissenschaft* (Berlin, 1930), pp. 522 ff.

[7] In 1811, for instance, Prussia enacted a *Klassen* or *Standessteuer*, a faculty tax assessed against presumed rather than actually determined income, which was imposed exclusively upon the inhabitants of rural districts and small towns. B. Moll, *op. cit.* p. 447. This faculty tax is not only interesting as a retrogression from the income tax principle, but also because American income taxes have frequently been justified on the ground that they would tend to ease the tax burden of the rural population. See National Industrial Conference Board, *State Income Taxes* (New York, 1930), I, preface.

[8] *Finanz-Archiv*, I, 308; II, 382; VII, 603, 611, 643, 559; X, 370; XII, 173, 778, 763, 255; XIII, 801; XV, 355; XVI, 719; XVII, 773, 797, 379; XIX, 152, 188, 243; XX, 281, 295; XXIII, 224, 250; XXVII, 812; XXVIII, 315, 307, 333, 348–9; XXIX, 810, 836; XXXI, 419, 465.

legislators, in contradistinction to their Anglo-Saxon confrères,[1] provided for so-called *Ergänzungssteuern* (supplementary taxes). These supplementary taxes were introduced because of a general conviction that income was not an adequate measure of ability. Virtually all income tax laws were sooner or later supplemented by *Ergänzungssteuern* or *Vermögenssteuern* (net-fortune taxes), levies which were measured by the net worth of the tax-payer.[2]

These *Vermögenssteuern*[3] differed from our general property taxes, in that they were not assessed against property as such, but against a given taxpayer's equities (net worth) in property.[4] Again, the German net-fortune tax differs from what is known in England and the United States as the capital levy,[5] in that it is a recurrent impost at a rate low enough to facilitate liquidation out of the current net yield of the equities taxed.[6]

Generally speaking, the net-fortune tax is an interesting modernization of the older property tax *in rem*. In connexion with the purpose of the present study it is of particular significance, because it is against the background of this fiscal device that some of the limitations of the concepts of income of German economists must be evaluated.

Prior to the Franco-Prussian War, which coincided chronologically with the widespread introduction of net income and net-fortune taxes in Germany, only four academic economists[7] had attempted to formulate concepts of income. Between 1871 and the turn of the century, some thirteen students[8] of distinction essayed the task. Often their definitions seem to be mutually exclusive. Most of these post-war scholars would be properly described as general economists, with the possible exception of

---

[1] See F. Meisel, *Britische und deutsche Einkommensteuer* (Tübingen, 1925), 'Introduction'.

[2] See above, p. 144, n. 8.

[3] The *Vermögenssteuern* should not be confused with the *Vermögenszuwachssteuer*. The latter tax was assessed, at a progressive scale, against land value increments.

[4] The Prussian Ministry of Finance outlined the following case in support of the net-fortune tax: (1) 'Income is not an adequate measure of ability to pay'; (2) 'The income tax cannot afford differential treatment to labour and investment incomes, but such a differential treatment must be insisted upon for reasons of equity'; (3) 'A net-fortune tax furnishes the best available fiscal instrument to accomplish the desired differentiation.' Prussian Ministry of Finance, 'Preussischer Gesetzentwurf wegen einer Ergänzungs-steuer', Begründung, *Finanz-Archiv* x (1893), 370 ff. It should be observed that Moll, as well as von Heckel, supports the position of the ministry. See Moll, *op. cit.* p. 544; M. v. Heckel, *Lehrbuch der Finanzwissenschaft*, I (Leipzig, 1907), 404 ff.

[5] Hugh Dalton, *The Capital Levy Explained* (New York, 1923), *passim*.

[6] For interesting exhibits of forms to be used by the taxpayer for the computation of net income and net-fortune taxes, see *Finanz-Archiv*, VIII (1891), 863 ff.; also K. Th. v. Eheberg, *Finanzwissenschaft* (Leipzig, 1915), pp. 287 ff. See also P. H. Wueller, *The Integration of the German Tax System* (New York, 1933), *passim*.

[7] Hermann (1832), Biersack (1850), Schmoller (1863) and Roscher (1869).

[8] Held (1872), Guth (1878), Weiss (1878), Sax (1887), Neumann (1889), Heckel (1890), Schanz (1892), Fürth (1892), Huene (1892), Volke (1892), Schäffle (1895), Schober (1896), Gärtner (1898).

Paul H. Wueller

Max von Heckel, who devoted himself primarily to problems of public finance, and Georg Schanz, editor of the *Finanz-Archiv*.

Hermann,[1] the first professional student who ventured a definition of income designed primarily for fiscal purposes, was exceedingly brief in his statement. According to this writer,

> while income is commonly expressed in terms of money, it is apparent that it is not money that is truly income, but the economic goods which money will procure for the individual. When we speak of income, we take it for granted that these economic goods flow with a certain regularity. Income is that portion of an individual's receipts which that individual may consume without injury to his capital stock. Not every expenditure represents consumption and not every receipt represents income. Income is the sum total of goods which come within the disposing power of an individual within a given time interval. These goods may be tangible or intangible.[2]

It would appear that the criteria (or tests) that form the components of Hermann's concept of income[3] are: (1) periodicity ('these economic goods flow with a certain regularity'),[4] and (2) preservation-of-source[5] ('receipts which that individual may consume without injury to his stock').

It would seem that Hermann's concept of income is unsatisfactory because his criteria, singly or in combination, do not establish definite limits. In the first place, as regards the periodicity criterion, Hermann fails to differentiate between the 'category' and the 'recipient' interpretations, leaving the status of windfall gains indeterminate. Again, the preservation-of-source criterion is of doubtful value without carefully elaborated limitations. Capital value is typically conceived of as a function of a series of

---

[1] F. B. W. Hermann, *op. cit. passim.*   [2] *Ibid.* p. 297.

[3] Throughout the subsequent exposition it is proposed to differentiate between concepts of income and income criteria or income tests. The terms 'income criteria' or 'income tests', which are used interchangeably, are employed whenever a component part of a concept of income is referred to. The above terminological conventions will be used in connexion with the presentation and discussion of all contributions, because it is felt that they will facilitate grouping and manipulation.

[4] See above. On the basis of the periodicity criterion, only those accruals which are likely to recur periodically are to be considered income. In connexion with this test or criterion, it is useful to differentiate between the 'category' and the 'recipient' interpretations. On the basis of the 'category' interpretation, accruals which are likely to recur if the economy of the group is considered are accorded income. Under the 'recipient' interpretation, only such net accruals as are likely to recur with the economy of a specific recipient are treated as income. In passing it should be noted that Professor Seligman apparently introduced the designation 'periodicity criterion' (the German equivalent is *Periodizitätstheorie*) into American public finance literature. Seemingly, however, Professor Seligman did not differentiate between the two interpretations suggested. It is nevertheless felt that the distinction is useful in connexion with the analysis of certain concepts to be presented in this study.

[5] On the basis of the preservation-of-source criterion, only that portion of an individual's accruals which may be economically disposed of (consumed or given away) without impairing the individual's net worth constitutes income.

discounted future income values. Other pertinent factors aside, the present value of a series of anticipated income values is a function of the interest rate. In other words, if the legislator would adopt the Hermann concept, strictly interpreted, he would have to permit the taxpayer a capital maintenance allowance that would vary with changes in rates of interest.

The second attempt to define income was made by the economist Biersack in 1850.[1] Apparently unaware of Hermann's contribution, Biersack approached the problem from a somewhat different point of view. He asserted that it is a generally accepted proposition that 'all receipts which flow from the application of an individual's productive power are taxable income'. And further,

according to this principle, all persons who, on the basis of the subsequently formulated definition, receive no true income should be exempt from taxation... Net income is that sum which is obtained when one deducts from receipts the amounts expended for the customary standard of living of an economically productive individual. It is difficult to define what is meant by 'customary standard of living'. From a practical standpoint, it is virtually impossible to take every individual's particular standard of living into consideration. As a general proposition, it may be said that the recipients of larger incomes should be permitted only the deduction of a smaller percentage of their income than individuals with smaller incomes.[2]

It will be observed that Biersack employs neither Hermann's periodicity nor his preservation-of-source criterion. Instead he proposes productivity as his sole test,[3] i.e. 'all receipts which are derived from the exercise of an individual's productive powers are taxable income'.[4]

In view of Biersack's admission that 'standard of living' cannot be adequately defined, his concept of income is identical with the productivity criterion. This heavy dependence on the productivity criterion would seem to imply that 'economic activity' has been previously defined. However, the author nowhere indicates what definition of productivity he considers pertinent for his purposes. Though the contour of Biersack's concept is too indistinct to permit its use for fiscal purposes, it is interesting to observe that the author, unlike earlier writers on the Continent, as well as in Great Britain, was conscious of the difficulties presented by the notion of 'standard of living'.

Gustave von Schmoller attacked the problem of defining income at a time when the shadow of income taxation loomed large on the fiscal

[1] H. L. Biersack, *Über Besteuerung, ihre Grundsätze und ihre Ausführung* (Frankfurt am Main, 1850), *passim.*
[2] *Ibid.* pp. 149 ff.
[3] The exponents of the productivity criterion assert that any accrual, in order to be considered income, must be traceable to 'economic activity' on the part of the recipient.
[4] See above, p. 146.

horizon of Germany.[1] His primary interest was policy. He seems to have been worried lest in the near future the taxation of income overshoot the mark and destroy his country's capital supply, His contribution is an emphatic restatement of the preservation-of-source criterion, a wearisome lamentation embellished with warnings that disregard of this criterion always foretells the doom of the national economy.[2]

Roscher,[3] who wrote during the same decade as Schmoller, incorporated his definition of income into a general treatise on economics. For Roscher,

receipts include all goods which enter the economy of a given individual within a given period of time. The term receipts covers all 'comings-in', such as gifts, lottery winnings, windfall gains, and inheritances. Income, however, includes only such receipts as accrue in consequence of the recipient's economic activities. Income is a sum of products and these products may be derived from either the application of labour or the investment of capital. The producer may use these products directly or he may exchange them for other products in order to satisfy his needs...the phrase 'secondary' or 'derived income' should be used to designate incomes which are obtained without the surrender of an economic equivalent.[4]

It will be observed that Roscher's concept of income, like that of Biersack, is in substance the productivity criterion. In the absence of a definition of economic activity or productivity, Roscher's concept of income would seem to be no more useful than Biersack's.

Adolf Held, the next German student to make a study of income, published his findings immediately upon termination of the Franco-Prussian War. Unlike his predecessors, he devoted an entire treatise to its analysis.[5]

By way of a first approximation, Held observes that

all goods which are necessary to maintain man's labour power must be considered income. Income is the sum total of all economic goods which rational human beings use in the satisfaction of their wants. All rational human beings will endeavour to set aside reserves in order to maintain their capital intact, unless unforeseen emergencies compel them to take a different course. No useful purpose is served by differentiating between gross and net income. It is convenient, however, to refer to that part of a person's income which remains after the person has satisfied his most urgent needs as 'clear' income.[6] This distinction is useful because 'clear' income may be transmuted into capital, whereas the amount of income spent for other purposes is predetermined by necessities. Again, this line of demarcation

---

[1] G. v. Schmoller, 'Die Lehre vom Einkommen in ihrem Zusammenhang mit den Grundprinzipien der Steuerlehre', *Zeitschrift für die gesamte Staatswissenschaft* (1863), pp. 52 ff.

[2] For criticism of the preservation-of-source criterion, see above, p. 146.

[3] W. Roscher, *Die Grundlegung der Nationalökonomie* (8th ed. Stuttgart, 1869).

[4] *Ibid.* pp. 305 ff.

[5] A. Held, *Die Einkommensteuer* (Bonn, 1872).

[6] Subsequently, the term 'clear' income was introduced into the American literature by Professor Seligman. See Seligman, *op. cit.* p. 21.

cannot be drawn with precision, because it is virtually impossible to determine, even if due consideration be given to the customs and standards of the period involved, the needs and requirements of individuals and families.[1]

Dissatisfied with this first formulation, Held shifts his point of reference and continues:

In view of the fact that the national income consists of the product of all those who engage in economic activity,[2] it appears that the national income is divided among those who participate in such activities. Only he who has participated in production can be said to have real, actual or primary income. Those whom a 'producer' permits to share in the fruits of his labours may be said to have 'derived' income. This 'derived' income is not income in any significant economic sense. It merely signifies a title to participate in the expenditure of the recipient of primary income.[3]

In the above passage Held substitutes the productivity criterion for the expenditure criterion previously suggested.

Then, apparently abandoning both these approximations, which are really mutually exclusive, he experiments with a third approach. This time he endeavours to evolve a definition of income via an income-computing technique—a procedure which is somewhat like putting the cart before the horse. After some consideration of the concept of national income, Held argues:

We have pointed out already that it is virtually impossible to measure the national income with any degree of accuracy. The question now arises whether or not it is possible to compute, with any degree of precision, the income accruing to a specific individual. This problem is important, because equitable assessment for income tax purposes depends upon the precision with which the income computation has been performed. Unfortunately, however, it must be pointed out that in our attempt to compute individual income we meet with some of the same difficulties which we encountered when we attempted to calculate national income. In addition the question arises whether or not individual income always and necessarily coincides with national income.[4] Because we cannot calculate national income, it is necessary for us to assume that national income is substantially the sum total of individual incomes. To further delimit the concept of personal income, we must confine the application of the term income, when used in conjunc-

---

[1] Held, *op. cit.* p. 75. On the basis of this general statement, it might be inferred that Held proposed to identify income with what in our literature is generally referred to as 'psychic income'. However, contrary to some contemporary American economists who equate 'psychic income' and 'true income', Held proposed to tax not only consumption expenditures, but savings as well.

[2] Held, like his predecessors, fails to define 'economic activity'.

[3] Held, *op. cit.* p. 78.

[4] This sentence suggests that Held is subscribing to the net product criterion. The net product criterion differs from the productivity criterion in that the first directs attention to the national or group economy, whereas the second is primarily concerned with individual or private economies. On the basis of the net product criterion, only that portion—if any—of an individual's accruals which constitutes a net addition to the group's income partakes of the nature of 'true' income.

tion with the individual economy, to that portion of a person's receipts which that person may expend without impairing his capital stock. Reasonable expenditures, in this connexion, include purchases of the necessities of life, outlays necessitated by the individual's social position and old age pension premiums. All these items of expenditure are made for the purpose of satisfying wants and it must be presumed that they do not impair the individual's capital... The above method, however, is not free from defects, because instances may occur where an individual's income is not part of the national income. A manufacturer, for example, may pay his wages and his interest. Upon balancing his books, however, he may discover that he has operated at a loss.[1] Under these conditions, the wages paid to the labourers and the interest paid to creditors are not part of the national income, because they have been drawn from the capital stock of the enterpriser... Another case of the same general type is met with in connexion with what we may call 'fictitious capital'. 'Fictitious capital' is represented by 'unproductive' loans such as are made coincident to the prosecution of war. In the case of such loans the funds are not put to a productive use and hence the interest paid on the loans does not represent the product of economic activity. Typically that interest is paid out of the public treasury, which in turn is replenished by means of taxes. Such interest payments do not constitute part of the national income. They partake of the nature of 'derived' income.[2]

In concluding his last argument, Held restates his position as follows: 'Wherever and whenever an individual comes into receipt of a part of the national income, part of that individual's income may be taken by the tax gatherer. In other words, everyone receiving a "primary" income is taxable.'[3]

Income as thus defined does not furnish an acceptable tax base. It is not acceptable for the very simple reason that there is no known technique which would facilitate identification of that part of an individual's 'income' which represents net product.[4]

---

[1] This seems to indicate that Held proposes to equate national net product and private profit. The setting up of such an equation, however, constitutes a denial of previously attempted distinctions.

[2] Held, *op. cit.* p. 103.   [3] *Ibid.* p. 106.

[4] Waiving for the moment the question of the availability of segregation techniques, it should be observed that American fiscal practice has never been concerned with the taxation of 'net product' no matter how defined. The purpose of American income taxes is the raising of revenue 'in accordance with the respective abilities' of the parties taxed. See *Colonial Records of Massachusetts Bay* (1853), I, 120; *Acts and Laws of His Majesty's Colony of Rhode Island and Providence Plantations, passim*; F. R. Jones, *History of Taxation in Connecticut, 1636–1776* (Baltimore, 1896), *passim; American State Papers*, Finance, I, 421 ff.; F. A. Wood, *History of Taxation in Vermont* (New York, 1894), *passim*; 'Sketch of Tax Legislation in Maryland', in *Report of the Maryland Tax Commission to the General Assembly* (Baltimore, 1888), Appendix; *South Carolina Statutes at Large*, II, 36 and III, 366; *Report of the Commissioners...Relating to Taxation and Exemption Therefrom* (Boston, 1875), *passim; The Congressional Globe*, 37 Cong. 2 Sess. (1862), pp. 1197 ff.; also 37 Cong. 1 Sess. (1861); *ibid.* 38 Cong. 1 Sess. (1864), pp. 1876 ff.; *ibid.* 39 Cong. 1 Sess. (1866), pp. 2783 ff.; *Report of the Secretary of the Treasury of the United States for the Year Ending June 30, 1861, passim; Public Laws of the Confederate States of America*, 1 Cong. 3 Sess. Act of April 24, 1863; *A Full Report of the Joint*

The attempts of Held were soon supplemented by Guth's[1] contribution. Guth's concept of income represents a combination of the preservation-of-source and the periodicity criteria. For Guth income is 'any increase in economic ability, which flows with a certain regularity from a given source. The recipient may enjoy income, consume it, or destroy it without impairing his "stock". Hence lottery gains, alms and gifts are not income. But alms and gifts to which the recipient has a certain claim are income.'[2]

Thus Guth, like his predecessor, Held, does not designate lottery winnings, gifts and alms as income; but where Held justifies exclusion of these items from the income category by reference to the productivity criterion, Guth's rejection proceeds from his subscription to the periodicity criterion.[3] Again, Guth like Held, differentiates between 'primary' and 'derived' income; but here, too, the differentiation is justified on different grounds. Guth speaks of 'primary' income when 'the income source is the property of the income recipient'[4] and of 'derived' income when 'the income source is not the property of the income recipient'.[5] Guth bases his distinction on a legal relationship, while Held distinguishes between the two income forms by reference to economic desiderata.

Weiss,[6] unlike both Guth and Held, disregards the preservation-of-source criterion and attempts to identify income by the exclusive application of a variant of the periodicity criterion. He approaches the problem as follows:

The satisfaction of human wants requires a continuous inflow of goods, which is called income. The essential characteristic of income rests on the fact that it furnishes us with a regular source from which we can satisfy our wants. It is not the creation of goods for the satisfaction of human wants that supplies the test by means of which we may identify income. It is the ultimate purpose of all economic

Special Committee on Taxation: Recommendations and Codifications Relating to the Laws of Taxation (Boston, 1894), pp. 33 ff.; *Report of the Special Commissioner of the Revenue Upon the Industry, Trade, Commerce...of the United States for the Year 1869* (Washington, 1869), *passim*; *Congressional Record*, 53 Cong. 2 Sess. (1894), xxvi, 572, 415, 1600, 3558 ff.; T. S. Adams, 'The Place of the Income Tax in the Reform of State Taxation', *Papers and Discussions, 23rd Annual Meeting, National Tax Association* (Princeton, 1911), pp. 302 ff.; *Reports of the Wisconsin Tax Commission*, 1919, 1920, etc.; *Final Report of the Pennsylvania Tax Commission to the General Assembly*, 1927, *passim*; *Congressional Record*, 61 Cong. 1 Sess. (1909), xliv, 502, 1692, 1363, 2243, 4285, 4524–685; Seligman, *op. cit.* pp. 631 ff.; Federal Income Tax of 1913, *U.S. Stats. at L.*, 63 Cong. 1913–15, xxxviii, Part I, Public Laws, pp. 166 ff.

[1] F. Guth, *Die Lehre vom Einkommen in dessen Gesamtzweigen* (Leipzig, 1878), *passim*.
[2] *Ibid.* p. 62.
[3] It may be pointed out that Guth adopts what has previously been called the 'recipient interpretation' of the periodicity criterion. See above, p. 146. Choice of the 'category interpretation' would oblige the author to treat gifts and lottery winnings as income.
[4] Guth, *op. cit.* p. 687.   [5] *Ibid.*
[6] B. Weiss, 'Die Lehre vom Einkommen', *Zeitschrift für die gesamte Staatswissenschaft*, xxxiv (1878).

activity to facilitate the satisfaction of our wants...it is but the origin of income that is conditioned by and varies with the economic functions which a given individual performs.[1]

Weiss's contribution represents a change of basic approach. With one stroke he discards not only the preservation-of-source test, but the productivity and net product criteria as well. Though he still operates with what he calls the periodicity criterion (literary tradition here reveals itself as a potent determinant of the forms of economic analysis), that designation now refers to a process that differs from the phenomenon contemplated by previous writers. The earlier writers, it will be recalled, used that term when they referred to regularly recurring revenue items. Weiss uses the same term to designate regularly recurring expenditure items. In fact, though he retains the terminology of his predecessors, he is actually describing behaviour of a different order. Terminology aside, Weiss differs from his precursors in that he was apparently the first German economist to formulate a concept of income of the 'disposition' type.[2]

Emil Sax, who wrote about ten years later than Weiss (1887), essayed a synthesis of the contributions of Weiss and earlier writers. For Sax, income is

that amount of goods which accrues to an individual in consequence of production and exchange activities within a given period of time, which that individual may consume for the purpose of satisfying his wants...The concept 'product' relates to goods in the process of production. The concept 'income', however, relates goods to the needs and wants of an individual...if the capital of a given individual economy is to remain intact, then those parts of the capital which have been used, that is, so to speak, destroyed coincident to the creation of a given product, must be replaced. It is only the residual product that remains after capital replacement has been made which can be considered income.[3]

In the terms of the conventional 'tests', Sax's concept of income rests on the preservation-of-source criterion.

The contribution of the economist Neumann, who presented his observations two years after Sax, differs in several respects from that of previous students. In the first place, Neumann critically appraises the works of his predecessors. Second, he takes issue with the income tax practice of his

---

[1] Weiss, *loc. cit.* pp. 687 ff.
[2] In order to clarify terminology, it should be noted that henceforth concepts of income shall be designated as being of the 'accrual type' whenever they focus attention upon inflow, or to use Alfred Marshall's phrase 'incomings'. The phrase, concepts of the 'disposition' type, on the other hand, will be used whenever the emphasis is upon 'expenditure' or 'disposition'. In passing it may be pointed out that the only other German author to advance a concept of income of the 'disposition' type was Mombert, who wrote during the [First] World War. See P. Mombert, *Eine Verbrauchseinkommensteuer für das Reich als Ergänzung der Vermögenszuwachssteuer* (Tübingen, 1916), *passim*.
[3] E. Sax, *Grundlegung der theoretischen Staatswirtschaft* (Vienna, 1887), pp. 364 ff.

period.[1] Third, his procedure is more systematic than that of those who preceded him.

Neumann opens the discussion by presenting a concept which he regards as faulty but which has merits as a tentative point of departure. He observes,

Income includes all valuable considerations and benefits that come within the disposing power of a given individual over a given period of time.

We may perhaps attempt a more definitive fixation of income by introducing the notion of periodicity. This has been previously attempted...[2] however, even with the periodicity notion suffixed the concept is not adequate, because (1) as a matter of conventional usage, alms and lottery winnings are not considered income although they may recur; (2) contrariwise, the legislator treats many receipt items as income though they do not typically recur.[3]

Can it be said that the 'incomes' of our painters, sculptors and architects are 'regular' or 'recurring'? Most of these incomes fluctuate considerably...The same may be said of part of the incomes of university professors and public officials, etc. An artist may devote the most productive years of his life to the creation of an outstanding production which will realize an immense price in the market. It would be unrealistic to contemplate the recurrence of such a price. Nevertheless, the price actually realized is treated fiscally as income, and correctly so, because if all receipts of this type were not treated as income, many shrewd merchants would never pay any taxes, whatever.[4]

The above considerations, while suggesting that there is a grain of truth in the periodicity criterion, nevertheless indicate that the exclusive use of that test is not likely to produce satisfactory results. Hence, it is not surprising that students of the subject have searched for additional criteria which, separately or in conjunction with the periodicity criterion, would permit of the formulation of a more satisfactory concept of income.

Some of these searches focused attention upon expenditure. It has been argued that expenditures are, in the nature of the case, continuous...In addition, it has been alleged that expenditure must of necessity coincide with income if a group of individuals is considered.[5]

---

[1] F. J. Neumann, *Grundlagen der Volkswirtschaftslehre* (Tübingen, 1889), *passim*.

[2] F. Guth, *op. cit. passim*. Also B. Weiss, *loc. cit. passim*.

[3] It is in connexion with the subsequent argument that the distinction between the 'recipient interpretation' and the 'category interpretation' of the *periodicity* criterion would seem useful. See above, p. 146.

[4] This was written in 1889.

[5] The universal validity of this contention is, to say the least, doubtful. It will be recalled that the writers who previously operated with the notion of national income apparently intended the term to mean what more recently has been referred to as 'income produced'. See above, pp. 149 ff. Also S. Kuznets, 'National Income', in the *Encyclopedia of the Social Sciences*, XI, 205–24, and *idem, National Income 1929–1932*, Senate Document No. 124 (Washington, 1934). It does not require laboured argument to show that 'income produced', when used as a synonym for national income, does not necessarily coincide with aggregate individual income. In fact, by way of broad generalization, it may safely be said that over a short period of time such as the fiscal year, the two forms of 'income' do not even tend to coincide as regards magnitude.

Paul H. Wueller

From the foregoing consideration, it has been concluded that expenditures would adequately measure income; income being conceived of as that part of an individual's receipts which he may consume without impairing his capital stock.[1]

On the basis of the above observations Neumann concludes that the introduction of anything approximating an expenditure test, even if de-limited by such an adjustment as the preservation-of-source criterion, must create embarrasing uncertainty. For, in Neumann's opinion, it is well-nigh impossible to determine 'economical' or 'just' expenditure.

In an attempt to escape what he considers the dilemma of his predecessors, Neumann suggests a 'new' criterion. He believes that the problems posited by the use of the preservation-of-source criterion may be overcome

if instead of insisting upon the permanency of a specific source, we attempt to think in terms of source types. That is to say, we should endeavour to think of capital in general and not of a *specific* capital investment as a source of in-come. If we choose this view, our difficulties are automatically and satisfactorily resolved.

The gains of speculators, merchants, architects and artists; the fees received by professional men, no matter how regularly or irregularly they occur; all must now be considered income, since both are derived from permanent source types. In the one case, their permanent source is represented by 'enterprisers' transactions'; in the other, by 'professional practice'. On the other hand, acceptance of our view[2] would lead to the exclusion of lottery winnings, inheritances and similar gains from the income category, for it cannot be maintained that they flow from permanent sources[3]...it would seem that the Prussian income tax has been built around the source criterion...[4]

The source criterion is not as 'new' as Neumann seems to believe. It is 'new' only if we choose to impute the 'recipient interpretation' of the periodicity criterion to the older writers. That imputation, apparently justifiable at times, is mere conjecture in other cases. Furthermore, Neumann limits its application without any supporting evidence whatever, unless his passing reference to current practice in Prussia is accepted as adequate substantiation.

[1] Neumann, *op. cit.* pp. 210 ff.
[2] In another passage Neumann refers to his modification of the periodicity criterion as the source criterion. It is apparent that source criterion is but another name for what was previously designated as the 'category interpretation' of the periodicity criterion. See above, p. 146. Henceforth, source criterion will be used as a synonym for that phrase. Source criterion seems preferable from a purely linguistic point of view, but the other phrase is more useful for purposes of conceptual manipulation.
[3] The permanency of a source is a function of the presence or absence of general cultural change. Capital is a 'permanent source' only in a society that takes advantage of the capitalistic mode of production. There seems to be no justification for the assumption that the institution of bequest is a less permanent source of gain than the institution of property. The same is true of lottery winnings.
[4] Neumann, *op. cit.* p. 115.

Possibly influenced by the breadth and freshness of Neumann's approach, Schanz,[1] in 1892, presented a concept of income that was more inclusive than any one previously offered by a German writer.

After a brief, preliminary discussion of the concepts 'net profit' and 'clear profit', Schanz suggests:

...these concepts ('net profit' and 'clear profit') are functionally related to a given enterprise. The concept of income, however, occupies an entirely different position. The concept of income is related to the economic ability of persons. When we wish to determine an individual's income, we must ask what economic power has accrued to a given person over a given period of time. In other words, we wish to know what means came within the disposing power of a given person, who, during the period in question, neither impaired his capital nor incurred personal debts.

We need a concept of income for various purposes. We need it if we wish to study the social structure (classification of individuals into income groups) and possible changes in this structure. We need it again if we propose to familiarize ourselves with the processes involved in the distribution of goods. Last but not least, we require it for fiscal purposes if taxation according to ability is to be an effective principle of our tax practice.

Continuing with his definition of income, by a method of differentiation and elimination, Schanz observes,

income...does not belong in the profit category. It is not to be considered the result of accounting conventions. Income is an entity which cannot be severed from a given individual and the satisfaction of his wants...the concept of income is but remotely related to production. From these considerations, it follows directly not only that income includes profits realized from the exchange of goods and other business transactions, but that it also covers such good as flows from the enjoyment of one's leisure, the use of one's house or one's garden. It is immaterial whether or not income is actually realized, that is to say, it is immaterial whether or not one actually lives in one's house! Discounting infrequent cases of extravagance, all satisfactions are functions of income. Continuous expenditure implies continuous income. It is for this reason that one is justified in looking upon income as a measuring-rod...Income covers and includes a changing multitude of factors. The multifarious forms of income must have but one element in common. They must be reducible to a common denominator, a monetary expression which permits the calculation of an approximate total.

It may be argued that Neumann and Schmoller, at least by implication, have carried the analysis up to this point. If so, we must add to their observations that in order to obtain a figure of significance, the monetary equivalent of advantages derived from the direct use of capital goods, houses,[2] gardens, etc.; the monetary equivalent of income in kind, lottery winnings, capital appreciation, inheritances, etc., must be included. For if one falls heir to an estate and consumes its substance,

[1] G. v. Schanz, 'Der Einkommensbegriff', *Finanz-Archiv* (1896), pp. 1–30.
[2] Already Neumann had observed that this form of income represented taxable ability.

Paul H. Wueller

one will not be poorer after having done with it than one was before.[1] In addition, adoption of the concept of income developed above points to the deduction of interest paid[2] and allows for capital depreciation deductions.

Summarizing his exposition Schanz concludes that income may be defined in one sentence as 'the net influx of wealth [*Reingewinn*] over a given period of time'.[3]

Not content with simply formulating a concept of income, Schanz proceeds to a critical examination of the principal criteria and concepts of his precursors. Challenging the acceptability of the productivity criterion, he queries: 'Who could deny that the student who is favoured with a stipend and the army officer who is subsidized by his father-in-law have incomes?'[4]

As regards the relevancy of the periodicity criterion, Schanz contends that

to insist that income be conceived of as regularly recurring net receipts is indicative of superficial observation. Neither sources, nor amounts from given sources are constant in time. Profit, wage and interest rates fluctuate. The merchant makes twenty thousand marks in one year, loses three thousand during the next and perhaps emerges with a five-thousand-mark profit in the third year...The periodicity criterion leads to absurd conclusions...If I should give a beggar one mark a day, that beggar, according to the periodicity criterion,[5] would have income. However, if a generous humanitarian should present my beggar with three hundred and sixty-five marks on the condition that for one year he abstain from begging, that beggar would have to be considered as having no income at least for the period of one year. Matters do not improve, if one...substitutes 'possibility' or 'probability of recurrence' for periodicity.

[1] It will be noted that Schanz completely abandons the net product criterion and, on the basis of this passage, the strict and universal interpretation and application of the preservation-of-source criterion as well.

[2] For a comprehensive analysis of the fiscal status of debts and interest payments see M. v. Heckel, *Die Einkommensteuer und die Schuldzinsen* (Leipzig, 1890), *passim*.

[3] Professor Robert Murray Haig designates the criterion implicit in this definition as the net accretion test. For convenience of reference, it will henceforth be referred to by that designation. R. M. Haig, 'The Concept of Income', in *The Federal Income Tax* (New York, 1921), p. 1.

[4] In addition to the exponents of the *productivity* criterion mentioned previously, the following writers endorsed its use: M. Haushofer, *Grundzügen der Nationalökonomie* (Stuttgart, 1879), p. 55; H. Schober, *Die Volkswirtschaftslehre* (Leipzig, 1896), p. 262; W. Vocke, *Grundzüge der Finanzwissenschaft* (Leipzig, 1894), p. 78; Heckel, *Lehrbuch der Finanzwissenschaft*, I, 202; R. Liefmann, *Ertrag und Einkommen auf Grundlage einer rein subjectiven Wertlehre* (Jena, 1907), p. 23; W. Lexis, 'Einkommen', *Wörterbuch der Volkswirtschaft* (Jena, 1911), p. 724; W. Lotz, *Finanzwissenschaft* (Tübingen, 1907), p. 445; F. W. Gärtner, 'Über den Einkommensbegriff', *Finanz-Archiv* (1898), p. 31.

[5] In addition to the exponents of the periodicity criterion already recorded, there is reason to believe that the economist Wagner was likewise inclined to adopt it. *See* A. Wagner, *Allgemeine oder theoretische Volkswirtschaftslehre* (Leipzig, 1879), p. 115.

From his critique of the periodicity criterion, Schanz turns to an analysis of the source criterion.[1] He states that

> the impossibility of achieving satisfactory results with the periodicity criterion has led Neumann to employ this concept in a somewhat different manner. Neumann believes that the important desideratum is not continuous flow or regular recurrence of a given income, but the permanence of a given income source. Neumann's income covers all goods, valuable considerations and use benefits (*Nutzungen*) which an individual derives from permanent sources within a given period of time, and which the individual may use in any way he chooses. Subscription to this concept, it is alleged, resolves many difficulties. The objections which may be urged against Neumann's criterion are many. Neumann seems to have anticipated some when he wrote, 'nevertheless some uncertainty remains'...Some uncertainty remains indeed! When we ask what is meant by the phrase 'permanent source', we find ourselves in a blind alley. Are capital investments 'permanent sources'? Buildings are destroyed, agricultural soil is exhausted, machines become obsolete... labour power, abstractly speaking, is perhaps a 'permanent source'.[2]

In concluding Schanz amplifies his definition of income. In his final revision he says:

> Income is the net inflow of economic ability over a given period of time, inclusive of use benefits (*Nutzungen*) and the valuable but not-compensated-for services rendered by a third party[3]...income includes all profits, all benefits, all valuable services, gifts, inheritances, legacies, lottery winnings, insurance annuities, speculative gains of all types minus interest charges and capital depreciation allowances.

Schanz's contribution differs from that of his predecessors in several respects. In the first place, he clearly states that his concept of income is to serve as a supplementary gauge of 'ability';[4] next, he discards all tests

---

[1] Subsequently the following writers attempted to exploit the possibilities of the 'source' criterion: B. Fuisting and G. Strutz, *Die Preussischen direkten Steuern* (Berlin, 1915), I, 162; J. Gruntzel, *Wirtschaftliche Begriffe* (Vienna, 1919), p. 9; E. v. Philippovich, *Allgemeine Volkswirtschaftslehre* (Tübingen, 1919), p. 339.

[2] Schanz seems unable to disregard some of the notions conventionally associated with the phrase 'periodicity' criterion. His last sentence indicates that the term 'permanence' still implies that a given individual is in permanent possession of a given permanent income source or that a specific captial good is permanent. However, there is no necessity for insisting upon a permanent nexus between a given individual and a given income source. If such nexus is not insisted upon—the phrase 'category interpretation of the periodicity criterion' avoids this difficulty—Schanz's objection seems ill-taken.

[3] The expression 'third party' which occurs frequently in the German literature of the period refers to any agency other than the State.

[4] The Prussian income tax statute of 1891 was patterned after the Schanz concept. At the time of its enactment, Schanz had not yet published his monograph. However, he had been prominent as an expert and adviser to governmental agencies. *See* F. Meisel, *Britische und deutsche Einkommensteuer, passim*. Also B. Moll, *Lehrbuch der Finanzwissenschaft, passim*.

previously proposed, except the preservation-of-source criterion.[1] This is, of course, implied in the net accretion criterion and hence, whatever other merits the Schanz concept may have, it raises questions similar to those previously encountered,[2] in connexion with this test.

Gärtner was the only German writer who seriously challenged the Schanz concept. By way of introductory remark, Gärtner[3] points out that a concept of income to be adequate must (1) not permit the taxation of capital gains under the income tax statute, and (2) 'serve the tax administrators as an unfailing guide'.

With this twofold purpose in view, Gärtner argues that

income presupposes antecedent expenditure of labour power. We may define labour power as the energy which the individual expends in order to obtain an income. No 'inflow', no accrual item may be considered income unless it can be related to antecedent application of labour power. For a net receipt to be income the recipient must have legal or equitable title to it...and the expenditure of labour power... constitutes the only 'natural' and legitimate claim to income. Whatever legally accrues to an individual without antecedent application of labour power belongs in the capital gain category.[4]

On the basis of the above observations it seems that Gärtner professes a preference for the productivity criterion. Presently, however, he broadens the range of this criterion in an unprecedented manner, when he asserts: 'Labour power expenditure must be presumed to have preceded the accrual of a given gain, even if the gain in question is but the result of a strategic decision.'

Elucidating the application of his variant of the productivity criterion, Gärtner observes: 'Declines in the value of government bonds may represent capital losses (in spite of the fact that their purchase involves the expenditure of labour power on the part of the capitalist) and they must be treated as such if the losses in question are not brought about by an independent economic act.' Likewise, capital appreciations are not to be considered income, if they do not arise in consequence of an independent economic act.

This illustration, in the absence of a definition of the phrase 'independent economic act', would not seem likely to furnish the 'tax administrator with

---

[1] In addition to the authors mentioned who operate with the 'preservation-of-source' criterion, the following writers lay considerable emphasis upon this test: L. H. v. Jakob, *Grundsätze der Nationalökonomie oder Theorie des Nationalreichtums* (Halle, 1825), p. 682; R. Meyer, *Das Wesen des Einkommens* (Berlin, 1887), p. 21; H. Pesch, *Allgemeine Volkswirtschaftslehre* (Freiburg, 1909), p. 298.

[2] For some of the difficulties which proponents of the 'preservation-of-source' criterion encounter, see above, p. 146.

[3] Gärtner, *loc. cit.* pp. 515 ff.

[4] Assignment of capital gain status to a given accrual does not imply tax exemption. See above, p. 145. Also below, pp. 159 ff.

an unfailing guide', and Gärtner hastens to supply the missing definition: 'In the above case the economic activity which involved the expenditure of labour power terminated with the purchase of the security, if the purchaser did not intend to sell the security with a view of realizing a profit.' Continuing his discussion of the phrase 'economic activity', Gärtner observes that a gift is not income because the recipient has neither 'a legal nor an equitable claim'; and he further remarks that 'anything that comes to an individual (e.g. treasure trove) without antecedent efforts on the part of the individual does not partake of the nature of income. It must be considered a windfall gain. However, if a professional prospector strikes it rich, his find is income because it is the result of his consciously directed economic activities.'

Turning from treasure trove to prosaic annuities, Gärtner finds that

the right to receive certain amounts annually (annuities) is acquired by a lump sum cash payment...The annual receipt of an annuity involves economic activity on the part of the recipient, because the annuity payments are only made when claimed and hence they must be considered income...Annuities are not to be treated as investment income but must be considered income which is derived in consequence of antecedent application of labour on the part of the recipient.

Schanz responded to Gärtner's concept by charging its author with inconsistency and impracticability.[1] After a brief restatement of Gärtner's treatment of annuities, Schanz remarks:

It is peculiar that the author who goes to such lengths to demonstrate the expenditure of labour power in connexion with the claiming of annuities...disregards all labour power expenditure when it comes to inheritances. For the author, receipt of an inheritance represents a capital accretion. He admits that the 'acceptance' of an inheritance constitutes 'economic activity'. Nevertheless, he argues that the 'activity' required is of no import whatever, because it does not precede accretion, but becomes operative only after accession is a *fait accompli*. It would seem that acceptance of the inheritance determines whether or not accession becomes actually effective. Typically the recipient of an inheritance carefully investigates whether or not acceptance would impose upon him liabilities in excess of the assets receivable upon exercise of his option.

In substantiation of his charge of inconsistency Schanz contends:

According to the author, waiters receive tips 'because of customs, hence waiters have an equitable claim to tips, hence tips are income'. In another passage the author nevertheless maintains that allowances granted by parents to their children for purposes of study are not income because the children have neither equitable nor legal claim to such allowances. It seems to me the claim of children is frequently more equitable than that of waiters. Again, the author insists: 'The alms of beggars do not belong in the income category because income is inseparable from antecedent economic activity and it is only by means of economic activity that legal or equitable

[1] G. v. Schanz, 'Gärtner's Einkommensbegriff', *Finanz-Archiv* (1898), pp. 530 ff.

title to income may be created.' Here again the author might be told by the pious and humane that the starving beggar, while without a legal right, nevertheless has an equitable claim. If the beggar's alms are not income, what are they? Capital accretions perhaps?

In addition even Gärtner will have to admit that some bequests represent payment for services previously rendered.

Schanz further feels called upon to reject Gärtner's concept because its usefulness is predicated upon the possibility of gaining reliable knowledge regarding the intent of the taxpayer. Schanz points out that

the author admits that intent is frequently his means of establishing the presence or absence of economic activity...in my opinion it is virtually frivolous to subject the taxpayer to such temptation as is inevitable if his 'intent' becomes the significant determinant of his tax liability. Anyhow the majority of people cannot say what they actually 'intended' when they purchased a security. They seldom remember whether or not they bought for resale purposes. What shall be done if the taxpayer affirms under oath that he does not remember what his intention has been? Shall we, in addition to the categories, income and capital, develop some such new conception as income-or-capital? Men change their minds. I may purchase a security because I anticipate an active market. But, contrary to my expectations, the market may not move and I may deem it more prudent to hold the security in my portfolio. Again, I may purchase a security because I consider it a good investment. A few hours after I may receive reliable information from a friend and resell my stock with a slight profit. Under these conditions which 'intent', the first or the second, shall guide the tax administrator?

I admit the subtlety in some of Gärtner's argument but I am still of the opinion that my concept[1] is preferable...from the point of view both of equity and administrative practicability.

The Schanz–Gärtner controversy represents the last attempt of German students of economics to arrive at a formal general definition of income for fiscal purposes.

In retrospect, a few summary generalizations concerning the German literature dealing with the concept of income seem justified. In the first place, contributions of the various writers are normative rather than analytical. Second, some of the earlier definitions reflect etymological habits of thought. Third, all German writers, save one, though they differ concerning the criteria which they choose, subscribe to concepts of the accrual type. Fourth, minor exceptions aside, successive writers offer increasingly more inclusive concepts. Fifth, the early emphasis upon net product recedes into the background with the progressive industrialization of Germany. Last but not least, the very objective of the net income tax base, and consequently the function of concepts of income as fiscal norms, was not clearly recognized until 1892 when Schanz applied a concise formulation together with the most inclusive concept of income ever presented.

[1] See above, pp. 155 ff.

11 The concept of income in economic theory

by Nicholas Kaldor*

Income, unlike some other notions which have been taken over into economics from everyday usage, is not generally subjected to any searching or systematic analysis in economic textbooks. Moreover, such discussion as there is usually proceeds from the standpoint of production and distribution theory and has no direct application to the problem of individual income that is relevant from the point of view of the measurement of taxable capacity. In the chapters dealing with taxation, on the other hand, the definition of income is generally taken for granted as something settled by the more fundamental notions of general economic theory. Even the orthodox textbooks on public finance, while they devote much space and argument to the question of how progressive taxation ought to be—to the problem of the 'ideal' scale of progression—tend to slur over the more fundamental question of how the base of progressive taxation should be determined.[1]

Thus Marshall in the *Principles* contented himself with the enumeration of a number of special issues in connexion with the notion of income and in effect, as Keynes said, 'decided to take refuge in the practices of the Income Tax Commissioners and, broadly speaking, to regard as income whatever they, with their experience, choose to treat as such. For the fabric of their decisions can be regarded as the result of the most careful and extensive investigation which is available, to interpret what, in practice, it is usual to treat as net income.'[2]

This empiricism may be justified if one, in the words of Marshall, 'deliberately adopts the *social*, in contrast with the individual point of

[1] This is true of the English literature, though the question has received far more attention in American literature; there was also an extended discussion among German writers on public finance from 1832 onwards and Italian writers in the first two decades of this century. The protracted controversy among German economists abated in liveliness after the publication of the famous paper by Georg Schanz, 'Der Einkommensbegriff und die Einkommensteuergesetze', *Finanz-Archiv*, XIII (1896), 23. Schanz's position was substantially that of later American proponents of the comprehensive concept of income (such as Haig and Simons), and his devastating criticism of narrower concepts evidently discouraged their academic protagonists.

[2] *General Theory*, p. 59.

* Professor of Economics, University of Cambridge.

view' and therefore thinks of income primarily as a measure of the 'production of the community as a whole'.[1] For, as will be argued below, the business concept of income which was gradually evolved with the progress of accountancy and which aims at isolating the net results of the ordinary activities of businesses, broadly aims at excluding much the same kind of things as an economist or social accountant would wish to exclude from 'income' in measuring the national dividend. The Income Tax Commissioners of the nineteenth century who looked upon the income tax not as a personal tax but as a tax on the revenue yielded by certain sources—an attitude that was probably justified when income tax was a proportional tax—were chiefly concerned with discovering what is the everyday business meaning of the notion in order to decide what is to be taxable and what is not. But with a system of progressive taxation which aims at taxing individuals according to their respective taxable capacities, this procedure is clearly question-begging from the point of view of taxation. Equally, from the point of view of economic theory, Marshall's empiricism can only be accepted 'for want of something better'—the aim of theory is to lay down clear and consistent general principles from which theoretically correct definitions can be drawn and on the basis of which the popular use of concepts can be criticized.

The fundamental theoretical work concerning the notion of income is of more recent origin. Apart from the brilliant but rather isolated work of Irving Fisher—who tried to gain acceptance for a concept of income that is free of ambiguity and capable of measurement, but which plainly does *not* correspond with the sense of the everyday use of the term—the main work was done by the writers of the Swedish School in the 1920s and 1930s, only very little of which is available in the English language.

In this appendix we shall review the various alternative theoretical approaches to income. We shall attempt to show that the meaning of income with which the Swedish approach is concerned is not the one which would provide a yardstick of taxable capacity; since the former is concerned with isolating accruals from revaluations, whereas the latter should be concerned with isolating the *real* increment of 'economic power' or 'spending power'—i.e. of a person's command over economic goods and services. We shall show that neither of these notions is capable of objective measurement; whilst the conventional notions of income provide a more reasonable approximation to the meaning of income that is relevant to accounting purposes or to national income estimates than to the one relevant to the measurement of taxable capacity.

[1] *Principles* (8th ed.), p. 76.

I. INCOME AS CONSUMPTION

Fisher's main work on the subject is contained in his *Nature of Capital and Income*, published in 1906. Fisher regarded the notions of income and capital as essentially correlative; '*a stock of wealth* existing at a given *instant* of time is called capital, a *flow of benefits* from wealth through a *period of time* is called income'. If we include human beings, as well as all forms of material wealth, under capital (since they are equally a source of income— the difference is simply that the capitalized value of human earning power is not valued in the market as, in a non-slave state, it cannot be bought and sold), income is simply the net benefit obtained from capital goods over a period; and the term 'net' is to be interpreted as what remains *after all double counting is eliminated*. This means, according to Fisher, the elimination of all such services (benefits flowing from capital goods) as serve the maintenance or the creation of other capital goods, and which are debited to the capital goods which received them, as well as being credited to the capital goods which yielded them. Hence the *net* yield of all capital consists of the total of goods and services received over a period by individuals in their capacity as consumers. On this definition income is simply consumption; saving is not part of income, since it is not part of the net yield of *all* capital goods taken together. By saving the stock of capital is enlarged and thereby the future yield of capital is enlarged, at the cost of reducing its current yield. But the increase in capital over the period is not part of its current yield, since it is merely a reflection of an increase in future yield; to regard it as part of the current yield means counting the same thing twice over—an element of the discounted value of future income is added to the undiscounted present income. (This point—that any notion of income which is *not* consumption implies adding together undiscounted values and discounted values—is really Fisher's main contention.)

If the expected income stream, for whatever reason, is rising, the value of the stock of capital will be rising too; but for any particular period of time the increase in the latter should not be added to the former, since this involves, in Fisher's view, circular reasoning in the sense of both the tree and the fruit being regarded as part of the same thing, instead of being treated as two different things. Similarly an expected fall in future income would be reflected in a decrease in capital value; but this decrease should not be treated as a *deduction* for arriving at current income; it is future income, not current income, which has fallen.

Fisher's approach has the virtue of yielding a simple and unambiguous result, but it does not accord with everyday notions on the subject; and in a sense, it only solves the problem by eliminating it. Keeping to Fisher's approach and terminology, the problem might be posed in this way. De-fining for the moment the 'net yield' of all capital as consumption, this 'net yield' will depend not only on the quantities and the productivity of different kinds of resources in existence, but also on the dispositions of their owners as between using these resources for purposes of current consumption and using them for future consumption. It is desirable to have a concept which is *not* dependent on this latter factor; and which shows, not the actual yield, but the 'potential net yield' of capital: the yield that would obtain if individuals neither saved nor dis-saved—or, in other words, that potential yield which, *in any given situation*, could be permanently maintained.[1] If we defined income as consumption, we should still re-quire another term to denote as potential income the consumption that would obtain if net savings were zero. Hence, apart from the trivial question of which is the right use of words, it is evident that income and consumption (as ordinarily understood) do not refer to the same thing, but to two different things; and if we reserved the term income for consumption we should still need another term for what would otherwise be called income; and we should still be left with the problem of how to define the latter.[2]

Returning then to the ordinary terminology, income is consumption plus net saving; the problem of defining income is really identical with the problem of defining net saving, which in turn is merely a different aspect of the problem of what is meant by 'maintaining capital intact'. A solution of any one of these three problems should therefore automatically carry with it the solution of the other two.

2. INCOME AS INTEREST

Starting from Fisher's basic premise, that income is a *flow* of wealth through a period of time, whereas capital is a stock of wealth existing at an instant of time, it is possible, as Lindahl has shown,[3] to look upon income not as the actual net yield of capital goods (i.e. the stream of services derived from them) but as the continuous appreciation in the value of capital goods due to the time factor.[4] For any given period, income in this sense can be regarded as the product of the capital value existing at the beginning of

---

[1] The qualification 'in any given situation' is important—as we shall see later when discussing other notions of Income [see p. 171 below].

[2] Fisher himself uses the term 'earnings' or 'standard income' to cover the meaning of the concept in this sense, as against 'realized income' which he defines as consumption.

[3] 'The Concept of Income', *Essays in Honour of Gustav Cassel* (London, 1933), pp. 399–407. [Reprinted as chapter 2 of this book.]

[4] This continuous appreciation, or augmentation, is of course merely another aspect of the net value created by production—or net excess of the things produced in a given period over the value of the things consumed in producing them.

the period and the rate of interest ruling in that period. This measures the appreciation in capital value that arises because the discounted future services (which make up the value) come nearer and nearer in time; in other words it measures the rate at which the value of capital goods increases through time (or rather would so increase if none of the value were withdrawn from it, for purposes of consumption).

In a world in which future events were accurately foreseen and there was no uncertainty, income thus defined[1] would be a measurable concept; it could be inferred from market prices. For in that world (i) there would be a single rate of interest, applicable to the discounting of future streams of net receipts accruing from all kinds of capital goods; (ii) the value of capital goods, at any point of time, would represent the discounted sum of these receipts; (iii) the difference in the value of capital goods between two points of time would be necessarily equal to the discounting factor (after appropriate adjustment for any 'withdrawal' of value into consumption during the interval); (iv) the rate of interest would measure the rate at which the *stock* of capital goods of all kinds would increase in time if none of the benefits accruing from capital goods were utilized for personal consumption.

But as soon as we step out of this textbook world this concept of income ceases to be objectively measurable, for several reasons.

1. In the first place, there is no longer a *single* rate of interest, applicable to the discounting of future returns of different types of assets. The so-called 'pure interest rates' applicable to loans of different duration themselves differ, both owing to the expectation of changing interest rates in the future, and the mere uncertainty of future rates. In addition, the rate of discount applicable to particular assets differs owing to various kinds of risks—lenders' risks and borrowers' risks. Hence each different kind of asset will appear to have a different *market* rate of interest attached to it—I use the word 'appear' advisedly, since the market value of assets, being the product of expected future returns and the rate of discount, does not enable us to conclude what the rate of discount is, without knowing the expected stream of returns which underlie this market value. (If a particular share A yields 5 per cent, while a share B yields 10 per cent, it is not possible to say how far the difference is due to the expectation

---

[1] This concept of income could be applied quite generally, to cover the income from land and labour, as well as the income from capital in the narrower sense; except that in a non-slave state, the capitalized value of personal earning power is a matter of subjective estimation only, since personal earning power cannot as such be bought or sold, and has no market price. Since there is in fact no *objective* measure of income derived from personal earning power other than actual earnings—with possibly some over-all allowance for the element of negative appreciation involved in the age factor—the particular question of income from work will not as such be further considered in this appendix.

of future returns being lower in the one case than in the other, and how far it is due to differences in the rates at which those returns are discounted, owing to their varying risk of uncertainty; it is doubtful even whether this is a legitimate question to ask.)[1] And even if we assumed that the correct *market* rate of interest applicable to each type of asset could somehow be elicited, the income thus obtained as the product of the particular rate of interest of each asset and its market value would no longer be an adequate measure of the psychic 'income' their owners derive from their possessing them. For assets which earn a low interest, owing to their safety, are productive of a higher psychic income to their owners, relative to their money-return, than other assets which owing to their riskiness have a high yield— the limiting case being cash, the money-return on which is zero. (The theoretically correct interest rates therefore, as Lindahl pointed out,[2] are not the objective (market) rates, but each individual owner's subjective estimation of these rates, based upon his own valuation of the risk factor.)

2. The income which is thus derived as the interest over a period on the capital value at a particular instant of time, is a forward-looking concept; it is the income *expected* for the coming 'period', or income *ex ante*. The income actually realized over a period can differ from this (i) if the stream of returns for the period in question (let us call it the 'first period') turns out differently from what was expected; (ii) if the expectations concerning returns in future periods (i.e. the returns expected for the second, third, etc., periods) were different at the end of the first period from what they were at the beginning; (iii) if the rate of interest changed during the first period; (iv) if the expectations concerning the interest rates in the second, etc., period are different at the end of the first period from what they were at the beginning.

These four types of differences between expectations and realizations, though analytically distinct, are not of course entirely independent of each other. Expectations are normally revised in the light of current experience (though they may be revised for other reasons as well—e.g. if some future event becomes expected that was previously unexpected) so that the differences between expectations and realizations in the first period normally involve changes in expectations concerning future periods, though there need be no correspondence between the two in magnitude, and it is even possible that positive changes in the one should involve negative changes in the other. Again it might be supposed that the difference between the actual and expected return of an asset over a period must be the same thing as the difference between the actual and expected interest over that period; yet the two are not the same, since the former might simply represent a

[1] See also pp. 168–9 below.   [2] See p. 57, n. 1 above.

change in the time-shape of receipts—as e.g. when certain particular receipts expected for the second period are actually realized in the first period, or vice versa.

The income that can actually be measured or observed from market data is the actual change in the value of assets over a period (adding back, for the purpose of this calculation, any value which was separated off during the period in the shape of dividend payments, etc.); in other words income defined as consumption plus *actual* capital accumulation. This is the meaning of income which was referred to as accrued income earlier in this chapter. But it automatically absorbs into the concept of income all changes which have resulted from changes in expectations (relating to future periods) between the beginning and the end of our income-period— whether they relate to the expectation of yields, or to interest rates. It therefore includes not only the differences between actual and anticipated accrual relating to the period in question but revisions of capitalizations due to changes in expectations (or in uncertainty) relating to the further future. It is generally accepted by both economists and accountants (for reasons that will be discussed presently) that the element of capital appreciation which is due to this change in expectations ought to be separated off from the element of capital appreciation which represents accrual—that part of capital appreciation, in other words, which would still have taken place if both the events and the states of mind over the period had been correctly anticipated at the beginning. It is only the latter which is a continuous *flow* in time (so much per week, or per month); the former is the result of a revaluation occurring in an instant of time.[1]

Income *ex post* is therefore not consumption plus actual capital accumulation but consumption plus actual capital accumulation excluding windfalls.[2,3] This latter concept cannot be inferred from observed phenomena

[1] This distinction between gains and losses on the one hand which occur at particular *moments* in time, and incomes and costs on the other which represent regular *processes* in time was first elaborated by Myrdal (*Prisbildningsproblemet och föränderligheten*, Uppsala, 1927).

[2] Professor Hicks in *Value and Capital* [see pp. 80–1 above] and, I believe, some other writers, use the terms 'income ex-post' to denote what we called, following American writers, *accrued income*—i.e. consumption plus *actual* capital accumulation. Yet this is not the proper interpretation of the Swedish *ex ante–ex post* approach. The distinction is used to denote the difference between anticipated and realized *interest* but it does not include in interest the change in capital value due to the reassessment of future prospects.

[3] The distinction can best be elucidated by an example. If a piece of land which is expected to yield £x in the year, and has a capital value (based on that expectation) of £k, actually yields £y, its capital value may have changed in consequence to £l. If we call £x the *ex ante* income from land, the *ex post* income is £y, and not £$y+(l-k)$; or else, if we call £$y+(l-k)$ the income *ex post* we still need another term for £y. So long as x and y are *money rents*, the situation is simple and obvious. The difficulties

any more than income *ex ante*. For to estimate it it is necessary to know what the value of assets would have been at the beginning of the period if the events of that period had been correctly foreseen; and if the states of mind relating to the second, etc., periods had been the same at the beginning of the period as at the end. Income then emerges as the difference between this hypothetical capital value at the beginning of the period and its actual value at the end.[1] It may be suggested that on this definition income is the product of the capital value ruling at the *end* of the period multiplied by the rate of interest that *has obtained* during that period (looking backwards); but this way of looking at the matter does not really get us any further, since interest *ex post* can no more be inferred from market price than interest *ex ante*; in both cases the concept depends on a hypothetical valuation: the expected value of assets at the end of the period in the case of the latter, and what may be termed their 'revised value', relating to the beginning of the period, in the case of the former.

3. INCOME 'EX ANTE' AND 'EX POST'

These relationships may be set out more clearly as follows. Let K_1 and K_2 be the *actual* values of assets at the beginning and the end of the period in question respectively (K_2 being calculated by adding back any value that was separated off during the period such as a formal interest or dividend payment). Let K_2' represent the value which the assets are *expected* to have at the end of the period, at the beginning of the period; and K_1' the *revised* value of the assets relating to the beginning of the period, as estimated at the end of the period (i.e., the value the assets would have possessed if the structure of expectations at the end of the period had been the same as at the beginning; and if the events occurring during the period had been correctly foreseen at the beginning). Let i represent the rate of interest for the period *ex ante*, and i' the rate of interest *ex post*. Then income *ex ante* is $K_2' - K_1$; income *ex post* is $K_2 - K_1'$;

$$i = \frac{K_2' - K_1}{K_1}; \quad i' = \frac{K_2 - K_1'}{K_1'}.$$

arise because x and y need not take the form of rents only but may consist, in varying degrees, of improvements in the land itself, etc., with the consequent need of separating that part of the actual capital appreciation which is part of y from that part which represents $l - k$.

[1] Something akin to this was the notion of income (as far as I understand it) that Keynes was after in chapter 6 of the *General Theory*: though he was mistaken, I believe, in thinking that the ambiguities due to changes in capital values only affect the notion of *net income* (i.e. net after deducting depreciation) and not of gross income (or what he called income *simpliciter*). As we shall argue below, the latter proposition is true as regards social income (or the income of enterprises which can be defined in an analogous way to social income) but not as regards individual income.

Under the postulate of perfect foresight, $K_2 = K_2'$ and $K_1 = K_1'$ hence $i = i'$, income *ex ante*, $K_1 i$, is identical with income *ex post*, $K_2[i'/(1+i')]$ and both can be written $K_2 - K_1$, in other words, the actual appreciation in capital, as measured by market values.

In all other cases, however, neither *ex ante* nor *ex post* income can be objectively measured, or inferred from market prices, for either concept depends on a hypothetical value, K_2' or K_1', which has not even any definite meaning if the different individuals' expectations or estimates are not unanimous.[1] The exception is the case of short term loans of perfect security made for the standard income-period, e.g. one-year Treasury bonds (assuming a year to be the standard period) where K_2' is independently given by the redemption value and therefore i or i' can be inferred from their actual purchase price, K_1.[2] If we could apply this particular rate of interest to all other assets, we could infer therefore K_2' and K_1' from our formulae—in other words, define and measure both *ex ante* and *ex post* income as $K_1 i$ and $K_2[i'/(1+i')]$ respectively. But this, as we have seen, is not the case; different assets earn different rates of interest, and there is no analogous method at hand for finding out what these are.[3] Thus if two-year bonds earn a different interest from one-year bonds, the calculation of interest by the method of the redemption-yield only gives the *average interest* for two years; the interest for the first year (*ex ante*) could only be determined if the expected value of one-year bonds a year hence were known. (Since a two-year bond half-way through its life is identical

[1] Since K_1 and K_2 are market values, K_2' and K_1' must also refer to expectations or estimates by the *market*—which can only be conceived of as representing some kind of average of different individuals' estimates and expectations; there is however no unique way of defining such an average. On the other hand if the expectation or estimates are taken to relate to each individual owner of assets separately, K_1 and K_2 must also be taken as the subjective value to the owner, which need not correspond to market values except in so far as the owner happens to be at the margin of indifference as a buyer or seller. This procedure avoids the major pitfalls but only at the cost of reducing income to a purely psychic concept which can neither be inferred from behaviour nor compared as between different individuals. (It would mean, for example, that two individuals could enjoy two different incomes from the ownership of two identical assets; but for that very reason, the one is not *in pari materia* with the other.)

[2] In the case of such one-year bonds i and i' can only differ for periods shorter than a year when, of course, the same difficulties emerge. But income itself is meaningful only when defined in relation to a standard period (which may be a year or only a week, but cannot be *both*) which means that we can ignore variations in interest (actual or expected) *within* that period (a year can begin, of course, every day of a calendar year).

[3] Since they cannot be inferred from market prices there is no way of *proving* that they are different either; all that one can say is that to assume them to be identical would require highly peculiar assumptions about the state of expectations which persisted in the light of continued conflict between anticipations and actual experience. Thus if a particular asset had a constant yield in time and its value (excluding the yield) was also constant, it would be difficult to contend that the excess of the yield over the 'standard' interest on the capital value was a recurrent windfall gain.

with a one-year bond.) Similarly the current price of one-year-old two-year bonds gives no clue to the 'pure interest' they earned in the past year, since the difference between this and their original value may include an element of windfall.[1] In the case of two-year bonds the accrued interest in the first year can only be inferred on the assumption that no change in the rate of interest is expected during its lifetime. The same holds for all other bonds (including perpetual annuities); while in the case of other assets, the rate of interest cannot be inferred, even on the assumption that no change in that interest is foreseen for the future.

4. INCOME AS 'STANDARD STREAM'

In his chapter on income in *Value and Capital* [reprinted as chapter 4 of this book] Professor Hicks suggests that the 'central meaning' of the income concept is to serve as a guide to 'prudent conduct'—to give people an indication of the amount which they can consume without impoverishing themselves. Following out this idea, he defines a man's income as 'the maximum amount which he can consume during a week, and still expect to be as well off at the end of the week as he was at the beginning.[2] He then finds that income is equal to the interest on the capitalized value of prospective receipts, if the rate of interest is constant; but if the rate of interest is not *expected* to remain constant, it is no longer equal to that (or to the amount which is left over after maintaining the capitalized value of the prospect constant); nor can it be described what it is, except in terms of the 'central criterion' itself. Hence, Professor Hicks concludes, 'we shall be well advised to eschew *income* and *saving* in economic dynamics. They are bad tools which break in our hands.'[3]

The novelty of this approach to the income concept is that it eschews any connexion between the notion of income and the notion of capital. Fisher, Lindahl, and the other writers on the subject invariably looked upon income as the yield derived from some *given source*: in the case of Fisher, it is the *net* yield of capital goods after elimination of all 'double counting'; for the others, it is *net* yield after deducting (or adding as the case may be) whatever is necessary to maintain the 'source' or the 'corpus' constant. In Hicks's approach the source or corpus from which the income is derived disappears altogether as a separate entity—capital appears only as the capitalized value of a certain future prospect and income as the

---

[1] The difference in the current price of *new* two-year-old bonds and two-year bonds issued a year ago, measures the difference between the *ex ante* interest of one-year bonds for the coming year and the average *ex ante* interest of two-year bonds for the coming two years: not the rate applicable for two-year bonds for the coming year.

[2] p. 75 above.   [3] p. 79 above.

'standard stream equivalent' of that prospect. Capital and income are thus two different ways of expressing the same thing, not two different things.

It is easily seen that the conditions under which this 'standard-stream equivalent' has no explicitly definable meaning are the conditions under which the income (in the more usual sense) derived from a given capital (in the more usual sense) is expected to change over time.[1] 'The maximum amount the individual can spend this week and still expect to be able to spend the same amount in each ensuing week' is thus not necessarily identical with 'the maximum amount the individual can spend this week after maintaining his capital resouces intact'; and when the two differ, the former notion ceases to have any operationally definable meaning.[2] The reason for this is that income and capital are separate but correlative notions; and neither could be endowed with a definite meaning in entire abstraction from the other.

This is not meant to imply that the notion of 'maintaining capital intact' is free from difficulties. From the point of view of the individual owner of resources *expected* diminutions in the market value of resources have the same significance whether they are due to physical depreciation or depletion, technical obsolesence or foreseen changes in demand. But this does not mean that *any* expected change in earnings could be allowed for in the depreciation provision, irrespective of whether it is reflected or not

---

[1] On Hicks's terminology an expectation of a change in income in the future is itself a contradiction in terms. Income is that magnitude which cannot be *expected* to change under any circumstances whatsoever, since all such changes are implicitly absorbed in the conversion into the standard-stream equivalent. This conversion however cannot really be accomplished when the change in income over time has other causes than the accumulation or decumulation of capital. Thus (taking the economy as a whole) a future increase in the yield of resources (due to greater productivity or prosperity) means the expectation of a rising income. It is not possible to express that future improvement in terms of a constant perpetual stream—since the 'interest rates' themselves are reflections of these yields, there is no method by which such a conversion could be accomplished.

Nor is it self-evident why, for example, an individual who expects to receive an inheritance in the future should, as a matter of 'prudent conduct', treat as part of his current income and saving the interest on the present value of that prospect. To say that 'when a person saves, he plans to be better off in the future' is not of course the same as saying that a person is saving *whenever* he plans or expects to be better off.

[2] It is not clear from Hicks's treatment either, how he would regard the case of a change in actual receipts relative to expected receipts (as against a change in future receipt-expectations). Assume that a man receives an unexpected sum in a particular week, which does not affect his expectations for the future. According as we regard his state of wealth before or after the accrual of these receipts the extra amount which he can spend during the week 'without impoverishing himself' is either equal to the whole of that sum, or to the interest on that sum. Clearly the man could spend the whole of that amount and still be 'as well off at the end of the week as he was at the beginning', but if he does he cannot 'expect to be able to spend the same amount in each succeeding week' as in that particular week.

either in the physical productivity or in the market value of capital resources. The difficulties surrounding the notion of capital and of 'maintaining capital intact' must imply a corresponding limitation in the income concept,[1] but these difficulties cannot be disposed of in the simple manner suggested by Professor Hayek[2] (and implied in Hicks's approach) of *defining* the maintenance of capital simply in terms of the maintenance of income. We cannot first define income as what is left after maintaining capital intact and then define the latter as what is required to maintain income intact, without getting involved in circular reasoning.

The Hayek–Hicks approach to income and capital does however focus attention on another basic difficulty. Suppose people *expect* a general fall in interest rates, is the resulting *expected* appreciation in capital value part of income? The textbook answer would be that in the textbook world a fall in interest rates means a fall in the expected yield of resources—since interest measures the productivity of capital, it is simply a reflection of the yield of resources in *general*. Hence a fall in interest could not lead to a general increase in capital values since *ex hypothesi* it is just sufficient to offset that fall in the market value of capital that would otherwise have occurred on account of the fall in the general yield of capital.[3] In the real world, however, the market value of all assets can rise and fall together with a change in the level of interest rates which is a bogus change, since it does not reflect any real change in the income derived from capital resources. To the extent, therefore, that people *expect* a general change in interest rates, the *ex ante–ex post* method of calculating true income does not succeed in excluding elements which represent revaluations and not accruals.

An analogous difficulty arises out of *expected* changes in the value of money. When prices, in general, are expected to rise, this is reflected in an expected appreciation of capital values. In other words, the interest on

---

[1] A useful guide-post to one's thinking on these matters is to remember that 'maintaining capital intact' has a fairly definite meaning (the word 'fairly' will be further explained later) when applied to the stock of resources of the community as a whole. This means that in making provision for 'depreciation' of particular assets all such expected value-changes can be allowed for as cancel out when the resulting net change in capital values is added together, but not those which would make the value of the net change in the total stock of capital something different from what it, in fact, is. But unfortunately this is no more than a guide-post: it does not enable us to lay down any definite or precise rules, for the use of accountants or others, as to how the depreciation provision should be calculated.

[2] 'The Maintenance of Capital', *Economica* (August 1935), p. 241.

[3] The owners of bonds would still make a capital gain in this case, but it would represent a genuine redistribution of income in their favour; since it would mean that *their* income from capital was maintained, while the income from other resources had fallen; and it would be offset, from the point of view of society as a whole, by the *fall* in the market value of other resources, i.e. that of their debtors.

capital—whether measured *ex ante* or *ex post*—goes up.[1] But this again introduces a bogus element in the calculation of income, since the resulting estimate of income (as measured in *current* prices) will exceed the true figure of accruals by the amount by which the expected increase in the value of assets exceeds the value of the increase in assets.

The general conclusion must therefore be that even if the windfall element in capital appreciation could be exluded—even, in other words, if we could discover by some objective test the values of K_2' and K_1' in the above denotation—the expectational approach would not really solve the problem of finding a measure of 'net saving' that corresponds to the real increase in 'resources'. It would only do so if the general level of prices was expected to remain constant; and if expectations concerning changes in the level of interest rates were consistent with, and reflected nothing else but, the expectations concerning the change in the yield of resources in general.

5. INCOME AS A MEASURE OF TAXABLE CAPACITY

We have left over until now the question whether the whole search for a concept of income which excludes the 'windfall element' is relevant from the point of view of a definition of income designed to measure the taxable capacity of individuals. The idea of excluding from income the casual or windfall element serves a clear and definite purpose in accountancy. For the main purpose of accounting is to exhibit, for the proprietors of the business, the actual results in terms as nearly comparable as can be to the expected results; in terms, in other words, which make it possible for the proprietors to judge whether the business is a 'success' and fulfils those expectations in the light of which they invested their capital, and which they alone are ultimately capable of deciding. The accountant is rightly in search therefore of a concept of income *ex post* which is as near a counterpart as can be found to the investor's income *ex ante*. In the light of the foregoing analysis, it is not surprising that the accountant's definition of income *ex post* is based, as it can only be based, on a series of admittedly arbitrary conventions whose value depends, to a large extent, on their status as time-honoured conventions—i.e. on their steady and consistent application.[2]

---

[1] This of course is Fisher's old proposition about the money rate of interest deviating from the real rate on account of changing prices; the difference is that only *expected* changes in the value of money enter into it.

[2] The nature of these conventions cannot be discussed here, but their net result (in accordance with the general accounting principle that it is better to err on the conservative side) is to bring more of the gains and less of the losses into the windfall category than

Similarly the economist who is mainly interested in a notion of income which corresponds to the value generated in the process of production (and from a social rather than an individual point of view) is in search of criteria by means of which the saving which reflects productive activity devoted to investment can be separated off from the saving which merely reflects the revaluation of future prospects. To a considerable extent therefore—though by no means the whole extent—the interests of the economist and the accountant run parallel, and income definitions based on accountancy notions can be adapted, with a number of adjustments, to serve the purposes of national income calculations.

From the point of view of the measurement of the individual taxable capacity, however, the problems that beset both accountants and economists are largely irrelevant and others take their place. For here the problem is to find a yardstick in terms of which the tax burden can fairly be apportioned among individuals; and whether an individual's taxable capacity is regarded as consisting in his personal spending power, or the 'net accretion of his economic power', the windfall character of gains (or losses) does not make the slightest difference. From the point of view of a man's ability to afford consumption goods or pay taxes it is a matter of indifference whether he makes his money at Monte Carlo or by selling shoestrings; and it may even be argued that unexpected gains possess a greater taxable capacity per £ than expected gains or returns since *ex hypothesi* they cannot have any effect on conduct. Windfalls, as Professor Pigou said, are the 'ideal objects of taxation in their announcement aspect'.[1]

The proper distinction for the purpose of the measurement of taxable capacity therefore is not between accruals and windfalls, or between expected and unexpected gains, but between genuine and fictitious gains. The exclusion of 'windfalls' from taxable income could in fact only be justified if it could be shown that the gains in the windfall category are of the fictitious kind, and not the genuine kind. But there is no such presumption. Fortuitous gains can be genuine; and as we have seen, expected gains can also be fictitious.

Capital appreciation represents a genuine gain whenever it secures for the recipient an increased command over both consumption goods and income-yielding resources—i.e. an increase in the purchasing power of his wealth in terms of commodities whether viewed as a *stock* or as a *flow*. In the normal case a gain which represents increased command in terms

could properly be regarded as belonging there. Thus the conventions for writing *down* assets are far more liberal than for writing them *up*. Occasionally, however, the conventions have the opposite results—as, for example, the depreciation of fixed assets on the basis of historical costs, in times of inflation.

[1] A. C. Pigou, *A Study in Public Finance* (3rd ed. revised, London, 1949), p. 156.

of the one also implies increased command in terms of the other. But it is possible to think of cases where this is not so. Thus when there is a general rise in capital values due to a general fall in interest rates, the purchasing power of capital resources in terms of consumption goods is higher than before. But the resulting capital appreciation does not (or at any rate need not) make any one capitalist better off relatively to others; it does not secure him an increased command over capital assets. Whilst the aggregate purchasing power (in terms of consumption goods) of his capital resources has gone up, the flow of real income that he expects to derive from his capital has not; so that his 'spending power' is not higher— or at any rate not appreciably higher—than before.[1] Similarly if in times of inflation there is a rise of ordinary shares, the gain of the shareholders is genuine enough in relation to other capitalists (whose capital values have not increased); yet, it would be wrong to treat such an appreciation as income in the same way as one which implied a corresponding increased command over consumption goods.

It follows from this that the ideal definition of income, as a measure of taxable capacity, is to be thought of, not as consumption plus *actual* capital accumulation (*à la* Haig) nor as consumption plus capital accumulation excluding windfalls (the accountancy ideal) but as consumption plus *real* capital accumulation, where the term '*real* capital accumulation' is to be understood as actual capital accumulation subjected to a double series of corrections: first, for the change in the general level of prices (of consumers' goods), and second, for the change in the general level of interest rates.

The correction for the change in the general level of prices could be regarded as an 'index-number problem'—i.e. a problem that is in principle capable of being dealt with in terms of approximative solutions though not of exact solutions.[2] But the correction for the general level of interest rates is not just an index-number problem: for the true change in interest rates,

---

[1] As we have seen earlier, an increase in the value of capital resources *in relation to income* does represent an increase in spending power, but this increase is not of the same order as one which secures for the recipient an equivalent appreciation of capital values and a correspondingly larger command over future income. Hence capital appreciation of the former type cannot be regarded as part of income in the same way as the latter type; and it may be considered that a more appropriate method of taxing benefits from capital appreciation which merely represent a fall in interest rates is through an annual tax on capital, rather than through a tax on capital gains.

[2] It must be borne in mind however that what needs to be corrected for price changes is not the saving, or the capital appreciation for the year, but the total value of assets at the end of the year by the change in prices in the course of the year. Such a correction is therefore only feasible for accrued income (which reckons unrealized capital appreciation, and not only realized) and not for realized income. Even if net realized capital gains were assumed to correspond to total net gains, realized and unrealized, it would not be possible to make the correction without knowing the total capital value at the beginning of the year.

as we have attempted to demonstrate above, is not something that can be inferred from market data. When the general level of share values goes up it is not possible to say how far the rise represents increased expectations of profits and how far it represents increased confidence resulting in a lower rate at which the expected profits are discounted. Thus the problem of *defining* individual income, quite apart from any problem of practical measurement, appears in principle insoluble.

6. SOCIAL INCOME AND INDIVIDUAL INCOME

Contrary to what is often supposed, the concept of social income does not suffer from quite the same ambiguity and vagueness as that of individual income; at any rate the arbitrariness in the former is of a different character, and raises less intractable problems than in the latter. The reason for this is that social income consists of the value of consumption plus the *value of the increase* in the stock of goods in existence (and not the *real increase in the value* of capital assets); and the measurement of a change in the stock of goods raises lesser problems than the measurement of the *real* change in their individual value. The change in the quantity of social capital, between any two dates, could in principle be measured by making an inventory of goods at each of the two dates and valuing the different kinds of goods at each at the same set of prices. To the extent that the actual goods in the two series are identical in character and only differ in the relative quantities in which they are available, the problem is the usual one of index numbers, of whether to take the prices ruling at the base date, and apply them to the end date, or vice versa.[1] It is only to the extent that the types of goods at the two dates are not identical—that new *kinds* of goods have appeared, and others have disappeared—that the problem of valuation emerges in the more acute form: since we have nothing to go on to show what the prices of the new goods would have been, had they been available on date 1, or what the prices of the vanished goods would have been had their kind still existed at date 2. To that extent the measurement of the change in capital must necessarily remain arbitrary.[2]

---

[1] Each particular piece of equipment will of course have changed its character: a two-year-old machine will have become a three-year-old machine, and so on. But so long as the two-year-old machine at date 1 can be taken as identical in character with the two-year-old machines at date 2, the values applied to two-year-old machines in *relation* to three-year-old machines do not present a problem, as the same price relatives are applied at both dates.

[2] All this is not to suggest that existing estimates of the national income are in conformity with these principles of measurement. But the point is that in the case of the national income there is a reasonably clear standard or 'ideal' to which existing techniques of estimation can, in greater or lesser degree, approximate.

From the point of view of national income estimates, moreover, the problem of depreciation can be ignored altogether for certain purposes, and the estimates confined to a measurement of the output of final goods realized during a period plus the net change in the stock of intermediate products. This corresponds to the gross income of enterprises (sales-proceeds less fuel and materials consumed) with a correction only for the element of price-change in the valuation of stocks.

But whilst the changes in capital values can thus be ignored when social income is taken in the aggregate, they cannot be ignored when it is a question of determining how command over wealth is divided among the different individuals. From the point of view of the individual, increased command over resources due to owning 'more things' is logically indistinguishable from increased command due to the possession of things which have gone up in price relatively to other things. The 'things' moreover are not the same *kind* of things in the two cases. Whereas the social capital relates to physical objects, buildings, plant and machinery and so on, the individual's assets consist mainly of titles—loans and shares in businesses valued not as collections of physical objects but as going concerns whose earning power depends on the efficiency with which the use of physical resources is organized, and not just on the physical resources they command. The methods that can be applied for separating quantitative from value changes, or the rules that can be adopted for measuring depreciation in the one case have no application (or meaning) in the other case. When the capital in question is the value of a whole enterprise it is meaningless to distinguish between increases which represent a greater quantity of 'real capital' and others which merely reflect a higher valuation put on 'goodwill'. The problem of measuring the 'real savings' of individuals raises therefore quite different issues from those involved in the question of the 'real savings' of business enterprises or of society as a whole.

7. INCOME AS DIVIDEND

Before we leave the subject we ought to introduce yet another concept of income, which differs from income as interest in that it confines itself to that part of interest which 'gets separated off' from the principal, in the shape of formal interest or dividend payments. Here the fact of *separation* is taken as the principal criterion of what constitutes income; and to distinguish it from what, in obedience to accepted terminology, we have here called income as interest, this conception might perhaps be designated as income as dividend. Income as dividend has the merit of coming nearest to conventional ideas of income; it is perhaps on that account one of the basic notions underlying our income tax legislation,[1] but logically there is nothing to be said for it, even as a kind of half-way house between income as consumption and income as interest. It falls short of income as interest, or, more accurately, of the measurable concept of accrued income, by the net amount of gains due to capital appreciation. It differs from income as consumption to the extent that the consumption of individuals exceeds or falls short of that part of their earnings which is formally distributed. Arguments which have been advanced (apart from administrative ones) for preferring it to income as interest as a tax base, are in fact identical with the arguments for preferring consumption to income as a tax base and are perhaps best shown in the following passage by Professor Pigou:

> Thus consider two men of equal wealth one of whom buys with £10,000 a property reckoned to yield a permanent income of £500 a year, and the other buys for the same sum a property of equal present value reckoned to yield...an income which begins at a low figure and is destined, and known to be destined, to grow progressively larger; that, for example, there is to be no income at all for ten years, and thereafter, a perpetual income of a large amount. A property tax in this case is not merely inconvenient, in that it forces a man to make payments (possibly by borrowing) before he has any income to pay with. It is also guilty of an inequity, for since the two series of incomes have *ex hypothesi* the same present value, they ought to be subject to taxes of the same present value. But whereas a permanent 10 per cent income tax on the first series beginning now will have the same present value as a permanent 10 per cent income tax on the second series, a permanent ½ per cent property tax beginning now on the property yielding the second series will have a substantially larger value than a permanent ½ per cent property tax beginning now on the property yielding the first series. What happens in effect is that the incomes which are to begin ten years hence are, under property taxes, assessed both when they arrive and also in anticipation of their arrival. There is here, clearly, a 'distributional evil'.[2]

The reader will note the complete analogy between this argument and the one used by Irving Fisher to justify his own definition of income as consumption. Indeed if one could be certain that individuals consumed the same amount, no more and no less, than that part of their income which is in fact distributed, income as consumption and income as dividend would amount to the same thing.

---

[1] This is true, even though the taxation of the undistributed profits of companies may be regarded as a tax on the potential capital appreciation of shares. But it is an indirect tax on the capital gains of shareholders as a class, not a tax on the capital appreciation of the individual owner of shares. It is not, therefore, even notionally a tax on 'income as interest'.

[2] *Op. cit.* pp. 135–6. Pigou is discussing here the relative merits of an annual tax on property and that of a tax on investment income. But since he is not concerned with differences in the rates of interest applicable to different assets, the argument is equally applicable to a comparison between using income as interest and income as dividend (in our sense) as the tax base. Hence for 'property tax' we can read a 'tax on income as interest' and for 'income tax' a 'tax on income as dividend'.

This, however, cannot be assumed—the man who receives no income from his property for ten years presumably will not live on air—so that the only argument in favour of income as dividend, as against income as interest, on the above lines, would be if it could be shown that the former is in fact *more closely related* to consumption than the latter. This, however, cannot be shown either; indeed the general presumption is the opposite. Two men of equal wealth will tend to live on an identical scale, and consume equal amounts if they have the same 'tastes and temperaments', quite irrespective of the forms in which they choose to invest their property. If they have different 'tastes and temperaments', and in consequence, consume unequal amounts again there is no presumption that the man who consumes more will invest in forms which yield more money income, and a smaller degree of capital appreciation, than the other—with the limited qualification that in so far as he is concerned to maximize the amount of his annual income readily available for spending he will avoid investing in property which is indivisible, and cannot be realized in small batches.[1] To the extent that the one form of income is taxed and the other is not, they both have the same incentive to invest their property in forms which reduce the tax liability; in fact the man who saves less, and spends more, may even have a stronger incentive than the other, since being more of a spendthrift, he is in greater need to save taxes.

Income as dividend comes off very poorly, therefore, as a tax base; it is neither a good income tax nor a good consumption tax; it does not manage to tax savings (as an income tax is supposed to do) since net savings are left untaxed if they take the form of capital appreciation; nor does it manage to tax consumption (as an expenditure tax does) since consumption is left untaxed if it is made at the expense of capital appreciation or out of capital; it is not a true 'half-way house' between the two—as for example a tax would be which taxed genuine consumption at one rate and genuine savings at some other.[2]

[1] Professor Pigou's argument that the man who receives no money income in his example would suffer in paying tax since he would have 'to make payments (possibly by borrowing) before he has any income to pay with' assumes in effect that the property is indivisible.
[2] Professor Pigou cannot be found guilty of inconsistency in this matter, in as much as in an earlier chapter of the same book he strongly argued in favour of expenditure, as against income, as the base for taxation. But he was clearly mistaken in thinking that in the absence of an expenditure tax, a tax on investment income is a kind of second best, and preferable *on distributional grounds*, to an annual tax on property. This is not so. His conclusions only follow if the consumption of the two men is more nearly related to their money incomes than to their properties—and this clearly cannot be assumed. If taxable capacity is conceived as spending power, and not actual spending, property provides a more reliable guide to taxable capacity than investment income; though, as we have seen, not an adequate guide except in the case where all property has the same interest (i.e. is expected to have the same net yield in time, in the form of both dividends or appreciation).

N. Kaldor

The conception of income as dividend is sometimes defended—apart from defence on the administrative consideration that it is more convenient to assess and to collect than any alternative—on the ground that any broadening of the conception of income would create more inequities than it would remedy. This of course is an admission that any conception of income, or at any rate any practicable conception, is bound to be inequitable as a tax base. But in point of fact it is a very questionable argument. The fact that fictitious gains and losses escape hardly makes up in equity for the exclusion of genuine gains and losses; and the argument entirely ignores the point that the division between income which takes the form of dividend and income which takes the form of capital appreciation is not fixed by nature but is subject to manipulation by the taxpayer. There are innumerable ways of converting income into capital appreciation against which specific provisions designed to prevent tax avoidance are quite ineffective.

In the foregoing chapter [not reproduced here] I carefully refrained from advocating expenditure as the basis of progressive taxation on the 'Fisherian' argument that income is really consumption, not consumption plus net saving. If income could be satisfactorily defined—in other words if true net saving could be ascertained and brought into charge, and the benefit derived from ownership as such brought into charge by an annual tax on property—then at least on a narrow view of equity which considers taxation in its immediate distributional aspects there would be something to say in favour of income. But income cannot be satisfactorily defined. Hence even if consumption plus net saving (and not consumption as such) is taken as the ideal criterion of taxable capacity, there is no presumption that any definition of income that is objectively measurable could provide a better, or even as good an index of that taxable capacity as expenditure.

There is therefore a case for taking expenditure as the tax base even on this particular view of equity. There is, however, as we suggested at the end of the last chapter, a wider conception of equity, which takes into account the social consequences of individual behaviour and on the basis of which consumption *is* the ideal criterion not consumption plus net saving. On the latter view expenditure is a superior tax base to income, quite apart from the problem of definition and measurement.

8. EXPENDITURE AND CONSUMPTION

It may be objected on the other hand that expenditure is not the same thing as consumption; what a man spends in a given period will differ from the value of his true consumption during that period on account of

(*a*) the net accumulation of decumulation of his stock of consumable goods;
(*b*) the notional income, or 'flow of benefits in kind' derived from that
stock. A proper tax on consumption, it may be thought, ought to make
adjustments both for (*a*) and for (*b*); and the question may be asked
whether the need for these adjustments does not reintroduce by the
back door, so to speak, the same problems with regard to the definition
of consumption as were found with the notion of income. Indeed,
Professor Hicks came near to suggesting in one place that the concept of
consumption suffers from the same ambiguity or vagueness as the concept
of income.[1]

Before considering the nature of the problems involved in making the
necessary adjustments for the differences between expenditure and consumption it is important to be clear that the problem created by consumers'
'capital goods' is not the same problem when the objective is to measure
consumption, and not income. Discrimination between taxpayers results
under an income tax when, because of the problems of valuation involved,
the income derived from consumers' capital goods—whether in the form
of a flow of benefits, or of capital appreciation—is ignored. On the principle
that an income tax taxes both savings and the fruit of savings, such income
from consumers' capital ought to be charged, regardless of the fact that
the initial purchase was made out of taxed income. From the point of view
of a tax on consumption, on the other hand, either the expenditure itself
(or its annual equivalent), or the annual benefit derived from the possession
of goods, ought to be subjected to charge, but not both.

Hence the problem of assessing the 'notional income' derived from
consumers' capital only arises in those cases where the acquisition of an
item is regarded as partaking primarily the character of investment and in
consequence the expenditure on that item is treated as part of savings
rather than of spendings. The most obvious example of this is the dwelling
house which requires a valuation of the annual use-benefit, in much the
same way as under our present conception of taxable income. The same
notion could be extended to other items (such as diamonds or valuable
works of art), the purchase of which could be excluded from chargeable
expenditure, provided an annual charge were imposed[2] and the sales-
proceeds brought into charge when the asset is sold, in so far as they were
spent. In this latter case the purchaser of a piece of consumers' capital
is treated in the same way as the man who saves a sum, consumes, and is

---

[1] p. 78 above.
[2] It is true that, apart from the case of the dwelling house, the proper amount of this
annual charge could not usually be determined by any market price (since diamonds,
Old Masters, etc. are not customarily hired out on an annual basis), and would have to
be assessed on the basis of an arbitrary percentage of the purchase price.

therefore taxed on, the income derived from his savings, and is also taxed on the principal if and when he spends his savings.

The real question is whether the difference between expenditure and consumption gives rise to conceptual difficulties analogous to those involved in the difference between income and consumption. This difference is the net saving in the form of consumers' goods; and it may appear at first sight that it raises the same problems of valuation (though on a smaller scale) as the net saving that is associated with income.

But the two kinds of 'savings' are not only quantitatively but *conceptually* different—and this is the basic reason why the one notion does not suffer from the same kind of ambiguity as the other. The net saving that constitutes the difference between expenditure and consumption is the *value of the change in the stock* of durable consumers' goods in the individual's possession; the net saving that constitutes the difference between income and consumption is the (real) *change in the value of the stock* of both consumers' goods and other forms of property. As we have seen above, the evaluation of the latter kind of change raises quite different problems from the former. The difference between expenditure and consumption raises the same problems (on a smaller scale) as are involved in measuring the net saving of enterprises or the net change in the stock of social capital. Ideally, if there is a secondhand market for each kind of durable commodity of each particular degree of wear, the change in the stock between two dates can be measured by the inventory method described above. Failing that the adjustment involves some estimate of depreciation—with the usual choice between historical or replacement cost, the straight-line method, the reducing-balance method, and so on. But there is no need to take account of the rise in the *value* of possessions as such—the rise in the price of old furniture or jewellery, the question whether this rise is a real rise or only a rise in money terms, whether it represents higher future returns or a fall in the rate of discount: all these problems would only become relevant in evaluating real capital accumulation which enters into income; they do not affect the evaluation of consumption in relation to expenditure.

In other words the theoretical problem here is not one of measuring net savings in the sense of *real* capital appreciation at all, but only of making the correct provision for depreciation. I am not suggesting that there are no conceptual difficulties about depreciation. But I hope the above analysis has convinced the reader that the problem of individual income is not *just* a problem of depreciation; it raises far more complex issues which, unlike the problem of depreciation, do not lend themselves to approximative solutions in relation to a standard of reference.

PART IV

MEASUREMENT OF BUSINESS INCOME

12 Price changes and income measurement

by Philip W. Bell*

Accountants and economists would still seem to be far from reaching a consensus on what, if anything, should be done to adjust for price changes in the accounts of the individual firm. There would seem to be implicitly four general positions one can adopt.

One position would have business firms adjust their *accounting methods* to individual items in the accounts, so as perhaps to reflect in part at least the fact of changing prices. Thus L.I.F.O. is substituted for F.I.F.O. in inventory accounting; an adjustment, with perhaps a reserve account, is made for rising replacement costs of fixed assets, and so forth.

A second position—one which seems to be gaining more and more adherents within the accounting profession in the United States—has been in the direction of making adjustments in all accounts for changes in the *general price level* on the basis, say, of the wholesale or consumer price index published by the federal government.[1] The proponents of such a move well recognize some of the limitations of such an adjustment, but they feel that it is all that is practicable at the present time and at least is a step in the right direction. Like adherents of the first position the motto of those behind making one price level adjustment in all accounts might be: 'Don't just stand there, do something!'

A third possible position is essentially a negative reaction to both of the first two positions. The motto of this group might be: 'Don't just do something, stand there!' Thus, Kenneth Boulding writes:

What the accountant tells us may not be true but, if we know what he has done, we have a fair idea of what it means. For this reason, I am somewhat suspicious of many current efforts to reform accounting in the direction of making

[1] Both the American Accounting Association and the American Institute of Certified Public Accountants have supported studies directed at making adjustments for changes in the general price level. *See* R. C. Jones, *Effects of Price-Level Changes on Business Income, Capital and Taxes* (Iowa City: American Accounting Association, 1956); *idem. Price-Level Changes and Financial Statements: Case Studies of Four Companies* (Iowa City: American Accounting Association, 1955); American Institute of Certified Public Accountants, *Reporting the Financial Effects of Price-Level Changes*, Research Study 6 (New York: The Institute, 1963).

* Provost, Merrill College, University of California, Santa Cruz.

it more 'accurate'. I am particularly suspicious of attempts to improve accounting by building into it an explicit recognition of the fact that the price level changes.[1]

A fourth position is that something does need to be done, but that it must be much more thoroughgoing and complete than either one or two above, taking account of *individual price changes* as well as changes in the general price level.

It is this fourth line of thought that will be developed in this chapter. What we shall attempt to do is present a shortened, simplified version of the concepts developed in *The Theory and Measurement of Business Income*,[2] indicate how they can be applied in practice, and then see if these results can serve to elucidate some facets of the various alternative approaches which have been suggested and/or are presently being tried to handle the accounting problems created by changing prices.

BASIC CONCEPTS

The basic premise of this section is that one of the primary uses of data on income within the individual firm lies in the evaluation of past decisions in order to make better decisions about the future, and that to do that properly there must be a clear delineation between *operating gains* on the one hand and *holding gains* on the other. Operating gains are defined as any excess over a period of the current value of output sold over and above the current cost of the related inputs. Holding gains are broadly defined as any increase in the value of a firm's assets (and decrease in the value of its liabilities) while held by the firm which results from individual price changes, i.e. a holding gain exists whenever the current value of assets held by the firm exceeds the original (historic) cost value of those assets. These two kinds of gains—operating gains and holding gains—normally result from quite different types of managerial decisions; for purposes of evaluation, therefore, the two must be clearly separated in the accounts. And as will readily be appreciated, this in turn necessitates accounting for *individual price changes* of different assets and liabilities rather than simply taking into account changes in the nation's *general price level*.

Operating gains are straightforward in concept. And they have all actually been realized, since the goods have been sold. But what holding gains should be included in over-all profit for a given period?

[1] 'Economics and Accounting' in W. T. Baxter and S. Davidson, eds., *Studies in Accounting Theory* (Homewood, Ill., 1962), p. 54.
[2] By Edgar O. Edwards and Philip W. Bell (Berkeley, 1961).

The 'realization principle' holds a strong position in accounting, and of course it would be most unfair to require tax payments on the basis of gains which have not as yet been (and may never be) realized. Therefore, what is needed is a measure of the holding gains which have in fact been *realized* during the period—gains which may have *accrued* during the current period or in past periods. Such gains may be realized in one of two ways—through *direct sale* of an asset which has risen in price or indirectly through *use of an asset which has risen in price in the production of output which is sold.* Operating profit is based on current values. If certain of the inputs have risen in price between the time of purchase and the time of use, the difference between current value at the time of use and historic (purchase) cost value is a *cost saving* to the firm—a gain accrued because of the timing of input purchase rather than as a result of current production and sale operations.

While realized holding gains are thus an important element of information on the business firm, for many purposes all *realizable* holding gains accruing to the firm *during the period in question* is the relevant complement to current operating profit; these two components together yield the true increase in the money value of net worth of the firm over the period. Some of these realizable gains accruing during the year in question may of course have also been realized within that year, either directly or indirectly as described above. It would be well to divide realizable gains into three categories: those realized through direct sale, those realized through use in production which is sold, and those which are as yet unrealized.[1]

Thus there are four possible components for the over-all concept, or concepts, of profit:

A. Current operating profit—the excess over a period of the current value of output sold over the current cost of the related inputs.

B. Realizable holding gains—the increase during the fiscal period in the current-cost value of assets while held by the firm, including (i) gains accruing and realized during the period through direct sale of the asset; (ii) gains accruing and realized during the period through use in production which is sold; (iii) gains accruing during the period but as yet unrealized.

C. Holding gains realized through direct sale—the excess of proceeds over (depreciated) historic costs on the irregular sale or disposal of assets. (Note that this will include *B*(i) above *plus* additional gains realized in the current fiscal period which had accrued in previous periods.)

---

[1] W. T. Baxter in exposition of the Edwards–Bell scheme suggests a twofold division—realized and unrealized. See his 'The Future of the Accountant. II', *The Accountant* (18 July 1964), pp. 68–9. Separate listing for the two categories of realization is urged because of certain practical problems in recording holding gains and losses on the direct sale of fixed assets considered below.

D. *Holding gains realized through indirect sale* (cost savings)—the excess of the current cost over the historic cost of inputs used in producing output which is sold. (Note again that this includes B(ii) above *plus* previously accrued gains which are realized in the current period.)

To illustrate briefly and simply these four basic concepts. Suppose that raw materials are purchased in Year 1, rise in price in Year 2 but are held to increase inventory stock, and rise in price again in Year 3 when they are used up in production for sale. A realizable (but unrealized) holding gain would be recorded in Year 2. In Year 3 a holding gain realized through indirect sale would be recorded—the gain consisting of the realizable gain in Year 2 plus a further realizable gain which must be recorded for Year 3. Similarly, suppose a fixed asset was purchased at the end of Year 1 which had a two-year life and an expected salvage value equal to one-fifth of the original purchase price of $100, and the price of this asset doubled at the beginning of Year 2 and remained stable to the end of Year 3 when it was sold. There is a realizable holding gain in Year 2 equal to the full increase in the value of the asset, i.e. $100. This realizable gain is then realized—$40 worth in Year 2, another $40 in Year 3 since in both years the current-cost value of use ($80) is greater than the historic-cost value of use ($40). Current cost depreciation is used to arrive at *current operating profit*; the difference between current-cost depreciation and historic-cost depreciation is a holding gain realized through use of the asset in production for sale. The remaining $20 of realizable gain accruing in Year 2 should be realized when the asset is sold, presumably for $40 rather than the originally expected $20.[1]

With this background one can now considers three concepts of profit in relation to the four profit components as follows:

	Profit elements included as	
	Operating profit	Holding gain
1. Realizable profit (for the year)	A	B
2. Realized profit (during the year)	A	(C+D)
3. Traditional accounting profit	A+D	C

The proposal, in essence, is to substitute profit concepts 1 and 2—both are needed and can be derived by relatively simple end-of-period adjustments to accounting records currently compiled—in place of concept 3 now universally used. A general price-level adjustment can *then* be applied to these money concepts if 'real-profit' figures are desired. But from the point

[1] A practical problem arises when the salvage value actually obtained does not match that expected. This really implies an error in the depreciation calculation, an error which should, correctly, be now applied to both years of use. In practice, the gain or loss will probably all be applied at time of sale.

TABLE I.

Company X: Income Statement for the Year 1965 (in thousands of dollars)

Sales, at current value		1450
Cost of goods sold, at current cost		
Raw materials	780	
Depreciation expense	262	
Other	398	
Total	—	1440
Current operating profit		10

	Holding gains accruing during the year				Holding gains realized during the year (accrued in 1965 and in previous years)
	Realized	Un-realized	Total		
On inventories	10	20	30	On inventories	20
On fixed assets	5	15	20	On fixed assets	42
On other assets and liabilities	2	6	8	On other assets and liabilities	12
Totals	17	41	58	Total	74
Total realizable profit			68	Total realized profit	84
(current operating profit plus realizable holding gains)				(current operating profit plus realized holding gains)	

Appropriations, etc.		
Tax liability	30	
Dividends	20	
Surplus for year:		
Realized	34	
Unrealized	41	
Total	—	75
Total appropriations, etc.	—	125

NOTE: Total appropriations for the year equal current operating profit plus all realized holding gains (accrued in this and former years) plus all unrealized gains (accrued in the current year).

of view of decision-making and evaluation such 'real-profit' figures will add little or nothing, It is the calculation of component B and the separation of A and D which are critical to the decision-making process.

Separation of A and D provides a proper delineation of operating and holding gains. If this separation is not made, users of accounting data may be badly misled. Consider, for example, a firm with an established plant in the East which now duplicates this plant on the West Coast. The West

TABLE 2.

Company X: Income Statement for the Year 1965 (in thousands of dollars)

Sales		1450	
Cost of goods sold			
Raw materials	760		
Depreciation expense	240		
Other	400		
Total		1400	
Net operating income		50	
Capital gains (losses):			
On fixed assets	20		
On other assets and liabilities	14		
Total	—	34	
Accounting profit		—	84
Appropriations, etc.			
Tax liability	30		
Dividends	20		
Surplus for year	34		
	—		84

Coast plant earns very low profits. Does this imply inefficiency? No, the fact of the matter is that the West Coast plant, which is newer, might be earning a *larger* current operating profit (component A) than the East Coast plant, but the latter's reported 'operating profit' is swollen by holding gains. (It had bought its capital equipment some years back when the price was very much lower than prevails currently and was running down inventory stocks which had been purchased also at lower prices perhaps two or three years ago.) One can argue that it is the task of the user rather than the accountant to 'figure this out', by noting that raw material costs and depreciation charges seem somewhat lower in the East Coast plant, but surely the accountant, who has access to the records on asset-purchase dates and so forth, could help out.

But it is the existence and availability of component B, not now reported in any form, which is perhaps of most importance for decision-making and evaluation. Not only should one know about *all* gains which have accrued, whether realized yet or not, but also one should know the full picture of the events of *this fiscal period*, to compare with events of other fiscal periods. To report *only* gains when realized means that profits are reported in one period which are attributable to events of past periods; the bulk of such realized gains may have little or nothing to do with this period's activities, although the income reported is supposed to represent events of the current period.

In short, it would seem to at least a few advocates of position four on means of accounting for price changes that an income statement such as given in Table 1 is more informative, giving a more accurate picture of events of the year, than a traditional income statement such as shown in Table 2. And a balance-sheet which gives *both* current and historic values is more helpful than one which gives only the latter.

MEASUREMENT IN PRACTICE

So much for conceptualization and the basic approach. What about difficulties in implementation? Surely to get such seemingly complicated and sweeping changes into general accounting practice will require a revolution comparable to that necessary to replace English measures by a metric system!

In the Edwards and Bell book a hypothetical example was worked out in detail showing journal and ledger entries as well as the nature of the computations necessary to put the full scheme into effect. The description went on for several chapters, although there were numerous analytical digressions. Peter J. Dickerson in 1963 took an important stride forward by successfully applying this system to the accounts of a small producer of moulded plastic articles—*at a cost of 45 hours of his time*, i.e. one week's work by one accountant, not connected with the firm or initially knowledgeable about its practices, to produce full beginning- and end-of-year balance-sheets, in current and historic costs, and an income statement similar to Table 1 both in money and 'real' terms.[1] The firm had only been in business since 1956, and so one would not expect large discrepancies for different profit concepts for the year 1962. Still, using traditional concepts, it had reported a net operating income of $82,000, whereas Dickerson's computation of current operating profit turned out to be $94,000. During the year there had been net holding losses of $12,000 largely because raw materials used during the year were lower in price in 1962 than at time of purchase. Furthermore, as one might frequently expect, a straight, price-level adjustment to net operating income *lowered* it to $78,000, i.e. moved it *away* from the true current operating profit figure.

Dickerson did encounter some practical difficulties, in particular with respect to fixed assets and intangibles. More thought and work are surely necessary on the side of practicability, and probably also on the theory. But feasibility *has* been demonstrated, and at very low cost.

[1] See 'A Case Study in the Implementation of *The Theory and Measurement of Business Income*' (duplicated Master's dissertation, University of California, Berkeley, 1963).

Then what about possible acceptance of the general scheme? Here matters are not so promising. Various accountants have raised objections of one kind or another to the proposed changes—some thoughtful and searching, some evidently resulting from misunderstandings. Perhaps the most disturbing element to most independent accountants involves the determination of current values for fixed assets. The arbitrary 'revaluations' of the 1920s are only too well remembered, or at least known about. But if component C in realized profit is clearly delineated, there is nothing lost from present records, or from price-level-adjusted records! All that has been attempted is the proper separation of operating and holding gains and *additional* recognition of unrealized gains occurring during the fiscal period. Even if the separation is sloppily done, it is very likely that it will yield a more accurate picture of events of the period than if it were not attempted at all. The federal government, of course, is not going to accept the separation for tax purposes until it can be satisfied that it can be accomplished uniformly and fairly, but this should not prevent business-men and accountants from attempting to improve the data used in decision-making and evaluation.

A greater obstacle to implementation is probably more political than theoretical or practical. When this scheme was proposed once before a group of accountants and business men under the auspices of a professional accounting organization, it was vehemently (and undoubtedly correctly) argued by one business man that fixed-asset inputs were steadily declining in price because of technological advance in his company, and this meant that current operating profit would usually be *larger* than what is reported using traditional practices today. The purpose of price-level adjustments, he maintained, was to make profits *smaller* for tax purposes, not larger. This is the sort of argument that cannot be countered.

13 The estimation of business profits in periods of changing prices

by F. W. Paish*

1. It is not the purpose of this memorandum to present in any detail the case for allowing such amounts to be set aside from business profits before tax as would enable the 'real', as opposed to the money, value of the capital of the business to be maintained intact. The commission has already heard much evidence on this point, and there is little that I could usefully add to it now. My main purpose is to attempt to find a convenient criterion for the maintenance of real capital intact, and to make suggestions about possible methods of achieving it. All that I wish to say here on the general subject is that I support a definition of business profits which would provide for the maintenance of real capital intact for reasons not only of equity but also of public interest. I believe that to base estimates of profit, both for tax and other purposes, on the maintenance merely of the money value of the assets of a business tends to promote over-spending and over-taxation in times of rising prices, and under-spending and under-taxation in times of falling prices. Thus existing methods of estimating profits tend to intensify both booms and slumps, unless indeed their effects are offset by deliberate Government action in the form of Budget surpluses in times of rising prices and of Budget deficits in times of falling prices. I consider that it would be most desirable to relieve the Government of this responsibility for providing a compensating mechanism to obviate the distorting effects on the economy of our present methods of estimating profits.

2. As a temporary offset to the excessive taxation imposed on businesses in times of rising prices by present methods of estimating profits, the Government granted in 1945, and increased in 1949, a specially high rate of depreciation allowance on new plant and equipment during the first year of its life. This initial allowance, which is now [1952] about to be withdrawn, probably brought the aggregate amount of depreciation allowances throughout the country up to something like the actual cost of maintaining the total of real fixed capital intact. While, however, the aggregate amount of depreciation allowed was probably about adequate between 1949 and 1951, the method used had at least four serious shortcomings: it was essentially

* Professor of Economics (with special reference to Business Finance), London School of Economics and Political Science, 1949–65. Professor Emeritus, University of London.

a temporary concession, for the more the depreciation allowed in the early years of a piece of equipment, the less there will be in its later years; its benefits were distributed between firms, not in proportion to the equipment they had to maintain intact but in proportion to the new equipment they installed; it made no attempt to deal with the problem of tax on book profits due to the rise in the recorded values of physically unchanged inventories; and above all it acted as a subsidy to new investment at a time when investment was in any case tending to outrun saving, and thus undid such anti-inflationary effects as it had through allowing businesses to increase their savings. Its discontinuance is therefore to be welcomed; but its absence makes essential its replacement by a more rational method of allowing businesses to set aside out of profits before tax sufficient provisions to enable them to keep their capital intact. The urgency of some new provision after the withdrawal of the initial allowance is clear if we consider the estimate of the finance of investment for 1951 given in the Economic Survey (Cmd. 8195, Table 26). This shows that in 1951, after setting aside £1,120 m. for depreciation and £530 m. for increased tax reserves, the undistributed profits of businesses were estimated at £780 m. But of this sum, no less than £700 m. was expected to be needed to cover the increased cost of stocks of unchanged size, leaving only £80 m. for actual increases in fixed or working capital. Now Table 6 of the National Income White Paper (Cmd. 8203) shows that out of £1,124 m. of depreciation allowed in 1950, £260 m. was due to the initial allowance. If, therefore, the initial allowance had not been in existence in 1951, provision for income and profits tax would have had to be more than £130 m. higher and net business savings would have been put at some £50 m. negative. In other words, taxes would have taken more than all the amounts that business was able to put aside after making provision to maintain its capital intact.

3. It is sometimes suggested that the correct method of deciding whether a business is setting aside sufficient amounts from its profits to maintain its real capital intact is to ascertain whether the amounts set aside would be sufficient, if reinvested continuously in the business, to maintain the assets of the business physically intact. This 'replacement cost' criterion, however, is not necessarily satisfactory, though it is likely to be a much closer approximation to a solution of the problem than the present 'original cost' criterion. The reason for the possible inadequacy of the 'replacement cost' concept is that all prices do not change at the same rates. Even in a time of a generally stable price level, some individual prices are rising and others falling. Owners of assets which rise in price relatively to the general level obtain a real advantage thereby. For owners of non-durable goods,

such as stocks of unhedged raw materials, this is fairly obvious. The owners of a large stock of raw cotton at a time of a short crop and a sharp rise in cotton prices will be in a favourable position as compared with other manufacturers whose stocks are small. If prices of finished goods rise commensurately with raw material prices, those with large stocks will benefit immediately. If, on the other hand, prices of finished goods do not show an immediate rise, those manufacturers who must buy raw cotton at the higher prices in order to produce at all will find production unprofitable and will be unable to continue to produce. Output of finished goods will, therefore, fall and prices rise until they reach their normal relationship with that of the raw material. Those with large stocks, who have been able to stay in business, will then reap an exceptional profit as long as their old stocks last.

4. The same considerations apply, though perhaps rather less obviously, to owners of durable assets of which the replacement cost has risen. Unless prices of finished goods also rise, anyone investing in new fixed assets at the higher prices will earn less than the return on other types of investment. Not only, therefore, will new competitors be deterred from entering the industry and existing competitors from expanding their output, but those whose assets wear out first will find that it does not pay to replace them. Output of the finished product will therefore fall, prices will rise and those with the longest-lived assets will find that for the remainder of their assets' lives they will make an abnormally large profit on their original cost.

5. Since other prices have, by definition, fallen slightly, the owners of these assets will obtain a higher yield not only in money terms but also in real terms. As they have obtained a real benefit from the rise in the value of their assets, there is no reason why this should not show as a profit in their accounts.

6. Similarly when all prices are rising, but some faster than others, owners of assets of which the replacement cost has risen unusually fast obtain a real advantage as compared with those whose assets have risen more slowly; and it is reasonable that this differential advantage, though not the whole rise in replacement costs, should be reflected in their taxable profits. It would, therefore, seem that it is only that part of the rise in their book profits which is due to the general fall in the purchasing power of money which should be excluded.

7. The obvious way of adjusting for a general change in the purchasing power of money is to calculate profits in exactly the same way as at present (subject to any changes which are thought desirable on other grounds) and then to make special adjustments at the end of each year in order to eliminate those book profits which are due to the change in the general

level of prices (or, in times of falling prices, add back book losses due to the same cause). For this we should need a general index of prices, and not merely an index of prices of any one commodity or group of commodities. No such general price index, covering industrial as well as consumption goods, exists at present; but it would not be difficult to construct one which would give a more satisfactory result than any now in existence. For purposes of illustration, I have made a very rough guess at such an index, based on 1938, which I give below, showing also for comparison the London and Cambridge Index of Retail Prices and the Index of Prices of Consumption Goods derived from the figures of consumption at 1948 and 1938 prices given in Cmd. 8203.

Averages for	Index of retail prices	Consumption index	General price index
1938	100	100	100
1946	150	157	162
1947	160	169	177
1948	173	182	189
1949	178	186	194
1950	184	191	201
1951 (prov.)	200	210	226

8. While the general price index is very rough, the difference made by more refined methods could hardly be very great; for so large a proportion of all goods and services used at home enters into personal consumption that no general index could depart very far from the consumption index.

9. The ways in which the price index would be used would depend on the class of asset involved. Business assets may be divided for our purposes into six main classes:

(i) Land, non-industrial buildings and other fixed assets on which no depreciation is allowed.

(ii) Plant, machinery and other fixed assets on which depreciation is allowed.

(iii) Stocks of raw materials, goods in process and awaiting sale. These will be referred to as 'inventories'.

(iv) Investments in the ordinary shares of other companies.

(v) Long and medium-dated fixed-interest investments.

(vi) Short-dated investments, debtors and cash. These will be referred to as 'money assets'.

10. The first class of asset would not be affected by any proposed adjustment. The second class would be depreciated as at present, and the depreciation allowance would then be increased by the amount of the rise in the general index since the year in which each particular asset was acquired (it would probably be convenient to regard all pre-war assets

as having been bought in 1938). The original depreciation would be deducted, as at present, from the value of the asset, and the adjustment would be placed to a special replacement reserve account.

11. As an example, let us assume that a firm has £200,000 of depreciable fixed assets which, for the sake of simplicity, we will say were all bought in 1946, and on which depreciation for 1951 on the existing basis would be £20,000. Since the general price index for 1946 was 162 and for 1951 was 226, the additional depreciation to be allowed would be

$$\text{£20,000} \times \frac{226}{162} - \text{£20,000,}$$

or £7,900, which would be deducted from taxable profits and placed to replacement reserve. If at some subsequent date the general index of prices should fall, so that in the current year it stood below its level in the year in which the asset was bought, there would be a deduction from the normal depreciation allowance which would be charged against the balance standing in the replacement reserve and added to the profits for the current year.

12. The present method of dealing with our third category of assets, inventories, is to include in taxable profit the whole of any increase in the book value since the beginning of the accounting period, even though in physical terms the closing stock may be smaller than the opening stock. It is desired to exclude from the total of taxable profits any book profits which are due merely to the rise in the general level of prices. If stocks are fairly stable in quantity throughout the year, it will be sufficient to deduct from book profit and to add to replacement reserve an amount equal to the difference between the book value of the opening stock and the same value multiplied by the percentage which prices at the end of the year are of those at the beginning of the year. Let us assume that the book value of a firm's inventory on 31 December 1950 was £180,000 and on 31 December 1951 £200,000. Let us also assume that the index of general prices stood at 204 in December 1950 and 235 in December 1951. The adjustment in profits for the effect on inventories of changes in the general level of prices will be

$$\text{£180,000} \times \frac{235}{204} - \text{£180,000,}$$

or £27,400. Together with the adjustment on the depreciation of the fixed capital there will be a total deduction from profits as at present calculated of £35,300.

13. Where the level of inventories changes markedly during the year a modification of this method will be necessary. A simple adjustment would be to take the average of the appreciation due to the rising general price

level in the opening and closing stocks: e.g. opening stock £180,000; closing stock, £100,000:

$$\frac{1}{2}\left(£180,000 \times \frac{235}{204} - £180,000 + £100,000 - £100,000 \times \frac{204}{235}\right)$$

equals $\frac{1}{2}$(£27,400 + £13,200) or £20,300.[1] Including the additional depreciation allowance, this would bring the total deduction from taxable profits to £28,200.

14. No action needs to be taken with regard to class (iv) of assets (equity investments), or at this stage to classes (v) and (vi) (fixed-interest investments and money assets). If a business financed wholly on equity capital decides to invest part of its capital in fixed-interest securities or money assets, it will suffer a real loss in times of rising prices in exactly the same way as a private investor would.

15. It is sometimes urged, in opposition to proposals for relieving productive industry from taxation on fictitious profits due to a fall in the general purchasing power of money, that since individuals or companies who hold money assets or fixed-interest securities lose part of their real capital in times of rising prices, it is only fair that owners of productive physical assets should also suffer a loss. This contention does not appear to be well founded. The ownership of productive assets carries with it many risks which are not shared, or are shared in a much smaller degree, by owners of claims fixed in terms of money. To require the owners of productive assets to carry, in addition to the risks peculiar to the function of entrepreneurship, the risks which are proper to *rentiers*, is not only unjust but likely to have undesirable social results. In particular, it makes the ownership of productive assets relatively less attractive in times of rising prices than the ownership of non-productive assets, and may well make the hoarding of goods a better hedge against inflation than a share in the ownership of a productive enterprise.

16. While, however, this particular criticism appears to be unjustified, it may well be based, perhaps sometimes unconsciously, on another which, though rarely expressed, has much more validity. This criticism is that, while a business in a time of rising prices is taxed on fictitious profits, it escapes tax on the benefit it receives from the diminution in the real burden of its liabilities. Thus, although the reductions in taxable profit as proposed above would be wholly apposite in the case of a business financed wholly on equity terms, for a business with substantial liabilities or fixed-dividend capital the resultant position would be much too favourable. For

[1] If the level of inventories shows large seasonal fluctuations, it may be necessary to estimate the amount of nominal profit which is due to the effect of the rising general level by reference to an average of monthly inventories instead of merely the opening or the opening and closing figures.

a completely satisfactory scheme for eliminating the distortions in taxable profits due to changes in the purchasing power of money, we must include adjustments not only for the rising prices of assets but also for the falling burden of liabilities.

17. The simplest way of allowing for the fall in the burden of liabilities would be to treat all liabilities and fixed-dividend capital as negative inventories, and to add back to profits the whole of the difference between their value at the beginning of the year and the same figure divided by the percentage which prices at the end of the year are of those at the beginning of the year. It will, however, be only fair to allow any fixed-interest investments and money assets to be offset against fixed-dividend capital and liabilities, and to calculate the benefit which the business has received from the effect of the rise in the general level of prices with reference only to the net values. Let us assume that at the beginning of 1951 the business we are considering had among its assets fixed-interest investments of £50,000 and money assets of £100,000, while its liabilities consisted of £200,000 of debentures and £50,000 of short-term debts. Deducting its fixed interest investments and money assets from its liabilities, we have net liabilities of £100,000 at the beginning of 1951. The gain from the fall in the real value of these during the year is

$$£100,000 - £100,000 \times \frac{204}{235},$$

or £13,200. As the amount to be deducted from profits on account of assets was £35,300, and the amount to be added to profits on account of liabilities is £13,200, the net amount to be deducted from taxable profits and placed to replacement reserve account is £22,100.

18. If the total of liabilities changed greatly during the year, it would be possible to average the adjustments between the opening and closing liabilities in the same way as we averaged the adjustments between the opening and closing stocks in the example given in paragraph 13.

19. In a period of falling prices, the adjustments made by the method suggested here would operate in the opposite direction. The fictitious losses made through the fall in the book value of assets due to the fall in the general level of prices would be added back to profits and deducted from the replacement reserve, while the real losses made through the rise in the real value of liabilities would be deducted from profits and added to the replacement reserve.[1]

---

[1] In view of the possible, though not at present very probable, event of prices falling so sharply that withdrawals exceeded the amount of the replacement reserve, some amendment of the existing Companies Act would be required to permit the scheme suggested here to be adopted in full.

20. It is extremely important that profits should be adjusted in this way, not merely for tax purposes, but also for the businesses' own purposes. Under the present system, high nominal profits in times of rising prices and apparent losses in times of falling prices may not only affect the amount of tax paid but also mislead directors and shareholders. This is especially important in times of falling prices, when the publication of fictitious losses may well cause unjustified pessimism and prevent profitable investment from being undertaken. Merely to add to tax liabilities at such a time would probably serve to intensify the pessimism and prolong the depression; but if accountants and directors could be brought to keep their accounts in such a way as to show an often substantial real profit in place of an apparent loss, the higher liability to tax would be more than offset by the more satisfactory profit position. If not only the Inland Revenue, but also business men in general could be brought to think in real, and not merely in money terms, it would go far to modify the violence both of inflationary and of deflationary movements.

14 Profit measurement and inflation

by R. Mathews* and J. McB. Grant†

THE MEASUREMENT OF ACCOUNTING PROFIT

The task that is performed in this chapter is the theoretical analysis of the effects of conventional methods of accounting on profits and finances in times of inflation. For this purpose it is necessary to examine the accounting theory of profit.

Profit measurement in accounting may be regarded as a process of matching with the revenue realized during a given period the costs and expenses incurred in producing revenue. This matching concept ensures that profit measurement is a logical process, but there are, nevertheless, a number of postulates and conventions underlying the accounting theory of profit which limit the usefulness of accounting profit as a measure of business surplus and hence as a basis for policy decisions.

Revenue is defined as the current (i.e. the non-capital) gross earnings or incomings of an enterprise. As a result of the realization postulate in accounting, revenue is brought to account only when realized, as for example by sale of goods. Costs and expenses are defined as the non-capital outgoings of an enterprise, incurred for the purpose of earning revenue. The historical record convention requires revenue, costs and expenses to be recorded as historical events with a view to making the accounts factual and objective. However, not all the costs and expenses incurred during a given period involve transactions in the market place with outside parties. Some relate to operations within the enterprise, such as the processing of raw materials or the using up of fixed assets, and therefore have no explicit market valuation. The historical record convention results in these operations being recorded in the books of account as though they were objectively measurable historical facts. The values accorded to such costs and expenses are estimates only, and to this extent a subjective element is introduced into the process of profit measurement.

Other assumptions underlying the accounting theory of profit measurement include the continuity assumption, which postulates that a business maintains continuity of existence for an indefinite period, and the accounting period convention, which assumes that the life of an enterprise can

* Professor of Accounting and Public Finance, The Australian National University.
† Professor of Applied Economics (with special reference to Accounting), University of Tasmania.

be divided into a number of arbitrary time periods, called accounting periods. For financial accounting this period is usually one year. The continuity assumption has important implications in the valuation of assets for balance-sheet purposes, and this indirectly affects the determination of profit. For example, as a result of the continuity assumption and the historical record convention, physical assets such as stocks and fixed capital equipment are taken into account on the basis of original cost and not replacement or realizable values. It follows that such assets are absorbed into costs and expenses on the basis of their original cost to the enterprise. What is assumed, in effect, is that the original cost of assets reflects their value to the enterprise as a going concern.

The application of the accounting period convention results in costs and expenses on the one hand, and revenue on the other, being allocated to accounting periods in order to measure profits by periods. It will be appreciated that this assumption is unrealistic, since the operations of the modern business are continuous. Costs and revenues relating to any given period can be estimated, but not precisely determined, so that the consequence of applying the accounting period convention is to introduce another subjective element into the process of profit measurement.

Finally, the measurement of accounting profit rests on the monetary assumption, which postulates that the recording processes in accounting are carried out in terms of the monetary unit of account. The application of the monetary assumption means that transactions involving different kinds of goods and services are all recorded in terms of a common unit of measurement. Such an assumption is basic to the whole idea of a systematic accounting record, but it must be recognized that the monetary postulate is responsible for some of the more serious limitations inherent in the measurement of accounting profit. The application of the assumption means that fluctuations in the value of money itself are ignored for accounting purposes. This introduces an unreal and misleading element into the accounting record when the value of money changes. The money values used to record transactions in the accounts do not necessarily reflect the current values of the goods and services entering the transactions. This limitation has particular significance when the value of money steadily falls (or steadily rises), as during a period of inflation (or deflation).

These are the important limitations of the accounting theory of profit measurement. In practice, however, the consistency and usefulness of the accounting records are further impaired by two kinds of financial manipulation having no justification in accounting theory. First, there is the doctrine of conservatism. It may be decided, as a matter of financial policy, to make adjustments to costs and revenues in order to ensure that costs are not understated in the accounts and that revenues are not overstated; or it may even be decided deliberately to overstate costs and understate revenues. This might be done, for example, by means of 'accelerated' depreciation, i.e. arbitrarily increasing depreciation charges above the amounts needed to write off the original cost of a fixed asset over its estimated working lifetime. A further example of conservatism as an accounting policy is the arbitrary reduction in closing stock values with a view to writing up the cost of stocks sold above their historical costs.

Procedures such as these undermine the whole foundation of accounting profit measurement, viewed as a systematic matching of costs with revenues. The practice of conservatism as an accounting policy is inconsistent with the accounting postulates mentioned above. Conservatism distorts profits, particularly as the overstatement of costs in one period will often be followed by the understatement of costs in subsequent periods. Excessive depreciation charges, for example, will inevitably be succeeded by inadequate charges in later periods, when the asset has been fully written off but is still in use. Conservatism, if applied as an accounting procedure, also distorts the relationship between the profit and loss statement and the balance-sheet, and makes the latter useless as a statement of the firm's financial position. The making of excessive depreciation charges or the writing down of stocks in effect transfers portion of the firm's profits to undisclosed reserves. Conservatism may still be justified as a financial policy, but only if its effects are clearly disclosed in the accounts.

The second kind of financial adjustment which has no justification in accounting theory is the revaluation of fixed assets to bring book values into line with current market values. This procedure conflicts with the historical record convention and the continuity assumption. Revaluation primarily affects the balance sheet, but the profit and loss statement may be influenced indirectly if subsequent depreciation charges are based on the revised values. Once again, there may be sound financial reasons for revaluation, but the results of any such procedure must be clearly disclosed if the value of the accounting reports is not to be impaired.

LIMITATIONS OF ACCOUNTING PROFIT

In theory, accounting profit is a reasonably definitive concept and one which can be measured fairly accurately, although in practice it may be distorted by the adjustments that have just been described. It is necessary to emphasize, however, that accounting profit is a measure of business surplus in historical money terms, derived by matching historical money costs with realized money revenues. For many purposes such a measure is unsatisfactory. In particular, there are two reasons why accounting profit cannot be accepted as a unique measure of business surplus, and both result from the application of the monetary assumption.

The first is that, when the value of money is changing, accounting profit does not provide a measure of current income, defined as the difference between revenues expressed in current prices and costs and expenses expressed in current prices. If the unit of measurement is itself fluctuating in value, then the values at which costs and revenues are recorded in determining profit are not consistent. The monetary units used to record revenues at one point of time are different from those used at another point of time. Costs and expenses are likewise valued in terms of monetary units which differ from one another, and also differ from the units used to measure revenue items. In these circumstances accounting profit does not measure current income. For purposes of policy-making in the firm it is the latter concept which is important. Current income is relevant, for example, in deciding upon changes in total output and the product composition of output. Preoccupation with accounting profit rather than current income not only tends to distort resource allocation but in addition changes the pattern of income distribution. Management should also have regard to current income, and not accounting profit, when considering policies affecting the financial stability of the enterprise.

The second defect of accounting profit as a measure of business surplus is that it fails to maintain the real value of the capital of the enterprise during a period of rising prices. Adherence to historical money costs means that the money capital contributed by shareholders is preserved as a result of the profit measurement process, but in times of inflation this original money capital will not command the same volume of stocks and fixed assets. This is the 'capital erosion' effect of conventional accounting procedures in times of rising prices. It may be possible to augment shareholders' funds by retaining portion of the profits in the company, but this will not be easy when taxation, dividends and indirectly wages are all related to the level of accounting profits. Unless profits can be retained the enterprise will become short of liquid funds or undercapitalized, and fresh capital will have to be raised to maintain the same volume of physical assets. Because this undercapitalization occurs as a result of conventional accounting procedures, management may not become aware of its existence until the financial position of the enterprise has been seriously weakened. In the initial stages of inflation many firms finance the replacement of stocks and fixed assets at higher prices by increasing short-term indebtedness. As a result their financial stability is undermined.

FINANCIAL STABILITY

The financial stability of a company depends first on the maintenance of a satisfactory relation between short-term assets and short-term liabilities, and secondly on the maintenance of a satisfactory relation between borrowed funds and shareholders' funds. The first relationship measures the short-term financial position of the company, and is usually expressed as the 'working capital ratio', that is, the ratio of current assets to current liabilities. However, because stocks will probably be difficult to realize in a time of financial crisis, it seems safer to use the ratio of quick assets (i.e. current assets other than stocks) to current liabilities as a measure of liquidity or short-term financial stability. Short-term financial safety requires that a company's quick assets should be sufficient to meet all the liabilities that may have to be satisfied on demand.

The relationship between borrowed funds and shareholders' funds, sometimes called the 'gearing ratio', gives some indication of the long-term financial position of a company. The size of the gearing ratio should be related to the degree of risk attaching to the enterprise. However, for any given company the higher the gearing ratio the more likely it is that the company will fail to survive a prolonged recession. The gearing ratio cannot be considered in isolation from the company's asset structure and its short-term financial position. In general, financial safety requires that increases in the value of stocks or fixed assets should be accompanied by such reductions in the gearing ratio as will maintain the liquidity position of the company. Unfortunately there is an inherent tendency for traditional accounting methods, based as they are on the monetary assumption, to produce both short-term and long-term financial instability.

ACCOUNTING PROFIT AND CURRENT INCOME

Despite the limitations imposed by the monetary assumption, accounting profit cannot be wholly discarded as a measure of business surplus. Its particular merit is that it is largely an objective measure derived by reference to actual transactions as they affect an enterprise, and the recording of these transactions on an historical basis means that accounting profit is largely factual or descriptive. While accounting profit must for these reasons be retained, a second concept of business surplus is required for purposes of policy-making. This is the concept of current income referred to above.

We have seen that accounting profit for a particular period is the difference between historical costs and revenues, it being assumed that all changes in the value of money may be ignored. We define current income for a particular period as the difference between costs and revenues, all expressed in current prices of the accounting period. For accounting purposes most items of revenue and cost are automatically expressed in prices of the current period; hence the cause of differences between accounting profit and current income can be narrowed down to the difference in the prices used to value items carried forward from one accounting period to another. The accounting theory of profit measurement requires these items to be valued in terms of historical prices, i.e. the prices of past periods, whereas to determine current income it is necessary that they be valued in terms of prices of the current period.

Certain items brought forward from past periods, such as prepaid and accrued expenses, revenue received in advance and accrued revenue, are so insignificant that for practical purposes they may be ignored. In any case these items usually represent money claims not affected by price changes. This leaves two major items of cost, depreciation of fixed assets and the opening stock element in cost of goods sold, which for accounting profit purposes are recorded in terms of prices appropriate to past accounting periods, but which should be valued on the basis of current prices in order to measure current income.

ACCOUNTING FOR DEPRECIATION

Depreciation as an accounting concept may be defined as the value, in terms of the original money cost, of that part of a fixed asset which is used up in producing revenue during a particular period. It is an expense related to the original money cost of the asset, not an allocation of revenue or profit to provide funds for the replacement of the asset. As a result of the profit measurement process the original money investment in the enterprise is maintained intact. In measuring current income, on the other hand, depreciation may be defined as the current cost of using fixed assets in producing revenue during the period. The current cost may be estimated by reference to the current replacement value of the asset.[1]

If the rate of depreciation conforms with the physical rate of deterioration or using up of a fixed asset, and if prices are stable, the accounting allowance for depreciation equals the current cost of using the asset. In times of rising (or falling) prices the depreciation charge needs to be related to the asset's current replacement cost in order to approximate the current

---

[1] The current replacement value may be taken to mean the current cost of an identical asset, if available, or if that is not available, the cost of an asset capable of achieving similar performance.

cost of using it over the given period. It is often argued that the periodic cost of using a fixed asset is determined only by its historical cost, since this is the only paid-out cost which the firm must bear. Where the enterprise has the alternative of using the asset itself or hiring it to other users, to take one example, this paid-out or original cost is irrelevant; the relevant cost concept is the alternative or opportunity cost, measured by the revenue forgone in using the asset as opposed to hiring it to other users. This opportunity cost will reflect the asset's current replacement cost. A similar argument applies when the company may sell the asset as an alternative to using it. This is one of the most powerful arguments in support of the use of current replacement cost as opposed to historical cost, and one with which economists have long been familiar. It is strange that it has received so little attention in discussion on this problem.[1] Ideally, the depreciation charge should maintain intact the real capital resources, or productive capacity of the enterprise. However, this may be difficult if prices rise continually over a number of accounting periods. To maintain the real value of capital it would be necessary to base depreciation on the replacement value at the time when the asset is replaced. This is not known in advance, and the only practicable alternative would be to make the depreciation charge in any period equal to the sum of the following:

(*a*) depreciation based on the current replacement value of the asset; plus

(*b*) the amount by which previous depreciation charges, based on the lower replacement values prevailing in previous periods, have been insufficient to provide for replacement on the basis of current values.

It is clear that the adjustment for (*b*), if included in the depreciation charge for the current period, would seriously distort the measurement of current income, which by definition equals current revenue minus current costs and expenses. For purposes of estimating current income, therefore, depreciation must be restricted to (*a*) above; that is, it must be based solely on the current replacement value of the asset. Current replacement value for this purpose may be defined as the average replacement value prevailing during the current accounting period, and during a period of steadily rising prices this will be approximately the same as the replacement value half-way through the accounting period. Depreciation calculated on this basis will not necessarily provide sufficient funds for replacement of the asset if its replacement value continues to rise in the future. It may approximately do so if it is invested in assets which themselves rise in value with

---

[1] This point is ignored, for example, in an excellent survey by A. R. Prest of the arguments for and against the use of replacement cost. See 'Replacement Cost Depreciation', *Accounting Research*, 1 (July 1950), 385 [reprinted as chapter 20 below].

the inflation, and not held in the form of cash balances and money claims. This applies, for example, if the business has a number of fixed assets, a constant proportion of which fall due for replacement each year.[1]

The relationship between accounting depreciation and current depreciation may be expressed in the following way:

$$\frac{\text{Current}}{\text{depreciation}} = \frac{\text{Accounting}}{\text{depreciation}} \times \frac{\text{Current replacement value of asset}}{\text{Original cost of asset}}.$$

This relationship holds irrespective of the method of estimating accounting depreciation. A simple example will make this clear. Let us suppose that an asset costs £100, and that on the basis of its estimated working life it is decided to write it off over ten years by equal instalments.[2] Accounting depreciation will therefore be recorded at £10 during each year of the asset's life. If the asset's average replacement value rises to £110 in Year 1 and to £120 in Year 2, the current cost of using the asset in Year 1 and Year 2 may be represented by $(\frac{1}{10} \times £110) = £11$, and $(\frac{1}{10} \times £120) = £12$ respectively.

The formula given above yields the same results:

$$\text{Year 1} \quad £10 \times \tfrac{110}{100} = £11,$$
$$\text{Year 2} \quad £10 \times \tfrac{120}{100} = £12.$$

If the annual depreciation charge is based on the reducing balance of the asset (i.e its original cost less previous depreciation) the same relationship holds. Let us suppose that an asset costs £100, and that it is decided to write it off by making a depreciation charge of 10 per cent p.a. on the reducing balance of the asset. With this method it will take longer than ten years to write off the asset, but we may assume that the estimated life and estimated scrap value of the asset have been taken into account in determining the percentage to be applied. Accounting depreciation under these circumstances will be 10 per cent of £100, or £10, in Year 1; 10 per cent of (£100 − £10), or £9, in Year 2; and so on. If the average replacement value rises to £110 in Year 1 and to £120 in Year 2, the current cost of using the asset in those years may be represented by 10 per cent of £110, or £11, in Year 1; and by 10 per cent of (£120 *minus* 10 per cent of £120), or £10·8, in Year 2. The general formula gives the same results:

$$\text{Year 1} \quad £10 \times \tfrac{110}{100} = £11,$$
$$\text{Year 2} \quad £9 \times \tfrac{120}{100} = £10·8.$$

[1] See Prest, p. 297 below, for an explanation of this point.
[2] This method is described as the fixed-instalment or straight-line method of recording depreciation.

The difference between current and accounting depreciation measures the accounting effect of inflation on company profits that results from rising replacement costs of fixed assets. This effect will be carried into the balance-sheet, thereby affecting the financial structure of the company, unless special steps are taken to offset it by transferring an equivalent portion of the accounting profit to the company's reserves.

ACCOUNTING FOR STOCKS

The other important item of cost, valued for accounting purposes in the prices of a past period, is the opening stock element in cost of goods sold. The accounting concept of cost of goods sold is defined as the original money cost of stocks brought forward from previous accounting periods, *plus* the original money cost of stocks purchased during the period, *minus* the original money cost of stocks carried forward into the subsequent accounting period. Cost of goods sold is deducted from the realized sales revenue in order to determine gross profit on trading, from which net accounting profit is derived by deducting other expenses.

To measure current income, on the other hand, it is necessary to determine the current cost of goods sold. Strictly speaking, this involves ascertaining the current cost price of each item of stock sold, at the time it is sold. However, this is not practicable, and we adopt the simplifying assumption that price changes within an accounting period may be ignored.[1] Current cost of goods sold may then be defined as opening stocks *plus* purchases *minus* closing stocks, all valued at current prices of the period. Since purchases and closing stocks are automatically valued at prices of the current period,[2] it is only necessary to determine the current cost of opening stocks. Current cost for this purpose is taken to be the recorded cost price of stocks most recently acquired. Opening stocks are thus revalued in the same prices as closing stocks, and the appreciation of stock values resulting from the inflationary rise in prices is recorded as a cost, and excluded from current income.

The difference between accounting cost of goods sold and current cost of goods sold is thus measured by the difference between (*a*) opening stocks valued at original prices and (*b*) opening stocks valued at current prices, i.e. the same prices used to value closing stocks. The effect of this in relation to the measurement of profit or income may be seen from the following

---

[1] This assumption means that we ignore price changes in respect of any physical changes in stocks during the period. The practical significance of this omission is small.

[2] It is implicitly assumed that stocks have turned over at least once during the year. We are indebted to Professor H. W. Arndt for this point.

simple example. Suppose a trading enterprise, maintaining a constant physical volume of stocks, has a series of monthly sales revenues:

$$r_1, r_2, r_3, \ldots, r_{12}$$

and a series of monthly stock purchases:

$$c_0, c_1, c_2, \ldots, c_{12}$$

where the subscripts in each case designate the month when the revenue was received or the cost incurred. The cost c_0 can be visualized as the original cost of stocks purchased in month o. These are the closing stocks in month o, the opening stocks in month 1, and are absorbed into cost when sold in that month. Accounting profit for the year is calculated as the sum of the differences $r_1 - c_0, r_2 - c_1, r_3 - c_2 \ldots, r_{12} - c_{11}$. Current income on the other hand is the sum of the differences $r_1 - c_1, r_2 - c_2, \ldots, r_{12} - c_{12}$. The difference between accounting profit and current income is thus $c_{12} - c_0$. This is the difference between opening stocks valued at closing prices of the current period and the same volume of stocks valued at original prices.

The same idea may be expressed in language more familiar to the accountant. Let us assume that a company commences an accounting period on 1 January with 1,000 units of stock, valued at the original cost of £1,000. During the year 1,000 units are sold for £1,150 and another 1,000 units are bought for £1,100, so that 1,000 units of stock are carried forward into the subsequent accounting period. What is the difference between accounting cost of goods sold and current cost of goods sold? For purposes of simplicity it is assumed that cost is interpreted on the first-in-first-out basis.[1]

To determine accounting profit, cost of goods sold is calculated from historical values:

	£	£
Sales		1,150
less Cost of goods sold		
Opening stock	1,000	
Purchases	1,100	
	2,100	
less Closing stock	1,100	
		1,000
Accounting gross profit		£150

However, the current cost of goods sold is £1,100, and the current gross income is calculated as follows:

	£
Sales	1,150
less Current cost of goods sold	1,100
Current gross income	£50

[1] This method of valuation assumes that stocks are disposed of in the order in which they have been acquired.

Alternatively, current gross income can be calculated by ascertaining the current cost of each element in cost of goods sold:

	£	£
Sales		1,150
less Current cost of goods sold		
Opening stock	1,100	
Purchases	1,100	
	2,200	
less Closing stock	1,100	
		1,100
Current gross income		£50

The difference between accounting and current cost of goods sold, also the difference between accounting gross profit and current gross income, is simply the difference between opening stock at current prices (£1,100) and opening stock at original prices (£1,000), i.e. £100. Another method of calculating current gross income would be to deduct this increment in stock values, or stock appreciation as it is called, from accounting gross profit:

	£	£
Accounting gross profit		150
less Stock appreciation		
Opening stock at current prices	1,100	
less Opening stock at original prices	1,000	
		100
Current gross income		£50

This increment in stock values provides us with a measure of the accounting effect of inflation on company profits (and hence on capital structures) arising out of conventional methods of calculating cost of goods sold. In the above illustration, for example, accounting gross profit may be analysed into two elements: (*a*) the trading profit arising out of sales, £50; and (*b*) the stock appreciation, £100. If the whole accounting profit were to be disbursed in the form of taxes and dividends, the capital structure of the enterprise would inevitably be weakened. Additional funds to the value of £100 would be required from some source to finance the holding of stocks at the higher prices. Unfortunately, it is only too often the case that these funds are obtained by increasing short-term liabilities or reducing liquid assets. This means that the ratio of quick assets to current liabilities is reduced, thereby indicating a weakening of the financial position of the enterprise. To avoid this situation it would be necessary to transfer portion of accounting profits, corresponding to the stock appreciation, to the company's reserves.

Mathews and Grant

THE ACCOUNTING EFFECTS OF INFLATION

To the extent that stocks and fixed assets are brought into account on the basis of original prices instead of current prices which are higher, accounting profit exceeds current income. Using the stock and the fixed instalment depreciation figures from the above examples, and assuming the same changes in current replacement values noted on pp. 208–10, it is possible to measure explicitly the accounting effects of inflation on the profits and financial structure of a company. For this purpose the following additional data are introduced. The only expenses are assumed to be wages, £20. The assets of the company at 1 January, in addition to stocks £1,000, and fixed assets £100, are cash and debtors £1,000; and the liabilities of the enterprise (creditors) at 1 January are £1,000. Accounting profit may be calculated as follows:

	£	£
Sales		1,150
less Cost of goods sold		
Opening stocks	1,000	
Purchases	1,100	
	2,100	
less Closing stocks	1,100	
		1,000
Accounting gross profit		150
less Expenses		
Wages	20	
Depreciation	10	
		30
Accounting net profit		£120

Having determined accounting profit, it is possible to estimate current income by making the following adjustments:

	£	£
Accounting net profit		120
less Adjustments to bring historical costs up to current costs		
Stock appreciation	100	
Depreciation	1	
		101
Current net income		£19

The adjustments necessary to convert accounting profit to current income measure the accounting effects of inflation on company profits.

If the whole of the accounting net profit is distributed, the balance-sheet at the end of the year may be contrasted with the opening balance-sheet as follows.

Assets		1 Jan.		31 Dec.
	£	£	£	£
Cash and debtors		1,000		1,010
Stocks (at historical cost)		1,000		1,100
Fixed assets (at cost)	100		100	
less Provision for depreciation	—		10	
		100		90
		2,100		2,200
less Liabilities				
Creditors		1,000		1,100
Shareholders' funds		£1,100		£1,100

This example illustrates the balance-sheet effect in relation only to the replacement of stocks at higher prices, but similar results would appear when the fixed assets have to be replaced. The example demonstrates that under the conditions postulated inflation has promoted undercapitalization, since the shareholders' funds at the end of the year no longer finance the same volume of stocks and fixed assets. The increase in stock values has been financed by borrowing from creditors. Alternatively it could have been financed by running down cash or debtors. In either event the short-term financial position of the company has obviously deteriorated. To avoid this result it is necessary to base distribution policy on current income rather than accounting profit. This involves transferring to reserves the amounts of the adjustments made in respect of stocks and depreciation of fixed assets. If this is done, and if the whole of current income is distributed, the balance-sheets at 1 January and 31 December will compare as follows:

Assets		1 Jan.		31 Dec.	
	£	£	£	£	£
Cash and debtors				1,000	1,011
Stocks (at historical cost)		1,000		1,100	
Fixed assets (at cost)	100		100		
less Provision for depreciation	—		10		
		100		90	
		2,100		2,201	
less Liabilities					
Creditors		1,000		1,000	
Shareholders' funds					
Capital	1,100		1,100		
Reserves	—		101		
		1,100		1,201	

Under these circumstances shareholders' funds again finance the whole of stocks and fixed assets, so that the opening position has been restored. The additional £11 in cash and debtors represents the funds made available from the depreciation allowance and the depreciation adjustment, and held, for example, against replacement of the fixed assets. The accounting effects of inflation have therefore been avoided.

The essential differences between the alternative distribution policies, one based on accounting profit and the other on current income, may be illustrated by comparative sources and uses statements:

	Distribution based on	
	Accounting profit	Current income
Sources of funds	£	£
Retained profits (increases in reserves)	—	101
Depreciation allowances	10	10
Reduction in working capital (other than stocks)	90	—
	£100	£111
Uses of funds		
Increase in stock values	100	100
Increase in working capital (other than stocks)	—	11
	£100	£111

To offset the accounting effects of inflation on both profits and financial structures it is therefore necessary to make the adjustments to accounting profits in respect of stocks and depreciation of fixed assets. The adjustments outlined constitute a general procedure for measuring the accounting effects of inflation on profits and financial structures.

15 The accountant's contribution to the trade cycle

by W. T. Baxter*

I

It is well known that a changing price-level can have curious effects on the accountant's figures for profit. A firm's inputs are normally charged in accounts at their acquisition price; and so—unless inputs and sale are simultaneous—the cost side of the income account must reflect an earlier price-level than the revenue side. When prices are rising, accounting costs are measured in £s that are older and worth more than the revenue £s, and so profit looks big; when prices are falling, accounting cost is relatively high and profit small. Perhaps we may—rather tendentiously—use the phrase 'time-lag error' to describe the gap between accounting profit and the profit figure that would be found if inputs were measured in the same £s as sales (i.e if the capital sunk in the inputs were restated, with the aid of a general index, in £s of the corresponding revenue dates); this latter profit may be called 'corrected profit'.

The time-lag error has been widely advertised during the post-war inflation, mainly by businessmen who feel their taxes—based on accounting profit—to be unreasonably high. But it has other aspects of importance, and notably its possible influence on the trade cycle.[1] Its alternate over- and understatement of profit seems likely to affect the size of the cycle— in particular, through its influence on mental attitudes, on the supply of credit, and on policies of consumption and investment. If this is true, the accountant must bear some of the blame for the major social ills of boom and slump.

2

There are accordingly plausible grounds for agreeing with the critics who accuse the accountant of *intensifying* an established upswing and downswing. Little has however been said so far about the *timing* of the accounting error. This point seems to demand study—since, if the error's size alters

---

[1] The trade-cycle effects have been explored, in particular, by Mr K. Lacey—see for example his *Profit Measurement and Price Changes* (London, 1952). They are also discussed in G. Haberler, *Prosperity and Depression* (New York, 1952), pp. 49–50; Erich Schiff, *Kapitalbildung und Kapitalaufzehrung im Konjunkturverlauf* (Vienna, 1933), pp. 113–34; and Delmas D. Ray, *Accounting and Business Fluctuations* (Gainsville, 1960).
* Professor of Accounting, London School of Economics and Political Science.

W. T. Baxter

much at critical points in the cycle, its impact is likely to be greater. Accordingly, the main part of this article is concerned with timing, and the more general argument is touched on only at the end.

To understand the timing issue, one must scrutinize the error's anatomy. The error arises if, during a time of changing prices, the date of buying an input differs from the sale date of the resultant output. By far the most usual inputs with such a time-lag are plant and materials (though sometimes the cost side of a capital-gain calculation may give scope for a large error); and so the suspect costs are those under the heads of depreciation and 'cost of goods sold'.

The error can in theory be measured easily enough. Let H be the historical cost, c the reading on an appropriate general price index[1] at the date of the input's purchase, and s the reading at sales date. ('Appropriate' obviously evades a lot of questions; but, difficult and relevant though these are in other contexts, they scarcely seem to demand answer for the narrow purpose of our present study.) Then the accounting error is $H\{(s/c) - 1\}$—i.e. this is the amount by which accounting profit exceeds corrected profit.

3

Let us take depreciation first. Here H is that part of the asset's historical cost which is shown as an expense in the income account—and is, by the straight-line method, a constant quantity in all years of the asset's life; c is the price-index of the asset's acquisition date, and therefore is also a constant throughout the asset's life; and s varies each year, since it represents the price-level at which output is sold during that year, i.e. it is the average of the price-indices at the dates of all sale transactions, weighted by their sizes. The error, $H\{(s/c) - 1\}$, thus alters in step with the price-level.

It may be helpful to get a rough picture of the error's results through diagrams. In Diagram 1 (a), we assume that plant is bought at the start of Year 1, when prices have just reached the median level of an imaginary cycle, and the index stands at, say, 100. Their course is then assumed to follow the unbroken curve AB. The annual depreciation charge in accounts,

---

[1] Some advocates of reform favour use of a *special* index—of price change for the given type of input—rather than a *general* index; the special index method is geared to the notion of maintaining physical capital, and is often called replacement cost accounting. This argument over type of index is hardly relevant to the trade cycle, and much space would be needed to set out my views clearly. In brief, these are that the special index gives the better figures for assets in a balance sheet or inputs in budgets for management decision, but the general index is satisfactory for income measurement. My reason is that, if the income statement raised the historical cost of input with the special index, then it should raise the revenue side too—by the input's real appreciation (historical cost multiplied by the excess of the special over the general index); if both sides of the account are raised in this way, the net effect on profit is the same as if the general index is applied to cost.

being always based on original cost, will follow the straight line *CD*. The vertical distance between *AB* and *CD* suggests the error's movements from year to year. When *s* exceeds 100 (as in the years till the end of 6), historical cost is less than its equivalent in terms of current £s—for instance, at the middle of Year 1, by *AC*; accordingly the accounts now understate costs and overstate profit. The error's contribution to the profit figures for each year may perhaps be best shown by the height of the pillars at

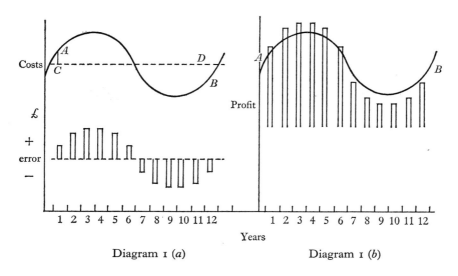

Diagram 1 (*a*)　　　　　Diagram 1 (*b*)

the foot of the diagram. Those pillars which rise above zero indicate an increase in the accounting profits; such an increase is found during all years with prices above 100. In Years 7 to 12 prices are below 100, and the error depresses low profits still further. The positive and negative errors will—in these improbably symmetrical conditions—exactly cancel over all the years of the cycle.

We can speak of the error's effect on *costs* with some certainty. However, its size relative to *profit* must vary from firm to firm. Depreciation may be large or small compared with profit; thus the error will be negligible where a firm owns little plant, but substantial in, for example, an electric power undertaking. Again, the given firm's profits may not move in proportion to price changes. But perhaps we are not over-simplifying too grossly if we picture corrected profits as following some such cyclical pattern as the curve *AB* in Diagram 1(*b*), while the accounting profits have an accentuated rhythm rather like that of the pillars. The error extends the pillars in good years, and cuts them short in bad years.

Had the plant not been bought at the mid-point of price movements, the error's pattern in Diagram 1(*a*) would not be symmetrical about *CD*, and the positive and negative errors would be less likely to cancel over the years. For instance, if the plant is bought at a price peak (as in Diagram 2), *s* will never rise above *c*, cost will always be overstated, and accounting

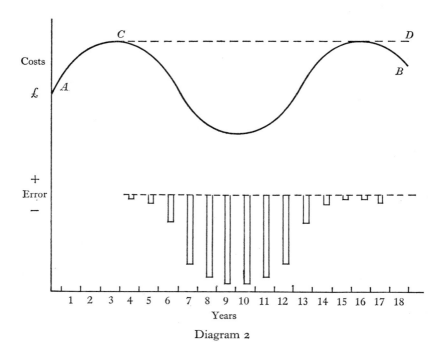

Diagram 2

profit will in consequence always be less than corrected profit; here the firm tends to set aside more depreciation funds than will be needed for replacing the plant at anything less than peak prices (if the price of this asset moves in much the same way as the general index), and so expands its real capital unwittingly. At the other extreme, where plant is bought at the nadir, accounting profit will tend in all years to be swollen because of the skimpy depreciation policy, and the firm may have to borrow extra funds at replacement day. In short, whatever the time of purchase, the error fluctuates in direct response to the price cycles.

If prices become stable (at any level other than that of purchase date), the error will persist but will no longer fluctuate. Suppose for instance that prices rise from year 0 (purchase date of an asset) to year 8, and then become steady, i.e. follow the curve *AB* in Diagram 3. As the pillars show, the error rises too, and then becomes stable in years 8–11. (It is odd that the agitation for tax concessions to offset the error dies down when a price rise is checked. A substantial depreciation error can persist thereafter—as the diagram indicates; firms with old plants have still as strong a case as ever for tax concessions.) But when the asset's life ends (Year 11), the

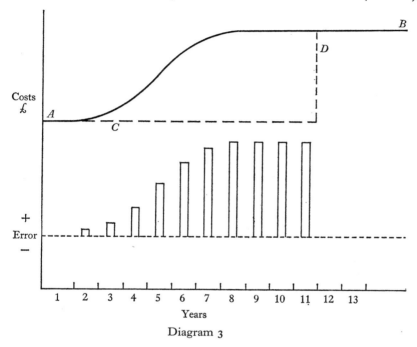

Diagram 3

understated cost goes too; probably the asset will now be replaced at increased prices, so that depreciation cost tends to rise abruptly (perhaps like *CD*); at any rate, the error disappears. The process of asset renewal must always limit the error's size, and make its description less simple.

After allowing for all such qualifications, however, it seems probable that movements of the depreciation error will approximately coincide—in timing and pattern—with movements in prices, and perhaps with those in correct profits. Thus the error is likely to serve the cycle as a prompt and often powerful ally by intensifying the prevailing mood.

4

In any discussion on stocks, one should keep in mind the form of calculation through which stocks alter accounting profit. A merchant's trading account (for, say, a calendar year during which the general index and the special index for these stocks both move from 100 to 120) may be set out somewhat like this:

	£		£
Cost of goods sold		Sales (1,000 units)	1,456
Opening stock (400 units)	380		
Purchases (1,000 units)	1,090		
	1,470		
Less Closing stock (400 units)	460		
Total	1,010		
Gross profit	446		
	£1,456		£1,456

The important things to note are that closing stock must mainly consist (on the usual first-in-first-out assumptions) of those purchases which were made in the later months of the trading year; and that, by subtracting closing stock at its purchase cost, we deprive these later purchases of all influence over this year's trading cost and profit. The 'cost of goods sold' might be set out more clearly by showing the various blocks of purchases in detail—for example, as under (supposing that extra stocks are built up in the spring to meet a sales peak in the autumn):

	Physical units		Average price	£	
Cost of goods sold					
Opening stock (bought July–					
December, last year, at index 95)	400		0·95		380
Purchases:					
January–June (this year)	600		1·05	630	
July–December (this year)	400		1·15	460	
	1,000			1,090	
Less Closing stock (bought July–					
December, this year)	400		1·15	460	
		600			630
Total		1,000	1·01		£1,010

Thus the £1,010 charged against the sales of the current accounting year is the cost of purchases made between the preceding July and the current June. As we have seen, the error is produced by this discrepancy between 'cost year' and 'revenue year'. (Where the units of stock are not homogeneous, some items will not be sold in strict order, and the figures will overlap a trifle; but the argument is not changed substantially.)

If the average general index for the above sales—weighted to allow for their pattern over the year—is 112, then the error is:

	£
Historical costs, at actual purchase prices, July–June—	
1,000 units at average index 101	1,010
£1,010 re-expressed in sales £s—1,000 units at average index 112	1,120
Error	£110

To correct the accounts, one might introduce an 'inflation charge' of £110, thus:

Cost of goods sold:	£
Historical	1,010
Inflation charge	110
Cost in current £s	1,120
Sales	1,456
Corrected profit	£336

The phrases 'inflation charge' and 'cost in current £s' are appropriate if the size of the charge is based on the general index (when this varies from the special index). Corrected profit is then the surplus after the purchasing power of the opening capital has been maintained. Use of the special index instead would result in the maintenance of physical capital— surely a less defensible aim. It will be seen that 'inventory profit' is scarcely a happy phrase with which to label the error. 'Inventory profit' is commonly used to mean the increase in the value of the given physical quantity of stock between opening and closing dates. Here this increase is only £80, whereas the error is £110. The £30 difference is due to the summer peak of stocks, which is not reflected in the opening and closing inventories. To take the extreme case, if a firm buys all its goods in the spring and sells out completely in the autumn, the error could be substantial, and yet opening and closing stocks, and presumably 'inventory profit', are zero. Many firms must have seasonal peaks in physical stock—e.g. after harvest or before the Christmas rush—even if it sinks back to its opening level at the end of the accounting year (often a date chosen just because stock is low then). Thus inventory profit will tend to be less than the error. Another cause of divergence—ignored in our simple example—is real change in stock value, i.e. discrepancies between movements in the general index and a special (stock) index. However, where physical changes and real price changes are not large, inventory profit may give a handy approximation to the error.[1]

---

[1] If general and special indices coincide, the stock error can be expanded to

$$s(B+P-E)-(Bb+Pp-Ee),$$

where B, P, and E are respectively the physical quantities of stock-at-beginning, purchases, and stock-at-end; and the average prices at which each of these quantities was

How does $H\{(s/c)-\mathrm{1}\}$ behave when we pass from plant to stocks? For most firms, the annual cost-of-goods-sold is a far bigger figure than depreciation, and so H is normally substantial. s is again the cost index at the weighted average date of the year's sale transactions—say, mid-year. c is the cost index at the weighted average date of the year's purchases of

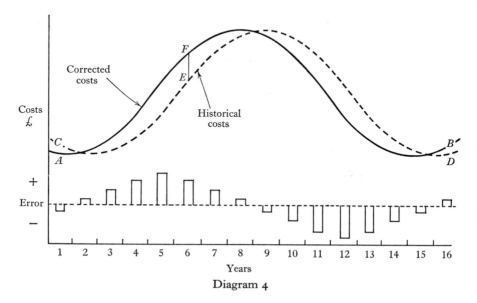

Diagram 4

stock. Because stock is normally sold within a few months from its purchase date, the cost of a batch of goods is not likely to be split up and charged against several years (as is the case with the cost of a machine), and so c is here a far more volatile quantity than when it relates to depreciation, and usually follows hard on the heels of s. The stock error may thus have a pattern quite different from the depreciation error.[1]

In Diagram 4, the curve AB represents the corrected cost of goods; it can also represent purchases if physical activity is constant. The curve for historical cost can be got simply by shifting AB to the right, by the space

bought—at beginning, purchase, replacement, and end—are respectively b, p, s, and e. If stock is kept constant, however, $B = E$. Then the error is $sP-(Bb+Pp-Be)$; whereas inventory profit is $B(e-b)$. Error and inventory profit are equal if $P(s-p) = \mathrm{o}$. This condition is satisfied if $s = p$, which is perhaps most likely to be the case where goods are replaced at the same time as they are sold, i.e. where stock is always constant.

[1] The difference would shrink if the life of the machine is short; for instance, where the life is only two years, c tends to catch up with s in a series of biennial hops. Where a range of long-lived machines is being steadily replaced throughout the cycle, c (based on the total cost of all the machines) tends to move at a sedate pace.

of the turnover period; it is shown as the dotted line *CD*. The error is due to the vertical distance between the two curves (e.g. in Year 6, *EF*). The total contribution by the error to each year's accounting profit may again be shown by the heights of the pillars at the foot of the diagram. In years of rising prices, $H\{(s/c)-1\}$ is positive and so the error restrains accounting cost and thereby lifts accounting profit. But, in contrast to the depreciation error, the stock error shrinks to *nil* when prices cease to rise (in a time not longer than the turnover period, as in the months about the end of Year 8); on the down-grade, the stock error is negative.

The stock error can move from its positive to its negative extremes either slowly or abruptly, according to the shape of the price curve. (With the depreciation error, this transition lasts from peak to trough.) Our curve in Diagram 4 rises at its fastest in Year 5, thereafter rises at a decelerating pace, and culminates in a gently rounded peak; corresponding movements take place on the down-grade. With such a 'sine-shaped' curve the error's upward trend is reversed (in Year 6) well before the peak is reached, at the point where *AB* and *CD* cease to run parallel and start to converge; and the new trend lasts till the curves are once more parallel (Year 12). When the price curve has a less rounded peak and trough than in our example, the error's trend will change more steeply. In extreme cases, where the curve culminates in a sharply pointed peak (i.e. where *AB* and *CD* are triangular or cusp-shaped) the transition from positive to negative is violent, and its damaging impact is concentrated on the period just after the peak; similarly a pointed trough may herald a sudden improvement in the accounts.

Thus the stock error seems likely to have earlier and more dramatic tendencies than the depreciation error. But whether the stock error in fact has noteworthy effects will depend on both the price curve and the methods of the firm in question. The impact on costs is the more likely to be big if any of the following conditions obtain:

(*a*) the price change is violent;

(*b*) the turnover period is long;

(*c*) material costs form a large part of total costs (e.g. where the firm deals in commodities).

Yet another condition must obtain before the change in costs is likely to have a dramatic effect on profit trends: the rate of gross profit is low.

Given suitable circumstances, accounting profit might be distorted as in Diagram 5. Here we assume the course of the price-index—shown as the unbroken curve *AB*—and the error to be the same as in Diagram 4; we also assume that corrected profit follows much the same pattern as the price-index. The height of the pillar for, say, Year 6 shows the correct profit for 6 (from the base up to the line *AB*) and then the error (from *AB* upwards—corresponding to the distance *EF* in Diagram 4). The dotted lines at the top of pillars 8–15 will be explained later.

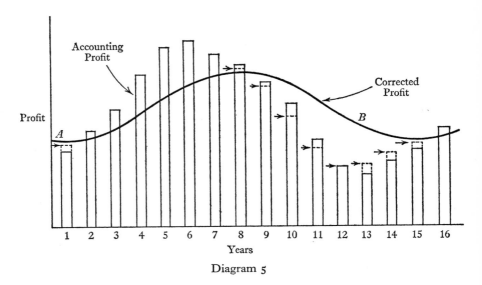

Diagram 5

In this particular example, accounting profit starts to wane in Year 7, although the peak in prices and profits is not reached till the middle of 8. The circumstances needed to bring about this premature fall are:

(1) As the summit draws near, prices must rise at a decelerating pace. And

(2) The error must be large relative to profit, so that the decline in the error outweighs the rise in correct profit (see Years 7 and 8).

Condition (1), it seems reasonable to think, will obtain not infrequently. Condition (2) depends on the factors listed in the preceding paragraph; however, even if these are not strong enough to make accounting profit fall, they will certainly damp its upward trend.

On the down-grade of prices, our example reflects the same forces. In Years 14 and 15, because prices are falling at a decelerating rate, the negative error moves so fast to zero that it raises accounting profit (though the nadir of prices and correct profits is not reached till the mid-point of Year 15).

If our diagram correctly shows a tendency found in a fairly large number of firms, then surely the error should play a bigger part than it has done hitherto in discussions of the trade cycle. Just as the 'accelerator' is said to alter the demand for capital goods before general activity reaches its turning points—perhaps thereby causing the general crisis or the recovery—so accounting may alter mental attitudes prematurely, and thus contribute to changes in activity.

It is not hard to find flaws in our diagram. In real life, the pattern of profits will doubtless not correspond closely to our curves. One reason is that firms are unlikely to carry constant physical stocks throughout the cycle; if stocks are reduced in the slump, the error will also dwindle at that stage,[1] i.e. will do less to encourage recovery than it did to bring about the fall. Another factor that may vary physically is sales; if, as seems likely, these grow in the boom and fall off in the slump, they will probably give a bias to corrected profit; but the error would not seem to be affected thereby (save by any consequential changes in physical stock). Again, selling prices may not be adjusted promptly when general prices change; in particular, they may lag because the firm fixes them at historical cost plus a constant mark-up—a policy likely to cause further changes in customers' demand, and so in physical volume of sales. Thus we cannot—till many empirical studies have been made—treat any abstract diagram as an accurate photo of profit patterns. The case against conventional accounting is not so clear as Diagram 5 suggests.

However, though we cannot say that accounting profit always anticipates the general trend of the cycle, we can hardly avoid the conclusion that accounting cost may have a most unfortunate influence at crucial points in the cycle. Just when confidence begins to waver, delayed high charges for goods find their way into the accounts; the stock error has its least desirable effect at the worst possible moment.

5

Another practice of accountants may aggravate the stock error's effects at the start of the down-grade. Our discussion has so far supposed that the closing stock figure in income accounts is always valued at historical cost (found on first-in-first-out assumptions), i.e. at the price level of a date preceding the end of the business year (on average, by half the turnover period). In fact, this may well not be true on the down-grade of prices. For then a normal practice of accountants is to abandon historical cost, in accordance with the over-riding rule of 'Cost or Market, whichever is the lower'. For example, if the business year ends on 31 December and stocks

---

[1] In general, stocks appear to have a cycle very like the sales cycle, but with a narrower amplitude and a lag of some months (the number of months varying with different types of stock)—M. Abramovitz, *Inventories and Business Cycles* (New York, 1950), pp. 93–6, 144–5.

were bought in August, the unsold items will at closing stocktaking be valued at the market prices of 31 December if these are lower than the cost prices of August. The precise interpretation of this cautious formula varies from firm to firm; but its general effect must on the down-grade be to depress stock values to below their historical cost.

This rule leaves our argument unchanged so far as the up-grade of prices goes. But in the year during which prices start to fall, market is substituted in the income account for the (higher) cost value of closing stock, though opening stock is—somewhat inconsistently—still shown at cost. Thus a smaller sum is deducted from the charges, and accounting cost is increased; in effect, the cost-of-goods-sold is loaded with both (i) the usual error for the year, and (ii) a bit of next year's error. Profit, under this double assault, may well fall abruptly. In Diagram 5, the decrease is shown by the dotted line cutting off the top of the profit column for Year 8.

In subsequent years of the down-grade, both opening and closing stocks are valued at market. This pessimism at both ends of the income account puts a brake on the rule's working. The net effect of the rule seems to be substantially as follows (assuming physical quantity of stock does not change violently, and the price curve is free from kinks). Profit is reduced so long as the price curve is falling at an accelerating pace (Years 8 to 11 in Diagram 5). If the pace becomes constant—for the space of an accounting year plus the preceding months during which opening stock is bought—profit is the same as if the rule did not exist (Year 12 in Diagram 5). If prices fall at a decelerating pace (Years 13 and 14), the rule actually makes accounting profit less conservative, and so speeds up the illusion of recovery—and perhaps the actual recovery too.[1] In the last year of the rule's

---

[1] Let E and B be the physical quantities of stock-at-end and -at-beginning in an income account for Year n. Let c_n and c_{n-1} be the prices at which stock-at-end and -at-beginning are valued at cost, and m_n and m_{n-1} at market. Then the inclusion of stocks in a revenue account raises profit by:

If stocks are valued at cost $\qquad\qquad\qquad\qquad Ec_n - Bc_{n-1}$

If stocks are valued at market $\qquad\qquad\qquad\quad Em_n - Bm_{n-1}$

So switching from cost to market depresses profit by $\quad E(c_n - m_n) - B(c_{n-1} - m_{n-1}).$

Suppose that physical stock is constant. Then E and B are equal: therefore the rule depresses profit if $(c_n - m_n)$ exceeds $(c_{n-1} - m_{n-1})$—i.e. if prices are falling at an accelerating pace; the rule raises profit if $(c_n - m_n)$ is less than $(c_{n-1} - m_{n-1})$; and it has no effect when $(c_n - m_n)$ equals $(c_{n-1} - m_{n-1})$.

If E and B are not equal, the pattern is modified. For example, if physical stocks sink during a depression and so E is less than B, the switch from cost to market depresses profit less than if stocks are constant; the dotted lines in Diagram 5 become higher in all years. But the modification seems to be slight unless physical stock changes to a remarkable degree.

operation, closing stock reverts to cost, but opening stock stays at market, and so still keeps down the cost-of-goods-sold, and raises accounting profit.

Thus, on the down-grade, the rule's effect is to reinforce the error, and to make accounting profit respond more skittishly to each change in price trends.

6

There are, however, important counter-arguments to the whole case against the error. These have been skilfully marshalled by Professor Delmas D. Ray.[1]

The main way in which the error could affect activity is generally thought to be via investment: cheerful profits give a rosy tinge to expectations, and thus tempt business men to expand. Professor Ray is unimpressed by this view. Relying largely on surveys of the reasons given by business men for their decisions, he suggests that technological needs for improved plant are a main cause of investment; and that, in cases where such needs are not predominant, the sales outlook rather than profit is what counts. He also reminds us that large firms may be less influenced by a wish to maximize profits than we formerly supposed; and that, even if business men want to invest more, their cash position puts a ceiling on their programmes. He adds that knowledge of the accounting error is now widespread and must tend to offset the error's impact, while high tax payments—based on the error—damp down the elation of the boom.

The error may also affect activity by changing the pattern of saving. During booms, exaggerated profit figures make management less tough with unions and shareholders, and these more importunate towards management. Thus potential savings of companies are distributed. The recipients are unlikely to save all this extra income, and so total saving sinks, and expenditure on consumption rises. The accountant's error may at such times increase demand in a second way: because he underestimates the firm's costs, its sales prices will be too low (on the assumption that many sale prices are based on cost-plus, and thus lag behind input prices). Professor Ray sets out these suggestions methodically, but then for the most part rejects them. Wages are raised mainly because of other factors (e.g. cost of living); dividends are limited by the cash balance, and for the most part go to a wealthy few whose consumption will not be changed much; the influence of cost-plus is weakening, and anyway its 'cost' is increasingly current rather than historical.

Professor Ray's criticisms are certainly persuasive enough to make one think with much more care about this aspect of accounting. But I doubt whether he has established a good case. Some of his minor contentions scarcely carry conviction. For instance, it is doubtless true that many

[1] *Op. cit.*

business men know that the accounting error exists, but probably few of them could say how big it is in their own firm and what are its results on the other figures; and the accounts are written and authenticated, whereas one's reservations are mental and untested. Total income from private firms is roughly as big as that from incorporated firms, so presumably erroneous figures can have a considerable influence through unsophisticated owner-managers if not through directors and wealthy shareholders. Again, the size of a firm's cash balance admittedly has some restraining effect on investment and dividends; but inflated profits make it easy to raise more money by new issues and bank loans (and the small investor or local banker is most unlikely to question the accountant's golden figures). Tax may indeed diminish the error's effects. But tax is not assessed at 100 per cent; some part of a profit increase remains to cheer the appropriation account. Again, the date at which tax is paid may seem remote—under British tax law, a spurt in profit is unlikely to raise tax payments until a year or more has passed, and so there is a long period before the cash is drained off.

However, the essence of the matter presumably is that so much depends on expectations, and no one (not even the decision-maker himself, in his most self-analytical mood) can measure the various influences that colour expectations. Professor Ray may conceivably be right in saying that accounting errors have scant effect. But the opposite view seems more plausible. Surely the business man's outlook must be influenced by marked changes in his profit figures—particularly when these synchronize with similar changes in the figures of most other firms, in dividend payments, and in quotations for company securities (sometimes highly geared). It is hard to believe that such repeated changes in so many quarters do not affect his views of the future and his willingness to shoulder risk.

7

To sum up. The accountant's devotion to historical data begets cost figures that lag behind prices. In consequence, accounting profits overpaint the state of trade. The depreciation error tends to make the high-price years (both before and after the peak) look better, and the low-price years look worse. The stock error lifts profits instead in all years when prices are rising, and depresses profit throughout the down-grade; it seems likely to exaggerate the rate of change in the trend of correct profit, and may on occasion produce falling profit figures before the price rise has ended, and rising figures before recovery has begun.[1]

[1] Where accounts include both depreciating assets and stocks, the errors' *composite* pattern will probably look rather like the pillars in Diagram 4, but the depreciation error will

It is reasonable to conclude that an error so widespread and so emphatic in its rhythm must have a considerable influence on business sentiment. In particular, the error is likely to strengthen the factors that link demand and investment (after a time-lag) with the rate of change of prices; it probably introduces a relationship analogous to the accelerator principle. If this argument is correct, the error must reduce the stability of the economy.[1]

Reform of accounting thus seems to offer one of the simplest and safest devices by which we might try to combat instability. Many business men have already suggested that the Chancellor should permit the use of current costs in computing their firms' taxable profit. By granting this privilege, on condition that the same costs are also used in the ordinary income accounts, reform could be achieved with little opposition from business.

push each pillar somewhat to the right (so that the highest error is nearer to, but still comes before, the price peak); the depreciation error will also give the accounting-cost curve a greater amplitude than the replacement-cost curve.

[1] See A. W. Phillips, 'Stabilisation Policy in a Closed Economy', *Economic Journal* (June 1954), pp. 311–14, for a mathematical demonstration that, when one component of demand depends on the rate of change of prices, the system is made less stable. The accounting error is presumably one of the reasons for such dependence.

16 Income and the valuation of stock-in-trade

by H. C. Edey*

It is possible to make at least one valid generalization on the valuation of stock-in-trade for income tax purposes. It is that no consistent principle can be found in the Income Tax Acts or in the decisions of the courts as a firm foundation for the valuation. It is true that it has long been generally accepted, on the basis of judicial decision, that in ascertaining the *quantum* of profit to be assessed to tax the following fundamental rule is to be observed: namely, that the ordinary principles of commercial accounting are to be followed except to the extent that they conflict with specific rules laid down by the Income Tax Acts. Reference was again made to this general principle in *Ostime* v. *Duple Motor Bodies, Ltd.*,[1] though it is not clear how far the decision in that case must be regarded as depending thereon. The Income Tax Acts are silent with respect to the method to be followed in stock valuation in a continuing business; hence, applying the principle, one might expect that any generally accepted accounting practice with respect to stock valuation would be acceptable. But *Patrick* v. *Broadstone Mills, Ltd*,[2] and *Minister of National Revenue* v. *Anaconda American Brass, Ltd.*[3] show that the courts are not prepared to follow this principle in all cases, and are prepared to reject methods of stock valuation that are fully acceptable for the purposes, for example, of presentation of accounts under the Companies Act.

It is, perhaps, worthwhile looking a little more deeply into the possible reason for this contradiction. At the root of the problem lies the fact that the Income Tax Acts do not provide a general definition of taxable income or profit. It might seem at first that this apparent deficiency in the statutes is not significant. If, indeed, one believed that annual profit was in some sense an objective phenomenon, one might well take the view that careful search was bound to disclose the appropriate formula, in the same way that a scientist by looking deeply into the nature of the real world is able sometimes to produce a formula describing, within very close approximations, a natural phenomenon, such as the propagation of

---

[1] [1961] 1 W.L.R. 739 (H.L.).   [2] [1954] 1 All E.R. 163 (C.A.).
[3] [1956] A.C. 85 (P.C.).

---

* Professor of Accounting, London School of Economics and Political Science.

light. But this is not the case. The terms 'profit' and 'income' are in fact used in our language to indicate a whole range of ideas. It is true that all these ideas have something in common. They all imply in some sense the receipt of a benefit during a given period of time. But there the common element ends. In fact, the systematic use of any one of the many concepts of income arises only because thereby a convenient social purpose is fulfilled; and for different social purposes it is convenient to use different concepts. There is no reason why the concept used for a particular social purpose should necessarily be appropriate for a different purpose.

If, for example, we look at the measurement of income as it is carried out by accountants for the purpose of company accounts, or for the purpose of a partnership deed, we are, I think, bound to conclude that the measurement is in essence designed to assist a group of parties, bound together in mutual contract, to settle, on a fairly rough and ready, approximate basis, on the division among themselves of certain accretions to their joint property. People come together in companies or partnerships with the object of receiving some return over and above the ultimate recovery of their initial investment. It became apparent long ago that in deciding how much of the return should be shared out annually among company members or partners, it was necessary to have a set of rules that could be applied without undue expenditure of time, and without an unduly subjective element of estimation entering into the calculation. In this way the ordinary rules of profit calculation, used in the financial accounts of companies and partnerships, arose. They were, and are, rough rules; but they are useful as a basis of a year-to-year sharing-out operation and, if all parties concerned accept them, no serious injustice is done. When the introduction of general limited liability gave rise to the need for company law to set some limit on distributions to owners, in the interests of creditors, the courts decided that the same rules, applied in good faith, were appropriate for the determination of divisible profit.

It has always been realized that these rules are too rough to allow their use on occasions when substantial changes in the relative rights of partners or company members are about to take place. When a partnership dissolves, a new partner is taken, or a change is made in the profit-sharing ratios of partners, the balance-sheet valuations (changes in which, over time, measure the accounting profit, after adjustment for capital paid in or withdrawn) are reconsidered carefully with an eye to the economic reality, as reflected by the market.[1] Similarly, when company reconstructions take place that in-

---

[1] It is true that partnership agreements may lay down a rule-of-thumb method for the valuation of partnership interests on such occasions. This does not affect the principle that different rules of balance-sheet valuation are appropriate.

volve a change in the relative rights of shareholders, it is usual to seek the advice of financial experts who are likely to be familiar with the current market situation. The asset valuations which arose from the applications of normal accounting principles are abandoned on such occasions.

It follows from this that the profit which would be obtained in the case of a partnership by taking the difference between the initial investment and the final valuation on dissolution (after allowing as usual for additional money paid in or money withdrawn by the owners) might be a different figure from that shown by summing over the same period the annual balances on the profit and loss accounts as prepared on conventional accounting lines. The same kind of comparison can be made by considering the life of a company from its beginning to the date of liquidation or of radical reconstruction accompanied by a revaluation of all the assets. This in itself is sufficient evidence for the proposition that profit, and the corresponding valuations that are made in the process of profit calculation, must be defined in relation to the particular purpose for which the figures are required.

Even from the point of view of management accounting, there is no clear-cut concept of profit available. It is common to use the profit figure that emerges from application of one or other of the normal accounting conventions as a rough measure of management success. But one has only to look carefully at how such figures are computed to realize with what caution they should be used. The major defect from which all the conventional figures suffer is their inability to reflect changes in the business potential. From the point of view of the management of the business, or the shareholders whom that management represents, the value of the business interest usually depends upon the ability of the directors to make good use in the future of the assets at their disposal. Any important change in their capacity to produce a future flow of dividends is of fundamental significance in assessing the value of the shareholders' interest. A succession of good reported profits, accompanied by good dividends, over a period of years, counts for nothing with respect to the future of the company if the factors that produced these dividends have disappeared. Yet these changes in the capacity of a business to produce dividends—which we may call changes in the goodwill of the business—are incapable of measurement by the normal accounting processes. It is inevitable that this should be so, for their assessment is subjective, and requires a good knowledge of the business itself.

There are other defects in the use of conventional accounting profit calculations for management purposes that can be eliminated by taking a wider view of the conventions that are appropriate. For example, a particular business might have improved its economic position as the result of a shrewd policy of investment in such fixed assets as freehold land and buildings. If it was not the main function of the company to trade in real property, the normal conventions would prevent the rise in value of its fixed assets from appearing as part of the profit reported to the shareholders. Yet from the point of view of the assessment of the management's competence, and from the point of view of judging whether the company has been successful, the calculation of the profit resulting from the rise in value of these assets may be of critical significance. Here there is a clear divergence between what may be of relevance for management purposes—which may justify the preparation of special management accounts—and what is regarded as appropriate for company law purposes.

If we consider stock-in-trade, it is the saleable value of the stock at any given time that is really significant from the point of view of the management; some accounts prepared for management purposes do in fact record stock on the basis of its expected realizable value. Here again there is a difference between the information appropriate for management and what would normally be regarded as appropriate for company accounts.

When we turn to the income tax law we are concerned, not with the guidance of management, or the relations of joint or common owners among themselves, but with the relation between, on the one hand, a group of people having a legal interest in any accretions to the value of their business and, on the other hand, the State, which has a special interest in the same accretions. The interest of the State is based on the need to achieve certain social ends by economic means. If a tax system could be constructed *de novo*, one might therefore expect the calculation of profit or income for the purpose of that system to be based on a careful consideration of these ends and means. For example, the effect of applying tax to profit as defined in a certain way would, one might expect, be considered with respect to its effect on business activity, on investment, on employment, and so on. There is no reason to suppose that the concept of profit arrived at after such consideration would necessarily coincide with that adopted by accountants for the rough-and-ready purposes discussed above, even assuming that the latter could be subsumed under one general principle (which is far from being the case in fact).

However, the Income Tax Acts were not constructed in this way. They are based essentially on an Act of 1803, and their present structure owes its existence in the main to a continued process of expedient tinkering over a period of more than a century. It is true that the rules have been reviewed by more than one Royal Commission. But this has not yet led to the laying down of any general principle for the calculation of profit or income. In fact, the Revenue authorities, and the courts, have in the main been prepared to accept the rule-of-thumb approximations used by accountants for other purposes. This approach is embodied in the general principle of law referred to above, to which lip-service is still paid, namely, that the ordinary principles of commercial accounting shall prevail except when the statutes say otherwise. The principle actually applied is however rather different. It is that the ordinary principles of commercial accounting shall be applied except when the courts decide that they shall not be applied (as in the *Broadstone Mills* case). That the courts would interfere with the ordinary principles of commercial accounting was inevitable. A rough-and-ready method of sharing property accretions may work well enough when all those concerned have roughly the same interest. But when one-half of those concerned stand to gain heavily if the share of the other half can be reduced by altering the rules, something must give way.

It might be assumed that the divergence between accounting profit calculated for the purpose of income taxation and accounting profit calculated for other purposes, though important, need not prevent the development of a general principle of profit calculation for tax purposes and hence of a principle for the valuation, *inter alia*, of stock-in-trade. It might be argued that behind the normal accounting principles which are acceptable for tax purposes, there can be found some rather general, yet definable and usable, concept of profit that has emerged over a long period as the result of the combination of accounting practice with judicial decisions. The difficulty of finding such a concept can be illustrated by considering normal accounting practice.

If we look at an accounting textbook, we find that the usual definition of profit runs in some such terms as: 'That surplus which remains after the maintenance of capital.' But we are seldom told what is meant by the 'capital' that is to be maintained; and consideration shows the difficulty of attaching a precise significance to the term. It might, for example, be argued that by capital here is meant the total capital value of the whole undertaking as measured in an actual or hypothetical market. To take this as the criterion, however, would imply that each year a reassessment was made of the capital value at the beginning of the year, so that at the end of the year one could determine how much cash could be distributed without encroaching upon that capital value. This clearly is not a procedure that is normally envisaged in business.

An alternative definition might be that capital is the sum of the individual market values of the separate assets, less the amount of the liabilities. But again it is common knowledge that no attempt is made annually to re-appraise the values of all the individual assets of a business in order to decide how much of that value has been maintained at the end of the year. The practical difficulties of doing so are obvious.

It might be said that the maintenance of capital implies the maintenance of a given level of dividend-paying capacity. If this were so, the annual assessment of profit would require an assessment of this capacity, implying the preparation of a financial budget for the future. Clearly this procedure does not form part of the conventional profit calculation.

It cannot be argued consistently that maintenance of capital should be defined by assessing capital through the application of normal accounting conventions, since this leads us into a circular argument. If we are trying to establish the rationale of the conventions by establishing some principle for which they are valid—and this is our object here—we cannot invoke these conventions for the purpose of setting up the principle.

I have so far refrained from mentioning the rather special problem to which so much attention has been devoted in recent years, the question of whether capital, however it be defined, should be measured in terms of constant price levels or in money terms. This, too, is a matter that must be considered if a principle is to be established.

Thus however hard we try we are unable to detect a usable general principle of profit calculation lying behind the existing conventional accounting procedures, other than the principle of reasonable compromise in given circumstances.[1] I do not think that the figures produced by applying decisions of the Revenue court to these procedures fit any better into a standard theory that can be used to settle all problems. This follows from the fact that, on the whole, the decisions of the courts, for example on matters of stock valuation, have merely specified the set of existing accounting conventions that are to be used in particular cases, or in general.

Dicta in the *Duple* case give perhaps the best rationale of the procedure that is in fact followed by the court. Lord Reid said: 'The most I can do is to try to bring common sense to bear on the elements of the problem involved,' and again: 'It appears to me that we must...simply ask what, in all the circumstances of a particular business, is a figure which fairly represents the cost of stock-in-trade and work in progress.'[2] If we apply these two statements, we arrive at the kind of rough and ready approach which

[1] It may be said that even a reasonable compromise implies the existence of some concept of profit and capital maintenance, however vaguely formulated. This is no doubt true. I would find it difficult, however, to detect behind the day-to-day approximations used in practice, any general idea of profit more definite than that of a very rough indicator of the rise in the dividend-earning capacity and therefore, in given circumstances, in the marketable capital value of the undertaking (after allowing for money paid in or withdrawn by the owners during the period), so far as this is due to the normal business activities and, in particular, excluding changes in the value of the undertaking's goodwill, or arising from changes in the general level of interest rates and yields or in the dividend yield thought appropriate for the undertaking in question.

[2] At pp. 753 and 754–5.

235

has always, I believe, lain at the base of the ordinary accounting conventions, namely, that of setting up a working rule that will be acceptable to both parties. Since, however, in matters of taxation the interests of the two parties conflict greatly, and since businesses differ a great deal, some form of arbitration procedure is necessary; this is provided by the Revenue court. Whatever may be the legal point of view, this seems to be a reasonable interpretation of the function of the court with respect to many of the problems of profit measurement. If this is so, we cannot expect the decisions of the court to be susceptible to over-close logical analysis in the sense that it is possible to fit them into any but the most general pattern of principle.

Nor does it necessarily follow that if any general principle of income determination were to be laid down by Parliament, this would in fact lead to a better situation; for despite what I have said above about piecemeal tinkering with the statutes, an attempt to set up a profit concept otherwise than by what would amount to piecemeal improvement of existing rules (e.g. by making available again the use of L.I.F.O.) would lead to difficulties. For example, Parliament might decide that, since the object of income tax is to assess burden broadly in terms of capacity to pay, profit should be calculated by making an overall valuation of all assets annually and taking the difference between the valuations at the beginning and end of the year (allowing as usual for capital movements into and out of the business). This would be a consistent and theoretically clear-cut principle; but that it would raise very severe difficulties in practical application I need hardly point out. Any general principle of this type seems likely to lead to similar difficulties.

It may be argued that to accept Lord Reid's dicta as the basis for the determination of income is inconsistent with a view of income tax legislation as an economic tool to be used in such a way as will best further national economic policy. To measure income on the basis of arriving at a reasonable and fair method suitable for a given type of business is not, it may be said, to adopt the criterion of national economic good. There are perhaps two points to be considered here. In the first place, and this is perhaps the more important point, it is doubtful, for the reason already given, whether any approach is possible that does not leave a good deal of freedom to the courts in interpretation unless a set of rules for profit calculation is laid down so rigid that it is likely to produce serious and irremediable injustice in certain contexts. Even so, such a set of rules would have to be formulated in very great detail, to meet most foreseeable situations, and would be likely to impose, in certain cases at least, a considerable amount of clerical work that would not otherwise be undertaken. It is most desirable that businesses should not be prevented from calculating such magnitudes as the value of stock-in-trade on the basis of the rule-of-thumb or statistical estimates that they think most useful for management purposes. An income tax system that forces a business to invest heavily in clerical labour or mechanical and electronic aids merely in order to achieve apparent precision in tax assessment is undesirable; quite enough national resources are already absorbed in the administration of the tax system. The possibility of reasonable flexibility provided by the present system of judicial decision is less restrictive in fact, from a point of view of economic policy, than might at first be thought. Judicial decisions which conflict seriously with broad economic aims can be set aside on an *ad hoc* basis in the annual Finance Act. This process of marginal adjustment is not necessarily a bad one, provided it is subject to continuing critical review and provided access to the courts is not too expensive: desiderata to which, perhaps, more attention should be paid. It is, however, desirable in the interests of clear thought that the fundamental basis of the judicial decisions should be made clear. There can be little advantage in claiming that, for example, the assessment of the appropriate value of stock-in-trade is based on some fundamental principle of 'accuracy' in profit determination (as was suggested in the *Broadstone Mills* case). It is better to make it clear that the judges, when they decide these cases, are being asked to make an assessment in the terms described by Lord Reid.

When it is accepted that the estimation of profit for income tax purposes is not a matter of adhering to a clear-cut principle, but rather of arriving at a reasonable compromise, the various methods of valuation that are used in practice appear in a new light. It becomes apparent that arguments about the relevance of including an element of overhead cost in the stock valuation, of including factory overhead cost but not general administrative overhead cost, and so on, are sterile. None of the different methods that are acceptable at present to the Inland Revenue, or that are acceptable if the Recommendations of the Council of the Institute of Chartered Accountants are taken as the criterion, conform to any particular principle other than that (with one limited exception—the valuation in certain limited cases of stock at net selling price) they all produce a 'cost' figure below the ultimate expected selling price and to this extent conform to the principle that 'profit shall not be realized'. They are all reasonable, but arbitrary, practical approximations.

If this is recognized, life becomes much easier. Instead of the search for some absolute criterion, stock valuation can be based for management purposes on that criterion which seems most likely to provide the management with useful information—which may differ for different managements;

and if this particular criterion conflicts, as it occasionally may, with those set by the income tax law or by the practice of company accounting, an alternative calculation can be made for the purpose of these on the basis of the simplest and cheapest procedure available.[1]

[1] So far as financial accounting is concerned I would, however, argue that the rules of stock valuation at present acceptable to most accountants are in fact unduly restrictive. It may well be that in certain instances better information would be given to shareholders if stock were valued on a realization basis at all times. However, this is a controversial matter and has no direct relevance to income tax problems.

17 Lower of cost and market in Britain and the United States: an historical survey[1]

by R. H. Parker

INTRODUCTION

> And out of olde bokes, in good feith,
> Cometh al this newe science that men lere.
>
> Geoffrey Chaucer (1340?–1400),
> *The Parlement of Foules*

The subject of this article is the history of the lower of cost and market rule of inventory valuation in Britain and the United States. It is not possible to discuss the rule in isolation either from the progress of financial accounting theory in general, or from the economic environment in which practitioners of and writers on accounting have found themselves. Some attention has therefore been given to these matters.

All periods were once 'modern' and any terminal point in an historical essay is clearly arbitrary. Convenience demands, however, that one stops somewhere. The approximate date chosen for this essay is 1947, the year of publication of *Research Bulletin*, no. 29 on 'Inventory Pricing' by the American Institute of Accountants (as it then was). The first recommendation on the valuation of stock-in-trade of the Institute of Chartered Accountants in England and Wales was published two years before, in 1945.

The general plan of the paper is as follows:

(*a*) a short discussion of the views of early British writers;

(*b*) a longer look at the environment in which the lower of cost and market rule became traditional in nineteenth-century England;

(*c*) a discussion of the influence, especially in the 1920s, of American academic accountants, especially Hatfield, Littleton and Paton;

(*d*) rules of inventory valuation as part of the search for accounting

---

[1] This article is partly based on a paper, 'Inventory Valuation Historically Considered', presented at the May 1965 meeting of the Australasian Association of University Teachers of Accounting held at the University of Melbourne. The author is greatly indebted for the comments, constructive and destructive, on this previous paper, of Mr R. P. Brooker of the University of Sydney and Dr H. P. Hain of the University of Melbourne.

R. H. Parker

principles of the 1930s and 1940s, mainly in the United States, but with some reference to British developments; and

(e) some conclusions which can be drawn from an historical survey of the lower of cost and market rule of inventory valuation.

EARLY BRITISH WRITERS ON INVENTORY VALUATION

What's aught, but as 'tis valued?

William Shakespeare, *Troilus and Cressida*, II. ii.

There was once a happy time when inventory valuation was not at all important. Raymond de Roover has written of medieval accounting that, 'Because of the prevalence of venturing, inventory valuation did not constitute a problem, and medieval merchants were accustomed to open a separate account for each lot or consignment and to leave it open until everything was sold.'[1]

It is not surprising therefore that there are very few references to the problem in early accounting literature. The early texts are in any case usually severely practical and devoid of theoretical discussion.

James Peele, citizen and salter of London, clerk of Christ's Hospital and father of George Peele the dramatist, wrote two books on double-entry bookkeeping in the second half of the sixteenth century. In his second book, *The Pathwaye to Perfectnes*...(1569), there is an account of 'fine clothes' in which 'there is founde at takinge of the ballaunce, to remayne vii. clothes'. These are 'valewed as the cost'.[2]

[1] R. de Roover, 'The Development of Accounting Prior to Luca Pacioli according to the Account-books of Medieval Merchants', in A. C. Littleton and B. S. Yamey (eds.), *Studies in the History of Accounting* (London, 1956), p. 117. In his recent book on the Medici bank, Professor de Roover writes: 'It was the custom of merchants, including the Medici, to open a separate account for each venture or lot of merchandise. Such accounts were charged with all outlays, costs, and expenses and credited with proceeds from sales. The difference remaining after conclusion of the venture represented either a profit or a loss and was usually transferred to an account, "Profit and Loss on Merchandise" (*Avanzi e disavanzi di mercatantie*). Thus profits from trade and from exchange were kept separate. This system of opening a separate account to each venture has been called "venture accounting" by accountants and students of the history of accounting. Venture accounting eliminated the necessity of inventory valuation. Since records were generally kept according to this system, it is not surprising that Luca Pacioli and other early authors on bookkeeping are silent on the subject of inventory valuation. Neither is it surprising that there are no examples of it in the Medici records.' *The Rise and Decline of the Medici Bank 1397–1494* (Cambridge, Mass., 1963), p. 148.

[2] *The Pathwaye to Perfectnes*...(1569). The paragraph in which these phrases occur is reprinted in B. S. Yamey, H. C. Edey and H. W. Thomson, *Accounting in England and Scotland: 1543–1800* (London, 1963), p. 108. For a reprint in modern spelling of Peele's first book (1553) see P. Kats, 'James Peele's "Maner and Fourme"', *The Accountant*, LXXXII (1930), 41–4, 88–91, 119–22. For further information on Peele and his books

240

John Smythe, a sixteenth-century Bristol merchant, usually valued his stock at cost but sometimes he used a possible selling price and sometimes something between the two.[1]

In 1741 Richard Hayes stated that it was 'usual with Merchants, when they make a general Balance of their Books, to value the goods that they have by them at the Market Price they then go at, at the Time of their balancing; but some do not so'. His own advice is valuation at the market price 'or at the Price they cost you'.[2] In the same year John Mair recommended valuation 'at the prime Cost'. Alexander Malcolm (1731) preferred cost to using 'the current Rates' of goods since 'it seems more reasonable to value them as they cost you; for otherwise you bring in Gain or Loss into your Accounts, which has not yet actually happened, and may, perhaps not happen'.[3]

Robert Hamilton (1743–1829), who was Professor of Natural Philosophy and later Professor of Mathematics at the University of Aberdeen, claimed in 1788:

It is much more proper to value the goods on hand in conformity to the current prices, than at prime cost: For the design of affixing any value is to point out the gain or loss; and the gain is in reality obtained so soon as the prices rise, or the loss suffered as soon as they fall.[4]

The most complete discussion of the rule before the nineteenth century is to be found in a book by the French writer Jacques Savary (1622–90).[5]

see: Yamey, Edey and Thomson, *op. cit.* pp. 162–6; C. Gordon, 'The First English Books on Bookkeeping', *Accounting Research*, v (1954), reprinted in Littleton and Yamey, *op. cit.*; and D. H. Horne, *The Life and Minor Works of George Peele* (New Haven, 1952), chapter 1.

[1] Jean Vanes, 'Sixteenth-Century Accounting. The Ledger of John Smythe, Merchant of Bristol', *The Accountant*, CLVII (1967), 361.

[2] Richard Hayes, *The Gentleman's Complete Book-keeper*...(London, 1741), chapter 8. See Yamey, Edey and Thomson, *op. cit.* p. 116.

[3] John Mair, *Book-keeping Methodiz'd*...(2nd ed. Edinburgh, 1741), p. 77 (see Yamey, Edey and Thomson, *op. cit.* pp. 108–9); Alexander Malcolm, *A Treatise of Book-keeping*... (London, 1731), p. 89, quoted in B. S. Yamey, 'Some Topics in the History of Financial Accounting in England 1500–1900', in W. T. Baxter and S. Davidson, *Studies in Accounting Theory* (2nd ed. London, 1962), p. 35.

[4] R. Hamilton, *An Introduction to Merchandise*...(2nd ed. Edinburgh, 1788), p. 285. This passage is reprinted in Yamey, Edey and Thomson, *op. cit.* p. 123. On Hamilton see D. Murray, *Chapters in the History of Bookkeeping, Accountancy and Commercial Arithmetic* (Glasgow, 1930), p. 49.

[5] On Savary see A. C. Littleton, *Accounting Evolution to 1900* (New York, 1933), p. 152; J.-H. Vlaemminck, *Histoire et Doctrines de la Comptabilité* (Brussels, 1956), pp. 128–30; and R. H. Parker, 'A Note on Savary's *Le Parfait Négociant*', *Journal of Accounting Research*, IV (1966), 260–1.

R. H. Parker

THE RISE OF A PROFESSION

> The whole affairs in bankruptcy have been handed over to an
> ignorant set of men called accountants, which is one of the greatest
> abuses ever introduced into law.
>
> Mr Justice Quain in 1875, quoted in A. H. Woolf,
> *A Short History of Accountants and Accountancy*, p. 177

It is doubtful if the writings dicussed so far have had much influence on
modern accounting theory and practice. The real beginnings of modern
accounting are to be found in the nineteenth century. Some time during
that century the lower of cost and market rule appears to have become
accepted as traditional. In 1862 Sawyer referred to the 'recognized principle
that stock should be valued at cost price (unless depreciated in value) and
that no profit should be estimated unless realized'.[1] George O. May tells
us that the rule was well established when he entered the profession in
England in 1892. He ascribes the rule to 'natural conservatism and a long
period of falling prices'.[2]

One suspects that the conservatism and the falling prices were not unrelated. Was the conservatism of late nineteenth-century accountants really
'natural' or was it a product of their environment? The English accountancy
profession grew up because of the need for accounts and statements of
affairs in connexion with bankruptcies, failures, frauds and disputes. It
was a profession which 'was born through bankruptcies, fed on failures
and frauds, grew on liquidations and graduated through audits'.[3] The
Royal Charter granted on 11 May 1880 to the Institute of Chartered
Accountants in England and Wales contains the following significant
paragraph:

the Profession of Public Accountants in England and Wales is a numerous one
and their functions are of great and increasing importance in respect of their
employment in the capacities of Liquidators acting in the winding-up of companies
and of Receivers under decrees and of Trustees in bankruptcies or arrangements
with creditors and in various positions of trust under Courts of Justice as also in
the auditing of the accounts of public companies and of partnerships and otherwise.

Auditing appears to be almost an afterthought and there is no mention
of taxation, secretarial or management work, none of which was important
at the time.

---

[1] J. Sawyer, *Bookkeeping for the Tanning Trade* (2nd ed. London, 1862), quoted in R. S.
Edwards, 'The Nature and Measurement of Income', *The Accountant* (July–October
1938), reprinted in W. T. Baxter, *Studies in Accounting* (London, 1950), p. 259.

[2] G. O. May, 'Concepts of Business Income and their Implementation', *Quarterly Journal
of Economics*, LXVIII (1954), 16.

[3] H. W. Robinson, *A History of Accountants in Ireland* (Dublin, Institute of Chartered
Accountants in Ireland, 1964), p. 30.

Cost and market in Britain and U.S.A.

It is instructive to look at some figures relating to liquidations, bankruptcies and falling prices. According to H. A. Shannon,[1] 25·6 per cent of the companies formed 1856–65, 30·3 per cent of the companies formed 1866–74 and 33·4 per cent of the companies formed 1875–83 ended in insolvency. For the whole period 1856–83, the average is just over thirty per cent. Of the companies formed 1856–65 half of the liquidations took place within the first six years of existence; of the 1866–74 liquidations half took place within the first five years of existence; of the 1875–83 liquidations half took place within the first four years of existence.[2]

A. H. Woolf, writing in 1912, stated that the Companies Act of 1862 'offered new fields of lucrative employment for accountants and no doubt did much to attract many ambitious young men to seek their fortunes in the profession'. The attraction was section 92 which created the position of Official Liquidator, to which in most cases a professional accountant was appointed. The Act was spoken of as 'the accountant's friend'.[3] The Bankruptcy Act of 1869 abolished Official Assignees in Bankruptcy and provided for the appointment of trustees to distribute the debtor's estate; this also 'brought grist to the accountant's mill' as most of the trustees appointed were professional accountants.[4] The 1883 Act provided for Official Receivers in the place of trustees appointed by the creditors, thus transferring much work away from professional accountants. Nevertheless, the young George O. May, articled to Thomas Andrew of Exeter, 1892–7, was engaged during his articles almost entirely in bankruptcy work.[5]

It has been the aim of the above paragraphs to suggest that the environment in which the English accounting profession was born has much to do with the accountants' conservatism, and does something to explain such rules as lower of cost and market. Their history has filled accountants, as Anthony Sampson has recently written, with 'a vivid sense of disaster'.[6]

The founders of our profession also lived in a period of almost continually falling prices after the boom year of 1873. The Rousseaux overall index illustrates this well (see Table 1).

[1] H. A. Shannon, 'The First Five Thousand Limited Companies and their Duration', *Economic History*, II (1932); H. A. Shannon, 'The Limited Companies of 1866–1883', *Economic History Review*, 1st ser. IV (1933), reprinted in E. M. Carus-Wilson (ed.), *Essays in Economic History*, I (London, 1954). See also D. H. Macgregor, 'Joint Stock Companies and the Risk Factor', *Economic Journal*, XXXIX (1929), and G. Todd, 'Some Aspects of Joint Stock Companies, 1844–1900', *Economic History Review*, 1st ser. IV (1932).

[2] Carus-Wilson (ed.), *op. cit.* p. 387.

[3] A. H. Woolf, *A Short History of Accountants and Accountancy* (London, 1912), p. 176.

[4] Woolf, *op. cit.* p. 177.

[5] P. Grady (ed.), *Memoirs and Accounting Thought of George O. May* (New York, 1962), p. 10.

[6] *Anatomy of Britain Today* (London, 1965), p. 525.

TABLE I. *Rousseaux overall price index, 1873–1900*

(Average of 1865 and 1885 = 100)

Year		Year	
1873	127	1887	81
1874	121	1888	84
1875	117	1889	84
1876	115	1890	87
1877	110	1891	86
1878	101	1892	82
1879	98	1893	82
1880	102	1894	74
1881	99	1895	72
1882	101	1896	73
1883	101	1897	74
1884	95	1898	78
1885	88	1899	84
1886	83	1900	91

Source: P. Rousseaux, *Les Mouvements de Fond de l'Economie Anglaise, 1800–1913* (Brussels, 1938), as reported in B. R. Mitchell with the collaboration of P. Deane, *Abstract of British Historical Statistics* (London, 1962), pp. 471–3.

In such an atmosphere conservatism was perhaps inevitable. In the 1880s the lower of cost and market rule was recommended by J. W. Best;[1] and by C. R. Trevor in an address to the Manchester Accountants Students' Society which was described at the time as 'thoroughly orthodox from beginning to end'.[2] In 1904 the rule was endorsed by J. A. Walbank in his *Encyclopedia of Accounting* and by the influential Arthur Lowes Dickinson in a paper read to the first International Congress of Accountants at St Louis.[3]

Dicksee, one of the leading English accountants of his day, has an interesting discussion of the general problem of asset valuation. Since it was the primary object of most ordinary undertakings to continue to carry on operations, 'it is but fair', he wrote, 'that the assets enumerated in a Balance Sheet be valued with that end in view'. He recognized the necessity of valuation on a 'going concern basis', and concluded that 'As a general rule, the amount at which *all* assets are stated in the Balance Sheet—except where a special statutory provision to the contrary obtains—should be regulated by the realizable value of such assets on the basis of a going con-

[1] *Accountants' Journal* (1 January 1886), cited in Littleton, *Accounting Evolution to 1900*, pp. 310, 319.
[2] S. Gilman, *Accounting Concepts of Profit* (New York, 1939), p. 439. Gilman gives a short historical review of the rule on pp. 436–45 of his book.
[3] Gilman, *op. cit.* p. 440.

cern'.[1] On the valuation of 'floating assets' (as they were still called) in particular, he wrote as follows:

It being the essential feature of these assets that the whole aim of the undertaking is to convert—or be able to convert—them into cash at the earliest possible opportunity, the element of immediate realization is an important factor in their value. The only point to remember is that, while a manufacturing profit is earned only when the manufacture is completed, a trading profit is only made when the sale is completed. Neither profit must be anticipated, but it does not appear to be invariably essential that manufacturing profit should be held over until a sale has been effected. It may be added that, where a manufacture consists of several distinct processes, and separate accounts are kept of the manufacturing profit earned under each process, there seems to be no great objection to each process being considered as a separate manufacture, so long, of course, as the goods are readily saleable at the usual trade price.

With regard to what is a trading profit, a most ingenious argument was once advanced by Sir Richard Webster (now Lord Chief Justice) before the late Lord (then Mr Justice) Field (in *Hordern v. Faulkner and others*), in which it was contended that the most scientifically correct method of valuing a stock-in-trade was to take it at selling prices, less the average trade profit; it being suggested that any profit realized in excess of the average was in reality a profit on buying, not on selling; and any profit realized less than the average a corresponding loss on buying. The argument passed muster at the time, appears to be plausible, and indicates a system that would doubtless prove very convenient in practice; but, unless the profit on different articles was very uniform, it would hardly be a safe one to adopt.[2]

Even Garcke and Fells, who were regarded by some as quite radical in their views,[3] were not free from the influence of conservatism:

The right principle undoubtedly is that in a manufacturing business a profit should not be considered to have been made until a sale has been effected, or until a contract for the delivery at a future date of goods already manufactured is entered into. But in the case of the production of raw materials and in those exceptional cases in which the stock of manufactured articles could be put upon the market and realized at their normal price, a modification of this principle would seem to be necessary; for in that case the product is generally saleable at an ascertained market price (or, at any rate, at an approximation to it), and it does not seem incorrect to say that the profit which that price leaves has been earned on the production of the commodity and not on its sale. *Nevertheless, even in this case, it would probably*

---

[1] L. R. Dicksee, *Auditing* (7th ed. London, 1907), pp. 197–201. The first edition was published in 1892. See also his *Advanced Accounting* (5th ed. London, 1916), p. 12 (first published 1903).

[2] *Auditing*, p. 202.

[3] A reviewer of the first edition of their book *Factory Accounts*, the most important early English work on cost accounting, in *The Accountant* of 5 May 1888, described their work as more theoretical than practical, and pedantic and involved 'in the nature of a work on political economy'. See R. S. Edwards, 'Some Notes on the Early Literature and Development of Cost Accounting in Great Britain', *The Accountant*, XCVII (4 September 1937), 313.

in the long run prove to be more judicious to price the commodity in the books at its cost, and only to credit profit and loss account with the profit when sales have been effected.[1]

Garcke and Fells were generally in favour of valuation at the cost of production (excluding 'standing charges' and interest on capital); but they considered that any deterioration undergone by the goods on hand 'should of course, be periodically written off' and stocks which became entirely obsolete 'should be reduced to their scrap value'. 'Old' material on hand should be valued for stock-taking purposes 'at the market value of such old material or at the price at which similar old material was last disposed of, unless such price be higher than the market price, in which case the lower value should be taken'. They were not in favour of constant adjustments for 'fluctuations in the market price'. They did not, however, give unqualified approval to 'inordinate reduction in the value of assets' and they recognized the possibilities of distortion of profits by 'taking undue advantage of facilities and opportunities which may exist at particular periods for writing down the value of assets'.[2]

Garner is of the opinion that, whereas in England practically all authorities recommended the lower of cost and market rule, in the United States it was not very popular at this time, at least so far as factory inventories were concerned.[3] In 1917 the rule was recognized by both the British Board of Inland Revenue and the U.S. Treasury Department.[4]

THE COMING OF THE ACADEMICS

> He was in logick a great Critick,
> Profoundly skill'd in Analytick.
> He could distinguish and divide
> A hair 'twixt South and South-West side:
> On either which he would dispute,
> Confute, change hands, and still confute.
>
> Samuel Butler (1612?–1680), *Hudibras*,
> Part I, Canto I

George O. May, writing in 1954, suggested that inventory accounting in Britain 'may be said to have had virtually no history for the last sixty years'.[5] Things were different in the United States; one reason may be

---

[1] E. Garcke and J. M. Fells, *Factory Accounts* (4th ed. London, 1893), p. 123. (My italics.) The first edition was published in 1887. In the 6th edition (1911) at p. 164, the following sentence is added: 'In the exceptional case of the market price being lower than cost, the market price should be taken'. [2] *Ibid.* pp. 123–4.

[3] S. P. Garner, *Evolution of Cost Accounting to 1925* (Montgomery, Ala., 1954), p. 321.

[4] Gilman, *op. cit.* pp. 436, 442.

[5] G. O. May, 'Concepts of Business Income and their Implementation', *loc. cit.* p. 16.

the very dissimilar ways in which academic accounting developed in the two countries. The importance of the second half of the nineteenth century in the history of accounting has already been stressed. This was also the period in which most of the English civic universities were founded. The new universities were established in busy industrial and commercial centres but accounting failed to take root in them. At the beginning of the twentieth century only Birmingham University, where Dicksee was Professor of Accounting 1902–6, the London School of Economics and Manchester University provided courses in accounting. A number of other universities followed later, but even in the 1960s English academic accounting is still not very well developed by American (or even Australasian) standards.

The American experience has been very different. Joseph Wharton in the deed of gift which made the Wharton School of Finance and Commerce at the University of Pennsylvania in 1881 the first school of business in the United States, specified that the staff should include 'One Professor or Instructor of Accounting or Bookkeeping, to teach the simplest and most practical forms of bookkeeping for housekeepers, for private individuals, for commercial and banking firms, for manufacturing establishments and for banks...'. During the rapid growth of collegiate business schools after the turn of the century every new school, without exception, provided instruction in accounting.[1] Thus, for over half a century now the United States has had a corps of academic accountants whose critical minds have not always been willing to accept such 'traditional' rules as the lower of cost and market.

One important group argued strongly that current market values had no place in accounting. A. C. Littleton of the University of Illinois was probably the most influential exponent of this school of thought.

Assuredly (he wrote in 1929) value is a vague sort of thing, subject to all the whims of mankind and turned by the least wind of altered circumstances...Whereas value is an estimate of what price ought to be, price itself is an established fact... When accounting is loosed from this anchor of fact it is afloat upon a sea of psychological estimates which, however important they may be to business management, are beyond the power of accounting, as such, to express.[2]

Littleton therefore recommended that inventories be consistently and uniformly stated at 'cost', 'accompanied of course by any reserves the management and auditor may agree upon and such supplementary parenthetical figures or footnotes as may be thought necessary to supply bankers and others with the information they expect'.[3]

[1] R. G. Cox, 'Accounting', chapter 14 of F. C. Pierson and others, *The Education of American Businessmen* (New York, 1959), p. 355.
[2] A. C. Littleton, 'Value and Price in Accounting', *Accounting Review*, IV (1929), 149, 150.
[3] *Idem*, 'Value or Cost', *Accounting Review*, X (1935), 272.

R. H. Parker

Not all writers were convinced of the superior objectivity of historical cost. Henry Rand Hatfield (1866–1945) of the University of California was concerned to point out some of the difficulties, especially in the case of self-manufactured articles.[1] Hatfield's views on inventory valuation can be found in his book *Accounting* published in 1927. He found contemporary practice 'curiously inconsistent and illogical',[2] but although he recognized the illogicality of the cost or market rule (he described arguments in favour of it as a 'brilliant...instance of flabby thinking')[3] he recommended only means of improving disclosure. Inventories should be shown in the balance-sheet at cost. Any significant decrease in value should be recognized by debiting profit and loss and crediting an account called allowance for decline in inventory value, the latter to be preferably shown in the balance-sheet as a deduction from the cost figure of the inventory. A marked appreciation in value should be credited not to profit and loss but to a reserve due to marking-up inventory, and the inventory should either be shown in the balance-sheet simply at present market value or as made up of two items, cost price and estimated appreciation, with the sum extended. When the goods are sold, 'so much of the credit to reserve due to marking-up inventory as is properly allocated to the goods sold should be transferred from this reserve to the general profit and loss account or to surplus'.[4]

Acceptance of either the lower of cost and market rule, or of the historical-cost-only doctrine implies acceptance of what we now call the realization convention. A number of academic writers were doubtful of the usefulness of this convention.

Hatfield, characteristically, cut through some of the more confused thinking on the subject:

> It is not always clear...whether a writer considers that there are unrealized as well as realized profits, the latter only being of interest to the accountant, or whether there is no such thing as unrealized profit. If the latter is true the phrase realized profits is evidently tautological. Much of the discussion of realized profits is confused by an uncertainty as to whether the writer...means that profits are not in existence until realized, or that profits are not available for distribution unless they have been realized.[5]

Hatfield noted that probably the most generally accepted view was that profits were realized when a sale was made. This he ascribed largely to the fact that a contract of sale offered 'objective evidence of the correctness of

---

[1] 'A Symposium on Appreciation', *Accounting Review*, V (1930), 14.
[2] H. R. Hatfield, *Accounting* (New York, 1927), p. 99.
[3] *Idem*, 'What is the Matter with Accounting?', *Journal of Accountancy*, XLIV (1927), reprinted in S. A. Zeff and T. F. Keller, *Financial Accounting Theory* (New York, 1964), p. 358.
[4] Hatfield, *Accounting*, pp. 102–3.   [5] *Ibid.* p. 251.

the estimated profit'.[1] He regarded the view that profits are realized when assets appreciate as 'logical' but not generally accepted because of the peculiar conservatism of accountants:

The accountant transcends the conservatism of the proverb, 'Do not count your chickens before they are hatched', saying 'Here are a lot of chickens already safely hatched, but for the love of Mike, use discretion and don't count them all, for perhaps some will die'.[2]

At this point Hatfield gives an example of the odd results of the 'realization convention' which in various guises has been repeated a number of times since.[3]

One may have bought $10,000 Second Liberty Loan bonds and $10,000 Third Liberty Loan bonds when both issues were selling at 90. Somewhat later, when both have risen, he may sell his block of the third issue at par and buy, at the same figure, a block of the second issue. If this has been done, he is conventionally allowed to show that the more recently acquired bonds are worth par and that he has made a 10 point profit in the transaction. But the identical bonds which he bought at an earlier date, in accordance with the [conventional] rule, must still be valued at 90 showing no profit from appreciation.[4]

Hatfield also pointed out that it is inconsistent to deny that profit can exist without a sale and at the same time to recognize accrued interest as income:

The exception in favour of accruing interest probably rests upon the idea that it is definitely calculable, its amount may be accurately determined. But if this is a satisfactory basis of differentiation, the rule for recognizing profits should be expressed in terms of calculability or certainty rather than made dependent upon the existence of a contract.[5]

W. A. Paton of the University of Michigan has never seemed wholly convinced of the 'cost only' doctrine. In 1918 he argued strongly for taking the present market value rather than cost;[6] in 1924 he thought that 'In general, actual cost furnishes the most satisfactory basis or starting point for the pricing of inventory in the trading field';[7] but he could still write

---

[1] *Ibid.* p. 255.
[2] *Ibid.* p. 256 n. 13. The passage is indexed under 'Mike, love of,'!
[3] Paton, in fact, gave a similar example five years before in 1922: W. A. Paton, *Accounting Theory* (New York, 1922; and Chicago, 1962), p. 467 n. 5. Essentially the same point was later made by E. A. Heilman, 'Realized Income', *Accounting Review*, IV (1929), 87; K. MacNeal, 'What's Wrong with Accounting?', *The Nation*, New York (7–14 October 1939), reprinted in Baxter and Davidson, *op. cit.* pp. 60–1; and J. W. Bennett, J. McB. Grant and R. H. Parker, *Topics in Business Finance and Accounting* (Melbourne, 1964), pp. 77–80.
[4] Hatfield, *Accounting*, pp. 256–7.   [5] *Ibid.* p. 257.
[6] W. A. Paton and R. A. Stevenson, *Principles of Accounting* (New York, 1918), p. 468, quoted in Hatfield, *Accounting*, p. 102.
[7] W. A. Paton, *Accounting* (New York, 1924), p. 373.

in 1926 that 'there are undoubtedly many cases in which, everthing taken into account, the most satisfactory method of inventory valuation involves the consistent use of market prices'.[1]

By 1934, however, he could state:

it seems to me that the matter of realizable values as associated with the prepara-tion of a balance sheet has been unduly emphasized in the case of inventories... Inventories, particularly in industrial plants, are substantially nothing more nor less than aggregates of cost factors which will be realized through the completion of the process of production...When it is more fully appreciated that the con-ventional balance sheet includes a mass of costs which have little or no relation to realizable values and immediate liquid position...a long step toward better accounting practice will have been taken.[2]

Littleton, Hatfield and Paton all appeared to be agreed upon one thing: the illogicality and unreasonableness of the cost or market rule. Most academic writers probably agreed with them. DR Scott even went so far as to contribute in 1926 what he termed an obituary notice of the rule. E. J. Filbey, commenting on Scott's paper, claimed, however, that 'the reports of the death of this rule have been greatly exaggerated'.[3]

Filbey was right, of course. Accounting is practice as well as principle, and the practitioners were by no means willing to abandon the rule.

PRACTICE AND PRINCIPLE

> Sir, you are so grossly ignorant of human nature, as not to know that a man may be very sincere in good principles, without having good practice!
>
> Dr Samuel Johnson as reported in James Boswell,
> *Journal of a Tour to the Hebrides*, 25 October 1773

From the early 1930s onwards the accountants of the English-speaking world have increasingly concerned themselves with the search for account-ing 'principles'. Most accountants have been convinced that they exist; but there has been plenty of disagreement about their nature and the way in which they should be found.

It is probably fair to say that practitioners have usually favoured an *inductive* approach, whilst academics have tended to favour a *deductive* approach. Both approaches were tried in the 1930s.

The first use of the phrase 'accepted principles of accounting' and the first attempt at a formal statement of 'accounting principles' are to be

---

[1] *Accounting Review*, I (1926), 30 (part of a comment on a paper by DR Scott).
[2] W. A. Paton, 'Aspects of Asset Valuations', *Accounting Review*, IX (1934), 123–4.
[3] DR Scott, 'Conservatism in Inventory Valuations', *Accounting Review*, I (March 1926), 18, 24.

TABLE 2. *Index of Common Stock Prices (United States)*

All stocks	1926 = 100
1926	100·0
1927	118·3
1928	149·9
1929	190·3
1930	149·8
1931	94·7
1932	48·6
1933	63·0
1934	72·4
1935	78·3
1936	111·0
1937	111·8

Source: United States Bureau of the Census, *Historical Statistics of the United States 1789–1945* (Washington, D.C., 1949), p. 281.

found in the Report dated 22 September 1932 of the American Institute's Special Committee on Co-operation with Stock Exchanges.

The date is of interest. We have already discussed the environment of the English accounting profession during its early years. The environment of the first set of accounting principles may perhaps be best understood by looking at an index of common stock prices (Table 2).

In its Report, the Institute's committee emphasized the need to 'bring about a better recognition by the public of the fact that the balance-sheet of a large modern corporation does not and should not be expected to represent an attempt to show present values of the assets and liabilities of the corporation' and to 'make universal the acceptance by listed corporations of *certain broad principles of accounting which have won fairly general acceptance*'.[1]

It was suggested that in the first instance the broad principles should be few in number. Five principles were set out which the committee thought should 'presumably' be included. The first one is relevant to the present discussion. It states that 'unrealized profit should not be credited to income account...either directly or indirectly'. The committee thought profit should be deemed to be realized 'when a sale in the ordinary course of business is effected'. It was perhaps an augury of the future that there were two qualifications: the collection of the sales price had to be 'reasonably

---

[1] Report of the Special Committee on Co-operation with Stock Exchanges of the American Institute of Accountants to the Committee on Stock List of the New York Stock Exchange, dated 22 September 1932; reprinted in G. O. May, *Financial Accounting* (New York, 1943), pp. 72–85. The quoted passages are from pp. 79 and 80. (My italics.)

assured'; and 'an exception to the general rule may be made in respect of inventories in industries (such as the packing-house industry) in which owing to the impossibility of determining costs it is a trade custom to take inventories at net selling prices, which may exceed cost'.[1] No mention was made of the lower of cost and market rule in the suggested list of principles, but it was mentioned in the Report as 'the most commonly accepted method of stating inventories'.[2]

A further important step in the inductive derivation of principles was the work of T. H. Sanders of the Harvard Graduate School of Business Administration, H. R. Hatfield, and Underhill Moore of the Yale Law School. They were asked by the Haskins & Sells Foundation to 'formulate a code of accounting principles which would be useful in the clarification and improvement of corporate accounting and of financial reports issued to the public'.[3] In their letter of transmittal the three authors noted that since 1933 a large and increasing majority of auditors' certificates were using the terms 'accounting principles' or 'principles of accounting' and that the demand for a statement of accounting principles had become insistent.[4] The report which they produced has been recently described as 'the first relatively complete statement of accounting principles and the only complete statement reflecting the school of thought that accounting principles are found in what accountants do—the school which emphasizes the *accepted* part of "generally accepted accounting principles"'.[5]

There is little doubt about what American accountants were *doing* in the 1930s. Writing in 1939, Gilman commented that the lower of cost and market rule had been so completely accepted that the great majority of all published balance-sheets displayed inventories which had been so valued. Of 197 companies reported in the *N.A.C.A. Bulletin* of 15 March 1937, 172 or over 87 per cent valued raw material inventories at the lower of cost and market.[6] A few years before, a New York court had accepted the rule as 'a correct accounting principle'.[7]

---

[1] G. O. May, *Financial Accounting*, p. 81.

[2] *Ibid.* p. 75. The five suggested principles were (with one addition) adopted as 'rules' by the American Institute in 1934. See *Accounting Research and Terminology Bulletins— Final Edition* (New York, American Institute of Certified Public Accountants, 1961), pp. 11–12.

[3] T. H. Sanders, H. R. Hatfield and U. Moore, *A Statement of Accounting Principles* (New York, American Institute of Accountants, 1938), p. xiii (letter of invitation to the committee).   [4] *Ibid.* p. xv.

[5] R. K. Storey, *The Search for Accounting Principles* (New York, American Institute of Certified Public Accountants, 1964), p. 31.

[6] Gilman, *Accounting Concepts of Profit*, p. 405.

[7] *Irving Trust Co. v Gunder*, 271 N.Y. Supp. 795 (1934). *See* S. I. Simon, 'Cost or Market Before the Bar', *Accounting Review*, XXXI (1956), reprinted in *Accounting and the Law* (Bureau of Economic Research, Rutgers, The State University, 1965) which also refers to other American cases supporting the rule, one as early as 1899.

In their introductory chapter Sanders, Hatfield and Moore pointed out that accounting followed certain conventional procedures. Two very different classes of information were used: first, an historical record of transactions, and secondly, the adjustment of historical amounts to 'something nearer to practical present-day conditions'.[1] The difficulty with views such as these is that almost any valuation practice can be justified. The authors to some extent limited this by favouring conservatism. The sixth in their list of 'General Principles' reads as follows:

The possible extent of unforeseen contingencies of adverse character calls for a generally conservative treatment of items to which judgment must be applied.[2]

The result was a set of principles which, *inter alia*, supported the lower of cost and market rule:

Only income realized by the sale of goods or rendering of service is to be shown in the income statement. Unrealized income should not be recorded,[3] nor utilized to absorb proper charges against earnings...Cost and expenses must include... inventory losses of the period...The proper showing of current assets requires... that the values in general be the lowest of cost, replacement, or realization, as may be applicable for the several items...[4]

In 1936 development of accounting principles and standards became one of the objectives of the American Accounting Association.[5] Its aim was to prepare a statement of accounting principles 'which *might* be adopted as fundamental to sound accounting'.[6] It was recognized that such a statement 'must inevitably embody some conflict with existing accounting practice, since existing practice is in conflict with itself at a hundred points'.[7]

The Association's 'Tentative Statement of Accounting Principles affecting Corporate Reports' was published in June 1936. The Statement expressed belief in 'a single coordinated body of accounting theory' and took as a 'fundamental axiom' the view that accounting is not a process of valuation, but 'the allocation of historical costs and revenues to the current and succeeding fiscal periods.'[8] The lower of cost and market rule was not specifically mentioned, but a way in which the rule could be 'reconciled' with a cost basis was provided:

Every business enterprise should eliminate from its accounts those costs which are applicable to assets no longer useful or salable, and should reduce the carrying values of assets in use or ultimately to be marketed to such amounts as may reasonably be expected to be recoverable in the course of future operations.[9]

---

[1] Sanders, Hatfield and Moore, *op. cit.* p. 2.   [2] *Ibid.* p. 114.
[3] Compare Hatfield's views in 1927! (see pp. 248–9 above).
[4] Sanders, Hatfield and Moore, *op. cit.* pp. 114–15.
[5] 'A Statement of Objectives of the American Accounting Association', *Accounting Review*, XI (1936).   [6] *Ibid.* p. 3.   [7] *Ibid.*
[8] 'A Tentative Statement of Accounting Principles affecting Corporate Reports', *Accounting Review*, XI (1936), 188.   [9] *Ibid.* p. 189.

R. H. Parker

There were now two ways in which the lower of cost and market rule could be supported. The first justification, perhaps becoming rather unfashionable, was an appeal to conservatism; the second justification was the newer doctrine of *recoverable cost*, which survived the first (1941) and second (1948) revisions of the 'Tentative Statement'.[1] In 1940 Paton and Littleton published 'an outline of the basic theory which underlies the Tentative Statement'.[2] They viewed inventories as 'essentially unrecovered costs...that portion of the stream of costs incurred in acquiring and producing goods which can reasonably be applied to revenues of the future'.[3] But they considered that this approach did not preclude the absorption in current charges to revenue of 'an appropriate portion of the cost of obsolete or damaged materials, work in process, or merchandise'.[4] They were at pains to point out that a clear distinction should be drawn between this kind of absorption and 'the substitution for recorded cost of figures designed to represent costs as they would be if the entire inventory were acquired or produced under the level of prices for the component factors obtaining at the inventory date'.[5] They regarded such a procedure as 'seriously objectionable'.[6] They did not support conservatism and clearly did not regard the deduction of an 'appropriate portion of the cost' as being connected in any way with the lower of cost and market rule.[7]

The American Institute's official statement on inventory valuation was published in 1947 as *Accounting Research Bulletin* No. 29.[8] It is described by Storey as 'a classic example of trying to please everyone'.[9]

[1] First revision, 1941: 'Costs of productive factors or other resources which are no longer useful should be reduced to realizable value, if any; and in the case of resources to be continued in use or held for sale only such portion of their costs as may reasonably be assigned to future periods should be carried in the balance sheet.' 'Accounting Principles Underlying Corporate Financial Statements', *Accounting Review*, XVI (1941), 135.

Second revision, 1948: 'The portion of recorded cost [of an asset] to be reported in the balance sheet is the amount assignable to future periods. Where an asset or asset group will be continued in use this amount is the portion of cost recoverable through the remaining useful services the asset is expected to yield...The residual cost should be carried forward in the balance sheet for assignment in future periods except when it is evident that the cost of an item cannot be recovered, whether from damage, deterioration, obsolescence, style change, over-supply, reduction in price levels, or other cause. In such event the inventory item should be stated at the estimated amount of sales proceeds less direct expense of completion and disposal.' 'Accounting Concepts and Standards Underlying Corporate Financial Statements', *Accounting Review*, XXIII (1948), 340–1.

[2] W. A. Paton and A. C. Littleton, *An Introduction to Corporate Accounting Standards* (Menasha, Wis., American Accounting Association, 1940), p. ix.

[3] *Ibid.* p. 77.   [4] *Ibid.* pp. 79–80.

[5] *Ibid.*   [6] *Ibid.* p. 81.   [7] *Ibid.* pp. 80–1, 126–9.

[8] *Accounting Research Bulletin* no. 29, 'Inventory Pricing' (New York, American Institute of Accountants, 1947); reproduced unchanged as chapter 4 of *Accounting Research Bulletin* no. 43 in 1953 (pp. 27–35 of American Institute of Certified Public Accountants, *Accounting Research and Terminology Bulletins. Final Edition*).

[9] Storey, *op. cit.* p. 50.

The primary basis of accounting for inventories, states the Bulletin, is acquisition and production cost,[1] but

> A departure from the cost basis...is required when the utility of the goods is no longer as great as its cost. Where there is evidence that the utility of the goods, in their disposal in the ordinary course of business, will be less than cost, whether due to physical deterioration, obsolescence, changes in price levels, or other causes, the difference should be recognized as a loss of the current period. This is generally accomplished by stating such goods at a lower level commonly designated as *market*.[2]

'Utility' is to be thought of in terms of the equivalent expenditure which would have to be made at the balance sheet date to procure corresponding utility. 'Market' therefore usually means current replacement cost, by purchase or by reproduction as the case may be. But this is not appropriate when the net realizable value is lower or where it appears that cost will be recovered with an approximately normal profit upon sale in the ordinary course of business.[3] Exceptionally, inventories may be valued at more than cost, but this must be justified by inability to determine appropriate approximate costs, immediate marketability at quoted market price, and the characteristic of unit interchangeability.[4]

In Great Britain the cost or market rule was never seriously challenged; it was, indeed, hardly ever *discussed*. The following statements from an influential textbook published in 1925 are typical:

> If all the assets were valued at the amount they are expected to realize if the business were closed down, a heavy loss would necessarily be shown. This method therefore is not adopted, but the valuation is made on the basis of a going concern... floating assets should not be valued above cost, as this would involve taking profit before it is realized; the proper basis of calculation being cost, market [i.e. replacement value] or realizable value, whichever is the lower [*sic*]...In no case should the value [of stock-in-trade] be higher than cost, even though the market value has risen, as this would result in taking profit before the sale is effected and the profit earned. On the other hand, a fall in the market value, due to a fluctuation in the price, need not be considered if the value has since risen. A permanent fall in value, however, must be taken into account.
>
> Stock...is bought for the purpose of selling again at a profit, and if at the date of the balance sheet it cannot be sold at a profit, a loss has already been sustained which must be provided for by bringing such stock into account at a reduced value. This operation...must also be effected in cases where stock has become obsolete or spoilt.[5]

F. R. M. de Paula devoted a chapter of his standard work on auditing (first published in 1914) to inventory valuation and verification. He regarded

---

[1] American Institute of Certified Public Accountants, *op. cit.* p. 28.
[2] *Ibid.* p. 30. [3] *Ibid.* pp. 31–2.
[4] *Ibid.* p. 34.
[5] E. E. Spicer and E. C. Pegler, *Practical Auditing* (4th ed. London, 1925), pp. 343–4, 168–9.

it as a 'basic principle' that inventories should not be valued above cost and as 'an accepted and wise principle' that any possible or probable losses in connexion with unsold inventories should be anticipated.[1] As far as he could judge, stores and raw materials were usually valued at the lower of cost or replacement value, and work in process and finished goods at the lower of cost or net realizable value. This inconsistency he regarded as incorrect and he suggested that the lower of cost and net realizable value should be the rule in all cases.[2] He argued that if replacement value is below cost 'no loss has arisen, or is likely to arise, provided that there will be a margin of profit upon the ultimate sale of the finished products'.[3]

At least one academic voice was raised to criticize such views. R. S. Edwards could see no merit in the lower of cost and market rule. Against de Paula he argued that it would be ignoring plain facts to say that one's stock of goods was worth more than other stocks of the same goods which could be acquired in the market.[4]

The views of such writers as Edwards seem to have had practically no influence on accounting practice. *Recommendation on Accounting Principles*, x, of the Institute of Chartered Accountants in England and Wales, probably reflected faithfully the views of most British practising accountants when it was issued in June 1945. It recommended that the basis of valuation should normally be the lower of cost and market value; the latter being interpreted to mean net realizable value. It was argued in the recommendation that the fact that at the time of valuation the goods could have been acquired at a sum less than their cost 'only indicates that the expected profit is less than it might have been had it been possible to acquire them at the accounting date'. This is not a trading loss but 'only indicates that the ultimate results under other conditions might have been better'.[5]

No mention was made in the recommendation of the concept of recoverable cost, but it is not completely unknown in the British accounting and economic literature of the 1940s. Norris, for example, although defining assets as 'deferred costs to be carried forward'[6] thought that common practice in inventory valuation was 'probably not seriously wrong so far as resulting figures are concerned'. It was his opinion that the saleability of particular items should be taken into account 'for the purpose only of deciding how much cost is to be carried forward'. This process should not be thought of as providing for losses.[7]

[1] F. R. M. de Paula, *The Principles of Auditing* (8th ed. London, 1936), pp. 96–7.
[2] *Ibid.* pp. 99–100. [3] *Ibid.* p. 103.
[4] Edwards, 'The Nature and Measurement of Income', *loc. cit.* pp. 265–6.
[5] Institute of Chartered Accountants in England and Wales, *Recommendations on Accounting Principles*, x, 'The Valuation of Stock-in-Trade', issued 15 June 1945.
[6] H. Norris, *Accounting Theory* (London, 1946), p. 18. [7] *Ibid.* p. 73.

Cost and market in Britain and U.S.A.

The economist P. W. S. Andrews approved the lower of cost and market rule and claimed that its justification did not lie in conservatism. His argument was as follows:

If market values have fallen...the costs expended on the stocks at the beginning of the next accounting year would be greater than the costs at which the business could *then* acquire similar goods. Now, it is essentially the purpose of the business to hold such goods for ultimate sale and to take the risks of the market. If they were carried at outlay-cost into the balance sheet at the end of the year, the next year would be saddled with what would be the consequences of financial risks which were really incurred in the earlier period, and the year in which the business acquired them would be avoiding one of the costs of its having done so—the fall in prices that has taken place...To value at market prices when prices are rising would falsify the cost position and cause the following year to be charged with costs which had not been incurred in fact...the accountant's rule here is a strict application of the logic of his principle of charging as costs the money outlays that have been incurred during any period.[1]

CONCLUSIONS

> 'Is that it?' said Eeyore.
> 'Yes', said Christopher Robin.
> 'Is that what we were looking for?'
> 'Yes', said Pooh.
> 'Oh!', said Eeyore. 'Well, anyhow—
> it didn't rain,' he said.
>
> A. A. Milne, *Winnie-the-Pooh*, chapter viii.

The astonishing thing about the lower of cost and market rule is its ability to survive attack. G. O. May was probably right in suggesting that most accountants are 'content to regard the demonstrated practical wisdom of the rule as outweighing any supposed illogicality'.[2] May embraced the doctrine of recoverable cost in order to 'avert the embodiment of the two rival concepts of cost and value in a single rule'.[3]

It might be suggested, however, that the lower of cost and market rule has survived precisely because it *does* embody the two rival concepts. Accountants are faced with a dilemma, as Littleton pointed out in 1929:[4] they are willing to accept neither a purely cost balance sheet, nor a purely appraisal balance sheet. In a purely appraisal balance sheet, they are worried about recognizing 'unrealized' profits; in a purely cost balance sheet, they are worried about showing an asset at a figure above that at which it could be currently sold or replaced. The 'practical' answer is

[1] P. W. S. Andrews, *Manufacturing Business* (London, 1949), pp. 41–2.
[2] May, *Financial Accounting*, p. 180. [3] *Ibid.* p. 184.
[4] Littleton, 'Value and Price in Accounting', *Accounting Review*, IV (1929), 148.

obviously a lower of cost and market rule, without worrying too much about 'theoretical' illogicality.

To Littleton the rule is the result of 'convenience and expediency'.[1] Vance, on the other hand, regards it as having grown in response to the needs of business men.[2] It does fulfil a need so long as accountants are unwilling to decide on the *objectives* of financial accounting. They cannot really have it both ways: either a balance sheet is a historical record or it is a statement of current resources. The concept of recoverable cost is not convincing; it is, as an Australian writer has put it, 'a rationalization of accepted accounting practices rather than an attempt to discover fundamental principles on which practices should be based'.[3]

The search for accounting principles goes on. It is unlikely that there will be agreement on inventory valuation so long as the more general problem remains unsolved.

[1] Littleton, 'A Genealogy for "Cost or Market"', *Accounting Review*, XVI (1941), 166.
[2] L. L. Vance, 'The Authority of History in Inventory Valuation', *Accounting Review*, XVIII (1943), 227.
[3] J. R. Ballantyne, at p. 129 of A. A. Fitzgerald (ed.), *Accounting* (4th ed. Sydney, 1963).

PART V

DEPRECIATION

18 A general mathematical theory of depreciation[1]

by Harold Hotelling*

In the older treatments of depreciation the cost, or 'theoretical selling price' of the product of a machine, was conceived of as determined causally by the addition of a number of items of which depreciation is one. In other words, depreciation was first computed by some rather arbitrary formula not involving the theoretical selling price, which was then found by the addition of depreciation to operating costs and division by quantity of output. It will be shown in this paper that depreciation and theoretical selling price must be computed simultaneously from a pair of equations which are frequently a bit complicated. The differences in the results obtained from the arbitrary and mathematical formulae are often very large.

The simple methods referred to, which still prevail generally in business, are analogous to the naïve type of economic thought for which the only determiner of price is cost and which fails to consider the equally important role played by demand.

The 'unit cost theory' gave the first recognition to the reciprocal relation existing between the value of a machine and the value of its product. It also deserves the credit for taking into account operating costs and output which, as in the present paper, are assumed to have been determined from experience. However, this theory in its usual form involves a number of serious errors of reasoning which have been pointed out by Dr J. S. Taylor.[2]

As an improvement on the unit cost theory Dr Taylor puts forward a method which, it is fair to say, is the only one that has been proposed which ever gives correct results. To it the present paper owes much. He assumes that unit cost-plus (defined as operating cost, plus depreciation, plus interest on the value of the machine, all divided by the number of units of output) is to be determined by the conditions that

(a) it is either to remain constant during the machine's life or is to increase in a specified manner; and

(b) it is to be made a minimum.

[1] Presented before the American Mathematical Society (Chicago meeting), 26 December 1924.

[2] 'A Statistical Theory of Depreciation Based on Unit Cost', *Journal of the American Statistical Association* (December 1923), pp. 1010–23.

* Professor of Mathematical Statistics, University of North Carolina.

This procedure is open to a possible criticism which he does not anticipate, namely that since the unit cost-plus depends on the distribution of depreciation charges, there is danger of the accountant deceiving himself into thinking that he has reduced costs when he has merely changed his system of charging depreciation to make the unit cost appear less. If unit cost is to be made a minimum in any useful sense, it is to be done by performing some operation on the machine itself, rather than by adjusting depreciation charges, or by any other process of bookkeeping. The criticism may be answered on Dr Taylor's behalf by the fact that he uses the test (*b*) above only to determine the time for the tangible operation of scrapping the machine, and then uses (*a*) to distribute the depreciation charge over the useful life.

But even if we admit the validity of (*a*) there remains a question concerning (*b*). Does the manufacturer desire to make his unit cost-plus, in the sense defined, a minimum? Or may not considerations of profit lead him to scrap the machine at some different time from that which makes unit cost-plus a minimum, or to shut down his factory or restrict the output of the machine? We shall indeed give a proof that in certain cases the tests (*a*) and (*b*) give correct results.

To one important element in the problem I find no allusion in the literature. The value of an old machine or other property must depend upon the operating cost. In all depreciation theories based on unit cost it is assumed that the operating cost is known, and the value is then calculated. But operating cost always includes elements which depend on the value. Hence we cannot know the operating cost until we know the value; that is, until the problem is solved. We shall resolve this difficulty by solving a simple integral equation.

The viewpoint of the present treatment is that the owner wishes to maximize the present value of the output minus the operating costs of the machine or other property. This quantity is, in fact, the value of the property. The first step is, therefore, to set up an expression for the value of the property in terms of value of output, operating costs, and the life of the property. Various hypotheses concerning the economic situation are then applied to evaluate the unknowns appearing in the equation. Depreciation is defined simply as rate of decrease of value. A mathematical formulation of the problem of depreciation is presented from which, it is believed, the whole of the valid portions of existing depreciation theories are readily deducible, and which also lays a foundation for further developments. This treatment is adapted to the consideration of depreciation in connexion with variation of such factors as prices and interest rates. The theory is in fact completely general. The property involved will be referred to as a machine purely for convenience of language. The amount of computation involved in a particular application will depend upon the degree of refinement of the data; in the present stage of knowledge of mortality tables of property the work can be made quite simple. A specimen problem is worked out numerically.

Continuous functions, instantaneously compounded interest, and integration will be used as better adapted to the needs of theory than the discontinuous functions and summation processes usually employed. The methods of the integral calculus also appear to me simpler than those of algebraic summation even where only integral numbers of years are involved; while the occurrence of portions of years, which does not seriously affect the integration process, is always a source of trouble when discontinuous functions are used.

Obsolescence is a risk of essentially the same nature as fire, earthquake, or burglary, and should be provided for in the same manner—namely, by an allowance out of operating expenses similar to an insurance premium. Even where no insurance or inadequate insurance is carried, an allowance should be made, Obsolescence is thus to be relegated, with insurance, to the category of operating expenses.

FUNDAMENTAL FORMULA

If a machine with operating cost per year $O(\tau)$ produces $Y(\tau)$ units of output per year at time τ and if the value ('theoretical selling price') of a unit of output is x, the annual rental value of the machine at time τ is

$$R(\tau) = xY(\tau) - O(\tau).$$

Now the value of a machine is the sum of the anticipated rentals which it will yield, each multiplied by a *discount factor* to allow for interest, plus the scrap or salvage value, also discounted.[1] In the most general case the

---

[1] The 'force of interest' $\delta(t)$ is defined as the rate of increase of an invested sum s divided by s:

$$\delta(t) = \frac{1}{s}\frac{ds}{dt}.$$

It follows by integration that $s = s_0 \exp\left\{\int_0^t \delta(v)dv\right\}$, where s_0 is the value of the invested amount when $t = 0$ and v is a mere variable of integration. Hence $s_0 = s \exp\left\{-\int_0^t \delta(v)dv\right\}$. That is, the present value s_0 of a payment to be made t years hence is the amount s of the expected payment multiplied by the *discount factor* $\exp\left\{-\int_0^t \delta(v)dv\right\}$. If $\delta(v) = \delta$, a constant, the discount factor is $e^{-t\delta}$. The discount factor takes the form v^t if we write $v = e^{-\delta}$; and $v = 1/(1+i)$ in this case, where i is the *rate* of interest in the ordinary

rate of interest will vary with the time. If $S(n)$ is a function giving the scrap or salvage value at the time n at which the machine is to be discarded, the value at time t is given by the following fundamental formula:

$$V(t) = \int_t^n [x\,Y(\tau) - O(\tau)] \exp\left\{-\int_t^\tau \delta(\nu)d\nu\right\} d\tau + S(n) \exp\left\{-\int_t^n \delta(\nu)d\nu\right\},$$

$$(1)$$

τ and ν being variables of integration representing time. In case the interest rate is constant (1) becomes

$$V(t) = \int_t^n [x\,Y(\tau) - O(\tau)]\,v^{\tau-t}d\tau + S(n)\,v^{n-t}. \tag{1a}$$

Since the value of a new machine is its cost c, we have for $t = 0$,

$$c = V(0) = \int_0^n [x\,Y(\tau) - O(\tau)] \exp\left\{-\int_0^\tau \delta(\nu)\,d\nu\right\} d\tau$$
$$+ S(n) \exp\left\{-\int_0^n \delta(\nu)\,d\nu\right\}. \tag{2}$$

Having once bought the machine, the owner wishes to conserve its value as far as he can. This, in the light of (1), is the same as saying that he hopes to get as much net rental as possible out of the machine, interest and scrap value being considered. We, therefore, adopt as the basis of our further work the simple postulate:

I. *Everything in the owner's power will be done to make $V(t)$ a maximum when $t > 0$.*

A second postulate of less general validity, which is often assumed tacitly or is thought to follow from I, is the following:

II. *The machine is always operated at full capacity.*

We shall assume II tentatively.

We suppose that c and the functions Y, O, S and δ of the time are known, but before we can evaluate the right member of (1) we must make some

sense, i.e. the interest payable at the end of a year on each dollar invested for the year. Then

$$\delta = \log_e(1 + i) = i - \frac{i^2}{2} + \frac{i^3}{3} - \dots$$

and

$$i = \delta - 1 = \delta + \frac{\delta^2}{2!} + \frac{\delta^3}{3!} + \dots$$

Since both these series converge rapidly they afford a ready means of passing from force of interest to rate of interest or vice versa. The difference between i and δ is ordinarily very small.

The value at time t of a payment to be made at time τ is evidently the amount of the payment multiplied by $\exp\left\{-\int_t^\tau \delta(\nu)d\nu\right\}$. If s is constant, this discount factor equals $v^{\tau-t}$.

hypothesis which will enable us to determine n and x. There are several possibilities.

(*a*) If the property has a known useful life n, (2) is a simple equation in x alone.

(*b*) If x is known, the most obvious way to find a value for n is to solve (2). This, however, can be justified only in very special circumstances. For if x is known in advance of the solution of our problem of depreciation, it must be determined by competitive conditions entirely beyond the control of the machine's owner. He may, for example, use the machine to do work usually done by some other process. In such a case (2) does not hold unless ideally fluid conditions of competition have acted to bring the price c of the machine to such a point as to justify its purchase when n is determined to best advantage. Thus to use (2) to find the best life to allow the machine, the owner must rest precariously upon the judgment of his competitors.

The correct procedure is as follows. Let m be the time, if it exists (if not, put ∞ for m), at which the ouput of the machine ceases to be worth the operating expenses. Then m is determined by the equation

$$x Y(m) - O(m) = 0.$$

We may for the sake of generality consider that x is a given function $x(t)$ of the time. In this case m is determined by $x(m) Y(m) - O(m) = 0$, which we may also write $R(m) = 0$. The sum of the possible future rentals of the machine, discounted at (say) a constant rate of interest is then

$$\int_t^m R(\tau) v^{\tau-t} d\tau.$$

This quantity will decrease until, at time n, it reaches the scrap value $S(n)$. Thus n is determined by

$$\int_n^m R(\tau) v^{\tau-t} d\tau = S(n),$$

where $R(m) = 0$. It is of course possible that these equations may have a plurality of solutions. The correct solution is then the one which makes $V(t)$ greatest.

(*c*) If, as is most common, both x and n are to be determined, we use the equation (2) connecting these unknowns, solving it simultaneously with an additional equation obtained by means of (1).

If all economic conditions are static, x is a constant. If economic conditions are not static but their trend can be estimated, we may consider that the value of a unit of output varies in a specified manner with the time, but that its general level depends upon an unknown parameter α. For example it may be supposed that x increases in geometric progression with known ratio r, but that the initial and final values are unknown. We then write $x = \alpha r^\tau$, or in general, $x = x(\tau, \alpha)$.

Take first the static case. Supposing all our functions continuous and with continuous first derivatives, we differentiate (1) and put $dV(t)/dn = 0$. The result of this operation becomes, after cancelling out the common factor

$$\exp\left\{-\int_t^n \delta(v)\,dv\right\}$$

and solving[1] for x,

$$x = \frac{O(n) + \delta(n)\,S(n) - S'(n)}{Y(n)}, \tag{3}$$

a condition independent of t, as it should be. This equation states that x, the cost of a unit of product, is found by adding the operating cost $O(n)$ of the machine (at the time n when it is least efficient and is about to be scrapped) to interest $\delta(n)\,S(n)$ on the scrap value and the rate of depreciation $-S'(n)$ of the scrap value, and dividing this sum by the machine's rate of production.

If conditions are not static we may still be able to write a known function

---

[1] The derivation of (3) given in the text is strictly accurate only in the case in which x is independent of n. If, as is generally the case, x is a function of n, the result of equating to zero the derivative of the right member of (1) with regard to n is

$$\frac{dx}{dn}\int_t^n Y(\tau)\exp\left\{-\int_t^\tau \delta(v)\,dv\right\}d\tau + [xY(n) - O(n) - \delta(n)S(n)$$
$$+ S'(n)]\exp\left\{-\int_t^n \delta(v)\,dv\right\} = 0.$$

To get rid of dx/dn we differentiate also the relation (2) between x and n, obtaining an equation exactly like the one above excepting that t is replaced throughout by 0. Eliminating dx/dn between the two we have

$$\begin{vmatrix} \int_t^n Y(\tau)\exp\left\{-\int_t^\tau \delta(v)\,dv\right\}d\tau & \exp\left\{-\int_t^n \delta(v)\,dv\right\} \\ \int_0^n Y(\tau)\exp\left\{-\int_0^\tau \delta(v)\,dv\right\}d\tau & \exp\left\{-\int_0^n \delta(v)\,dv\right\} \end{vmatrix} [xY(n) - O(n) - \delta(n)S(n) + S'(n)] = 0.$$

If the factor in the square brackets vanishes we have (3). But it must vanish, for the determinant becomes, when the upper row is multiplied by $\exp\left\{-\int_0^t \delta(v)\,dv\right\}$,

$$\begin{vmatrix} \int_t^n Y(\tau)\exp\left\{-\int_0^\tau \delta(v)\,dv\right\}d\tau & \exp\left\{-\int_0^n \delta(v)\,dv\right\} \\ \int_0^n Y(\tau)\exp\left\{-\int_0^\tau \delta(v)\,dv\right\}d\tau & \exp\left\{-\int_0^n \delta(v)\,dv\right\} \end{vmatrix},$$

which can vanish only if the terms in the first column are equal. This would imply that $\int_0^t Y(\tau)\exp\left\{-\int_0^\tau \delta(v)\,dv\right\}d\tau = 0$, which is impossible (excepting for $t = 0$) because we suppose $Y(\tau)$ positive for all values of τ less than n.

$x(\tau, \alpha)$ for x in (1) and (2), and $x(n, \alpha)$ for x in (3). We then solve (2) and (3) simultaneously for n and α and substitute in (1). This parallels a method suggested by Dr Taylor in the paper cited above, but is slightly more general.

There is of course nothing in the theory to preclude the possibility that n may become infinite.

OPERATING EXPENSE DEPENDENT ON VALUE

It has been assumed up to this point that when we set out to solve a particular depreciation problem we know a function $O(t)$ giving the operating expense at all times in the life of the article. But certain elements of operating cost always depend upon the value of the article at the time, which value we do not know until we have solved the problem. Thus taxes are supposed to be proportional to the value, and insurable risk, if not insurance, certainly is. The risk of obsolescence enters here.

If we write $O(\tau)$ in (1) as a function of $V(\tau)$ and τ we have an *integral equation* to solve for the unknown function $V(t)$. Now the study of integral equations is a new and incomplete branch of mathematics, so that an integral equation written down at random can probably not be solved until pure mathematics has advanced further than at present. By rare good luck, however, the cases which usually arise in practice are of type leading to one of the few integral equations whose theories are well developed, the *Volterra* equation. This is because the dependence of operating cost upon value is ordinarily *linear*. Thus taxes and insurance premiums are directly proportional to the value, and not to its square or some other function. Hence we may write

$$O(\tau) = A(\tau) + B(\tau) V(\tau),$$

where $A(\tau)$ and $B(\tau)$ are functions which, like $Y(\tau)$ and $\delta(\tau)$, are supposed to have been determined, or at least estimated, on the basis of experience. Substituting this value of $O(\tau)$ in (1) we have

$$V(t) = \int_t^n [x Y(\tau) - A(\tau)] \exp \left\{ -\int_t^\tau \delta(v)\, dv \right\} \delta\tau + S(n) \exp \left\{ -\int_t^n \delta(v)\, dv \right\}$$
$$- \int_t^n B(\tau) V(\tau) \exp \left\{ -\int_t^\tau \delta(v)\, dv \right\} d\tau. \quad (4)$$

This integral equation admits of a very easy solution by reduction to a differential equation as follows. Differentiate (4) and add each member of the resulting equation to the product of $-\delta(t)$ by the corresponding member of (4). Several terms cancel out, leaving[1]

$$\frac{dV(t)}{dt} - [\delta(t) + B(t)]\, V(t) = -x\, Y(t) + A(t). \tag{5}$$

Let us write for brevity $\gamma(t) = \delta(t) + B(t)$. The solution of (5), found by elementary methods, is then

$$V(t) = \exp\left\{\int_0^t \gamma(v)\,dv\right\}\left[\int_t^n [x\,Y(\tau) - A(\tau)] \exp\left\{-\int_0^\tau \gamma(v)\,dv\right\} d\tau + k\right],$$

where k is the constant of integration. To evaluate k we may use either the fact that $V(0) = c$ or that $V(n) = S(n)$. In the first case we find

$$V(t) = \exp\left\{\int_0^t \gamma(v)\,dv\right\}\left[c - \int_0^t [x\,Y(\tau) - A(\tau)]\exp\left\{-\int_0^\tau \gamma(v)\,dv\right\} d\tau\right];$$

in the second case we obtain the equivalent form

$$V(t) = \int_t^n [x\,Y(\tau) - A(\tau)] \exp\left\{-\int_t^\tau \gamma(v)\,dv\right\} d\tau + S(n) \exp\left\{-\int_t^n \gamma(v)\,\delta v\right\}, \tag{1a}$$

which differs from (1) only in that $\gamma(v)$ replaces $\delta(v)$ and $A(\tau)$ replaces $O(\tau)$.

The problem of value and depreciation is now solved exactly as in the simpler case. Equations similar to (2) and (3) are derived and used in the same manner as before, δ being everywhere replaced by γ and $O(t)$ by $A(t)$.

EXAMPLE

Suppose that the data available from experience justify the expectation that

$$Y(\tau) = ae^{-\lambda\tau}, \quad A(\tau) = be^{\mu\tau}, \quad S(n) = 0, \quad \text{and} \quad \delta(v) + B(v) = \gamma, \text{ a constant.}$$

Then, by (1a),

$$V(t) = \int_t^n [x a e^{-\lambda\tau} - b e^{\mu\tau}] e^{-\gamma(\tau-t)}\, d\tau$$

$$= e^{\gamma t}\int_t^n [x a e^{-(\lambda+\gamma)\tau} - b e^{(\mu-\gamma)\tau}]\, d\tau$$

$$= xa\frac{e^{-\lambda t} - e^{\gamma t-(\lambda+\gamma)n}}{\lambda+\gamma} + b\frac{e^{\mu t} - e^{\gamma t+(\mu-\gamma)n}}{\mu-\gamma}.$$

From an equation similar to (3) we have, since $S(n) = 0$ and therefore $S'(n) = 0$, $x = A(n)/Y(n) = be^{(\lambda+\mu)n}/a$.

[1] If we solve (5) for x we have the well known expression for cost of output in terms of operating costs, yield, interest and depreciation on the machine.

Substituting above we have

$$V(t) = \frac{b}{(\lambda+\gamma)(\mu-\gamma)} \{(\mu-\gamma)e^{-\lambda t+(\lambda+\mu)n} - (\lambda+\mu)e^{\gamma t+(\mu-\gamma)n} + (\lambda+\gamma)e^{\mu t}\}.$$

For $t = 0$ this gives

$$c = V(0) = \frac{b}{(\lambda+\gamma)(\mu-\gamma)} \{(\mu-\gamma)e^{(\lambda+\mu)n} - (\lambda+\mu)e^{(\mu-\gamma)n} + \lambda+\gamma\},$$

which on rearrangement becomes

$$e^{(\lambda+\mu)n} + \frac{\lambda+\mu}{\gamma-\mu}e^{(\mu-\gamma)n} + \frac{\lambda+\gamma}{\mu-\gamma} - (\lambda+\gamma)\frac{c}{b} = 0.$$

This equation for determining n, it will be observed, contains b and c only in the ratio c/b, and does not contain a at all. Since commensurable values may always be taken for γ, λ and μ it reduces to an algebraic equation. It may be proved mathematically that in every case there is just one root for which $n > 0$, and that n approaches zero and infinity with c/b.

Let us take $\gamma = 0.09$, $\lambda = 0.06$, $\mu = 0.14$, $c/b = 20$. The equation becomes $e^{0.20n} - 4e^{0.05n} = 0$. Hence

$$e^{0.05n} = \sqrt[3]{4}, \quad \text{and} \quad n = \tfrac{1}{3}\log 4/0.05 \log_e = 9.244 \text{ years}.$$

Therefore

$$V(t) = \frac{b}{0.15} [e^{-0.06t+0.20n} - 4e^{0.09t+0.05n} + 3e^{0.14t}]$$

$$= \frac{b}{0.15} [4^{4/3}(e^{-0.06t} - e^{-0.09t}) + 3e^{0.14t}].$$

Calculation from this formula gives the following results for $b = 1,000$.

t	$V(t)$	$V(t-1) - V(t)$
0	20,000·00	
1	16,553·86	3,446·14
2	13,327·50	3,226·36
3	10,345·07	2,982·43
4	7,638·10	2,706·97
5	5,246·63	2,391·57
6	3,220·65	2,025·98
7	1,621·75	1,598·90
8	524·96	1,096·79
9	20·97	503·99
9·244	0	

The decrease in value shown by this table for the first year is more than $1\frac{1}{2}$ times that indicated by the straight-line law, and is more than double that calculated by means of the equal-annual-payment or sinking-fund method with interest at 6 per cent.

Depreciation has been defined as rate of decrease of value:

$$D(t) = -dV(t)/dt.$$

The *total depreciation* over a period is the difference between the value at the beginning of the period and that at its end. It equals the average value of the depreciation times the length of the period; for

$$\int_a^b D(t)\,dt = -\int_a^b [dV(t)/dt]\,dt = V(a) - V(b).$$

The total depreciation in the value of an article over its whole life is thus $c - S(n)$. The average depreciation is therefore

$$\frac{c - S(n)}{n}. \tag{6}$$

RELATION TO OTHER DEPRECIATION THEORIES

The formula (6) for average depreciation is so simple that if accuracy is not worth while, and if the useful life n is known with some degree of definiteness, it may be assumed that the depreciation of each year is equal to this average depreciation. Or if we are considering the composite depreciation of a large number of similar machines whose times of installation have been uniformly distributed over n years, (6) gives a rough approximation. This *straight-line law* is often used in cases in which it gives rise to large errors.

Let us suppose that $O(t)$ and $Y(t)$ are constants q and y, respectively, for a certain number of years of the machine's life and then change abruptly in such a way as to make it clear that the end has come. The supposition that $O(t)$ is constant means, of course, that $B(t) = 0$, that is, that neither risk nor a tax on value exists. Let the scrap value be s, a constant, and let $\delta(t) = \delta$, a constant. Let x also be constant. Then (3) does not hold because its derivation assumed $O(t)$ and $Y(t)$ continuous. But n is now known, so that we can find x from (2) alone.

In this case (1) becomes

$$V(t) = \int_t^n (xy - q) v^{\tau - t} d\tau + s v^{n-t}$$

$$= (xy - q) \frac{1 - v^{n-t}}{\delta} + s v^{n-t}.$$

Putting $t = 0$ we have the equation, like (2),

$$c = (xy-q)\frac{1-v^{-n}}{\delta}+sv^n.$$

The result of eliminating $xy-q$ between these two equations is

$$\begin{vmatrix} V(t)-sv^{n-t} & \dfrac{1-v^{n-t}}{\delta} \\ c-sv^n & \dfrac{1-v^n}{\delta} \end{vmatrix} = 0.$$

Now add $-s\delta$ times the second column to the first. Then subtract the second row from the first. Finally, multiplying the second column by $(1+i)^n$ and remembering that $\bar{s}_{\overline{n}|} = [(1+i)^n-1]/\delta$, we have

$$\begin{vmatrix} V(t)-c & -\bar{s}_{\overline{t}|} \\ c-s & -\bar{s}_{\overline{n}|} \end{vmatrix} = 0.$$

From this we find at once

$$V(t) = c-(c-s)\frac{\bar{s}_{\overline{t}|}}{\bar{s}_{\overline{n}|}} = c-(c-s)\frac{s_{\overline{t}|}}{s_{\overline{n}|}}.$$

Hence

$$V(t)-V(t+1) = (c-s)\frac{(1+i)^t}{s_{\overline{n}|}}. \tag{7}$$

This gives a proof of the correctness, under the circumstances assumed, of the equal-annual-payment and sinking-fund methods of calculating depreciation. But these methods are almost always misleading because the assumptions take no account of the almost universal tendency for operating costs to increase and for output to decrease with age. Consequently they understate the depreciation in the early years.

We may further enquire in what circumstances particular depreciation methods are valid. The test here is supplied by (5), which we now write in the form

$$P(t) = \gamma V(t)-\frac{dV(t)}{dt}, \tag{8}$$

where $P(t) = xY(t)-A(t)$. Let us, for simplicity, consider γ constant, and let us call $P(t)$ the *gross rental*.

According to the straight-line method,

$$V(t) = c-(c-s)t/n.$$

Substituting this expression in (8) we find

$$P(t) = c-s+c\gamma-(c-s)\gamma t/n.$$

This is such a special condition that we must in general discard the straight-line method as a valid rule where accuracy is required.

The reducing-balance method supposes that depreciation is a constant percentage of value. It follows that $V(t) = ce^{-kt}$, k being determined by $s = ce^{-kn}$. From (8) we have in this case the condition $(P)t = ce^{-kt}(\gamma - k)$.

Similarly the condition for the validity of the sinking-fund method (7) is

$$P(t) = \gamma - \frac{c-s}{(1+i)^n - 1} [B(t)(1+i)^t + \gamma],$$

which is constant if $B(t) = 0$.

Thus the three methods in most common use depend for their validity upon the satisfaction of conditions which involve no disposable constants and which are so special that the chances are overwhelmingly against the satisfaction of any of them in a particular case.

Dr Taylor[1] defines unit cost-plus by a formula which, in terms of continuous functions, becomes

$$x = \frac{O(t) + \delta(t) V(t) - [dV(t)/dt]}{Y(t)},$$

which is equivalent to (5), and reduces to (3) when $t = n$. We may now derive his criterion of minimum unit cost-plus as follows. The value of the machine being given by (1) in terms of x and n, and these unknowns being connected by (2), we seek the value of n which will make x a minimum. This can be found from (2) alone. For, differentiating with respect to n and putting $dx/dn = 0$, we have (3). The simultaneous solution of (2) and (3) will then yield the same values of x and n as those found under (C).

Thus Dr Taylor's treatment yields the same results as those found under (C), save for the discrepancies arising from the use of discontinuous functions which suppose all changes to occur by yearly steps. It is better adapted to calculation than the theory of the present paper in many cases in which $B(t) = 0$, that is, in which there is no element of operating expense such as risk, insurance and taxes. But even under this severe restriction it does not seem a logical foundation for a theory of depreciation without a demonstration, such as the one above, that the life to be allowed a machine to make it most valuable to its owner is also that which makes unit cost-plus a minimum. This proposition is not obvious, and is false in case of the failure of our postulate II.

Dr Taylor in the same paper mentions as an alternative to that discussed—though without advocating it—a theory based on the assumption that 'unit cost', defined like unit cost-plus except that interest is not in-

[1] J. S. Taylor, *op. cit.*

cluded, should be made a minimum. This assumption lacks even the justification given for minimizing unit cost-plus. Like the straight-line law, it has nothing to recommend it but simplicity.

FURTHER DEVELOPMENTS

What can be said in case of the failure of postulate II—that the property is used to full capacity? There are very important cases, such as those of mines, in which the postulate is not even approximately true. In this connexion we must consider as unknowns not only useful life, value, and depreciation but also the functions $Y(t)$ and $A(t)$. The owner, that is, may voluntarily run the machine at less than full capacity, and wishes us to tell him just how fast to let it run in order that his profits may be a maximum. If we do not tell him, he will guess to the best of his ability. The demand function must be known in order to give a solution.

In all such cases the guiding principle is that the right member of (1), representing discounted future profits, is to be made a maximum. Even if the capitalist system is to give way to one in which service and not profit shall be the object, there will still be an integral of anticipated utilities to be made a maximum. Since we must find a function which maximizes an integral we must in many cases use the Calculus of Variations. But the problem here transcends the questions of depreciation and useful life, and belongs to the dawning economic theory based on considerations of maximum and minimum which bears to the older theories the relations which the Hamiltonian dynamics and the thermodynamics of entropy bear to their predecessors.[1]

The question of charging depreciation as a function of output rather than of time has been discussed of late.[2] It is more natural to consider the depreciation of an automobile in terms of miles than of years. Since interest is an element, this is strictly possible only in case the rate of output $Y(t)$ is known for the whole life of the property; but in this case the arguments commonly advanced for the proposed method fail.

However, an answer may be given to a question of some interest which

---

[1] For the solution of a special problem in the new 'entropy' economics see G. C. Evans, 'The Dynamics of Monopoly', *American Mathematical Monthly*, XXXI (2 February 1924), 77–83. A thorough working knowledge of the Calculus of Variations is a prerequisite to the development of this type of economic theory—which doubtless explains why it has not developed further.

All hedonistic and eudaemonistic ethical theories, which declare that the total of pleasure or happiness should be made a maximum, really reduce the question of right conduct to a set of problems in the Calculus of Variations and in the more general theory of maxima of functionals.

[2] E. A. Saliers, *Depreciation, Principles and Applications* (New York, 1922), pp. 172–8.

arises in this connexion in case operating cost depends on a controllable rate of output and not merely on the time. What is the additional cost of taking a short trip in an automobile? More generally, what is the additional net cost of a slight increment in output of a machine? We suppose that the increased output extends over a time so short that interest for this period is negligible. The operating cost $A(t)$ per unit of time, exclusive of items such as risk and taxes which are proportional to value, may usually be divided into three classes. One class of costs depends only on the age of the machine, one on age and the amount of current use, and one on the total of past use. We may thus write as an approximation which is probably good enough for all existing data,

$$A(t) = \alpha(t) + a(t)\,Y(t) + b\int_0^t Y(\mu)\,d\mu.$$

The additional cost of a small temporary increment z to the total output, concentrated in a time dt, consists partly of increased operating cost at this time and partly of depreciation due to subsequent increase in operating cost. The first part is obviously $za(t)$. The second part depends upon the increment of the integral

$$\int_0^\tau Y(\mu)\,d\mu.$$

This increment will be z for every time τ later than the time t at which the increased use takes place. Thus the future rentals of the machine are decreased by an amount bz per unit of time. The decrease in its value is the discounted sum of these decreases,

$$\int_t^n bze^{-\gamma(\tau-t)}d\tau = bz\,\frac{1-e^{-\gamma(n-t)}}{\gamma},$$

if γ is constant.

SUMMARY

(a) The value of a machine and that of a unit of its output are *interrelated*, each affecting the other. This economic truism must underlie a correct theory of depreciation.

(b) The fundamental formula (1) gives the value of a machine in terms of time, value of output, operating cost, scrap value, useful life and rate of interest. One relation between these quantities, given by (2), is due to the fact that the cost of the machine when new is its value at that time.

(c) Two postulates are introduced, one equivalent to the supposition of completely rational action with a completely selfish motive; the second, to which we attach less permanent importance, excludes from consideration the possibility that the owner may seek to increase his profits by slowing down production.

(*d*) Methods are given for finding the value function $V(t)$ when we know either the useful life *n* of the machine or the value *x* of a unit of output, and also when we know neither *n* nor *x*.

(*e*) The hitherto untouched difficulty of operating expenses proportional to value is resolved by means of an integral equation.

(*f*) A numerical example is worked out which is believed typical of a large class of cases.

(*g*) The depreciation methods hitherto used are tested and all excepting that of Dr Taylor are found in general to give false results.

(*h*) When postulate II is abandoned and the rate of output considered controllable, the methods of this paper are capable of further elaboration to cover a great deal of economic and even ethical theory.

(*i*) Depreciation cannot, as has been proposed, be charged as a function of output alone, the omnipresence of interest preventing this. The increase of depreciation with output can however be calculated by means of our formulae, given adequate experience tables.

Since this article was written, two papers bearing on the subject have appeared: 'Economics and the Calculus of Variations', by G. C. Evans, *Proceedings of the National Academy of Sciences*, XI, 90; and 'A Note on the Theory of Depreciation', by J. S. Taylor, *Bulletin of the American Mathematical Society*, XXXI, 222.

19 Towards a general theory of depreciation

by F. K. Wright*

For the past hundred years accountants have been searching for the 'true' depreciation method which would allocate the cost of the machine over its lifetime in accordance with the rate at which it is actually being 'used up'. They have reluctantly concluded that there is no 'true' depreciation method, and that all the methods used or proposed are mere conventions, the choice between which is a matter of convenience.[1]

In the thirteen years since the above was expressed by the Lutzes, nothing has been published which need cause them to revise their pessimistic view of depreciation theory.[2] It is true that they had underestimated the reluctance of accountants to give up the search for the 'true' method: several articles have appeared recently, each claiming to describe a theoretically sound depreciation method.[3] None of these, however, is free from the hidden assumption to which Preinreich drew attention many years ago,[4] and on which the pessimism of the Lutzes was presumably based.

Here it will be argued that there is, in principle, only one theoretically sound method of depreciation, though its application would require a greater degree of foresight than is likely to be realized in practice. The foundations of this theory of depreciation were laid by Hotelling[5] and Canning[6] nearly forty years ago; it is hoped that this article will go some of the way towards completion of the structure which they began.

[1] F. and V. Lutz, *The Theory of Investment of the Firm* (Princeton, 1951), p. 7.

[2] I wish to except from my generalization a paper which came to my attention only after the present article went to press: H. D. Lowe, 'The Essentials of a General Theory of Depreciation', *Accounting Review*, xxxviii (April 1963), 293–301.

[3] H. R. Anton, 'Depreciation, Cost Allocation and Investment Decisions', *Accounting Research*, vii (April 1956), 117–34; R. L. Dixon, 'Decreasing Charge Depreciation—A Search for Logic', *Accounting Review*, xxxv (October 1960), 590–7; I. N. Reynolds, 'Selecting the Proper Depreciation Method', *Accounting Review*, xxxvi (April 1961), 239–48; H. Bierman, Jr., 'Depreciable Assets—Timing of Expense Recognition', *Accounting Review*, xxxvi (October 1961), 613–18; S. H. Sosnick, 'Depreciation: The Offsetting-Interest Method', *Accounting Review*, xxxvii (January 1962), 59–66; H. R. Hudson and R. Mathews, 'An Aspect of Depreciation', *Economic Record*, xxxix (June 1963), 232–6.

[4] G. A. D. Preinreich, 'Annual Survey of Economic Theory: The Theory of Depreciation' *Econometrica*, vi (July 1938), 233–41.

[5] H. Hotelling, 'A General Mathematical Theory of Depreciation', *Journal of the American Statistical Association*, xx (September 1925), 340–53 [reprinted as chapter 18 above].

[6] J. B. Canning, *The Economics of Accountancy* (New York, 1929), chapters xii–xiv.

* Professor of Commerce, University of Adelaide.

276

THE PROBLEM OF DEPRECIATION

For a specific asset, objective verifiable values based upon external transactions are available at only two points of time: at the moment of acquisition, and at the moment of disposal. If these two events occur within the same accounting period, no depreciation problem arises. But where the events are widely separated in time (as is usually the case with fixed assets), determination of periodic income is impossible without establishing a value for the asset at the end of each intervening period. The problem of depreciation accounting is the problem of establishing these needed values without the objective verifiable basis which only external transactions can provide.

There have been two distinct approaches to the solution of the depreciation problem which might be designated the 'accounting approach' and the 'economic approach', respectively. The accounting approach requires the cost of an asset less salvage, if any, to be distributed over the life of the unit 'in a systematic and rational manner'.[1] The economic approach, on the other hand, ignores cost as an irrelevant datum: the value of an asset at any point of time is simply the sum of its discounted future services (including salvage if any).[2]

It seems clear that the accounting approach does not really represent an attempt at valuation: indeed, it has been officially described as 'a process of allocation, not of valuation'.[1] It is probably not unfair to say that the accounting profession, recognizing the extreme difficulty of valuing fixed assets, has abandoned the attempt and is prepared to accept any method of arriving at book values which can claim to be 'systematic and rational'. With this practical judgment it is difficult to quarrel; in our search for a theory of depreciation, however, we must abandon the accounting approach as sterile. Only the economic approach represents a theory of valuation, and without a theory of valuation we cannot have a theory of depreciation.

PROBLEMS OF VALUATION

If we adopt the economic approach to the valuation of an asset, we encounter three main problems: (1) the problem of forecasting the future services of the asset; (2) the problem of valuing those future services; (3) the problem of determining the appropriate rate (or rates) of discount.

This article does not purport to solve the first of these problems; and it will be convenient to defer discussion of the third until a later stage. The

[1] *Accounting Terminology Bulletin* no. 1, Review and Résumé (American Institute of Certified Public Accountants, 1953), p. 25.
[2] *See* Irving Fisher, *The Nature of Capital and Income* (New York, 1906), p. 189.

F. K. Wright

second problem, that of valuing the future services of an asset, holds the key to the depreciation problem: it is failure to solve this problem completely which has prevented the construction of a satisfactory theory of depreciation.

As a general rule, accountants solve their valuation problems by defining value as 'value-in-exchange' and look to an exchange transaction to supply them with a book value. But as we have seen, this method breaks down when we have to account for a long-lived asset: we must then define value as 'value-in-use', a much more difficult concept to apply.

What is the value of the services of an asset already owned by a firm? Reversing the well-known concept of opportunity cost, we may say that their value is equal to the cost, loss or sacrifice which would have to be incurred if the firm did not have those services. Opportunity cost is measured by the most valuable alternative forgone; conversely, 'opportunity value' (if we may coin this phrase) is measured by the least costly of the alternatives avoided through owning the services.[1]

The problem of valuing the services of an asset thus reduces to the problem of determining the alternatives to ownership of that asset, assessing the costs or losses associated with those alternatives, and selecting the least of those costs or losses to represent the value of the services.

UTILITY AND REPLACEMENT

The alternatives to ownership of an existing asset may be divided into two groups: those which involve cessation of production of the services provided by the existing asset, and those which involve producing those services in some other way. We shall define the term 'utility' to mean the cost of the cheapest alternative in the first group, and 'replacement cost' to mean the cost of the cheapest alternative in the second group. The opportunity value of the services of an asset at any point of time will then be the lower of utility or replacement cost. Thus, if the utility of the service is below its replacement cost, the value of the service to its owner will equal its utility; if the utility exceeds the replacement cost of the service, its value to the owner will equal its replacement cost.

It seems reasonable to assume that the value of the services of a newly

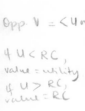

---

[1] The concept of opportunity value is not new. It was clearly understood by Canning who used the term 'opportunity differential' to describe the difference between what we have called the opportunity value of the services of an asset, and the operating costs incurred in their extraction: see his *op. cit.* p. 241. For subsequent references to the concept see the citations collected by D. Green, Jr. and G. H. Sorter on p. 436 of their article 'Accounting for Obsolescence—A Proposal', *Accounting Review*, xxxiv (July 1959), 433–41.

acquired machine is equal to their replacement cost: at this stage, the utility of the services to the firm is usually so great that it would pay to continue to provide them even if the existing machine were suddenly destroyed. It may also be assumed that, for every service now being provided, there will come a time when its utility falls below replacement cost— in other words, the supply of the service will not continue to be required for ever.

REPLACEMENT COST UNDER STATIC CONDITIONS

Let us consider the case of a service whose utility exceeds its replacement cost, so that its value is cost-determined. On the simplest assumptions, namely, stable prices and static technology, the most economical method of providing the service, should an existing machine be suddenly destroyed, would be by the purchase and operation of an identical machine. The assumptions of stability also imply that the replacement cost of the service will be constant from period: we can therefore define replacement cost as the (constant) average unit cost of obtaining the service from a hypothetical substitute for the existing machine. This average unit cost will be a minimum if the substitute machine is operated for the optimum number of years; the minimum average cost may therefore be determined by solving for R in the equation

$$C = \sum_{n=1}^{r} [RQ(n) - E(n)](1+i)^{-n} + S(T)(1+i)^{-T} \tag{1}$$

where

C is the capital cost of the substitute machine,

$Q(n)$ is the number of units of service produced by the machine during the nth period of its life,

$E(n)$ is the operating expense incurred during that period,[1]

i is the rate of interest, expressed as a fraction per period,

$S(n)$ is the salvage value of the machine at the end of the nth period, and

T is the economic life of the machine, i.e. that life which leads to the minimum value of the average unit cost R.[2]

Now, on our assumption of stable prices and static technology, the value of C, and the functions $Q(n)$, $E(n)$, and $S(n)$, will be exactly the same for the hypothetical substitute machine as for the existing machine.

---

[1] For greater ease of discounting it has been assumed that all services are received, and all operating expenses incurred, on the last day of the period.

[2] *See* Hotelling, above, pp. 263–4: our R corresponds formally to Hotelling's 'theoretical selling price', *x*.

F. K. Wright

Hence the value of the existing machine at the end of the tth period of its its life is given by

$$V(t) = \sum_{n=t+1}^{T} [RQ(n) - E(n)](1+i)^{t-n} + S(T)(1+i)^{t-T} \qquad (2)$$

and its depreciation during the tth period by

$$D(t) = V(t-1) - V(t) \qquad (3)$$
$$= RQ(t) - E(t) - iV(t-1) \qquad \text{[see Appendix]}$$

where R is the minimum average cost of service defined by equation (1) above.

Canning, who gave this depreciation formula many years ago,[1] apparently did not realize that it depends for its validity on the rather special assumptions of stable prices and static technology.

OPPORTUNITY VALUE UNDER VARIABLE CONDITIONS

If we now relax these special assumptions, we lose the convenient simplicity of constant opportunity values. The replacement cost of a unit of service may now vary over time and must therefore be expressed as a function of time. We must also recognize that, for any given machine, the constant unit cost obtained by striking an average over its economic life has no unique claim to be regarded as *the* cost of its services: we must be prepared to accept as equally valid any cost function $F(n)$ which satisfies the equation

$$C = \sum_{n=1}^{T} [F(n)Q(n) - E(n)](1+i)^{-n} + S(T)(1+i)^{-T} \qquad (4)$$

where $F(n)$ is the cost of a unit of service from the machine, expressed as a function of time,[2] and T is the economic life of the machine, i.e. that life which maximizes the value of the right-hand side of equation (4).

For any given machine, there is an infinite number of functions $F(n)$ which satisfy equation (4). Whilst for a single machine, therefore, no unique cost function can be found, we shall show that it is possible to define the replacement cost of a given service as a unique function— namely, that function of time which makes the most efficient machine available in each period appear as a marginal investment when its expected services are valued at the lower of utility or replacement cost.

[1] *Op. cit.* p. 300.
[2] We shall assume, for convenience, that changes in the cost function only take place at the end of an accounting period, so that $F(n)$ may be considered constant within each period. This is not a restrictive assumption, since the duration of accounting periods may be made as brief as we please.

Suppose that at the beginning of period $(h+1)$, for the first time, the expected net utilities of the most efficient machine available have a present value which is less than the cost of the machine. Then the opportunity value of the services in period $(h+1)$ and subsequent periods will be their utility, so that their replacement cost need not be found.

If period h is the last period in which the present value of the expected net utilities from a machine exceeds its cost, then it is also the last period for which a replacement cost must be determined. The required figure, $R(h)$, will be that value which makes the most efficient machine available at the beginning of period h appear as a marginal investment when its services in that period are valued at $R(h)$ and those of every subsequent period at their utility. Similarly, $R(h-1)$ will be that value which makes the most efficient machine available at the beginning of period $(h-1)$ appear as a marginal investment when its services in that period are valued at $R(h-1)$, those of the next period at $R(h)$, and those of each subsequent period at their utility. Overall, we have h unknown values of $R(\tau)$, where τ stands for absolute time, measured in 'periods'; and we have h equations similar to equation (4), representing the characteristics of the most efficient machine available in each of the next h periods. In principle, therefore, the replacement cost function is a determinate one.

The mathematical determination of that function, however, would require forecasts of the capital cost, operating costs, and production rates of the most efficient machine in every future period up to the time when the utility of the service falls below its replacement cost, and forecasts of the utility of the service beyond that time. Thus, there is very little hope of the necessary forecasts ever being obtained; and since the opportunity value of the service must be known in order to calculate the correct depreciation charge, there is equally little hope of obtaining a mathematical solution of the depreciation problem in this way.

An intuitive approach to the problem may, however, prove more practicable than a strictly mathematical one. Intuitively, one would expect the replacement cost of a service to fall if the efficiency of machines is being improved more rapidly than equipment prices are increasing, and to rise if the rate of price increase exceeds the rate of technological advance. On the basis of broad expectations of this kind, an estimate might be made of the likely trend in the replacement cost of the service over the expected life of the machine—indeed, such an estimate is really implicit in any forecast of economic life.[1]

Since replacement cost is defined as that function of time which makes the most efficient machine available appear as a marginal investment, it

---

[1] *See* G. Terborgh, *Dynamic Equipment Policy* (New York, 1949), p. 108.

follows that the machine for which we are seeking a depreciation pattern should also represent a marginal investment when its services are valued according to that function.[1] One test of the reasonableness of our forecast of replacement costs is therefore provided by equation (4), and our initial estimate of $R(n)$ may have to be revised to enable it to take the place of $F(n)$ in that equation.

The resulting function $R(n)$ would then replace the constant R in equation (3), and we would estimate the appropriate depreciation charge by the equation

$$D(t) = R(t)Q(t) - E(t) - iV(t-1). \tag{5}$$

That is to say, the appropriate depreciation charge is equal to the drop in the capital value of the machine, future services being valued at their estimated replacement cost.

In the absence of perfect foresight, we must of course be prepared for changes in the expectations on which our estimates of replacement cost were based. In particular, it will often happen that unforeseen obsolescence results in a downward revision of expected utilities or replacement costs. When this happens, the book value of the asset should be written down to the present value of its future services based on the changed expectations about opportunity values.[2]

DETERMINING THE RATE OF INTEREST

When one considers the difficulty of forecasting the opportunity value of future services, the choice of a rate of interest is seen to be a problem of very minor importance. Canning took the view that for practical purposes interest could simply be ignored: to make allowance for it in calculating depreciation charges would be 'as absurd as trying to correct for the earth's rotation in a snowball fight'.[3]

Since this article is concerned with the theory rather than the practice of depreciation, however, a few remarks about the determination of the interest rate may not be out of place. The appropriate rate for any period will be the opportunity cost of funds during that period. In the case of a firm whose growth is not restricted by the amount of funds it can raise, the opportunity cost of funds will usually be the average cost of raising additional funds, though in some cases it might be the rate at which surplus funds can be placed in the market.[4] In a firm whose growth is effectively

---

[1] If we assume that the decision to acquire the machine represented a rational choice, and that its expected economic life does not extend beyond the replacement horizon h.

[2] See Green and Sorter, *loc. cit.*   [3] *Op. cit.* p. 297.

[4] For a full discussion of this point see E. Solomon, *The Theory of Financial Management* (New York, 1963), chapters III–V.

limited by the amount of finance available to it, the opportunity cost of funds will be 'the expected rate or set of rates marginal to future investment budgets of the firm'.[1]

COMPARISON WITH OTHER THEORIES

Other theories of depreciation fall mainly into three categories:

(1) traditional accounting theory which seeks to 'match' the capital cost of each asset with the net revenues to which it gives rise;

(2) theories based upon discounting or expected net revenues from the asset (usually at its 'internal rate of return'); and

(3) theories which aim at stabilizing net earnings after depreciation, such as Professor Sosnick's 'offsetting-interest method'.[2]

All three types of theory are based on the assumption that, in respect of each asset, there are specific revenues which can be identified as attributable to it. The validity of this assumption is in many cases open to considerable doubt. But even if we accept, for argument's sake, this assumption of identifiable asset revenues, we still face the problem of justifying the book values which result from the proposed methods of depreciation.

Traditional matching theory does not seriously attempt such a justification —indeed, it was developed largely for the purpose of by-passing the valuation problem which lies at the root of most of our difficulties with depreciation.

Discounted revenue theory does formally resemble an economic theory of valuation. But Preinreich pointed out some years ago that the valuations to which it gives rise have *objective* validity only when the discount rate equals the opportunity cost of funds; book values obtained by discounting expected net revenues at any other rate are in fact based upon some (usually unrecognized) subjective assumption about 'the continuous time shape of the profit' from the investment.[3] There would thus be as many equally valid methods of depreciation as there are possible assumptions about the time shape of the profit—in other words, an infinite number.

But worse is to come. Although there is an infinite number of depreciation patterns which Preinreich regards as equally valid, that number does *not* include every possible pattern: he rules out, as leading to a contradiction, all time shapes of profit which do not terminate with an earning rate equal to the opportunity cost of funds.[4] This would exclude from the

---

[1] Ed Renshaw, 'A Note on the Arithmetic of Capital Budgeting Decisions', in E. Solomon (ed.), *The Management of Corporate Capital* (Glencoe, 1959), p. 213n.
[2] See p. 276 n. 3 above. [3] Preinreich, *loc. cit.* p. 237. [4] *Ibid.* pp. 237–9.

category of valid depreciation methods those which discount expected net revenues at the internal rate of return, unless that rate happens to coincide with the opportunity cost of funds (i.e unless the investment is a marginal one). It would also rule out the offsetting-interest method, excepting once again the case of the marginal investment.

To this radical criticism it might perhaps be objected that the contradiction pointed out by Preinreich would not bother anyone except a theoretical purist, and that the time shapes implicit in the discounted-revenue or stabilized-earnings method are really quite reasonable. Let us therefore leave this argument on one side, and turn to the question how the revenue attributable to a particular asset may be identified.

This would not be too difficult a problem if it were true, as Preinreich apparently believed,[1] that a market price can generally be found for the product of any machine. But this assumption had been severely criticized by Canning some years earlier. 'In a plant in which tractors are manufactured for sale,' Canning had asked, 'how much of the service of bringing in the dollar-receipts from a given sale is attributable to coal burned under the boilers, how much to the service of the boiler, how much to the various devices in foundry, machine shop, assembly floor, how much to the firemen, moulders, machinists, and night watchmen?'[2] It seems clear that any valuation theory which depends upon having a market price for the services of each machine to be valued will be applicable to only a very limited range of assets.

In the absence of such a market price, it would appear that the only way of measuring the contribution which a particular machine will make to the revenues of a firm is to use the 'differential cash flow' approach commonly employed in connexion with investment decisions. Indeed, several recent writers on depreciation seem to have taken it for granted that the differential cash flows which should have been forecast in the course of arriving at an investment decision also represent an appropriate basis for asset valuation, and hence for depreciation policy.

Thus Bierman has written:

the proper depreciation charge is determined at the moment the decision to invest is made. At that time the cash proceeds of the future periods are discounted back to the present and compared to the cost of the asset. In a sense the cost of the asset consists of the cost of purchasing the proceeds of different periods. Thus the depreciation charge of the period will be related to the forecasted net cash proceeds which formed the basis of the decision to invest in the asset.[3]

We shall argue, however, that there are important differences between the problems posed by an investment decision and the problems of asset

---

[1] Preinreich, *loc. cit.* p. 236.   [2] *Op. cit.* pp. 232–3.
[3] *Loc. cit.* pp. 613–14; also Anton, *loc. cit.* p. 119, and Reynolds, *loc. cit.* pp. 243–4.

valuation; with the result that cash flows relevant to the former will frequently be inappropriate for the latter purpose.

For the purpose of arriving at an investment decision, it is usually convenient to measure the cash flows resulting from the purchase of a proposed machine against *the best alternative not involving capital expenditure*. Thus the differential cash flow from a proposed machine might be the difference between the cost of operating that machine and the cost or loss which would result from dispensing altogether with the service which the machine could provide; or it might be the difference between the cost of operating the machine and the cost of purchasing its services (where this is possible, and cheaper than other alternatives); or it might be the excess costs avoided by not continuing to operate and maintain an existing obsolete or worn-out machine.

Differential cash flows computed in this way may be discounted at the opportunity-cost rate, to yield a 'present value' for the proposed machine— a value which will often be greatly in excess of its cost. But such a surplus of present value over the cost of the machine does not necessarily mean that the machine should be bought: it merely shows that it would be preferable to buy this machine rather than nothing. Usually there will be other machines capable of supplying a similar service. Differential cash flows for those other machines must be calculated on exactly the same basis (i.e. against the same best-alternative-not-involving-capital-expenditure). The present values of the various machines may then be compared with their respective costs. The machine showing the highest surplus of present value over cost should be chosen as it will represent the most profitable of the mutually exclusive investment projects under consideration.

We see, therefore, that in many investment decision problems involving a choice among several more or less comparable machines, the alternative of 'no capital expenditure' does not really enter into the final comparison: it merely serves as a convenient benchmark from which to measure the cash flows of the various machines in order to determine their relative merits.

It should also be evident that the present value of a machine, based on its cash flows relative to buying nothing, is often a fictitious value in the sense that no rational buyer would pay this much for the machine as long as substitutes are available. Of course this fact in no way detracts from the usefulness of such a figure when used for investment decisions in the manner just described; but it makes that figure quite unsuitable as a basis of asset valuation.

The essential difference between the cash flows of capital budgeting and our concept of opportunity value is simply this: differential cash flow is measured by comparing the situation which would result from a proposed capital expenditure with the best alternative available *without incurring capital expenditure*; opportunity value is measured by comparing the existing situation with the best alternative currently available, *whether that alternative involves capital expenditure or not.*

By not excluding alternatives involving capital expenditure, the concept of opportunity value avoids certain features of differential cash flow which make the latter concept unsuitable for asset valuation: the double counting of revenue from complementary machines,[1] and the fiction that the services of a machine can be worth more to the owner than it would cost him to provide them by alternative means.

CONCLUSION

The essential ingredients of a general theory of depreciation can be found in the pioneering contributions of Hotelling and Canning. Canning developed the concept of opportunity value, but apparently failed to see that in a dynamic economy this value must be allowed to vary over time. Hotelling understood the need for expressing his 'theoretical selling price' as a function of time,[2] but lacked the opportunity value concept necessary to defend his theory against the objections later put forward by Preinreich.[3] When these complementary concepts are brought together, a general theory of depreciation begins to emerge.

In view of the difficulty of applying this theory, it is unlikely to be used in practice except in very rare instances. But a theory of depreciation should not be judged by its practical usefulness, but rather by its theoretical soundness, its generality, and the light it throws on accounting practice.

The opportunity value theory of depreciation is superior to the traditional matching approach because it is firmly grounded in valuation theory. As compared with the discounted-revenue and stabilized-earnings approaches, it has the advantage of avoiding the difficulties arising from jointness of revenue among complementary machines, and of being free from arbitrary assumptions about the 'time shape of the profit'.

Opportunity value theory firmly supports the traditional accounting practice of valuing newly acquired machines at cost: accountants need no longer feel apologetic about doing so even though discounted-cash-flow calculations may show a present value in excess of cost.[4]

---

[1] Where several machines can only operate profitably in conjunction with one another, the revenue from all those machines could be included in the differential cash flow of a proposed replacement for any one of them.

[2] p. 264 above.   [3] *Loc. cit.* p. 234.

[4] *See* Bierman's suggestion that in such a case the asset might be recorded in the books at its present value and the excess over cost credited to an 'Unrealized Profit' account: *loc. cit.* p. 616.

Again, the theoretical justification of decreasing-charge depreciation has recently been the subject of debate.[1] With the aid of opportunity value theory it is easily shown that this practice could be justified by ordinary technological obsolescence, even in the absence of any physical deterioration of the machine.

APPENDIX

1 *Proof of equation (3)*

$$D(t) = V(t-1) - V(t)$$
$$= V(t-1) + iV(t-1) - iV(t-1) - V(t)$$
$$= (1+i) V(t-1) - V(t) - iV(t-1)$$
$$= (1+i)\left\{ \sum_{n=t}^{T} [RQ(n) - E(n)] (1+i)^{t-n-1} + S(T) (1+i)^{t-T-1} \right\} - V(t) - iV(t-1)$$
$$= \sum_{n=t}^{T} [RQ(n) - E(n)] (1+i)^{t-n} + S(T) (1+i)^{t-T} - V(t) - iV(t-1)$$
$$= RQ(t) - E(t) + \sum_{n=t+1}^{T} [RQ(n) - E(n)] (1+i)^{t-n}$$
$$\qquad\qquad\qquad\qquad + S(T) (1+i)^{t-T} - V(t) - iV(t-1)$$
$$= RQ(t) - E(t) + V(t) - V(t) - iV(t-1)$$
$$= RQ(t) - E(t) - iV(t-1).$$

2 *Arithmetical illustration*

Consider a machine with the following characteristics:

$C = 1,000$

$Q(n) = 36 - n^2$ i.e. $Q(1) = 35$, $Q(2) = 32$, etc.

$E(n) = 10 + n^2$ i.e. $E(1) = 11$, $E(2) = 14$, etc.

$S(n) = C(0.8)^n = 1,000.(0.8)^n$ i.e. $S(1) = 800$, $S(2) = 640$, etc.

and assume $i = 0.10$.

To find the economic life of this machine, assuming stable prices and stable technology, solve for R in equation (1) using varying values of T, and choose the T which yields the lowest R.

Suppose $T = 1$,

then $1,000 = (35R - 11) (1.1)^{-1} + 800(1.1)^{-1}$

i.e. $311 = 35R$ $\qquad\qquad\qquad\qquad\qquad\qquad\qquad$ $R = 8.8857.$

Suppose $T = 2$,

then $1,000 = (35R - 11) (1.1)^{-1} + (32R - 14) (1.1)^{-2} + 640(1.1)^{-2}$

i.e. $596.1 = 70.5R,$ $\qquad\qquad\qquad\qquad\qquad\qquad$ $R = 8.4553.$

[1] R. L. Dixon, *loc. cit.*; A. N. Lorig, 'On the Logic of Decreasing Charge Depreciation', *Accounting Review*, XXXVII (January 1962), 56–8; G. J. Staubus, 'Decreasing Charge Depreciation—Still Searching for Logic', *Accounting Review*, XXXVII (July 1962), 497–501.

Suppose $T = 3$,

then $1,000 = (35R - 11)(1 \cdot 1)^{-1} + (32R - 14)(1 \cdot 1)^{-2} + (27R - 19)(1 \cdot 1)^{-3} + 512(1 \cdot 1)^{-3}$

i.e. $866 \cdot 71 = 104 \cdot 55R$, $\qquad\qquad\qquad\qquad\qquad\qquad\qquad R = 8 \cdot 2899.$

Suppose $T = 4$,

then $1,000 = (35R - 11)(1 \cdot 1)^{-1} + (32R - 14)(1 \cdot 1)^{-2} + (27R - 19)(1 \cdot 1)^{-3} +$
$$(20R - 26)(1 \cdot 1)^{-4} + 409 \cdot 6(1 \cdot 1)^{-4}$$

i.e. $1,132 \cdot 981 = 135 \cdot 005R$, $\qquad\qquad\qquad\qquad\qquad R = 8 \cdot 3921.$

For higher values of T, even higher values of R would be obtained. The lowest value of R, $8 \cdot 2899$, occurs at $T = 3$, which therefore represents the economic life of the machine.

We can now use equation (3) to calculate the depreciation charges:

$D(1) = (8 \cdot 2899 . 35) - 11 - 0 \cdot 1 . 1,000$
$\quad\quad\ = 290 \cdot 15 - 11 - 100 = 179 \cdot 15$

$D(2) = (8 \cdot 2899 . 32) - 14 - 0 \cdot 1(1,000 - 179 \cdot 15)$
$\quad\quad\ = 265 \cdot 28 - 14 - 82 \cdot 09 = 169 \cdot 19$

$D(3) = (8 \cdot 2899 . 27) - 19 - 0 \cdot 1(1,000 - 179 \cdot 15 - 169 \cdot 19)$
$\quad\quad\ = 223 \cdot 83 - 19 - 65 \cdot 17 = 139 \cdot 66.$

Check: $1,000 - 179 \cdot 15 - 169 \cdot 19 - 139 \cdot 66 = 512 \cdot 00$, which is $S(3)$, the salvage value at the end of three years.

Now suppose the facts to be the same as in the first illustration, except that technology is not stable: the introduction of new models is expected to reduce the unit cost of services by 10 per cent per annum, i.e.

$$R(n + 1) = 0 \cdot 9R(n)$$

i.e. $\qquad\qquad\qquad\qquad R(2) = 0 \cdot 9R(1), \ R(3) = (0 \cdot 9)^2 R(1),$ etc.

This time, let r stand for $R(1)$. Again, we first must find the economic life, i.e. that which minimizes r (and hence $R(2)$, etc.).

Suppose $T = 1$,

then $r = 8 \cdot 8857$, as in previous illustration.

Suppose $T = 2$,

then $1,000 = (35r - 11)(1 \cdot 1)^{-1} + (32 . 0 \cdot 9r - 14)(1 \cdot 1)^{-2} + 640(1 \cdot 1)^{-2}$

i.e. $596 \cdot 1 = 67 \cdot 3r$, $\qquad\qquad\qquad\qquad\qquad\qquad\qquad r = 8 \cdot 8574.$

Suppose $T = 3$,

then $1,000 = (35r - 11)(1 \cdot 1)^{-1} + (32 . 0 \cdot 9r - 14)(1 \cdot 1)^{-2} +$
$$(27 . 0 \cdot 81r - 19)(1 \cdot 1)^{-3} + 512(1 \cdot 1)^{-3}$$

i.e. $866 \cdot 71 = 95 \cdot 90r$, $\qquad\qquad\qquad\qquad\qquad\qquad\qquad r = 9 \cdot 038.$

Still higher values will be obtained for $T = 4$, etc., so that $T = 2$ represents the economic life of the machine.

Then $R(1) = r = 8 \cdot 8574$, and $R(2) = 0 \cdot 9 . 8 \cdot 8574 = 7 \cdot 9716.$

288

Now calculate the depreciation charges, using equation (5):

$$D(1) = 8.8574.35 - 11 - 0.1 . 1,000$$

$$= 310.01 - 11 - 100 = \qquad 199.01$$

$$D(2) = 7.9716.32 - 14 - 0.1(1,000 - 199.01)$$

$$= 255.09 - 14 - 80.10 = \qquad 160.99.$$

Check: $1,000 - 199.01 - 160.99 = 640.0 = S(2)$, the salvage value after two years.

20 Replacement cost depreciation[1]

by A. R. Prest*

This article is intended to appraise the arguments used in the recently revived controversy[2] about depreciation allowances at replacement cost which has come to life on both sides of the Atlantic.[3] We do not seek to make any lengthy statistical arguments, but the aim is rather to illuminate the underlying economic principles involved, a task which has grown increasingly difficult amid the welter of argument aroused. And we shall further restrict ourselves even within this limited area. In general the discussion will range around the sum of money which a business should attempt (or should be allowed) to accumulate over the course of the life

[1] I wish to thank S. A. Goldberg and R. W. Goldsmith for valuable remarks on this article.

[2] This cry seems to emerge regularly under inflationary conditions, e.g. the report of the U.S. Steel Corporation for 1920 shows special charges to income and allocations to reserve to meet increased inventory and fixed assets costs. And in Germany a number of works appeared in the 1920s, for example, Schmalenbach, *Die Dynamische Bilanz*, and Schmidt, *Die Industriekonjunktur—ein Rechenfehler*. A summary of Schmidt's ideas is to be found in his article 'The Basis of Depreciation Charges', *Harvard Business Review* (1930), p. 257.

[3] From the British side see: F. S. Bray, *Precision and Design in Accountancy*; H. W. Singer, *Standardised Accountancy in Germany*; A. Macbeath, *Depreciation and Renewal of Assets having Fluctuating Values*; Association of Certified and Corporate Accountants, *Working Party Reports: Some Accounting and Economic Aspects*; R. Kristensson, 'Errors in Accounting due to Inflation', *Economic History* (February 1940); S. P. Chambers, 'Taxation and the Supply of Capital for Industry', *Lloyds Bank Review* (January 1949); L. T. Little, 'Replacement Costs—an Economist's View', *Accounting Research* (November 1948); W. T. Baxter, 'Accountants and the Inflation', *Transactions of Manchester Statistical Society* (1948–9); K. Lacey, 'Profit Measurement and the Trade Cycle', *Economic Journal* (December 1947); 'The Finance of Industry', *The Times* (23 and 24 April 1949); 'Taxation and Shortage of Industrial Capital' (duplicated, Federation of British Industries).

See also numerous articles in *The Economist* (for example, 26 March 1949, pp. 549–51) and *The Accountant* (for example, 15 January 1949, Recomendation XII of Council of Institute of Chartered Accountants, 'Rising Price Levels in Relation to Accounts').

From the American side see: G. Terborgh, *The Bogey of Economic Maturity* and *Dynamic Equipment Policy*; Machinery and Allied Products Institute, *Depreciation Policy and the Post-war Price Level; Capital Goods Industries and Tax Reform*; Bulletin No. 2119; L. H. Kimmel, *Depreciation Policy and Post-war Expansion*; Profits Sub-Committee of Joint Committee on the Economic Report, *Summary Report on Corporate Profits Hearings* (December 1948); A. H. Dean, *Business Income under Recent Price Levels* (Study Group on Business Income); W. Adams, 'Accounting Practice and the Business Cycle', *Journal of Business* (University of Chicago) (April 1949); W. Froelich, 'Income Determination and Investment', *American Economic Review* (March 1948).

See also numerous articles in *Harvard Business Review*, *Accounting Review* and *Journal of Accountancy*.

---

* Stanley Jevons Professor of Political Economy, University of Manchester.

of a fixed asset, and we shall not deal, except in passing, with the criteria by which the length of life should be judged, or with the principles on which the accumulation should be spread over the different years of this life. Finally, we shall restrict ourselves fairly closely to a discussion of fixed assets, though, of course, many of the arguments used can be extended without difficulty to inventories.

There seem to be two main lines of reasoning lying behind the mass of literature on this subject. First, there is the argument that the accounting principles on which business firms work should be such that they do not simply attempt to recover the original, historical cost of capital equipment, but in some sense or other, replacement cost. Second, we have the theoretically less clear but more popular position, where the main objective is for various reasons to secure reductions in taxation on industrial profits, and the idea of depreciation at replacement cost (or, more generally, enhanced depreciation allowances), is propagated as a means of attaining this objective. Of course, the two lines of reasoning are not completely separate from one another, but it will be convenient to explore each of them in turn and to indicate the specific points of contrast as they arise.

I REPLACEMENT COST THEORY ARGUMENTS

1 *Main argument*

The main argument of the first school is based on the teachings of economic theory about the nature of income and capital. It is quite clear that any calculation of income which allows for depreciation at replacement cost approximates more closely to Dr Hicks' 'central concept'[1] than does one which simply allows for the recovery of the original money capital invested in fixed assets. It is, of course, fully recognized that even estimating depreciation allowances at replacement cost (whether current or anticipated) is by no means equivalent to estimating capital consumption—to do that we need to estimate the reduction in the aggregate (discounted) value of the prospective stream of services which would occur in any given timeperiod irrespective of changes in expected interest rates and prices and irrespective of windfall losses or gains of an extraordinary character. But, as has been pointed out often enough before, this is not a very precise definition, let alone a concept susceptible to statistical measurement, and therefore some rough attempt to allow for price changes is perhaps the best that can be done in making statistical estimates of capital consumption.

[1] *Value and Capital*, ch. XIV [chapter 4, above]. The criterion for measuring depreciation postulated by the same author in a subsequent article, 'Maintaining Capital Intact: A Further Suggestion', *Economica*, 1942 [chapter 9, above] also demands the same treatment.

A. R. Prest

Now the above argument is clearly of immediate and direct relevance when estimates of the net national income are being prepared. Any estimate of net national income in which allowances are only made for maintaining original historical value of capital intact is obviously biased upwards in a period of rising prices and biased downwards when prices are falling. And although any corrections to be made on this account might not in normal times be very significant, in a period such as the last few years the bias introduced may be of some importance.[1]

Now should these economic concepts which are so clearly relevant to the calculation of social income be applied in the determination of business income? Traditionally, of course, business accounts have normally allowed only for the recovery of original sums invested, and the great weight of opinion in accounting circles on both sides of the Atlantic has firmly endorsed this position.[2] The basis of this convention is in fact to be found at the very roots of double-entry bookkeeping in fifteenth-century Italy. At that time loans were made for specific short-period ventures and therefore price changes were of little significance, and the recovery of capital could be conceived purely and simply as relating to the original sums of cash lent to the entrepreneurs. Moreover, the first joint-stock companies[3] in the modern sense were formed to finance the excursions of the Elizabethan venturers, and these were, of course, specific short-term undertakings. Finally, it should be remembered that accountancy crystallized into a profession and accounting conventions were elevated into principles in the latter part of the nineteenth century—a period of relatively stable prices.

[1] Various attempts have been made to correct the official estimates of United Kingdom net national income on this point, for example, A. R. Prest, 'National Income of the U.K., 1870–1946', *Economic Journal* (March 1948), and D. Seers, *Oxford Bulletin of Statistics* (October 1948). Mr Seers is obviously right in correcting my estimates for upward bias introduced by my treatment of Government depreciation allowances, but he seems to err in suggesting that wartime disinvestment is not allowed for. Perhaps one may say that the correction to be made to the official figures was of the order of £250–300 million in 1945–6, that is, an addition of about 35 per cent to depreciation allowances and a deduction of about 3 per cent from net national income. Unfortunately it is impossible to extend this technique of estimation to more recent years owing to the introduction of special initial allowances in 1946. Moreover, it may be true that manufacturers have been more willing to replace machinery in the post-war period before the expiry of 'normal' life with the idea of claiming obsolescence allowances (reasoning that tax rates and therefore these allowances were likely to fall rather than rise). Both these mitigating factors must be taken into account in assessing the amount of upward bias in net national income figures during this period.

[2] See W. A. Paton, *Accountants' Handbook* (4th ed. p. 711): 'The essential conception is that of assigning the cost of property to the accounting periods included in useful life.' F. S. Bray, *op. cit.* p. 121; '...historical costs are in point of fact the only real objective dependable data available for the construction of accounting records'.

[3] See W. R. Scott, *Joint Stock Companies to 1720*, vol. I.

But, it is now argued, the application of such venerable principles in measuring the activities of the modern business corporation is a convention which cannot be justified on theoretical grounds. A distinguishing feature of such enterprises is that they are not short-period ventures destined to close down after a single period of operations but, in fact, they continue in operation for generation after generation. In other words one can regard business corporations today as a microcosm of society at large and therefore the principles relevant for measuring capital consumption in a social sense are directly relevant to business enterprise too.

2 Some supporting arguments

This is the fundamental argument for depreciation accounting on a replacement basis, but before considering its merits we must look at some reinforcements which have been marshalled in support. It is argued by one school[1] that the duty of the entrepreneur is to accumulate sufficient funds by depreciation charges, not necessarily to preserve the stock of physical assets intact, but to maintain the real value of the money capital originally subscribed in terms of some index of purchasing power. Another line of argument[2] is that the prime duty of the accountant is to match revenues and costs of the same time-dimension and, therefore, the only correct evaluation of the services of capital equipment in any time-period is on the basis of the replacement costs prevailing in that period. Possibly another way of interpreting this view is to go to the limit and consider the case where no depreciation accounting and major replacement is practised, but physical deterioration of fixed assets is made good by repairs and partial replacement and charged to current account. Clearly in that case all expenses are in the same time-dimension as revenues, and so, it may be argued, what grounds are there for different treatment in the more usual case of depreciation accounting? The argument also seems to relate to the accountant's budgeting problem—of deciding the costs to be taken into account in the pricing of goods to be sold in the future—for it is argued that in this case too replacement rather than original capital costs should be the standard.

[1] Machinery and Allied Products Institute, *Depreciation Policy and the Post-War Price Level.*

[2] E.g. Paton, *Accounting Review* (April 1948); Macbeath *op. cit.*; and Dannenberg, 'Depreciation and Capital Replenishment', *Journal of Accountancy* (April 1942), p. 340. A similar idea seems to be at the root of the article by T. H. Silcock, 'Accountants, Economists and the Valuation of Fixed Assets', *Economic Journal* (September 1949).

A. R. Prest

3   Arguments based on the consequences of not using replacement cost standards

Aside from the set of protagonists principally concerned with the relations between accounting statements and economic concepts *per se*, we have those who emphasize the dire consequences of not setting up accounting statements in such a fashion. First and foremost we have the argument that it is an accepted convention that industry should finance its own re-equipment. Therefore, unless the individual firm accumulates sufficient sums in its depreciation funds to finance re-equipment, it will in any prolonged period of rising prices find itself unable to carry on operations on the same scale, or at best it will be in an 'unsound' financial position. In its most extreme form this argument goes even further than pleading for depreciation at replacement costs, for it leads to the contention that if replacement costs rise after, say, the first five years of a machine's life, and subsequently stay constant, then not only should the remaining years of life be depreciated at the higher price level, but also an adjustment should be made to the original allowances for the first five years—in order that by the date of final retirement a sufficient sum should be accumulated to finance replacement.[1] Second, there is the view[2] that conventional accounting methods of valuing fixed assets and inventories tend to exaggerate cyclical booms and slumps. The line of reasoning here is that current accounting methods lead entrepreneurs to believe that profits are larger than they really are in the boom, and to trade union agitation for higher wages. Apart from the last point, the converse is held to occur in the slump. Third, it is urged that not only does 'over-expansion' take place in the boom, but also that it is unbalanced, in the sense that those firms with equipment purchased in the slump (or before any upheaval such as a war) have lower depreciation charges to meet (if they only seek to recover original costs), and therefore make greater profits and hence are more tempted to expand activities than those with newer equipment. Similarly, this argument can be extended to industries which have provided themselves with a large proportion of old equipment as against those with a small proportion, for if with stable prices industries of both types yield the same average rate of return on capital, any sudden general price change will tend to benefit the former type as against the latter. Similarly, industries with a high ratio of capital to total costs will probably also

---

[1] This general viewpoint has been put forward many times in the past. A recent statement in which it is embodied is R. F. Harrod, 'Planning for Four Years', *Soundings* (February 1949), p. 14, 'firms should be allowed to write off their existing plant by a total amount equal not to its original cost but to its present true replacement cost'.

[2] See K. Lacey, *op. cit.* W. Froelich, *op. cit.*

derive 'too much' encouragement. Fourth, we have the views of those interested in imposing standardized systems of accounts. If these accounts are to be anything more than a uniform system of presentation,[1] if they are to be used for comparisons of economic efficiency (either between firms at a given time point or for a single firm over time), then we need some system analogous to that developed in Nazi Germany where costing systems were developed in which all price and interest changes were eliminated.[2] Fifth, we have the statistical convenience argument put forward by the social accountants—the national or social income should allow for depreciation at replacement costs, but the national income is most easily conceived as the end-result of a consolidation process of private accounts; therefore, to be consistent, private accounts should be made up on the same depreciation principles. Analogous arguments can be put forward by those interested in measuring national capital.

Therefore, a number of powerful representations can be put forward in favour of replacement cost accounting. What arguments can be marshalled against them?

1 Main counter-argument

The central point on which issue must be joined is the concept of the rôle and nature of the modern business corporation. Now it is perfectly clear that replacement cost accounting is likely to give us a more accurate measure of 'social' income and it is also perfectly clear that the latter concept has relevance for the individual corporation. For the modern firm is a continuing enterprise (though whether, on the average, it outlives its buildings is a questionable point), and any measure of income from current production must therefore take into account the implications for future production, in exactly the same way as the measure of income for society must take into account any implied encroachment on future income. But is this the only facet of the firm? Surely it can be very strongly argued that 'capital' does mean two things to the individual firm corresponding to the two rôles of business enterprise and legal entity. It is *not* good economics to apply a social concept of income *simpliciter* to the business corporation. From the viewpoint of society the structure of debts and credits so characteristic of modern economies cancels out (apart from loans from or to foreigners, of course), and therefore the relevant concept of 'capital' is the sum total of physical assets. But for the individual firm the position

---

[1] The new 'uniform' system of accounts in France seems to be no more than this.

[2] See H. W. Singer, *Standardised Accountancy in Germany*. The results of applying such principles to the accounts of nine major steel companies in the U.S.A. are shown by R. C. Jones, 'Effects of Inflation on Capital and Profits', *Journal of Accountancy* (January 1949).

is not the same, and the simple fact that the firm has obligations to its shareholders—the principal one being to assure the solvency of the firm rather than the extent of its future operations—as well as to society as a whole, must always be remembered.[1,2] Indeed, it can reasonably be maintained that many, if not all, firms when faced with a difficult decision ask themselves primarily the effect on the structure of their assets as measured by, for example, the ratio of current assets to current liabilities or the effect on their relations with their shareholders rather than the effect on income from trading ten years hence. Nor can it be argued with great conviction that the interests of shareholders are best served by a measure of capital consumption which preserves income permanently intact, for even though it may be true that an individual may so wish to arrange his affairs as to preserve income intact *for his own lifetime*, that is no justification for assuming that the firm should act so as to preserve its income at the same level for ever. In fact, it is very hard to see any real reason for supporting this latter idea at all, for although we may agree that the firm today is a continuing organism, there the analogy with society as a whole ends. Whereas we may agree and hope that society as a whole will at least preserve its stock of physical assets intact from one generation to another, to argue that every individual firm must do so is surely unwarranted. And quite apart from the logic or equity of the matter, we always have to take account of the legal background, and in England, at any rate, any deliberate attempt to account on a replacement cost basis might possibly be construed as being against the legal rights of shareholders.[3]

Therefore the first point we challenge is that 'the' correct *motif* of action for the individual firm is to aim at preserving intact its stock of physical assets. Logically the next step is to examine the closely connected argument (listed in section 3 above) that, if this idea were accepted, the individual firm should account on a replacement cost basis to be sure of having 'sufficient' cash for such purposes. We have already seen that in the extreme form this argument asserts that not only should current and

[1] This basic idea seems to have inspired the famous series of judgments given by Mr Justice Brandeis (see Dean, *op. cit.* pp. 83–5).

[2] Although we are not principally concerned here with seeking the most appropriate concept of income for the individual, it should be observed that the argument developed here in respect of business income has relevance also for the private individual. For it can obviously be maintained that if a man is solvent or has quick assets equivalent to quick liabilities he is in an important sense keeping the 'capital' intact. Therefore the distinction between rival concepts of income and capital should perhaps be drawn in respect of social income on the one hand and personal and business income on the other (despite the fact that Hicks' concepts of income and capital were originally developed in relation to the private individual, see *Value and Capital, loc. cit.* [chapter 4 above]).

[3] *See* Black and Edwards, 'British Income Tax and Company Finances', *Review of Economic Studies* (1937–8).

future depreciation allowances be based on replacement cost but adjustments should be made to any previous allowances based on a lower replacement cost.[1] It is submitted that this argument is fallacious—and this because, fundamentally, it is an over-simplification to think in terms of one firm owning one piece of capital equipment only. Let us examine this problem in detail, for its understanding is an essential link in our chain of argument.[2]

In the first place, we may note that any problem of deficiencies in depreciation allowances 'over the first five years' will only occur if the rate of re-equipment is irregular. Suppose, for instance, we have a firm owning ten machines each of which lasts ten years, and also assume further that the age-distribution is rectangular, that is that one machine is replaced every year. Now suppose that costs of replacement are constant at £100 per machine for ten years and then suddenly double. If we think solely of the machine which is due to be replaced in this particular year, and if we conceive it to have a depreciation fund of its own, then obviously this fund will not suffice to pay for a new machine as it will only be £110—£90 accumulated at £10 a year for nine years and £20 allowed for the current year. But clearly this is not the right way of looking at the problem. In fact, the firm has a common depreciation fund for all ten machines and this fund is credited with £200 in the current year. Therefore the exact amount needed for purchasing the machine is available. This argument, however, essentially rests on the idea of a constant re-equipment rate, and as soon as we relax this stipulation the original contention is seen to have some force, particularly in the limit where the firm only has one machine and therefore only replaces it every ten years, although even here the shortfall depends on whether the price rise takes place soon after the asset is installed or near the end of its life.[3] At the same time, we should observe that such a shortfall can occur even though no price rise takes place. If we take the firm with ten machines, of which it normally replaces one every year, but owing to some circumstance (for example, war) has to suspend replacements for five years, then it will find itself with five machines instead of ten (or if the over-age machines are not physically discarded, with ten

[1] See p. 294 above.
[2] Since this part of the paper was written a similar argument has been put forward by H. Norris ('Depreciation Allowances in Relation to Financial Capital, Real Capital and Productive Capacity', *Accounting Research*, July 1949). As, however, the treatment is somewhat different and the conclusions derived very different from my own, I have left my argument as originally written.
[3] Even in this case it is not necessarily true that the depreciation on an original cost basis will lead to a shortfall, for accumulated funds may be in the form of securities or other assets which appreciate in value sufficiently to compensate for the rise in replacement costs.

machines having twice the normal average age), and with £350 accumulated in depreciation funds, that is (£90 + 80 + 70 + 60 + 50). Therefore if the firm wishes to replace all five of the worn-out machines at once its funds will be 'insufficient', even in the absence of any price rise. This point, however, does raise some issues of where the line should be drawn between replacements and additions to capital stock and we shall have occasion to revert to it later.[1]

Now, of course, it may well be argued that firms do in fact only re-equip at irregular intervals and that therefore our reply is not very helpful. But then, surely, we can make the point that even though the re-equipment for the individual firm is irregular, that for society as a whole is much less so. Therefore, even though for some firms depreciation allowances granted are not 'sufficient' for re-equipment, the total amount available to all firms is sufficient. This point surely exposes the fallacy of the whole idea of close correspondence between sums recovered as depreciation allowances and sums needed for re-equipment for the individual firm. For the question of sufficiency will depend in large measure on the structure of industry, on how far firms are a replica of society as a whole. This in turn depends largely on the size of the (financial) unit and the multiplicity of operations carried on. In other words, the apparent preciseness of the concept of a firm's own depreciation funds being adequate for its own re-equipment purposes disintegrates on close examination.

But all that we have shown so far is that the relation between recovery of funds at replacement rates and funds needed for re-equipment is not exact. We have not shown that depreciation at replacement costs may provide more funds than is necessary to finance re-equipment. In fact we have shown rather that if the total stock of capital equipment is to be replaced at a uniform rate, depreciation at replacement rates is necessary. This carries the obvious implication that if the replacement rate for all industry is not uniform, then even this measure of depreciation may be inadequate. How much substance is there in this implication?

One way of looking at this problem is to think of a firm in which a machine, installed at a cost of £100, is destined to last ten years. Assume that five years later a similar machine is again installed (at the same price). Then by the end of ten years on a straight-line basis of depreciation £150 will have accumulated, but only £100 of this is needed to buy the new machine needed to replace the first. Therefore there is a 'float' which will fluctuate

---

[1] How much the present 'inadequacy' of depreciation reserves in the United Kingdom is due to the war and post-war price rises and how much to the enforced hiatus in replacements is a most interesting point, but unfortunately it is not easily resolved in quantitative terms.

between £50 and £150, with a mean size of £100. If prices of new equipment do not change at all, then from the point of view of financing purchases of new equipment, though not, of course, from the viewpoint of
preserving the solvency of the firm, our firm will have funds to spare.
On the other hand, if prices of new equipment rise but depreciation
allowances continue to be made on the basis of orginal costs, the 'float'
will rapidly disappear, and the firm will find itself unable to finance re-
equipment on the same scale from its depreciation funds. At first sight
this argument seems conclusive, but in fact it is not so, for it fails to take
into account an extremely important factor—the possibility of net investment. In so far as the firm is continuously growing in size, then in the
absence of price changes the 'float' will increase with the increase in capital
stock. If, in fact, price changes do occur and depreciation on new assets
is charged according to the new prices, the size of the 'float' will depend
on a complex combination of circumstances: the original cost of assets,
the rate of growth of the capital stock, the rate of price rise, the age-
distribution of the stock of equipment. Furthermore, if accumulated depreciation funds are invested in securities or other assets that appreciate
in value, there is yet another reason why the 'float' may increase in size.
Therefore when net investment is taking place—circumstances which are
after all highly characteristic of modern capitalist economies—it cannot
be lightly assumed that failure to depreciate at replacement cost when prices
are rising will in fact make it impossible for firms to finance replacement
of equipment out of accumulated depreciation funds. Nor, it should be
noticed, can any question of insolvency arise so long as depreciation is
made on the basis of original costs. To summarize, therefore, we may say
that price changes are not the only—perhaps not even the most important—
reason why discrepancies may arise between funds accumulated by depreciating at original cost and funds needed for re-equipment. Such discrepancies inevitably occur where there is net investment or disinvestment
and, if the rate of net investment is large enough, the effect of any price
rise may be smothered. The converse holds if a high rate of net disinvestment co-exists with a falling price level. It is only in the limiting case of a
constant stock of capital that price movements have clear-cut influence
and even then the effects of a price rise are not as severe as has sometimes
been maintained. When we reinforce these considerations by reminding
ourselves that depreciation funds are not the only means of finance available
for replacement of capital equipment—that, in fact, only about 50 per cent
of the cost of capital replacement in the U.S.A. is currently financed in
this way,[1] that firms usually have liquid resources available through capital

---

[1] Terborgh, *The Bogey of Economic Maturity*, p. 127.

surplus or earned surplus, that conceivably it is not impossible to borrow or even raise new capital for such purposes,[1] and that, after all, if depreciation charges on a replacement-cost basis were not earned then it would be possible to have no liquid resources available for replacement despite the most conscientious accounting, the idea that failure to depreciate at replacement cost will in fact delay re-equipment, the belief that in some sense or other an entrepreneur has to wait until he has accumulated 'sufficient' funds in respect of any single machine, is seen to be a chimera.[2]

2 Other counter-arguments

We may now pass on to some of the other arguments put forward in support of replacement-cost accounting. The most persuasive of these is that advanced by Mr Terborgh and reiterated in various pamphlets issued by the Machinery and Allied Products Institute (of which Mr Terborgh is Research Director), on the desirability of preserving intact the real value of the original money capital rather than the stock of physical assets corresponding to that money capital. Now clearly this is a more subtle point than the general argument we have dealt with so far, and at first sight it seems very persuasive, despite practical difficulties such as deciding whether to use an index of prices of capital goods or consumers' goods as deflator.[3] But what are the implications of such an attitude? In the first place, is it true that the supply schedule for savings is so interest-elastic as Mr Terborgh assumes? Surely the risk of depreciation or appreciation of the general purchasing power of money is accepted by an investor in just the same way as he accepts the chance of a gain or loss in the (relative) price of the security he holds. To argue that the chance of depreciation of the value of money is in fact much greater than that of appreciation as a long-run possibility, that sooner or later investors will realize this and hence the supply of savings will be reduced, is to postulate an elasticity of supply which so far lacks empirical evidence. Nor does the matter rest there, for

[1] The usual objection to this practice is against one firm doing it, that is, to the exceptional nature of the practice rather than the practice itself. If tradition were so modified that all firms engaged in it, this point would lose much of its force.

[2] Whereas American manufacturing corporations reported depreciation reserves of 20 billion dollars in 1939, the excess of current assets (including inventories) over current liabilities was only 17·5 billion dollars (Gainsburgh and Krassa, 'Compiled Balance Sheet of Manufacturing Enterprises', *Studies in Income and Wealth*, vol. XII). If in fact current liabilities were to exceed current assets for any one firm, then it would stand to gain from a rise in prices.

[3] This clearly turns on what the proprietors would do if their capital were returned to them—would they re-invest in physical assets, or consume the whole amount or a mixture of the two? It is only fair to add that this difficulty is explicitly recognized by the adherents of this school. Other points, however, such as whether this principle is meant to apply to bonus shares issued by firms or even to capital surplus do not appear to be answered.

not only is it assumed that the supply of savings is elastic but also that the demand is inelastic. Clearly if firms had to guarantee repayment of money in real terms, the risk of investment would obviously increase and there would be a tendency on this score for the level of investment to *fall*, the exact opposite of what the adherents of this viewpoint so ardently desire. Finally, if the Terborgh principle were once admitted, would it not also have to apply to government cash and debts? In the light of these considerations there can surely be little disagreement with the general teachings of economic history about the desirability of a rising price level which reduces the real value of debts.

Now we must turn to the argument about matching current costs and current revenues. Although this argument has been put forward in one form or another by several authors,[1] there has generally been some hesitation in clarifying the precise meaning of 'costs' and 'revenues'. But such a clarification is essential, for the argument (and the counter-argument) is very different if one conceives these terms in an *ex post* sense to what it is if one takes them in an *ex ante* sense. If we are concerned with matching *ex post* or realized costs and revenues then surely the problem reduces to one of net income earned, for prices and output for the time-period under consideration are now bygones. In other words, the problem is how to determine capital consumption and the argument for replacement-cost accounting can only be defended if 'capital' is interpreted in the physical sense. Because in a system of replacement by annual repairs the annual charges incurred broadly suffice to maintain physical capital intact,[2] as well as (presumably) maintain the solvency of the firm, it does not follow that in a system of depreciation accounting the first as well as the second component is a prerequisite. If, on the other hand, we are concerned with matching *ex ante* or expected costs and revenues then the argument is entirely different, for then our main interest is in determining the optimum output or price. Now in the short period the only element of capital consumption which enters into marginal cost is user cost. In so far as capital consumption is purely a function of time and not of output at all, user cost is zero and therefore no problem arises at all. But if user cost is positive then in practice there are two points to resolve: what is the total sum which must be accumulated over the life of the asset and how much of this sum must be allocated to the current output and time-period? In other words, those who argue that replacement cost is the correct basis of measurement in this case prejudge the issue of what is meant by 'capital' for the business

---

[1] See p. 293 above.
[2] If the machinery is not actually in use and therefore not contributing to current output, then any such 'repairs' are really a form of capital accumulation rather than maintenance.

firm. In fixing long-period marginal costs the problem simply disintegrates; replacement cost and original cost are one and the same thing once an asset has been scrapped.

Thus it does not seem that the adherents of this line of thought are on very solid ground even when the arguments are put forward in respect of the individual firm. The consequences of *all* firms raising prices to cover the margin between replacement and original costs will be explored later.[1]

We may briefly discuss the other arguments put forward by those who fear the consequences of not adopting replacement-cost accounting. Dr Singer[2] has pointed out a number of objections to the 'cycle-exaggeration' line of argument[3] and to these others may be added. The most important is the idea that high current profits necessarily lead to over-confidence and expansion. This, surely, underrates the intelligence of the business man. For the profitability of new investment must depend *inter alia* on the current costs of purchasing equipment; simple extrapolation of current profits reckoned on the basis of *past* capital costs is a path which surely few would follow. The very fact that business men are at the moment expounding to their stockholders in nearly every company report that depreciation allowances as given by the tax authorities are not sufficient for replacement purposes, shows that they are not so completely deceived by the existence of large paper profits as the adherents of this school would have us believe.[4] Another point, into which we shall go more fully below, is the implication of the tax changes involved in replacement-cost accounting. Nor, for similar reasons, does the unbalance argument carry very deep conviction; how clear is the evidence that profit-projections are based on current profits net of depreciation rather than gross of such charges? When

---

[1] See p. 305 below.

[2] *Economic Journal* (December 1948), p. 594.

[3] The most important point raised is the counter-fluctuation in the ratio of undistributed to total net profits. Whereas in 1932 corporate undistributed profits in the U.S.A. were −6·0 billion dollars, in 1939 1·2 billion dollars and in 1948 12·8 billion dollars, corporate profits after tax were −3·4 billion dollars, 4·9 billion dollars and 20·4 billion dollars. (*Survey of Current Business, National Income Supplement*, July 1949). Comparable detailed figures are not available for the United Kingdom, but the White Paper on National Income and Expenditure and *The Economist* sample figures appear to show broadly similar trends. It has also been observed elsewhere that there is some evidence that business men do raise depreciation charges in boom years, over and above what is allowed by the taxation authorities or what would be justified on a historical cost straight-line basis (*see* Ruth P. Mack, *Flow of Business Funds and Consumers' Purchasing Power*, p. 36). It is somewhat surprising in the light of these considerations that Mr Lacey makes the following statement: 'It can be stated that profit distributions do tend to be increased in the boom and reduced in the slump to an extent not actually warranted by the actual circumstances.' ('How the Last-in-First-Out Principle Encourages Economic Stability', *Journal of Accountancy* (March 1949), p. 201.)

[4] See, for example, the chairman's remarks at the annual meetings of Lever Bros. and Unilever Ltd. in 1948 and 1949 (*The Economist*, 28 August 1948 and 13 August 1949).

we examine the standardized accountancy approach more closely, we see that there is really no argument for valuing capital charges on a *current* cost basis. All that is maintained is that valuations must be made on a *similar* cost basis; that is, to compare the annual capital charges incurred by two firms, if one has a new machine and the other is using a ten-year-old one, we can make these charges comparable either by reducing both to the current cost basis or both to the cost level ten years ago or in fact any other year. Finally, we have to deal with the arguments of the social accountants. If we are to measure capital consumption for society as a whole, we have agreed that we need something like estimates of depreciation at replacement costs. Perhaps it is not too much to ask that each firm, in publishing its accounts, should make some rough estimate of the correction factor applicable to any depreciation allowances based on original costs. Even though this estimate is not of prime significance for the individual firm it would obviously provide invaluable information for those dealing with statistics of national aggregates.

We have now dealt with all the various theoretical advantages claimed for accounting on a replacement-cost basis and to complete this section of the article we need to enumerate some of the more practical disadvantages of any such system. These points are all well known and are included for the sake of completeness rather than with any claim to originality. First, there is the point that replacement cost is not a simple concept. Technology does not stand still and as a result re-equipment is very rarely done with identical machinery, but with machinery which for some reason or other has advantages over the previous equipment. Therefore, any attempt to act on a simple replacement-cost basis, whether current or anticipated, may well mean that it is the (aggregated) quantity of inputs rather than the (aggregated) quantity of outputs that is maintained. Second, there is never any certainty about the exact date of replacement of equipment. Therefore the number of years over which a depreciation allowance can be spread is never known exactly. Any idea that, by costing on a replacement-cost basis, the exact sum needed for re-equipment can be obtained, will therefore be nullified on this ground alone. Of course, this means that original cost may not be exactly written-off either by the date of retirement of the machine but, if neither original cost nor replacement cost is likely to be exactly covered, this surely is an argument for sticking to the simpler and more precise concept of the two. Third, we have the institutional limitations imposed by tax regulations and legal restrictions. Is it conceivable that any tax regulations could really be keyed to a replacement-cost basis? And in the United Kingdom, at any rate, the retention in the firm of legally distributable profits is a questionable procedure, as we have already seen. Finally, is any business man really prepared to support a system of accounting which would entail increased taxation burdens in the slump years?

2 TAXATION REDUCTION ARGUMENTS

So far we have confined our attention to those who believe in thorough-going replacement-cost accounting, more or less for its own sake, and without any real regard for the implications of such accounting for business taxes. Now we come to those who advocate something like replacement-cost accounting mainly with the idea that if any such system were associated with appropriate modifications of tax-free depreciation allowances, generally beneficial results would follow. A number of different strands can be found in the thoughts of this group, ranging from those who advocate replacement costs at all times (with suitable tax adjustments) to those who simply believe that the weight of taxation on business enterprise is for some reason or other too heavy. In between, there are people who advocate replacement costs in times of rising prices like the post-war period, but not in the downswing, and people who plead for special initial or retirement allowances when equipment is newly installed or retired. We shall not explore all these ramifications in detail, but shall investigate the results of the adoption of a replacement-cost basis by the Inland Revenue authorities, principally with an eye on such a period as the post-war years but, it is hoped, with sufficient generality to make the analysis easily applicable to other circumstances. We shall first ask what the main results of such an innovation would be and then, secondly, consider whether such results can be deemed desirable from any points of view.

The first main problem to consider is: what is likely to happen to the propensity to save if tax allowances are granted at replacement costs in a period of rising prices? The most naïve answer is to say that a reduction in business taxation in the upswing will mean an increased level of net profits; this will enable a firm to increase its dividends or add to its reserves in some form or other. And frequently the argument is left at this point.

But obviously this is not sufficient. We need to consider the more general case where tax allowances at replacement cost are accompanied by the adoption of a replacement-cost accounting system. And we must also go more deeply into the effects of such a system on the different sectors of the community. Let us first ask what will happen if replacement-cost accounting is adopted but prices of end products are not changed in consequence. In such a case the individual firm will find, if replacement costs are greater than original costs, that its charges to gross profits are greater than before (by the amount of the difference between the old and new depreciation charges, less the reduction in taxation) and therefore it must either reduce dividends or the amount which is undistributed. In view of the tendency in the past for the ratio of undistributed to gross profits to rise in boom years,[1] there seems quite a strong probability that the second alternative will be adopted, but in either case gross business savings will be greater than before. But can we assume that prices will be unaltered? And what sort of effects may we expect if they do alter? If we consider a single firm, the answer to the first query depends on how far we assume that direct taxes and depreciation charges enter into (short-run) cost. There are some fairly clear-cut answers available here if we look at instances such as public-utility rate-fixing in the U.S.A. or the price-control system in industry in the United Kingdom today. But under a free price system the argument is (apart from the element of user cost[2]) nothing else but the old marginal versus full costs squabble, which we cannot pretend to explore at any length here. If, however, it can be assumed that the firm can pass its increased costs on to consumers there will, in the limiting case, be no reduction in the net profits available for dividends or free reserves. If we now turn to consider all firms the situation is somewhat different. If they all raise prices to compensate for the net effect of larger depreciation charges and smaller taxation,[3] the incidence of any *initial* rise will not be entirely on final consumers, but will spread between them and industry itself, depending, broadly speaking, on the relative volumes of inter-industrial sales and sales to final consumers. Whilst this point may be legitimately ignored in the case of the individual firm, when we consider society as a whole it is obviously of considerable importance[4] and it is not reasonable to assume that industry as a whole can in fact easily pass on the whole of its increased charges to final consumers.

The next point to follow up is the effect of reduced taxation receipts on the Government accounts. At the most the Government will reduce expenditure by an amount equal to the reduction in taxes,[5] and in practice

---

[1] See p. 302 above.   [2] See p. 301 above.

[3] This would clearly not mean equal proportional price rises all round.

[4] *See* Leontief's estimate that total sales of the main section of the U.S.A. economy (agriculture and foods, minerals, metal fabrication, fuel and power, textiles, leather and rubber, railways, other industries) were 133 billion dollars in 1939. Of this total 71 billion dollars were inter-industrial sales and only 62 billion dollars went to households. ('Output, Employment, Consumption, Investment', *Quarterly Journal of Economics*, February 1944).

[5] If the system of depreciation at replacement cost involved writing up assets in times of boom, then the reduction might be mitigated, in the U.S. at any rate, by increased receipts from the capital gains tax. Price changes could obviously influence both receipts from other taxes and expenditure items, but for simplicity these effects could perhaps be assumed to cancel out.

may not retrench as much as this. Government savings will therefore probably decrease.

When we turn to personal savings, we must ask first of all about the income effects. These will be a compound of various changes—on the one hand, any reduction in dividends paid out to profit-earners or in Government expenditure,[1] and on the other, increased prices of goods sold to final consumers. The final effect on savings will depend on the extent to which different income groups of the community are affected and on their relative marginal propensities to save. Secondly, there may be effects on capital account. For instance, if the remission of taxation gives a general fillip to Stock Exchange prices, and therefore capital values appreciate, there may be some tendency for the profit-earning classes to increase consumption expenditure.

Thus the over-all effect of the imposition of any replacement-cost accounting system, combined with appropriate tax changes, on the propensity to save, is by no means simple to discover. The supporters of such a system may possibly be right in asserting that the propensity to save will increase in a period of rising prices, but even if this is true, it is not the end of the story. We must also ask if the change in the composition and sources of savings is likely to reduce or increase the imperfection of the capital market. And the answer to this is by no means easy to see on *a priori* grounds, involving as it does such issues as whether corporate savings are more likely to be 'intelligently' invested than personal savings.[2]

Most of what we have said can be applied without difficulty to situations where prices are falling. There are one or two points to be noticed, however, when we consider longer periods of time embracing both rising and falling prices. First, if there is a tendency for tax rates to rise in boom years and be reduced in slump years, then over a period of time business firms will obviously pay less in taxation by replacement-cost accounting than they would if original-cost accounting were used. Second, we should observe that over the course of history the value of money has declined and, therefore, if it can be shown that a replacement-cost system will in fact increase the propensity to save in boom periods, over the long period we may perhaps expect on the average a similar result, even though the

---

[1] This effect, of course, will not be the same as the total reduction in Government expenditure if any of this is a reduction in amounts paid to business firms for their goods and services, there being no necessary correspondence between the amount paid by the Government sector to business and that paid by business to persons. Strictly we should also allow for reductions in undistributed profits due to Government attempts to prevent dissaving on its part.

[2] Another point which is of substantial importance, though not germane to our main argument, is the restraining effect which reductions in recorded net profits may exert on trade union pressure for higher wages.

propensity to save may decrease (relatively to what it would be under original-cost accounting) in slump years.

We have now spent some time discussing the effects of replacement-cost accounting on the propensity to save. What is likely to happen to the profitability of investment? If it is thought, on such grounds as those mentioned in the preceding paragraphs,[1] that the amount of taxation payable over the life of an investment is likely to be reduced, then obviously the schedule of marginal efficiency of capital is raised, and there is a stimulus to investment. Moreover, there will be differential advantages such as those accruing to firms engaged in especially risky enterprise, or those firms with large ratios of depreciation charges to gross income. Such points as these have been treated often enough before in the textbooks[2] and there is no need to labour them here. What is not perhaps quite so frequently emphasized is that there may be a stimulus to investment from the other side, that is, a reduction in lender's risk charges on loans or a reduction in the cost of bringing borrower and lender together, if there is any reduction in the imperfection of the capital market.[3]

We are now in a position to bring the two sides of our argument together and to examine the general effect on the economy of introducing replacement-cost accounting. When one considers all the relevant factors it is very difficult to be dogmatic about the likely course of events over the cycle. But it is clear that the situation is not nearly so simple as the school of thought represented by Mr Lacey would have us believe.

Over the longer period, on the other hand, it does seem that there would be increased opportunities for private investment, and an increased annual flow of savings. This, however, does not necessarily mean that the total stock of capital equipment would be larger after a period of time than it would be under original-cost accounting,[4] for we must remember that in

---

[1] Another point might be that if the incidence of investment over the cycle is such that the greater part of the life of capital equipment is spread over the upswing years, then the profitability of investment increases. The average length of life of capital equipment is sufficiently long, however, to make this point of secondary importance.

[2] *See* U. K. Hicks: *Public Finance*, chapter XII.

[3] Another point which, although theoretically invalid, may have some practical importance, is the unwillingness of business men to replace existing equipment if it has a substantial remaining book value. Obviously, in a period of rising prices, replacement-cost accounting would mean a smaller remaining book value than would original-cost accounting for a machine of the same age. Some light on whether this point is of real importance is shed by *Bulletin* no. 2119 of the Machinery and Allied Products Institute (U.S.A.), which found that 60 per cent of entrepreneurs replied in a questionnaire that they were not influenced by such ideas.

[4] We do not explore here the ramifications of long-period disequilibrium—a disequilibrium which is 'dynamic' in the sense of R. F. Harrod—between the rates of changes of the demand for and supply of savings, but clearly they have to be fully taken into account in considering the likely changes in the stock of capital equipment.

modern communities, and particularly in the United Kingdom, the Government may be responsible for a good deal of capital investment. The amount which it does undertake may be subject to argument, depending on whether we consider only accumulation of material capital and therefore exclude human capital,[1] but if industry were relieved of some of its taxation burdens any subsequent increase in the level of private investment might well be at the expense of Government investment expenditure.

We have now traced in some detail the likely results of any system of replacement-cost accounting. We are unable to be dogmatic about the cyclical effects, but it does seem likely that over the long period the average profitability of investment would increase and the propensity to save would also increase. Now it is, of course, possible to claim that these are consummations earnestly to be desired—for on the one hand it can be argued that the rate of increase of national income, in the U.S.A. at any rate,[2] was at its highest level in the latter part of the nineteenth century (when the rate of capital accumulation was higher than it has been in recent decades), and on the other hand that the concurrent increase in investment profitability and thriftiness is precisely what is needed to keep the economy more or less on an even keel through time. But obviously such issues as this raise very wide questions which cannot be dealt with here. We may, however, make three remarks on these points: first, it is necessary to keep one's sense of proportion in these matters. How much difference would the adoption of replacement-cost accounting really make to the average level of investment over the long period? We have already seen that formal depreciation accounting does not apply to many sections of the economy and it must be remembered that changes over the cycle may very well cancel out, leaving only such points as the secular upward trend of prices as an influential factor. There seems to be no way of quantifying this point unless we are prepared to work with very wide margins of error, but it may be noted that the advocates of this line of thought are remarkably reticent when it comes to hard-and-fast figures. Second, the main arguments themselves cannot be accepted without reservations, quite apart from the

---

[1] Obviously this distinction is extremely important in the United Kingdom where such a large expansion of health and education services is taking place. Quite aside from the present argument, may not an answer be found here to those who bemoan what in their view is the low level of current investment in material capital? The most important reason for the vast discrepancy between Chinese and American production *per capita* may well be found in the different levels of human rather than of material capital.

[2] The data on capital formation and national income for the U.S.A. can be obtained from Kuznets, *National Product since 1869* (national incomes data for the United Kingdom are available in Prest *op. cit.* and some capital formation estimates are given by Clark, *National Income and Outlay*, p. 185). It should be noted, however, that all the nineteenth-century figures are subject to wide margins of error and that even if we do accept them the postulates given above essentially depend on the events of the late 1920s and 1930s.

statistical limitations. Many factors were at work in the late nineteenth century promoting rapid increases in the national income per head (population growth, increasing volume of world trade, freedom to emigrate, etc.), and these are no longer operating or at least are not operating so powerfully. This is not to deny that a high rate of capital investment to national income is a mainspring of progress or of recovery in the immediate post-war circumstances of Britain.[1] But it is a warning against facile, allegedly statistical, arguments. And the claim that the concurrence of an increase in investment and an increase in thriftiness is highly desirable obviously rests on the assumption of equilibrium conditions—if thriftiness were tending to outrun investment opportunites *à la* Hansen then clearly upward changes in *both* schedules would not contribute to stability. Third and last, are we, as economic theorists, as yet in any position to make anything like unanimous judgment on the socially optimum division between investment and consumption, between increments in future and current satisfaction? Until we are, then surely we are in no position to adopt a dogmatic attitude on such issues as those we have raised.

[1] This does not mean that we must necessarily accept some of the exaggerated notions of what is needed to restore the pre-war volume of capital assets in the United Kingdom. There is indeed an ambiguity about the concept of net investment, for the amount of new installations needed for replacement purposes depends on whether we simply want to restore the pre-war number of machines or the pre-war age distribution. War and post-war conditions have caused many firms to keep plant and equipment running long after the normal date of retirement—effectively a sort of negative obsolescence.

21   The accountant in a golden age[1]

by G. C. Harcourt

In Mrs Robinson's celebrated article, 'The production function and the theory of capital',[2] it is not made clear whether the 'man of words', whose doings are contrasted with those of the 'man of deeds', is an economist or an accountant. It is assumed in this article that he is an accountant; and it is proposed to examine how accurate is the accountant's measure of the rate of profit under 'Golden Age' conditions where uncertainty is absent, expectations are fulfilled, and the rate of profit has an unambiguous meaning.[3] The following question is asked: would the answer obtained by using the accountant's measure of the rate of profit correspond with what is known, under the assumed conditions, to be the right answer, namely, that the *ex post* rate of return equals the *ex ante* one. This does not seem to be an entirely pointless exercise, since a number of 'men of words', economists this time, have used the accountant's measure in their empirical investigations,[4] and conclusions have been drawn from both the relative and absolute sizes of their estimates. Thus Minhas used cross-section studies of the rates of return in the same industries in different

---

[1] The writer is especially grateful to Professor H. F. Lydall for suggesting the research project on which this article is based and for his comments and help. He would also like to thank Mr R. D. Terrell, members of the Departments of Economics and Commerce, University of Adelaide, and members of the Joint D.A.E.–Faculty Seminar, University of Cambridge. Miss J. M. Higgins checked the mathematical results.

[2] *Review of Economic Studies* (1953–4), pp. 81–106, portion of which is reprinted in her *Collected Economic Papers*, II (Oxford, 1960), 114–31. All subsequent references are to the second source.

[3] 'To abstract from uncertainty means to postulate that no such (unexpected) events occur, so that the *ex ante* expectations which govern the actions of the man of deeds are never out of gear with the *ex post* experience which governs the actions of the man of words, and to say that equilibrium obtains is to say that no such events have occurred for some time or are thought liable to occur in the future' ('The production function and the theory of capital', p. 120). These conditions are assumed to prevail in this article.

[4] See, for example, Simon Kuznets, 'Long-term changes in the national income of the United States of America since 1870', pp. 78–88, in Simon Kuznets (ed.), *Income and Wealth*, Series II (International Association for Research into Income and Wealth, Cambridge, 1952); E. H. Phelps Brown and B. Weber, 'Accumulation, productivity and distribution in the British Economy, 1870–1938', *Economic Journal* (June 1955), especially p. 272 and pp. 283–8; T. Barna, 'The replacement cost of fixed assets in British manufacturing industry in 1955', *Journal of the Royal Statistical Society*, Series A (General), (1957) especially p. 25 and p. 30; 'On measuring capital', chapter 5 of F. A. Lutz and D. C. Hague (eds.), *The Theory of Capital* (London, 1960), pp. 82–5; B. S. Minhas, *An International Comparison of Factor Costs and Factor Use* (Amsterdam, 1963), chapter 5; E. Nevin, 'The cost structure of British manufacturing, 1948–61', *Economic Journal* (December 1963), especially p. 646.

countries to test his hypothesis about factor-reversals; and Nevin was depressed by the stable, low level of rates of return in British manufacturing in the post-war period. But if it can be shown that the measure is faulty even in the equilibirum conditions of a 'Golden Age', it is unlikely to prove a realistic measure in real world situations.

The article is in six sections. In section 1 the various cases which are examined and the assumptions of the article are outlined; the following sections deal in detail with each case; and a concluding section draws the findings together. The principal conclusion is that the accountant's measure of the rate of profit is extremely misleading, even under 'Golden Age' conditions. The measure is shown to be influenced by the pattern of the quasi-rents associated with individual machines in a stock of capital, the method of depreciation used, whether or not the stock of capital is growing, and by what assets are included in the stock of capital. What is more, no easy 'rules of thumb' which would allow adjustments for these factors to be made in the estimates emerge from the analysis.

I

Four main cases, each of which contains further sub-cases, are considered. The first case is that of the rate of profit, as measured by an accountant, in a business which has a balanced stock of identical machines. The second case concerns the rate of profit in a business, the gross investment in machines of which grows at a constant rate each year. Then, following a suggestion by Mr H. R. Hudson, variants of the two cases are examined: in the balanced stock case, it is assumed that the accumulation of financial assets, which are purchased as a result of allowing for depreciation as the stock of machines builds up but before any replacement expenditure occurs, is included in the capital of the business; in the constant growth case, it is supposed that the accumulation of financial assets, which occurs from the beginning of the firm until the first year of replacement, plus the further accumulation associated with the difference between current depreciation allowances and replacement expenditure of subsequent years (the 'Domar effect'), are included in the capital of the business. The first two cases might be regarded as representative of stationary and growing 'Golden Age' economies respectively, because the capital in them consists entirely of physical assets. The second two cases can be regarded as representative of firms which hold financial assets as well, and which operate in 'Golden Age' economies. (Holdings of financial assets, of course, cancel out for an economy as a whole.)

For each of the four general cases, four special cases are considered: first, it is assumed that the machines are 'one-hoss shays' and that the expected quasi-rents of each year of operation are equal. This is referred to as the case of the constant q's, where q_i is the expected quasi-rent of year i ($i = 1, ..., n$, n being the life of the machine) and $q_1 = q_2 = ... = q_n$. (With the present assumptions, expected and actual quasi-rents always coincide.) Cases (2) and (3) are those of falling and rising q's respectively; for con-

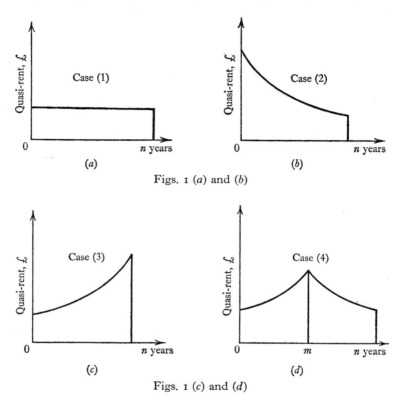

Figs. 1 (*a*) and (*b*)

Figs. 1 (*c*) and (*d*)

venience, it is assumed that $q_i = bq_{i-1}$ ($i = 2, ..., n$), where $b < 1$ [case (2)], and $q_i = aq_{i-1}$ ($i = 2, ..., n$) and $a > 1$ [case (3)]. Case (4) is a combination of cases (2) and (3); it is assumed that up to q_m ($m < n$), $q_i = aq_{i-1}$ ($i = 2, ..., m$), $a > 1$; and from q_m on (but not including q_m), $q_j = bq_{j-1}$ ($j = m+1, ..., n$), $b < 1$. The patterns of the quasi-rents over the life of a machine are shown for the four cases in Fig. 1. The cases most likely to be met in practice are cases (1), (2), and (4), with $m < \frac{1}{2}n$; perhaps (2) is the most common case. Prices and wages are assumed to remain constant so that the various patterns show the changes in productive efficiency over the lifetimes of the machines.

Let r be the expected rate of profit of each machine. The expected rate of profit in a 'Golden Age' is the internal rate of return—the rate of discount which makes the present value of the expected quasi-rents equal to the supply price of each machine. Then, because expectations are always realized in a 'Golden Age', and the rate of profit is uniform throughout the whole economy, it is known that each machine, and each business, is in fact earning r. The question which is analysed in this article is whether the accountant's measure of the rate of profit gives a value of r for each of the four patterns of surpluses for each of the four cases. To answer it, two further sub-cases are introduced, the first assuming that the accountant uses straight-line depreciation when calculating annual accounting profit and the *book* value of capital, the second assuming that he uses reducing-balance depreciation. The accountant's measure of the rate of profit is taken to be the ratio of annual accounting profit to the average of the opening and closing book values of the assets in the business concerned. It is assumed, as is reasonable in a 'Golden Age', that any financial assets owned by a business themselves earn r. Expressions for the accountant's rate of profit for the two sub-cases of the four patterns of surpluses of the four types of businesses are presented in the remaining sections and their values for particular ranges of values of the relevant variables are examined. Where no clear-cut patterns in the accountant's rate of profit were discernible when, for example, the length of life of machines was varied, the numerical values of the rate of profit were found by running a programme on a computer.[1]

It is not suggested, of course, that an accountant could actually find employment in a 'Golden Age'. Rather, the article is concerned with what would happen if he were to use his customary box of tools in 'Golden Age' conditions. In non-'Golden Age' situations, the only way of finding out whether expectations concerning rates of profit have been realized is to ask accountants—or use their tools.

2

The first general case considered is that of a business, the capital of which consists of machines only; it is assumed that it owns a balanced stock of machines, which is already established. The accountant calculates depreciation by the straight-line method.[2] The following notation is used:

L number of machines in any age group and purchased in any year;

n length of life of a machine;

[1] The writer is indebted to Dr M. V. Wilkes, Mathematical Laboratory, University of Cambridge, for the use of EDSAC and to Dr L. J. Slater and her assistants for programming the expressions.

[2] This case was first analysed by Joan Robinson in her paper, 'Depreciation', *Collected Economic Papers*, II, 216–19.

q_i expected quasi-rent in year i;

r expected rate of profit;

S supply price of machine: $S = \sum\limits_{i=1}^{n} \dfrac{q_i}{(1+r)^i}$;[1]

$S^* \sum\limits_{i=2}^{n} \dfrac{q_i}{(1+r)^{i-1}}$;

$Q \sum\limits_{i=1}^{n} q_i$; $Q^* = \sum\limits_{i=2}^{n} q_i$;

K value of capital for the year as a whole;

k book value of capital for the year as a whole (no subscript indicates that straight-line depreciation is used, subscript RB indicates that reducing-balance depreciation is used);

d rate of reducing-balance depreciation; $d = 3/2n$;

A accounting profit (no subscript: straight-line depreciation; subscript RB: reducing-balance depreciation);

R^* accountant's measure of the rate of profit; $R^* = A/k$.

If the accountant were to value capital as the sum of the discounted values of the expected quasi-rents, using r as the rate of discount, the value of capital for the year as a whole[2] can be shown to be:

$$K = \frac{L}{2r}[(Q+Q^*)-(S+S^*)].^3$$

---

[1] In a 'Golden Age', the supply prices of machines are always equal to the present values of the expected quasi-rents, the uniform rate of profit being the rate of discount. (See 'The production function and the theory of capital', p. 123.)

[2] Capital is valued for the year as a whole rather than at its beginning or end, because this procedure accords with the accounting practice of averaging the opening and closing values of assets when calculating annual rates of profit.

[3] Suppose that machines are bought at the beginning of each year and that incomes accrue at the end. The value of a balanced stock of capital at the *beginning* of any year (K^*) is:

$$K^* = L\left(\frac{q_n}{(1+r)}\right) + L\left(\frac{q_{n-1}}{(1+r)}+\frac{q_n}{(1+r)^2}\right)+...+L\left(\frac{q_1}{(1+r)}+...+\frac{q_n}{(1+r)^n}\right).$$

By gathering up terms and forming the appropriate geometric progressions,

$$K^* = \frac{L}{r}(Q-S)$$

is obtained.

Similarly, the value of capital at the *end* of any year (K^{**}) can be shown to be:

$$K^{**} = \frac{L}{r}(Q^*-S^*).$$

For the year as a whole, therefore,

$$K = \frac{L}{2r}[(Q+Q^*)-(S+S^*)].$$

The accounting profit for any year is:

$$A = L(Q-S),$$

so that R^*, *in this instance*, is

$$\frac{2r(Q-S)}{[(Q+Q^*)-(S+S^*)]}$$

which is approximately equal to r. That is to say, in this particular instance, if the accountant uses the economist's definition of the value of capital (in a 'Golden Age') and his own measure of accounting profit, the resulting expression for the rate of profit gives approximately the right answer. Once growth of the capital stock occurs, though, he would also need to use the economists' measure of depreciation (the decline in the value of capital from year to year), not one of his own, in order for this approach to give approximately the right answer.[1]

However, the accountant is more likely to use the average *book* value of capital for the year as his measure of the value of capital. This can be shown to be $\frac{1}{2}LnS$;[2] and, it follows,

$$R^* = \frac{2(Q-S)}{nS}. \tag{1}$$

In general, this expression is not equal to r. In the 'one-hoss shay' case,

$$R^* = \frac{2}{n}\left\{\frac{nr}{1-\{1/(1+r)\}^n}-1\right\}. \tag{1a}$$

---

[1] H. R. Hudson discussed this point and gave the formula for 'correct' depreciation in an unpublished paper which was read to the Seminar on Economic Growth held in the University of Adelaide in August 1960. See also H. R. Hudson and Russell Mathews, 'An aspect of depreciation', *Economic Record* (June 1963), pp. 232–6.

[2] At the beginning of any year the *book* value of the machines in the business (k^*) is:

$$k^* = LS+L\left(S-\frac{S}{n}\right)+...+L\left(S-\frac{(n-1)S}{n}\right).$$

By gathering up terms and forming the appropriate arithmetic progressions,

$$k^* = \frac{LS(n+1)}{2}$$

is obtained.

Similarly, the *book* value at the end of any year can be shown to be:

$$k^{**} = \frac{LS(n-1)}{2}$$

For the year as a whole, therefore, $k = \dfrac{LnS}{2}$.

The remaining expressions in the article may be obtained by following procedures similar to those in this footnote and n. 3, p. 314.

G. C. Harcourt

As $n \to \infty$, $R^* \to 2r$. However, the approach is not monotonic increasing: at $n = 1$, $R^* = 2r$; it then falls to a minimum value, which is always greater than r, at values of n which are related to r itself. For example, when $r = 5$ per cent, the minimum value of R^* occurs between the tenth and twentieth year; when $r = 30$ per cent, it occurs between the fifth and tenth year. That, is, in the 'one-hoss shay' case, the accountant's measure of the rate of profit will give different answers for two businesses which are alike in every respect except that the machines of one are longer-lived than those of the other. If, for example, the rate of profit is 30 per cent, the accountant's answer for $n = 5$ years is 42·1 per cent and for $n = 30$ years, 53·4 per cent.

In passing, it could be mentioned that American studies show that some business men estimate rates of return as the ratio of accounting profit to the *gross* (that is, undepreciated) value of assets. The book value of capital when straight-line depreciation is used is half the gross value. If the investment projects concerned are 'one-hoss shays' and n is large, the accounting rate of profit would approximately equal r. Expression ($1a$) may therefore provide a theoretical justification for this business practice.[1]

The corresponding expressions for cases (2), (3), and (4)—falling; rising; and rising, then falling quasi-rents—are:

$$R^* = \frac{2}{n}\left\{ \frac{(1-b^n)(1+r-b)}{(1-b)[1-\{b/(1+r)\}^n]} - 1 \right\};$$ (1b)

for case (3) read $\qquad\qquad a\,(>\,1)$ for b; (1c)

$$R^* = \frac{2}{n}\left(\frac{\dfrac{a^m-1}{a-1}+a^{m-1}\left(\dfrac{b(1-b^{n-m})}{1-b}\right) - \dfrac{1-\{a/(1+r)\}^m}{1+r-a} - a^{m-1}\left\{\dfrac{b[1-\{b/(1+r)\}^{n-m}]}{(1+r-b)(1+r)^m}\right\}}{\dfrac{1-\{a/(1+r)\}^m}{1+r-a} + a^{m-1}\left\{\dfrac{b[1-\{b/(1+r)\}^{n-m}]}{(1+r-b(1+r)^m}\right\}} \right)$$

(1d)

In case (2), $R^* \to 0$ as $n \to \infty$. There is a value of n where $R^* = r$, as R^* is greater than r for $n = 2$. The rapidity with which this occurs, for certain values of the variables, is shown in Table 1.

Would it be too fanciful to suggest that the low levels of rates of profit which Nevin found in British manufacturing may in part be due to a combination of quasi-rent patterns similar to those of case (2) and rather large n's?

In case (3), the value of R^* is greater than r (and the values of R^* for cases (1) and (2)) at small values of n, falls slightly as n increases, but then quickly increases, approaching ∞ as $n \to \infty$. With $a = 1\cdot1$, $n = 20$ years,

---

[1] The writer is indebted to Professor F. K. Wright for bringing this practice to his notice.

316

TABLE 1. *Values of R*, case (2) (balanced stock,*
physical capital) (percentages)

(non-bracketed figures, $b = 0.5$; bracketed figures, $b = 0.9$)

n (years)...	2	5	10	20	30
r					
5	6·7 [7·4]	3·7 [5·7]	2·0 [4·9]	1·0 [3·8]	0·1 [3·0]
10	13·4 [n.a.]	7·4 [n.a.]	4·0 [n.a.]	2·0 [n.a.]	1·3 [n.a.]
20	n.a. [30·3]	n.a. [24·4]	n.a. [21·4]	n.a. [16·4]	n.a. [12·5]
30	40·8 [46·0]	22·5 [37·9]	12·0 [33·5]	6·0 [25·2]	4·0 [18·9]

TABLE 2. *Values of R*, cases (2), (3), and (4), varying values of m (balanced*
stock, physical capital, straight-line depreciation) (percentages)

$R*$	m (years)		
	5	10	15
Case (2)	3·3	3·3	3·3
Case (4)	6·3	13·3	24·3
Case (3)	36·3	36·3	36·3

and $r = 30$ per cent, R^* is already 108·8 per cent; with $a = 1.5$, the corresponding figure is 796 per cent! (R^* is not defined for the case of $1 + r = a$.) Case (4) is a combination of cases (2) and (3). For given values of n, the value of R^* lies in between the values of R^* of the two previous cases.[1] As $m \to n$, the case (3) result comes to dominate the expression; as $m \to 0$, the case (2) result comes to dominate. This is illustrated in Table 2 where certain values of R^* for cases (2), (3), and (4) are shown; $r = 10$ per cent, $a = 1.3$, $b = 0.7$, and $n = 20$ years. Just by a fluke of counterbalancing forces, the accountant's measure could give the right answer in case (4).

In the article referred to in footnote 1, p. 315, Hudson and Mathews show that if the quasi-rents decline at a particular linear rate, stright-line depreciation is 'correct'. Substituting this pattern in (1) gives $R^* \simeq r$ for moderately large n, say > 10. ($R^* = r$, whatever n, if annual accounting profit is averaged as well as the annual book values of capital.)

[1] There is an exception to this statement when $m \leqslant 1$; but this result can be ignored as it has no economic relevance.

TABLE 3. *Values of R^*_{RB}, case (1) (balanced stock, physical capital, reducing-balance depreciation) (percentages)*

			n (years)			
r	2	5	10	20	30	50
5	10·1	5·2	3·7	3·4	3·4	3·6
10	20·3	10·7	7·9	7·5	7·8	n.a.
30	62·6	35·5	28·1	28·0	28·6	n.a.

If the accountant calculated annual depreciation by the reducing-balance method, the general expression becomes

$$R^*_{RB} = \frac{Q - S}{S\{\frac{1}{2}(2n - 1) - e\}}, \qquad (2)$$

where

$$e = \frac{d(n-1)(1-d) - d^2(1-d^{n-1})}{(1-d)^2}.$$

The expressions for cases (1) to (4) are not shown but can be derived easily from expression (2). In case (1) at $n = 2$, $R^*_{RB} > r$; it then quickly drops below r, reaches a minimum and, as $n \to \infty$, $R^*_{RB} \to r$. (See Table 3.)

The results for cases (2), (3), and (4) are similar, in the sense that they show the same general patterns for variations of n, to those for the corresponding cases using straight-line depreciation. For $n = 2$, $R^*_{RB} > R^*$; otherwise, for all computed values, $R^*_{RB} < R^*$. Again, there is one particular pattern of decline of the quasi-rents which makes reducing balance the 'correct' depreciation[1] and for which $R^*_{RB} \simeq r$.

3

The next main case to be analysed is that of a business, the gross investment of which grows at a constant rate each year. However, it is convenient, first, to comment briefly on the case of a balanced stock where the financial assets which have accumulated over the years o to n and which earn r, are included in the capital of the business. By the year n, the value of financial assets (F), in the straight-line depreciation case, is $\frac{1}{2}LnS$, which is the same as the book value of physical assets. Once the year n is reached, the balanced stock is established. Therefore, for all $n+j$ years afterwards

---

[1] 'An aspect of depreciation', *op. cit.* pp. 234–5.

TABLE 4. *Values of R* for n* = 10 *years, a* = 1·5, *b* = 0·5,
r = 10 *per cent* (*percentages*)

	Straight-line depreciation		Reducing-balance depreciation	
Case	Physical capital	Total capital	Physical capital	Total capital
(1)	12·5	11·3	7·9	8·3
(2)	4·0	7·0	2·5	4·0
(3)	22·7	16·4	14·3	13·4
(4)	10·5†	10·3†	6·6†	7·3†

† *m* = 5 years.

(j = 0 in year n, then 1, 2, ...), the book value of physical and financial assets in the year $n+j$ is: $k_{n+j}^T = LnS$. Accounting profit in year $n+j$ is:

$$A_{n+j}^T = L\{(Q-S) + \tfrac{1}{2}rnS\},$$

so that

$$R_{n+j}^{*T} = \frac{(Q-S) + \tfrac{1}{2}rnS}{nS},$$

which it is convenient to write as

$$R_{n+j}^{*T} = \frac{(Q-S)}{nS} + \tfrac{1}{2}r. \tag{3}$$

Now,

$$\frac{Q-S}{nS} = \frac{1}{2}\left\{\frac{2(Q-S)}{nS}\right\},$$

which is *half* the general expression for the balanced stock, physical capital case (see expression (1)). The accountant's rate of profit in this case, then, is always equal to half its value for the corresponding physical capital case, plus a constant, $\tfrac{1}{2}r$.

The corresponding general expression if reducing-balance depreciation is used is:

$$R_{RB,\,n+j}^{*T} = \frac{Q}{nS} - \frac{1}{n} + \frac{r(\tfrac{1}{2}+e)}{n}. \tag{4}$$

Again, while the values for particular cases show the same pattern of variation around r as n changes, the disparity between the accountant's measure and r is always less. That is to say, in general the influence of financial assets is to reduce the discrepancy between the accountant's measure and r. The explanation is obvious: the accountant's measure now includes in the numerator and denominator elements, namely financial assets and the income earned on them, which if expressed as a ratio equal r. The influence of the inclusion of financial assets in capital on $R*$ is illustrated in Table 4 where the accountant's values for balanced stocks of machines with lives of 10 years and r = 10 per cent are shown.

4

The next main case considered is that of a business, the gross investment each year of which is the stream: $LS, cLS, \ldots, c^{n-1}LS, \ldots$ $(c > 1)$. It has been argued already (see p. 315 above) that, if the capital stock is growing, the use of conventional accounting methods of reckoning depreciation prevents $R^* \simeq r$, even if capital is valued 'correctly'. If straight-line depreciation is used,

$$R^* = \frac{2(1+r-c)\left[\sum_{1}^{n} c^{n-i}q_i - (S/n)\{(c^n-1)/(c-1)\}\right]}{\sum_{1}^{n} c^{n-i}q_i + \sum_{2}^{n} c^{n+1-i}q_i - c^n(S+S^*)};$$

if reducing-balance depreciation is used,

$$R^*_{RB} = \frac{2(1+r-c)\left[\sum_{1}^{n} c^{n-i}q_i - S(x)\right]}{(\alpha)},$$

where

$$x = 1 - \frac{d(1-d^{n-1})}{1-d} + \frac{cd^n\{1-(c/d)^{n-1}\}}{d-c}$$

and

$$\alpha = \sum_{1}^{n} c^{n-i}q_i + \sum_{2}^{n} c^{n+1-i}q_i - c^n(S+S^*).$$

Neither of these expressions, in general, approximately equals r.

Expression (5) is the general expression for R^* for the constant growth case in the $(n+j)$th year (that is, after replacement expenditure has started) when the *book* value of physical capital and straight-line depreciation are used.

$$R^*_{c,n+j} = \frac{2n(c-1)^2\left\{\sum_{1}^{n} c^{n-i}q_i - S(c^n-1)/n(c-1)\right\}}{S(\beta)} \qquad (5)$$

where

$$\beta = \{(2n-1)c^{n+1} - (2n+1)c^n + (1+c)\}.$$

This expression is independent of c^j (though the expressions for accounting profit and the book value of capital contain it), but not of c itself. The patterns of behaviour of R^* as n changes appear to be the same, for the four types of machines, as for the balanced-stock cases. However, *in general*, the higher is the rate of growth of the capital stock, the closer, for given n, are the values of the accountant's rate of profit to the correct value. This is illustrated in Table 5, where values of R^* are shown for rates of growth between 0 and 20 per cent.

TABLE 5. *Values of R*, for c = 1·0, 1·01, and 1·2, r = 30 per cent, a = 1·5, b = 0·5, and straight-line depreciation (percentages)*

			n (years)	
Case	c	5	10	20
(1)	1·0	42·1	44·7	50·3
	1·01	41·8	44·0	48·7
	1·20	36·8	34·8	33·5
(2)	1·0	22·5	12·0	6·0
	1·01	23·1	12·9	7·1
	1·20	31·6	26·9	24·6
(3)	1·0	60·9	122·4	796·0
	1·01	59·7	116·7	713·4
	1·20	41·5	49·1	88·0
(4)†	1·0	34·7	39·6	75·9
	1·01	34·7	39·5	74·5
	1·20	35·2	35·0	50·0

† $m = \frac{1}{2}n$.

The general expression for the constant growth case when reducing-balance depreciation is used is:

$$R^*_{RB,c,n+j} = \frac{2(1-c)(1-d)(c-d)\left\{\sum_1^n c^{n-i}q_i - S(x)\right\}}{S(y)}, \qquad (6)$$

where

$$y = (1-d)(c-d)(1+c-2c^n)$$
$$- d(1+c)\{(1-d^{n-1})(c-d) - c^n(1-d)(1-(d/c)^{n-1})\}.$$

(Expressions for the four types of machines can be easily derived from expressions (5) and (6).) Except for the case of n = 2, R* for the reducing-balance case is usually less than the corresponding value for the straight-line case. For values of n below twenty years, anyway, the effect of growth is usually to make R* closer to r than in the corresponding balanced-stock case.

5

To complete the analysis, the case of constant growth where the accumulation of financial assets occurs is briefly examined. The accumulation of financial assets consists of two parts:

(1) the accumulation over the first n years before any replacement expenditure occurs;

(2) the net addition to this fund in subsequent years $(n+j)$, because current depreciation allowances exceed current replacement expenditure. The summation of the two relevant parts gives the financial capital for the year $n+j$, on which r is earned, and these income/capital ratios combined with expressions (5) and (6) respectively, give the general expressions for $R^{*T}_{c,n+j}$ and $R^{*T}_{RB,c,n+j}$:

$$R^{*T}_{c,n+j} = \frac{2n(c-1)^2 \left\{ c^j \left(\sum_1^n c^{n-i} q_i - (S/n)\{(c^n-1)/(c-1)\} \right) + \tfrac{1}{2} r S(g) \right\}}{S(h)}, \quad (7)$$

where

$$g = \frac{2n(c^n-1)}{c-1} + \frac{c(c^j-1)(c^n-1)}{(c-1)^2} - \frac{(\beta)}{(c-1)^2} - n\left(\frac{c^j-1}{c-1}\right)$$

and

$$h = 2n(c^n-1)(c-1) + c(c^j-1)(c^n-1) + (c^j-1)(\beta) - n(c^j-1)(c-1);$$

$$R^{*T}_{RB,c,n+j} = \frac{2\left\{ c^j \left(\sum_1^n c^{n-i} q_i - S(x) \right) + \tfrac{1}{2} r S[(p) + (t)\{(c^j-1)/(c-1)\}] \right\}}{S(u)} \quad (8)$$

where

$$u = \frac{c^j}{(1-c)(1-d)(c-d)}(y) + (p) + (t)\left(\frac{c^j-1}{c-1}\right),$$

$$p = 1 + \frac{d(1+c)}{1-c}\left\{\frac{1-d^{n-1}}{1-d} - \frac{c^n(1-(d/c)^{n-1})}{c-d}\right\};$$

and

$$t = d\left(\frac{c^n(1-(d/c)^{n-1})}{c-d}\right) + \frac{c-1}{c} - \frac{d(1-d^{n-1})}{1-d}.$$

Expressions for the four types of machines can be derived from (7) and (8). These expressions contain a new term, c^j, so that values were computed for a number of values of c^j (the range was: $j = 1\tfrac{1}{2}n{-}3n$). For the range of values of j examined, though, the values of R^* were hardly affected by variations in j. For example, with $a = 1\cdot5$, $b = 0\cdot5$, $c = 1\cdot01$, $n = 20$, and $r = 5$ per cent, the range was $8\cdot6$–$8\cdot8$ per cent, in the straight-line cases, and $6\cdot96$–$6\cdot98$ per cent in the reducing-balance cases. Again, while the patterns of change of R^* with respect to n have the same general shapes as those of the corresponding constant growth, physical capital cases, the discrepancy between the values of R^* and r, for given n, is usually reduced. Moreover, because the influence of growth is also usually to improve the accountant's measure, the discrepancies between R^* and r, for given n, are least of all of the cases examined. This is illustrated in Table 6 where values of R^* for the balanced stock, total capital and constant growth, total capital cases for $n = 10$ years, $a = 1\cdot5$, $b = 0\cdot5$, $r = 30$ per cent and $c = 1\cdot1$ are compared.

TABLE 6. *Values of R* for n = 10 years, a = 1·5, b = 0·5, c = 1·1, r = 30 per cent (balanced stock, total capital; constant growth, total capital) (percentages)*

	Straight-line depreciation		Reducing-balance depreciation	
Case	Balanced stock	Constant growth	Balanced stock	Constant growth
(1)	44·7	36·0‡	28·1	30·2‡
(2)	12·0	23·3‡	7·5	18·7‡
(3)	122·4	62·0‡	77·1	53·8‡
(4)	39·6†	35·3†‡	24·9†	29·6†‡

† m = 5 years. ‡ j = 30 years.

6

The article is concluded by summarizing briefly the variations of R^* with respect to n for the various cases examined. The following diagrams illustrate, schematically, the patterns of variation with respect to n.

(1) *Straight-line depreciation, balanced stock, physical capital*

Case (1):

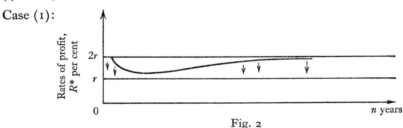

Fig. 2

(The arrows show the influence of growth and financial capital on R^*.)

Case (2):

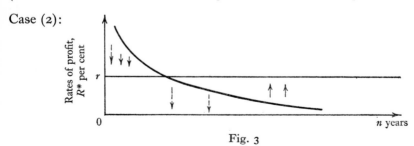

Fig. 3

(Dotted arrows show the influence of changes in b—the smaller is the value of b, the faster is the approach to zero.)

Case (3):

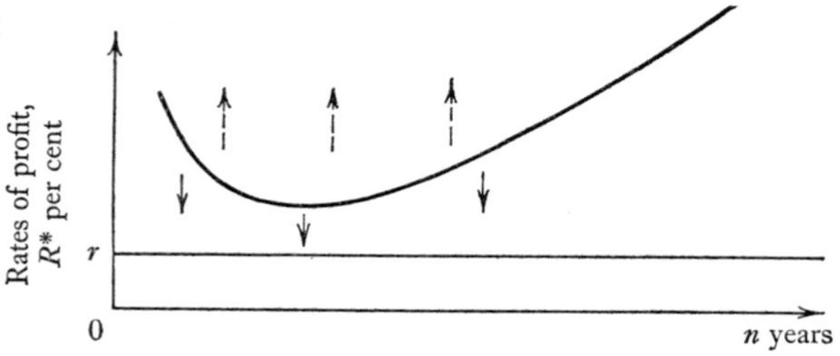

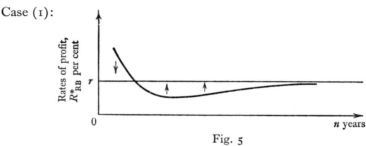

Fig. 4

(Dotted arrows show the influence of changes in a—the greater is the value of a, the faster is the approach to ∞. The function is not defined at $1+r = a$.)

Case (4): This case cannot be shown in a general diagram because it depends on the ratio, m/n. Its value approaches that of (2) as $m\ (< n) \to 0$.

(II) *Reducing-balance depreciation, balanced stock, physical capital*

Case (1):

Fig. 5

Cases (2) and (3) are similar to those for straight-line depreciation but, for $n > 2$, $R^*_{RB} < R^*$.

The implications of the analysis of the article are rather disheartening. It had been hoped that some rough 'rules of thumb' might be developed; and that these would allow accounting rates of profit to be adjusted for the lengths of life of machines, the patterns of quasi-rents, rates of growth, and the method of depreciation used. However, it is obvious from the calculations that the relationships involved are too complicated to allow this. A systematic presentation of the values of R^* for the various cases has not been attempted (though they have been computed). Nevertheless, on the basis of the above analysis it seems safe to add to the already well-known defects of accounting data on profits and capital,[1] the main conclusion of

---

[1] See, for example, Russell Mathews, *Accounting for Economists* (Melbourne, 1962), chapters 5, 6; Harold Rose, *Disclosure in Company Accounts* (Eaton Paper I), pp. 31–40.

this article, namely, that as an indication of the realized rate of return the accountant's rate of profit is greatly influenced by irrelevant factors, even under ideal conditions. Any 'man of words' (or 'deeds' for that matter) who compares rates of profit of different industries, or of the same industry in different countries, and draws inferences from their magnitudes as to the relative profitability of investments in different uses or countries, does so at his own peril.

PART VI

NATIONAL INCOME ACCOUNTING

22 The construction of tables of national income, expenditure, savings and investment

by J. E. Meade* and J. R. N. Stone†

I. INTRODUCTORY

The national income may be defined in a number of different ways. Differences in definitions, which are all too infrequently given with precision by writers on this subject, may lead to great confusion in economic discussion. It is the purpose of this paper to show that the construction of balance-sheets of national income and expenditure clears up some of these problems of definition and provides a powerful statistical instrument for the cross-checking of various methods of estimating the national income. Such tables may serve two further useful purposes. First, they make it possible for the statistician to provide estimates of the national income and expenditure in the various forms which are most useful to the economist for the elucidation of many economic problems. Secondly, if a form of tables of this kind could be generally accepted, international comparisons of national incomes would be greatly facilitated.

Tables A, B, C, D and E [pp. 344–6 below] are suggested outlines of the fundamental tables which serve the dual purpose of presenting the estimates in a form which is of most interest to economists and which enables the maximum amount of statistical cross-checking.

2. TABLE A

This table presents the basic material for a national income enquiry in three forms:

(i) *The Net National Income at Factor Cost* measures the money value of the income produced by, and accruing to, the various factors of production in any period of time—e.g. the rent of land, profits of business enterprises, interest on capital and the earnings of labour. Statistically for the United Kingdom, these estimates would be based principally upon

* Professor of Political Economy, University of Cambridge, 1957–68, Fellow of Christ's College.
† P. D. Leake Professor of Finance and Accounting, University of Cambridge.

income-tax statistics and upon statistics of the number of workers in employment and upon the average earnings of such workers.

(ii) *The Net National Output at Factor Cost* measures the value added to the product in various branches of economic activity. Statistically, these estimates would be obtained primarily by the Census of Production method of estimating the net value added in various industries, together with supplementary information on such items as the net income from foreign investment.

(iii) *The Net National Expenditure at Factor Cost* mesures the amount of the net national income (or output) which is used for various purposes—e.g. for personal consumption, for current government purposes and for additions to the community's capital. Statistically, the estimates would be based mainly upon public finance figures (for items 16, 17 and 18), upon a large number of different quantity and price series (for items 15 and 19),[1] and upon figures of foreign trade and other foreign transactions (for item 20).[2]

If the terms in the three columns of Table A are properly defined, the three totals (items 5, 14 and 21) must balance. Columns I and II are in effect merely different ways of enumerating the incomes earned by the various factors of production—land, capital and enterprise, and labour. In column I these incomes are enumerated according to the factors which earn the income, and in column II according to the various industries in which they are earned. In column I items 1 and 2 include the income received by the Government from State-owned property and the net income received from abroad by the Government and by the owners of foreign investments. The latter source of income is included in item 13 of column II, and the former in the various other items of column II. Item 12 of column II includes the salaries of civil servants and the pay of the armed forces—i.e. the factor incomes earned in Government service, which will not be included in the other items of this column.

Column III of Table A enumerates the expenditures which give rise to the factor incomes enumerated in columns I and II. Thus income is generated by personal expenditure on consumption and by the Government demand for goods and services. One preliminary matter which needs explanation is the reason for the insertion of items 17 and 18 in column III of Table A. Income, output and expenditure (items 5, 14 and 21 of Table A) are estimated 'at factor cost' and not 'at market prices'. If we consider

---

[1] For some items of personal consumption and of investment the Census of Production figures would, no doubt, have to be used, so that there would not be complete statistical independence between the estimates of national output and of national expenditure.

[2] See Table D, p. 346.

the production of any particular commodity (e.g. for personal consumption) we may measure either the income received by the factors of production from the sale of that product or the amount spent by consumers on that product. The former will be less than the latter if a tax is levied on the purchase of the commodity; and it will exceed the latter if the State pays a subsidy on its production. In order, therefore, that national income and expenditure may balance, we may—as is done in Table A—subtract indirect taxes from, and add subsidies to, the market value of the goods and services bought, in which case national income, output and expenditure are measured 'at factor cost'. Alternatively, we may add indirect taxes to, and subtract subsidies from, the national income and the national output, in which case income, output and expenditure would be measured 'at market prices'.

Column III also enumerates various expenditures—on personal consumption (item 15), on goods and services currently consumed by the Government (item 16), and on additions to the domestic equipment of capital (item 19)—regardless of the fact that these goods and services may be produced at home or may be imported from abroad. But it is only expenditure on home-produced goods and services which generates the factor incomes enumerated in columns I and II. Item 20 of Table A makes the necessary adjustment.

From Table D it will be seen that foreign investment (item 20 of Table A) is equal to income generated by receipts from abroad less current expenditure abroad. By including item 20 we are therefore adding to the other expenditures enumerated in column III of Table A the income generated by receipts from abroad (e.g. the sale of exports), and are deducting those current expenditures which are made abroad (e.g. the purchase of imports) and which do not therefore generate factor incomes at home.

Item 19 of Table A raises a number of difficulties of definition. In the first place, income, output and expenditure (items 5, 14 and 21 of Table A) have been defined as 'net'. Income is said to be reckoned 'net', and not 'gross', when deduction is made from the receipts of gross profits to allow for the depreciation, renewal, repair, etc., of capital equipment; and expenditure is reckoned 'net' when a similar deduction is made from gross investment. Income, output and expenditure may be reckoned 'gross' if profits (item 2) are estimated before deduction of these allowances, if the values added to the product in different industries (items 6–10) are estimated before deduction of the expenses which must be incurred to maintain the capital of each industry intact, and if home investment (item 19) is estimated in such a way as to measure gross rather than net expenditure

331

on fixed capital goods (i.e if item 19(*b*) is omitted from column III of Table A).

The problem of estimating 'net' investment raises fundamental problems of definition of income. (*a*) Income may be defined in terms of money values in the following way. We may say that a man's money income in any period is equal to the money value of his consumption plus the increase in the money value of his capital assets. For the sum of these two is the amount which he could have spent on consumption *while maintaining the money value of his capital stock intact*. (*b*) On the other hand, a man's income may be defined as the value of his expenditure on consumption plus the value of any increase in the real amount of his capital assets. For the sum of these two is the amount he could have spent on consumption *while maintaining the real amount of his capital stock intact*.

(*a*) If the first principle is adopted, home and foreign investment (items 19 and 20 of Table A) must be measured in such a way as to record the *increase in the value* of domestic fixed capital, of domestic stocks and of foreign assets. Similarly, in columns I and II income from profits must be defined so as to include the appreciation in the money value of all these assets, as well as the accounting profit which remains after deducting from current receipts the current cost of replacing the physical assets which are used up or depreciated in the process of obtaining those current receipts.

(*b*) The adoption of the second principle means that home and foreign investment must be defined as the *value of the increase* in all real assets, and that profits must be defined as the accounting profit resulting from the difference between current receipts and the current cost of replacing all real factors of production used up in current production.

The inclusion of item 19(*d*) in Table A needs some explanation. In the investment of savings, use is made of certain services—e.g. those of stock-brokers and lawyers. In so far as the cost of these services is reckoned as a current cost of production by any business which is investing funds, it will have been included as one of the factor costs which must be covered by the market prices of the goods produced by the business. In this case the value of the services in question will already have been covered by the market value of the goods and services enumerated in other items of column III of Table A. But in so far as these services are not so accounted for, they must be regarded as an item in the cost of providing new capital equipment for the community; and if expenditure on services of this kind were not separately enumerated, the sum of income-generating expenditures enumerated in column III of Table A would be incomplete.

3. TABLE B

This table shows the form in which estimates may be presented of personal incomes and of the uses to which personal incomes may be put (i.e. through expenditure on different forms of consumption or through savings). The first column of Table B ('The Composition of Personal Incomes') illustrates the way in which an estimate of personal incomes may be derived from the Net National Income at Factor Cost (item 5 of Table A).

If we start with the Net National Income at Factor Cost, we must first (Table B, item 2) add transfer incomes paid by the State (such as interest on the national debt, unemployment allowances paid by the State to the unemployed, etc.). For in Table A these items of transfer income are excluded (i) from the national income (which records only the incomes earned by the factors of production for productive work done), (ii) from the national output (which records only the value of the net output of various productive industries), and (iii) from the national expenditure (which in item 16 of Table A excludes expenditure by the State of a purely transfer character).[1]

We must next (item 3 of Table B) deduct all direct taxes paid on income in order to obtain the sum of incomes after deduction of direct taxes. We must next deduct those elements of this total of tax-free incomes which are not paid over to persons—namely, (i) Government income from property or from trading profits (item 4 of Table B), which is not paid over to individuals but is used as a part of Government revenue to finance Government expenditure, and (ii) undistributed profits (item 5 of Table B), which represents elements of tax-free income obtained from profits or interest or

---

[1] It may be thought that the balance of Table B will be upset if item 2 includes only transfer payments from the Government to individuals. For there are a number of other forms of transfer income. For example, a son may receive an allowance from his father, or a pauper may receive a transfer income from a charitable organization. The balance of Table B is, however, preserved by excluding such transfers both from personal incomes and from personal consumption. In the case of a son's allowance, since the father's 'expenditure' in giving the money to his son is excluded from personal expenditure (item 9 of Table B), the balance is preserved by excluding the receipt of the son's allowance from item 2 of Table B. A similar problem arises in the case of betting gains. Expenditure on betting leads (i) to the receipt of income by those engaged in the betting industry and (ii) to the receipt of a transfer income by those who win bets. In columns I and II of Table A the incomes of those engaged in the betting industry will be recorded; and, against this, item 15 of Table A (and so item 9 of Table B) must include only that part of expenditure on betting which is not transferred to those who win bets. The balance of Table B is thus preserved by excluding from transfer incomes (item 2) the money obtained from betting gains. Receipts of transfer incomes from charitable institutions may be regarded—as in the case of a father's allowance to his son—as a transfer between individuals, provided that suitable definitions of income and expenditure are adopted in the case of such institutions. [This problem is dealt with at greater length below, see pp. 340–3.]

rent, which are saved directly by companies without being paid to individuals.

We then obtain (item 6 of Table B) an estimate of the total of personal incomes after deduction of direct taxes. This sum can be divided (as in the second column of Table B) to show the distribution of the total of personal incomes between groups of income-recipients ranged according to the size of their incomes. It must also be equal (*see* the third column of Table B) to the sum of personal expenditures on various forms of consumption and personal savings.

The columns of Table B present the information about personal incomes in a way which should be of interest to economists. For it shows (*a*) the relations between the net national income and transfer incomes and impersonal incomes, (*b*) the distribution of personal incomes between income classes and (*c*) the way in which personal incomes are spent or saved. The total of personal incomes, its distribution among income classes, and personal expenditures on various types of goods or services are the raw material from which—with the supplementary aid of information about the prices of various groups of consumption goods and services—personal demand functions and propensities to consume may best be analysed.

The columns in Table B may also serve as a statistical cross-check. The sources used for the estimates in column I (in addition to the sources used for item I of Table B, which is the same as item 5 of Table A) are certain public finance figures (for items 2, 3 and 4) and figures of business accounts (for item 5). If income-tax statistics and figures of wages are used to make estimates of column II of Table B, there is little statistical cross-check between the totals of column II and of column I, item I of which is largely based on the same material. But if estimates for column II could be obtained from sample family budget enquiries, an independent estimate of the total of personal incomes might be obtained. In column III of Table B still other data could be used for the estimates—for item 9 a large number of series of production, prices or sales of different goods and services, and for item 10 an enumeration of the increases in all the different types of asset (cash, securities, etc.) held by individuals.

4. TABLE C

A third table may be constructed to illustrate the flow of savings. Savings may be made by persons (item I of Table C) or by businesses (item 2 of Table C); and they may be used either to finance investment (item 4 of Table C) or the excess of current expenditure over current revenue of the Government (item 5 of Table C). But while Table C presents information about savings and investment in a form which may be of interest to economists, it does not provide any additional statistical cross-checking; for if item 5 of Table C is properly defined, Table C is simply a re-arrangement of certain items of Tables A and B.

This fact can best be seen by means of Table B'. We know that item 5 of Table A should be equal to the sum of items 15, 16, 17, 18, 19 and 20 of Table A. In other words, item 1 in column I of Table B' is equal to the sum of items 7, 8, 9, 11 and 14 in column II of Table B'. The remaining items in column I of Table B' are identical with the remaining items in column II of Table B'; for example, item 2 of Table B' is the same as item 10 of Table B'.

But the items in column I of Table B' are the same as those in column I of Table B, which represents the composition of personal incomes after deduction of direct taxes. It follows, therefore, that column II of Table B' must measure the sum of personal consumption and personal savings, or that personal savings equals the sum of items 8, 9, 10, 11, 12, 13, 14 and 15 of Table B', or that

Personal savings + undistributed profits − investment
  = current Government expenditure on goods and services, subsidies and transfers
  − Government revenue from direct and indirect taxes and from Government income.

The above equation is the same as the balance between the uses and sources of savings as shown in Table C, if the right-hand term of the above equation is defined as the budget deficit. Or in other words, if this definition of the budget deficit is adopted, Table C must be regarded merely as a re-arrangement of Tables A and B.

5. THE INTERPRETATION OF PUBLIC FINANCE

The use of this definition of the budget deficit requires some explanation. In the first place, the budget deficit refers to the total transactions of all public authorities; and a combined statement of revenue and expenditure must be drawn up for (e.g.) the central Government, the local authorities and various extra-budgetary public funds. All transfers between these various authorities must be excluded from both revenue and expenditure. For example, grants-in-aid paid by the central Government to the local authorities must be excluded from central Government expenditure and from local authorities' revenue; and State contributions to extra-budgetary funds for social insurance must be excluded from central Government expenditure and from the revenue of extra-budgetary funds. When this is done a combined revenue and expenditure account of the following type may be drawn up.

Combined Revenue and Expenditure Account of all Public Authorities

Revenue	Expenditure
(a) Direct taxes, fines and gifts	(f) Transfer payments to private sector of the economy
(b) Indirect taxes	
(c) Government income from property and profits of trading services	(g) Subsidies
(d) Balance, or budget deficit	(h) Net current expenditure by the Government on goods and services:
	(i) Total expenditure on goods and services,
	less
	(ii) revenue from sale of goods and services to private sector of the economy,
	less
	(iii) Government purchase of capital assets
(e) Total revenue	(i) Total expenditure

It will be seen that this combined revenue and expenditure account gives a definition of the budget deficit which corresponds to that which is necessary for the balancing of Table C. Item (*h*) of the Combined Revenue and Expenditure Account corresponds to item 16 of Table A. This item excludes from Government expenditure on goods and services an amount equal to the revenue of the Government from the sale of goods and services to the private sector of the economy (e.g. sale of postage stamps, rent from municipally owned houses, etc.). For such expenditures (e.g. the purchase of postage stamps by individuals or for business purposes) will already have appeared in Table A, column III, either directly as an element of personal expenditure (item 15 of Table A), or as an element in the business costs, and so in the market prices of other goods and services produced for sale to persons, to the Government, for domestic capital construction or for export (items 15, 16, 19 or 20 of Table A). Item (*h*) of the Combined Revenue and Expenditure Account must also exclude Government expenditure on goods and services for investment purposes (e.g. for the extension of post office equipment or for the building of publicly owned dwelling-houses), in so far as these expenditures are included in home investment (item 19 of Table A).

There is, however, a certain degree of arbitrariness in deciding what items of Government expenditure should be regarded as investment expenditure. But the principles to be adopted for the purpose of balancing the tables are clear. If, for example, expenditure on roads and on battleships is excluded from current expenditure by the Government, then it must be included in home investment, and vice versa. The State may also spend money on taking over property from the private sector of the economy. It may, for example, buy land or other property from private-property owners or it may in wartime take over existing stocks of commodities from private owners. In these cases, if these expenditures are included in current Government expenditure on goods and services, home investment must be reduced by an amount equal to the net value of the property or stocks transferred from private to Government ownership.[1]

The definitions of indirect taxes, subsidies and Government income from the profits of trading services (items (b), (g), and (c) of the Combined Revenue and Expenditure Account) also raise certain problems of definition. For example, a State monopoly may be so run as to make an abnormally large profit on the goods or services sold. If part of the price of the commodity is considered to be an indirect tax, then a similar amount must be excluded from the Government profit from trading services, with the result that items 2 and 18 of Table A will be correspondingly diminished (algebraically). If the Government runs a trading service at a loss in order—for social reasons—to sell the goods or service concerned at a low price, then this loss may *either* be deducted from Government income from profits *or* may be included in subsidies. In the latter case both items 2 and 17 of Table A will be greater than they would have been in the former case.

The distinction between direct taxes and indirect taxes also raises certain problems of definition. The fundamental distinction is a clear one. Tax payments which are not deducted from current receipts as a cost before determining incomes are direct taxes[2] (e.g. the income tax), while those which are deducted from current receipts from market sales before determining incomes (e.g. taxes on the sale of beer or tobacco) are indirect taxes. In certain cases (e.g. excess profits tax), a tax which, for economic reasons, it is desired to treat as a direct tax, may be deducted from profits before determining income for income-tax purposes. In order to treat such taxes as direct taxes, in item 5 of Table A income must be reckoned before the deduction of such taxes, and they must be excluded from item 18 of Table A.

[1] There is a certain lack of symmetry in colum III of Table A. Current expenditure for personal consumption and for consumption of goods and services by the Government are shown separately (items 15 and 16). But investment (items 19 and 20) is divided between home and foreign investment and not, in addition, between investment financed by the Government and investment privately financed. It would, of course, be possible to divide total investment between privately financed investment and Government investment, if this were considered desirable for any economic purpose.

[2] It is convenient throughout the tables to treat such payments as gifts to the Government and fines paid to the Government, which are not deducted as an expense chargeable against income and which do not represent expenditure by persons on the purchase of goods and services, as direct taxes. A separate category for such payments could, of course, be devised if it were thought desirable.

Stamp duties may be regarded partly as direct taxes and partly as indirect taxes, or wholly as indirect taxes. Stamp duties—such as stamps on cheques by businesses—are to be regarded as a business cost of production, and are deducted from current revenue to calculate income from profits. They are therefore to be regarded as indirect taxes. Duties such as stamps on cheques drawn by individuals for their personal expenditure may be regarded as indirect taxes if they are added to item 15 of Table A and regarded as an addition to the market price paid by individuals for their purchases. If, however, they are not added to the market price of consumption expenditure, they must be regarded as a direct tax paid out of individual's income. Stamp duties on the transfer of property may be treated as an indirect tax if they are included in item 19(*d*) of Table A, and are thus included in the 'market price' of the goods and services used for production of additions to capital assets. If, however, they are not so included, they must be treated as a direct tax which is paid by an investor whenever a purchase of property is made.

For certain purposes it may be convenient to divide direct taxes into two groups: (i) those 'paid out of income' (e.g. income tax and surtax), and (ii) those 'paid out of savings' (e.g. death duties). This division would affect Tables B and C. If in item 3 of Table B only 'direct taxes paid out of income' are deducted, then business savings (item 5 of Table B) and personal savings (item 10 of Table B) must together be increased by a similar amount, so as to represent savings inclusive of that part of savings which is used to finance the payment of 'direct taxes paid out of savings'. For example, personal savings would be reckoned as the increase in capital assets held by individuals, before deduction of the amount of assets taken away from them by the State in payment of death duties, as property passed from one owner to another as a result of death. In Table C a new item—'direct taxes paid out of savings'—would have to be added to column II, since the Government would absorb part of the savings of individuals as now defined, through the capital assets which it took over from them in the form of death duties.

It may also be useful to draw a distinction between (i) payments of direct taxes in any period and (ii) accruing liabilities to tax payments in that period. This distinction is of economic importance, if there is any considerable time-lag between the earning of income and the date when tax is paid on it and if the total of incomes and rates of taxation are rising or falling. The current liability of taxpayers to pay taxes out of their current incomes at current rates of tax will be considerably in excess of the actual amount of tax being currently paid, if these tax payments have been assessed on lower past incomes and at a lower rate of tax than the current rate of tax.

If item 3 of Table B shows current liabilities to direct taxation, as opposed to current payments of direct taxes, then items 5 and 10 of Table B must be shown as institutional and personal savings after deduction not only of current payments of direct taxes but also of the excess of current liabilities to, over current payments of, direct taxes. In other words, savings will now be shown as the net amount of income which is free to be saved after putting aside all that is necessary to meet the current liability to direct taxation. In Table C a balancing figure must be included, and the current budget deficit must be reduced by an amount equal to the excess of current liabilities to, over current payments of, direct taxes. A comparison both of the budget deficit and of savings before and after making this adjustment is of interest in any period of rapid fluctuation of the national income or of rates of taxation.

6. TABLE D

This table shows how foreign investment is equal to the excess of current receipts from abroad over current expenditure abroad, and it also provides a statistical cross-check of the calculation of foreign investment (for item 20 of Table A). The principle of the balance of this table is self-explanatory. The sum of the increases in different foreign assets (item 4 of Table D) must be equal to the excess of current receipts of funds from abroad over current expenditure of funds abroad; for it is only through such an excess that a net sum of foreign funds may be acquired for investment abroad.

7. TABLE E

From Tables A and D a table may be obtained which shows home investments as equal to the excess of income generated by expenditure at home over current expenditure at home. If we subtract (algebraically) items 17 and 18 of Table A from columns I and III of Table A, we obtain figures of Net National Income and Net National Expenditure at Market Prices (as opposed to Income and Expenditure at Factor Cost).[1] If we then deduct coumn I of Table D from column I of Table A and column II of Table D from column III of Table A, we obtain Table E. Item 1 of Table E is the difference between the total Net National Income at Market Prices and that part of it which is due (e.g. through the sale of exports) to payments received from abroad. Item 3 of Table E is the difference between current National Expenditure at Market Prices and that part of it which is spent

---

[1] See pp. 330–1.

abroad (e.g. in the purchase of imports). The difference between these two (item 4 of Table E) is equal to expenditure on capital development at home.

8. METHODS OF ENSURING THE BALANCE IN TABLE A

In the preceding paragraphs and the accompanying tables an outline has been given of the main problems of definition which must be solved in order to ensure that the tables balance. There are, however, a thousand and one small problems of definition which arise in attempting to measure the individual items in the different tables. It is impossible to treat all these minor definitional problems at length; but the sort of problems which arise and the way in which they may be solved can be illustrated by means of an example.

We may consider the problem of treating the revenue and expenditure of hospitals in such a way that the balance between columns I and III of Table A is preserved. In the economic system as a whole a host of transactions are taking place which either involve the payment of money from one owner to another or may be imagined to be accompanied by such a money transaction.[1] Some of these payments of money (e.g. the purchase of consumption goods) will be recorded as part of the Net National Expenditure in column III of Table A (N.N.E.). Some of these receipts of money (e.g. the payment of wages) will be recorded as part of the Net National Income in column I of Table A (N.N.I.). Any one transaction (e.g. the transfer payment of an allowance by a father to his son) may be recorded neither as N.N.E. nor as N.N.I. A transaction (e.g. the payment of wages in a productive business) may be such that its payment is not recorded as N.N.E. but its receipt is recorded as N.N.I. Another transaction (e.g. the purchase of imported consumption goods) may be such that its payment is recorded as N.N.E. but its receipt is not recorded as N.N.I. The principle to be adopted is that as money flows round in different transactions of payments and receipts it shall be recorded alternately as N.N.E. and N.N.I. and not twice running as N.N.E. or twice running as N.N.I.

[1] An example of this latter type of transaction is the payment to (e.g.) domestic servants of part of their income in kind (e.g. in food and lodging) by their employers. If we wish to record their wages in item 4 of Table A as inclusive of their money wages and of their wages in kind, we may imagine that the employer pays to the domestic servant the whole of this wage in money, and that the domestic servant then purchases from the employer the food and lodging provided in kind. In order to preserve the balance between columns I and III of Table A, if the whole of the wages of domestic servants is included in item 4 the whole of it must also be included in item 15 as personal expenditure on domestic services.

We may apply this principle to a combined revenue and expenditure account of all voluntary hospitals. Such a combined account may be presumed to contain the following items:

Revenue		Expenditure	
	Transaction last re- corded as:		Transaction next re- corded as:
(a) Gifts from individuals	N.N.I.	(f) Food, drugs, etc., purchased	N.N.E.
(b) Gifts from businesses	N.N.I.	(g) Salaries, wages, etc.	N.N.E.
(c) Net income from property	N.N.I.	(h) Repairs and maintenance	N.N.E.
(d) Fees for medical services performed	N.N.I.	(i) Balance, being sums saved or accumulated by hospitals	N.N.E.
(e) Government grants	N.N.I. or − N.N.E.		

We must examine each item of hospitals' revenue to see whether each item when it has been received was last recorded as N.N.I. or N.N.E., and we must examine each item of hospitals' expenditure to see whether it is next recorded as N.N.I. or N.N.E.

If definitions are adopted of such a kind that the whole of the revenue and expenditure is *either* first recorded as N.N.I. and then as N.N.E., *or* first recorded as N.N.E. and then as N.N.I., the treatment is such as to preserve a proper balance between columns I and III of Table A.

(a) Gifts from individuals are paid out of individuals' incomes, and the incomes from which they are paid are recorded in Table A as a part of N.N.I. So long as gifts from individuals to hospitals are not recorded in item 15 of Table A as an element of personal expenditure, this item of revenue is recorded in Table A as N.N.I.

(b) Gifts from businesses are paid out of profits, which are recorded in Table A as a part of N.N.I. Since the payment of a gift from a business to a hospital is not recorded in N.N.E. in Table A, this item may also be marked N.N.I.

(c) Net income from property. This item is included in item 1 or 2 of Table A, and may therefore be marked as N.N.I.

(d) Fees for medical services are paid out of income (N.N.I.). If they are not recorded as an item of personal expenditure[1] in item 15 of Table A, this item must also be marked as N.N.I.

(e) Government grants. If Government expenditure on grants to hospitals

---

[1] They should not be recorded as an item of personal expenditure, if—as is suggested below—items (f), (g) and (h) which represent the actual purchases of goods and services for medical purposes are so recorded.

were included in item 16 of Table A, this item would need to be marked as N.N.E. But if we exclude this item of Government expenditure from item 16 of Table A and treat it as a transfer payment to the private sector of the economy, we must consider the sources from which the necessary revenue was raised to transfer to hospitals. If it were raised by direct taxes, from Government income or from borrowing, it would come out of income (N.N.I.). If it were raised by indirect taxation it would be recorded in item 18 of Table A as −N.N.E., which for balancing purposes is equivalent to N.N.I.

(*f*), (*g*) and (*h*). These current expenditures by hospitals may be recorded as N.N.E. if they are added to item 15 of Table A as an item of personal expenditure.

(*i*) Savings of hospitals. This item, in so far as it represents expenditure by hospitals on investment in (for example) hospital buildings, is recorded in item 19 of Table A as home investment (N.N.E.). If the savings are lent to other borrowers, it is not recorded directly as investment in Table A; but the expenditure of these savings by the borrowers will be so recorded (N.N.E.).

9. THE DIVISION OF THE ECONOMY INTO GOVERNMENT, BUSINESS AND PERSONAL SECTORS

In the above paragraphs and the accompanying tables the economy has been divided into three sectors—Government, business and persons; and the interrelations between the income, expenditure and savings of these three parts of the economy have been examined. It would appear that this division leaves no room for the transactions of various institutions—such as clubs, charities, trade unions, etc.—which are neither Government institutions nor business institutions. In order to avoid unprofitable complications of the tables which would arise if an attempt were made to introduce a fourth sector, it is convenient to treat such institutions merely as a channel through which persons receive and spend income. The way in which this may be done is best shown by taking one such institution as an example.

We can illustrate the method by taking again the treatment of the revenue and expenditure of voluntary hospitals. All the items of hospitals' revenue (in the revenue and expenditure account of hospitals shown on page 341 above) may be treated as being recorded in personal incomes in column I of Table B, and all the items of hospitals' expenditure may be treated as being recorded in personal expenditure or savings in column III of Table B.

(*a*) and (*d*). Gifts from individuals and fees paid by individuals are paid out of the total of individual incomes included in item 6 of Table B.

(*b*) The profits from which gifts are paid by businesses to hospitals are recorded as an element of item 1 of Table B, and provided that they are not deducted in undistributed profits (item 5 of Table B), this item will also be recorded as an element of personal incomes in item 6 of Table B.

(*c*) The income from property of hospitals is recorded in item 1 of Table B; and since it is not deducted in items 3, 4 or 5 of Table B, it remains in the total of personal incomes (item 6 of Table B).

(*e*) Government grants to hospitals, being treated as an item of Government transfer expenditure, will appear in item 2 of Table B, and therefore in the total of personal incomes (item 6 of Table B).

(*f*), (*g*) and (*h*). These expenditures must be recorded as elements of personal consumption (item 9 of Table B).

(*i*) Savings through hospitals must then be recorded as an item of personal savings, and the increase in the various assets held by hospitals must be included in the increase in assets held by individuals for the purpose of calculating item 10 of Table B.

We are, in fact, by these means regarding gifts from businesses, grants from the Government and the income obtained from property owned by hospitals as supplements to personal incomes, which enable individuals to purchase medical services or to save through the medium of hospitals.

[Tables A–E overleaf

TABLE A

I Net National Income at factor cost	II Net National Output at factor cost	III Net National Expenditure ,at factor cost
1. Rents 2. Profits and Interest 3. Salaries 4. Wages	6. Net output of agriculture 7. Net output of mining 8. Net output of manufac- turing 9. Net output of transport 10. Net output of distribution 11. Net value of personal services 12. Net value of Govern- ment services 13. Net income from abroad (see Table D, item 1 (*d*) and (*e*))	15. Personal consumption at market prices 16. Current Government ex- penditure on goods and services 17. Government subsidies 18. *Less* indirect taxes 19. Home investment: (*a*) Gross home investment in fixed capital (*b*) *Less* depreciation, re- newals, repairs, etc. (*c*) Home investment in stocks (*d*) Costs involved in trans- fer of property. 20. Foreign investment
5. Total Net National Income at factor cost	14. Total Net National Output at factor cost	21. Total Net National Ex- penditure at factor cost

TABLE B

I Composition of personal incomes	II Distribution of personal incomes	III Personal consumption and savings
1. Net National Income at factor cost (Table A, item 5) 2. Transfer incomes from the State 3. *Less* direct taxes 4. *Less* Government in- come 5. *Less* undistributed profits	7. Personal incomes: (*a*) gross personal incomes below £200 per head per annum *Less* direct taxes on above incomes (*b*) gross personal incomes £200–£500 per head per annum *Less* direct taxes on above incomes, etc.	9. Personal consumption at market prices (Table A, item 15): (*a*) food, drink and tobacco (*b*) rent and rates (*c*) clothing (*d*) travel, etc. 10. Personal savings: (*a*) Net increase in cash held by individuals (*b*) Net increase in secur- ities held by indi- viduals (*c*) Net increase in other assets held by indi- viduals
6. Personal incomes after deduction of direct taxes	8. Personal incomes after de- duction of direct taxes	11. Personal consumption and savings

I Personal incomes	Cross- reference to other items	II Personal consumption and savings	Cross- reference to other items
1. Net National Income at factor cost	Table A, item 5	7. Personal consumption	Table A, item 15
2. Transfer incomes from the State	Table B, item 2	8. Current Government expenditure on goods and services	Table A, item 16
3. *Less* direct taxes	Table B, item 3	9. Government subsidies	Table A, item 17
4. *Less* Government income	Table B, item 4	10. Government transfer expenditure	Table B, item 2
5. *Less* undistributed profits	Table B, item 5	11. *Less* indirect taxes	Table A, item 18
		12. *Less* direct taxes	Table B, item 3
		13. *Less* Government income	Table B, item 4
		14. Home and foreign investment	Table A, items 19 and 20
		15. *Less* undistributed profits	Table B, item 5
6. Personal incomes after deduction of direct taxes	Table B, item 6	16. Personal consumption and savings	Table B, item 11

TABLE C

I Sources of savings	II Uses of savings
1. Personal savings	4. Home and foreign investment
2. Undistributed profits	5. Budget deficit
3. Total savings	6. Total savings

TABLE D

I Income generated by receipts from abroad	II Current expenditure and investment abroad
1. Income generated by receipts from abroad: (*a*) Value of home-produced exports (*b*) Value of export of services (e.g. shipping, finance, etc.) (*c*) Receipts from foreign tourists (*d*) Net income from foreign property (*e*) Net government receipts from abroad	3. Current expenditure abroad: (*a*) Value of retained imports (*b*) Value of imported services (*c*) Expenditure abroad by tourists 4. Foreign investment: (*a*) Net increase in holding of gold (*b*) Increase in holding of foreign money *Less* Increase in domestic money held by foreigners (*c*) Increase in holding of foreign securities and other assets *Less* Increase in domestic securities and other assets held by foreigners
2. Income generated by receipts from abroad	5. Total current expenditure and investment abroad

TABLE E

I Income generated by expenditure at home	Cross-reference to other items	II Current expenditure and investment at home	Cross-reference to other items
1. Income generated by expenditure at home: (*a*) Net National Income at market prices	Table A, item 5, *less* items 17 and 18	3. Current expenditure at home: (*a*) Personal consumption and current Government expenditure on goods and services	Table A, items 15 and 16
Less (*b*) Income generated by receipts from abroad	*Less* Table D, item 2	*Less* (*b*) Current expenditure abroad	*Less* Table D, item 3
		4. Home Investment: (*a*) Net increase in domestic fixed capital (*b*) Net increase in domestic stocks (*c*) Costs involved in transfer of property	Table A, items 19 and 20, *less* Table D, item 4
2. Total income generated by expenditure at home		5. Current expenditure and investment at home	

23 Economic growth in Australia and its measurement

ECONOMIC GROWTH: MEANING AND DEFINITION

1. Among the objectives of the Commonwealth Government's economic policy stated in the preamble to the terms of reference are a high rate of economic growth, increasing productivity and rising standards of living. It is desirable to define these objectives as precisely as possible and in ways which lend themselves to measurement, even if only in very broad terms.

2. The economic nature of these three objectives means that they are concerned mainly with goods and services. Productivity is concerned with the flow of goods and services *produced*, usually expressed per unit of labour employed in producing them. Standards of living are concerned mainly with the flow of goods and services *available for use*, expressed per head of population, or per consumer, some regard being paid to their distribution, as well as to their average level. The kinds of goods and services included and how they are measured are considered later. The rate of economic growth of a country refers to the rate of increase in the flow of goods and services; but whether these are the goods and services produced in the country, or available for use in the country, is not implied in the term itself. The answer must be sought in the usage of the term.

3. The term 'economic growth' as applied to a country has come into use, mainly since the war, in connexion with three fields of study. One is the study of the ways in which industrialized economies can achieve long-term advances in their economic wellbeing, as distinct from merely avoiding economic fluctuations, or eliminating unemployment. Another is the study of ways in which poor and under-developed economies can set in motion and sustain advances in their economic wellbeing. A third field is the comparative study of rates of economic growth in countries of different ideologies. This is part of the study of comparative power and international influence, and has political rather than economic purposes.

4. In pre-war economic discussion, the question whether a country was better off in one year than another, or whether one country was better off than another, tended to be answered in terms of goods and services available. The statistical measure used was real national income, either

347

aggregate or per head of population. In post-war discussions of economic growth, it is clear that the statistical measures employed largely relate to the aggregate of goods and services produced, rather than available. The statistical measure generally used is gross national product at constant prices.

5. The differences between the two types of statistical measure are discussed in the next paragraph. 'Economic growth' does not appear to be generally used in the sense of expansion in an economy's capacity to produce goods and services, except in occasional contexts where it is used synonymously with 'economic development'—and in these contexts it is not generally used in a quantitative sense. It refers rather to the actual flow of goods and services themselves. However, the actual production of goods and services in conditions of full employment is sometimes identified with production at full capacity. Besides this, it is generally agreed that the periods selected for the measurement of growth trends should be long enough to prevent short-term fluctuations in employment from disturbing the trend. To this extent economic growth so measured is related to the growth of the economy's capacity.

6. The distinction between goods and services produced and goods and services available for use can be described by reference to the principal measures used to represent each type of concept:

(*a*) *Gross national product* (G.N.P.) is the total value of the goods and services produced in a country in a given period, usually a year, after deduction of the value of all goods and services, (except depreciation of capital equipment), used up in the course of production.[1] By revaluation of all goods and services at the prices of a base year, G.N.P. may be adjusted for the direct effects of price changes, and the result is *G.N.P. at constant prices*, the most common indicator of economic growth.

(*b*) Some of the goods and services are exported and are therefore not available for internal use. The value of these exported goods and services can be expressed in terms of their purchasing power over imported goods and services; this modification results in *G.N.P. at constant prices, adjusted for the terms of trade*, which is a frequently used indicator of economic growth in Australia. This is one measure of 'goods and services available', but it is possible to go further.

(*c*) Part of the value of the goods and services forming G.N.P. is not available for current use because it represents depreciation allowances required to keep capital intact. Another part is not available for internal use because it is paid overseas in the form of investment income. Deduction

---

[1] This is the same as 'gross domestic product' in the terminology of the United Nations *System of National Accounts*.

of depreciation allowances and net income payable overseas[1] gives a measure of aggregate income accruing to residents, referred to as national income. This can be expressed in terms of purchasing power over consumable goods and services by being divided by the consumer price index, and the result is *real national income*, the traditional measure of the economic wellbeing arising from the annual flow of goods and services available.

7. In terms of current prices, the relationship between G.N.P. and national income is:

G.N.P.

    less indirect taxation (*less* subsidies),
    less depreciation allowances,
    less net income payable overseas,

equals national income.

Thus there is a general measure of goods and services produced: G.N.P. at constant prices; and two measures of goods and services available for use: G.N.P. at constant prices adjusted for the terms of trade, and real national income.

8. As G.N.P. at constant prices is the most commonly used measure of economic growth, it can be concluded that economic growth is generally regarded as being associated with the flow of goods and services produced, rather than available. Nevertheless, the other two measures, which relate to the flow of goods and services available, have important uses and, especially in the circumstances of Australia, can be considered as useful alternative measures of economic growth. When expressed per head of population, they are also relevant to living standards. The general relationships of the concepts and their measures, expressed in the aggregate and per head, can be illustrated by means of a diagram:

Economic growth, i.e increase in flow of goods and services:			
Produced	Available	Productivity	Living standards
Aggregate measures		Per-head measures	
(1) G.N.P. at constant prices	(2) G.N.P. at constant prices adjusted for terms of trade	(1) G.N.P. at constant prices per person employed	(2) G.N.P. at constant prices adjusted for terms of trade, per head of population
	(3) Real national income		(3) Real national income per head of population

[1] And of indirect taxes less subsidies (see paragraph 11).

For these indicators of economic growth, the questions relating to concept and measurement which need to be answered are: What kinds of goods and services should be included? How are the indicators to be used? How accurately can they be measured? The answers which follow, except where otherwise stated, relate to all three concepts and measures discussed. Statistical practices differ slightly between countries; the details of the description given relate to Australian official practices.

KINDS OF GOODS AND SERVICES INCLUDED IN MEASURES OF ECONOMIC GROWTH

9. The goods and services to be included in measures of G.N.P. or national income are not identifiable by a single test. If they are sold for money they are included, but some goods and services not sold for money are also included, for example, the value of the foodstuffs produced and consumed on farms. In Australia, this can be estimated readily from the local value of such foodstuffs where they are sold as cash crops. (For countries where subsistence agriculture predominates, however, this valuation presents a serious problem, and the estimates of economic growth in such cases may be of doubtful value.) Similarly, the 'imputed income' derived by a house-holder from the dwelling he owns is included, valued at the rental value of similar dwellings which are tenanted. The services of public authorities, although not sold on a market, are also included among the measurable elements of G.N.P. and national income. For this purpose, they are valued at the 'factor cost' appropriate, that is, at the cost of the wages and salaries of the Government employees who perform the services. This may or may not be equal to the price that the Government or the community would have been prepared to pay for these services if they had been sold on a market. For purposes of estimating G.N.P. or national income no attempt is made to value the 'output' of public authority services at some set of notional market prices; instead, the public authorities are regarded as communal purchasers, on behalf of the public, of the services of their employees and the materials they use to do their work, the services of the employees being the net contribution of this 'industry' to G.N.P.

10. The uncharged services performed by members of the family in private businesses or households are not included in the goods and services entering into the measurement of G.N.P. or national income. Nor are the services performed by an individual for himself, even though, as in the case of driving a motor vehicle, they may replace a service which he formerly paid for as a passenger on the public transport system, and which was therefore included in G.N.P. and national income. Other services not in-

cluded are those provided by Government assets for which no charge is made to the consumer, for example, the services of parks, art galleries, and public roads and bridges. On the other hand, there is no means of allowing for the (negative) value of disservices arising from the production of other goods and services, for example, smoke from factory chimneys, traffic congestion and noise.

METHODS OF MEASUREMENT

11. The goods and services described as entering into the content of G.N.P. and national income are valued at their market prices, where sold on a market, for purposes of G.N.P., and at factor cost for purposes of national income. The difference between market price and factor cost consists of:

(*a*) Any indirect taxes forming part of the market prices but not accruing as income.

(*b*) *Less* any government subsidies accruing as income but not forming part of the market price.

(*c*) Depreciation allowances.

Where the goods and services are not sold on a market, they are valued in the ways described in paragraph 9—at the cost of wages and salaries in the case of public authority services. The same method is used for the services of financial enterprises, such as banks, which do not sell their services for a price but cover their costs from net interest receipts.

12. G.N.P., as pointed out, is the market value of the nation's output of goods and services, less the value of those used up in production, but with no deduction for the depreciation of capital equipment. The movement of G.N.P. at constant prices within a period is estimated by revaluing it at the prices of a given year selected as a base for comparison. Thus, if it is desired to estimate the change in G.N.P. at constant prices between 1953-4 and 1956-7, the G.N.P. of 1956-7 could be expressed at prices of 1953-4 and the result compared with the actual G.N.P. of 1953-4. The revaluation could be either a direct revaluing of individual quantity series, or an indirect revaluation carried out by dividing the value of output by a price index for the component items. As there is nothing permanent about the set of prices ruling in any given year, it is possible that the selection of a different year as base would produce a different trend in the revalued figures; this problem is discussed later.

13. The significance of G.N.P. at constant prices and real national income as measures of growth can be illustrated by reference to the operations of a single firm. A firm engaged, say, in manufacturing or distribution,

makes a contribution to G.N.P. consisting of the value of its current sales of goods and services (together with stock increase), less the value of its current purchases of goods and services. At constant prices, this is equal to the value of sales (and stock increase) revalued at base-year prices less the value of purchases revalued at base-year prices. Broadly speaking, G.N.P. at constant prices for the country as a whole is the aggregate of this figure for all firms in the country, including farmers and all other self-employed persons. Because the sales of one firm are, in part, the purchases of others, the process of consolidation produces an aggregate, termed gross national turnover, which is the aggregate of all sales to *final users*—that is, to consumers, to buyers of capital equipment and holders of stocks, to public authorities and financial enterprises, and to export markets. The deduction from gross national turnover of all purchases from *external suppliers*—that is, imports of goods and services[1]—gives G.N.P. G.N.P. at constant prices for Australia is, in fact, estimated by the Commonwealth Statistician by revaluing imports and gross national turnover (in the form of gross national expenditure and exports) and deducting one from the other.

Thus the following relationships exist in any period, both at current prices and at constant prices:

G.N.P.	Personal consumption expenditure
	plus current expenditure on goods and services by public authorities and financial enterprises,
	plus fixed capital expenditure,
	plus increase in stocks,
	equals gross national expenditure,
plus imports of goods and services	*plus* exports of goods and services,
equals gross national turnover	*equals* gross national turnover

14. To return to the individual firm, its contribution to national income, as distinct from G.N.P. is, broadly speaking, the sum of the incomes payable within the country from the proceeds of its trading operations, that is, what is left after deduction of depreciation allowances and indirect taxes paid, and interest and profits payable overseas. These incomes consist of wages and salaries, and profits, payable within Australia. To express these incomes in 'real' terms, it is necessary to use an index number which measures the changes in the prices of the goods and services on which the incomes may be spent. A consumer price index is used for this purpose, although not all income will be spent on consumer goods; some will be saved. Real national income, is, therefore, a measure of *purchasing power* over available goods and services rather than of the goods and services themselves.

---

[1] Including imports of finished goods distributed in Australia.

15. Thus, the firm makes a contribution to G.N.P. at constant prices equal to its gross trading margin revalued at selected base-year prices for both sales and purchases. It makes a contribution to real national income equal to the sum of its wage and salary payments and its net profits, before tax, accruing within the country, expressed in terms of purchasing power over all consumer goods and services. For the economy as a whole, the same is broadly true of the corresponding aggregates for all individual firms—including farmers and all other self-employed persons.[1]

16. The third type of measure—G.N.P. at constant prices, adjusted for changes in the terms of trade—is especially useful in a country like Australia, for which overseas trade is important. The terms of trade are the rates at which exports may, in effect, be 'exchanged' for imports, and are measured by the ratio of the export price index to the import price index. If the export price of wool, for example, rises and there is no change in other prices, the terms of trade will rise (become more favourable to Australia), that is, more goods can be bought from overseas with the proceeds of each bale of wool. Such a rise cannot affect the measure of G.N.P. at constant prices, because in the calculation wool production will have been revalued at the prices of a base year. In the adjusted version of G.N.P. at constant prices, exports of goods and services are revalued, not at the export prices of the base year but in terms of what they would buy in imports. To achieve this, the value of these exports is divided by an import price index instead of an export price index. The tabulation in paragraph 13 illustrates the effect of this. As the components of gross national expenditure, that is, personal consumption, current purchases by public authorities and financial enterprises, and purchases of capital equipment, are all goods and services entering final use *within* the economy, the conversion of exports into purchasing power over imports transforms the measure of the goods and services *produced* into one expressed at constant prices of the goods and services on which the proceeds are *spent*.[2] This version of G.N.P. is thus

---

[1] For public authorities, for owners of dwellings, and for financial enterprises like banks, as pointed out earlier, there are special ways of measuring gross product and income; these are described in greater detail in the Commonwealth Statistician's *Australian National Accounts, National Income and Expenditure, 1948–49 to 1962–63*, which provides a more comprehensive account of the meanings of all the terms under discussion.

[2] The method of calculating G.N.P. adjusted for the terms of trade, compared with that for calculating G.N.P. at constant prices is:

G.N.P. at constant prices	*G.N.P. adjusted for terms of trade*
G.N.E. at constant prices,	G.N.E. at constant prices,
plus exports at constant prices,	*plus* exports divided by import price index,
less imports at constant prices,	*less* imports at constant prices,
equals G.N.P. at constant prices.	*equals* G.N.P. at constant prices, adjusted for terms of trade.

closer to real national income than the former one. But, unlike real national income, it relates to the gross value of the product from which income is yielded rather than to income itself, and it is expressed in terms of purchasing power over the whole range of goods and services which the economy as a whole might purchase, including capital equipment and the services of public authorities, as well as the goods and services entering into personal consumption.

USES OF THE INDICATORS

17. The growth of G.N.P. at constant prices is relevant to discussions of economic growth in certain contexts; in other contexts, the growth of real national income is more relevant. Of the two alternative aspects of goods and services being considered, if availability to satisfy wants is accepted as the ultimate object of production, then real national income is the more basic measure.[1] A more 'ultimate' object still is goods and services available *per head of population*, for which an appropriate indicator would be real national income per head. This is referred to again in the discussion of standards of living.

18. Like real national income, G.N.P. at constant prices adjusted for the terms of trade is in one sense a measure of goods and services available, and not of those produced, because it substitutes purchasing power over imports for the value of exports at constant prices. However, it is still a gross measure, in the sense that it is estimated without deduction of depreciation allowances. Goods and services used to replace worn-out capital equipment are not themselves available, either for consumption or for adding to the productive capacity of the economy. The apparent simplicity of the two 'gross' indicators of economic growth, based as they are on the direct aggregation of the values of goods and services produced, therefore conceals a limitation of some importance. Often, the national income concept itself comes under criticism in this respect. Critics tend to attack the *method* of estimating depreciation allowances used in calculating national income from G.N.P. It has often been said that, ideally, national income should be estimated after deduction of depreciation provisions sufficient to replace at current market prices the amount of capital equipment used up in the course of the current year's production. This is not the sort of provision normally made in commercial accounting, or allowed by the

---

[1] Because part of national income is saved, it is not all 'available' to satisfy consumers' wants; nevertheless, it is useful to have a measure in terms of consumer purchasing power of what the national income would have bought had it all been spent on consumer goods and services.

taxation authorities. It is difficult for statisticians to estimate depreciation in this sense, and few countries have attempted it. In estimating national income, the official statisticians of most countries use the depreciation allowances acceptable for income-tax purposes. The problem, in fact, goes beyond the choice between depreciation at tax rates and at replacement cost. The view of a business about its own income will not necessarily correspond to either of those types of depreciation allowance; a variety of choices is available, representing different combinations of methods of valuing depreciable assets, methods of spreading the charges over the life of the assets, and methods of assessing the life of the asset itself. In so far as business decisions are based on the views of businesses, any of these methods may have relevance. This element of conceptual uncertainty attaching to the estimation of aggregate depreciation provisions is perhaps one reason why national income no longer has the predominance in economic discussion that it had before the war, but is overshadowed by the newer concept of G.N.P., whose definition is more clear-cut.

19. Nevertheless, depreciation of assets is a real charge against current production from the standpoint of economic wellbeing and, even if it cannot be given great precision in national income estimation, it should not be ignored in the study of economic growth. This is one reason why a number of indicators of economic growth are worthy of study. Besides the three indicators under discussion, it is also relevant to examine the trends of personal income and personal disposable income in terms of purchasing power over consumable goods and services, and the trend of personal consumption expenditure at constant prices. These are rather narrower in content than what is usually looked for in an indicator of economic growth, and are discussed in chapter 6 [not reproduced here] among the statistics relevant to living standards. However, they have the advantage of being unaffected by the particular statistical method used in estimating depreciation allowances, except those of unincorporated businesses, where the method used affects personal income and personal disposable income.

20. Each of the three statistical indicators mentioned has its uses, not only in connexion with a particular aspect of economic growth, but also in connexion with the growth of particular types of economies. The more the economy is dependent on the use of capital, on foreign capital and on international trade, the more differentiated will the three measures be. To take an extreme case, in a hypothetical primitive economy with no foreign trade and no capital engaged in production, and therefore no foreign capital, G.N.P., with or without adjustment for the terms of trade, would be equal to national income, because there would be no depreciation pro-

visions and no income payable overseas. And because the goods and services produced would be the same as the goods and services consumed, real national income (in terms of purchasing power over the consumer price index) would be the same as G.N.P. at constant prices (of the goods and services produced). If in such an economy an influx of foreign capital occurred, say, by investment in a new venture to produce oil for export, the three measures could at once diverge. G.N.P. could diverge from national income because of depreciation provisions and income payable overseas, and the consumer price index would cease to reflect all the prices entering into production. Besides this, G.N.P. adjusted for changes in the terms of trade would tend to follow its own trend, in so far as movements in the export price of oil diverged from movements in the import prices of drilling equipment and supplies. Choice among the three alternatives would depend on one's interest: if it were in the total production of the economy, including that of the oil company, G.N.P. at constant prices would be indicated; if it were in the wellbeing of the residents, excluding the foreign shareholders, real national income would be the measure; and if it were in the purchasing power of the whole economy over all the types of goods and services it was buying, including the imported drilling equipment and supplies of the oil company, G.N.P. at constant prices, adjusted for changes in the terms of trade, would be the appropriate indicator. Australian production relies heavily on capital, much of it foreign-owned, and the ratio of exports and imports to production is high. For Australia, therefore, the differentiation of the three indicators of economic growth may be significant.

21. The possibility of divergence in the trends of the three measures of growth outlined in the example given, with the introduction of the complication of overseas trade, overseas investment and capital equipment into a simple economy, also serves to illustrate an important fact about the significance of G.N.P. at constant prices, considered as an indicator of economic wellbeing. This significance becomes less certain as the economy becomes more complex, and the flow of goods and services entering production as a result departs further and further from identity with the flow of goods and services entering personal consumption. This is partly due to the importance of non-measurable elements of economic growth in complex economies, and partly to the limited precision of the available indicators already referred to, the reasons for which are now discussed.

THE LIMITATIONS OF MEASURES OF GROWTH

Difficulty of definition

22. The device of valuing a series of aggregates of different goods and services at the prices of a given year is an attempt to bring into measurable terms the idea of 'economic quantity'. This is distinguishable from quantity such as the number of thermal units represented by different fuels, or the amount of calories represented by a quantities it foodstuffs, or the tonnage of different goods making up a cargo. It is important to make clear that values of unlike goods at constant prices are in no sense measures of physical quantity, or even approximations to such measures. For a single product, value divided by price is obviously quantity, but not for aggregates of different products. For these, value divided by a price (index) is a different kind of quantity. 'Economic quantity' or 'quantum', as expressed in value at constant prices has common measurement based on the market price of each item in a base year. A pound of butter is twice a pound of margarine if it cost twice as much in a base year. This is a statement of a method of measurement rather than a definition, but no attempt to find a more basic definition has so far succeeded. However, this does not make the thing itself meaningless or useless. The Director of the National Income Division in the United States Department of Commerce has observed:

It is quite possible to do useful and significant work relating to the causes and consequences of economic growth, and as to the implications of these for action, without ever having defined and measured the concept of growth precisely.[1]

In this respect, economic growth and 'economic quantity' probably resemble a number of other concepts used in the social sciences, the measurement of which has proved useful long before it has been possible to give the concept itself a rigorous definition.[2] The limitations to be discussed

---

[1] George Jaszi: 'The Measurement of Aggregate Economic Growth', a review of key conceptual and statistical issues as suggested by United States experience. *Review of Economics and Statistics*, XLIII, no. 4 (November 1961).

[2] Compare, for example, the remarks of a well-known psychologist on the measurement of intelligence: 'In discussing the measurement of intelligence I think it is necessary first of all to squash one widely held misconception. It is often believed that intelligence tests are developed and constructed according to a rationale deriving from some sound scientific theory; it is also widely believed, however, that however "scientific" the measurement of intelligence may be, its practical value is very poor, particularly because of certain inherent difficulties in going from the ivory tower to the market place, and the alleged inapplicability of psychological science to practical problems of applied life. In actual fact the position is exactly reversed. Intelligence tests are not based on any very sound scientific principles, and there is not a great deal of agreement among experts regarding the nature of intelligence. Arguments about this subject were very popular in the 1920s and 1930s, but they have pretty well ceased now because it is realized that

in the following paragraphs do not mean that eco. .
be envisaged or measured, but they do mean that its
used sensibly for fine analytical purposes.

23. The difficulty of defining the concept is not the
fact, pointed out earlier, that for purposes of economic gr
types of goods and services can be measured. The non-mea
arise out of the fact that for many services of economic
no market price, and no possibility of valuing them at a satis
thetical price. The difficulty of definition referred to here r
limitation of market price itself as a basis for measurement—
unlike products—even within the measurable part of econom
No satisfactory theory has been devised to enable a pound's worth
at constant prices' to be interpreted as a standard unit of undiffer
'product'. The significance of 'pounds at constant prices' as u
measurement in economic aggregates is derived from economic
relating to an individual consumer's preferences in respect of cons
goods, at a point of time. When applied to G.N.P. at constant prices
theory is, in effect, extended pragmatically to the whole community,
the whole range of goods and services in production—whether consume
goods or capital equipment, Government services or exports—and to comparisons over time. On such a basis, 'pounds at constant prices' used as
units for aggregative purposes have a rather uncertain significance. This
is probably less of a problem for simple homogeneous communities, whose
production is mainly consumer goods sold on internal markets, than for
more complex communities.[1] In the case of real national income, the
definition offers problems of a different kind: the consumption standard
underlying the consumer price index is being applied as a standard of
value to the total income of the nation, not merely the part spent by consumers. Here again, the problem increases with the complexity of the
community.

'Index-number relativity'

24. This problem sets a limit to the precision of both definition and
measurement. If revalued at the prices of two different years, the annual
values of a given flow of goods and services during a period may show two

they were largely verbal and did not permit any reasonable solution. On the other hand,
intelligence tests, right from the beginning, have been outstandingly successful in their
practical application; we shall consider shortly what is meant by saying that an intelligence
test is "successful", but the evidence on this point is so overwhelming that no one
familiar with even a small part of it is likely to regard this statement as an exaggeration.'
H. J. Eysenck, *Know Your Own IQ* (London).

[1] Although in primitive economies problems arise in the valuation of subsistence food
production, for which there is no market price.

divergent trends, and there is no theoretical basis for choosing between them. The possibility of divergence appears to be greater in production indexes than in consumption indexes, and may be particularly great in certain industries, for example, manufacturing. It also appears to be greater in production indexes than in price indexes, at least in indexes of consumer or wholesale prices. The reason probably lies in a tendency for the output of certain individual products to increase relative to the average while their prices decrease relative to the average. Indexes based on different years, whether price or production indexes, tend to move closely together only if the individual items in the index do not have such a consistent tendency for movements in price and quantity to be correlated. However, in production series, strong inverse correlations of this kind appear likely to occur from time to time, for example, a new product with a high initial price like television receivers may tend to combine rapidly rising production with a tendency to falling prices. The result will tend to make the value of production, or G.N.P., rise faster when valued at the prices of an early year than when valued at the prices of a late year. The existence of this problem does not make the results of such revaluations meaningless, but it is a source of imprecision which should always be remembered, especially, as is often the case, when data are available for revaluation at the prices of one year only.[1]

25. Where information is available to enable the trends in values at the prices of two different years to be compared, something can be done to test the extent of the uncertainty due to index-number relativity. Strictly speaking, the two estimates of trend obtained in this way do not necessarily represent limits,[2] but it is of interest, nevertheless, to know the extent of their divergence. If the two base years are not themselves the terminal years of the period being studied, the divergence between them can be projected in such a way that estimates of the trends in values at 'start-of-

---

[1] On this and other aspects of index-number theory and practice underlying the measurement of economic growth and productivity, see Irving H. Siegel, *Concepts and Measurement of Production and Productivity*, U.S. Bureau of Labor Statistics (Washington, D.C., 1952).

[2] They do not provide any conclusive reason for believing that the trend that would be obtained by valuing the series at prices of a third year would fall within the range of the two base years. But it seems reasonable to assume that, if the third year fell between the other two, the trend obtained by using its prices would fall within the range of the other two trends. (See G. Jaszi, 'The Measurement of Aggregate Economic Growth', *Review of Economics and Statistics*, XLIII, no. 4, November 1961, p. 325 for remarks on the persistency of such trends in United States experience.) Besides this, however, the range itself depends on the level of detail at which the revaluation of the component items was done. If it were done only for broad groups, by means of group price indexes, it could be different from the range obtained if it were done for individual commodities, with individual price series. (See R. J. Nicholson and S. Gupta, 'Output and Productivity Changes in British Manufacturing Industry, 1948 to 1954', *Journal of the Royal Statistical Society*, CXXIII, Series A, 1960, p. 427.)

period' prices and 'end-of-period' prices can be made. An example is given in paragraph 39. This procedure involves an assumption about the persistence of the divergence throughout the whole period, but it is a way of making the most use of the available information in assessing the margin of uncertainty surrounding the estimates.

Limitations of data

26. The third type of limitation to be considered is that arising from the inevitable lack of data for estimating purposes. This has already been mentioned in connexion with the question of depreciation allowances. However, the main type of data problem met in estimating the indicators of economic growth lies in the application of the formula for making estimates at constant prices. The formula presupposes that the values of the goods and services can be represented by prices and quantities, forming continuous series throughout the period in question. In fact, many goods and services, not being homogeneous or in continuous production, cannot be represented by price and quantity series, but only by their market value. This is true even of many consumable goods and services, but it is specially true of capital equipment, buildings, etc. used by industry or public authorities, much of which is specialized and custom-built, or subject to frequent changes of specification. In addition, there are problems concerning the introduction of new products and the treatment of products whose quality has changed. Unlike most other types of estimation in national accounts, constant-price estimating has a formula but hardly a definition. The expression 'value of goods and services at constant prices' is only a formula in words and, if there are no prices for some of the goods and services, there is no obvious method of approximation. The general aim in handling these problems is to make an assumption about how the price of the given product would have moved if price series for it had existed in the period in question. A typical situation is that statistics of the value of expenditure of a certain kind are available—for example, retail sales of electrical goods—and price series are available only for certain types of products in this class of expenditure, excluding non-standard products and new types of product which have only just become available. There is no acceptable alternative in these circumstances to assuming that the prices of non-standard and new products, had they existed, would have moved proportionally with those of the standard products for which prices do exist. This is the general solution adopted in these circumstances: a price index for the standard products is divided into the value of sales of all products in the class. Even in the case of products for which prices are available, there are great statistical difficulties in recognizing and making

allowances for quality changes. Much is done by statisticians by way of dividing products into as many quality classes as possible, with their characteristics clearly specified, and compiling separate price series and quantity series where possible for each. However, the problem of joining together a price series broken by a straight change of model has not yet been solved, and it is unlikely that any unique and generally acceptable solution will be found. Like the problem of the changing weight-pattern in a price index, the consequences of this can only be judged subjectively.

27. It is not necessarily true that, because no statistical method can adequately measure quality changes, any existing estimates of the growth in G.N.P. at constant prices must be understated. This is a subject of continuing debate among economists and statisticians, and only tentative observations are offered at this stage:

(*a*) For a quality change to be ignored in a series of values at constant prices, it must have occurred either in a quantity series which is assumed to have been homogeneous but is in fact not—such as the tonnage of coal produced in a country, not classified according to quality, or in a price series which is assumed to have related to standard products but in fact has not. As pointed out in the previous paragraph, statisticians attempt to specify in great detail the qualities of the goods included in their output series and price indexes and to collect separate series for each quality specified. In so far as they succeed in this, the changes in average quality will be reflected in the estimates of value at constant prices.

(*b*) Even in cases where the statistician has not succeeded in specifying standard qualities, his measure of the increase in values at constant prices is not necessarily understated. Quality changes are not necessarily always 'improvements'. A person faced with a choice at a point of time would probably always choose the better quality, prices being the same, but this is not the point. Over a period, quality may change not only because consumers are demanding better goods and services; it may also change because the circumstances of both production and consumption have radically changed. Mass production of consumer goods may produce cheaper goods with a quite acceptable loss of 'quality'; they may be sold to a new class of consumers, or the loss of what was formerly regarded as intrinsic quality may be offset by some new property such as convenience in use. Today's consumers may have a different view of quality from yesterday's. They may buy less well-made clothing than they used to because they now prefer fashionability to durability. They may buy groceries at self-service stores because they would rather dispense with service than be kept waiting. Producers will tend to produce the goods and services demanded by today's consumers, just as yesterday's producers tended to produce the goods and services demanded by yesterday's consumers. What the consumers of each period demand is determined partly by their mode of living, as well as their standard of living, and partly by the types of goods and services available to them. Advances in design and technology probably tend to improve the quality of certain types of goods, such as motor vehicles, other durable consumer goods, and houses, and these improvements may not be allowed for in price indexes. Even this is hard to demonstrate by example, as it is necessary to distinguish quality changes from price changes and fashion changes. However, for other classes of goods it is more difficult to judge which way the change in quality may have gone. Moreover, for capital equipment, the problem involves some deep questions of economic theory, and it is an unsettled issue whether quality changes should be allowed for at all.[1]

(*c*) The main conclusion is that because changes in 'quality' are inevitable, and also changes in consumers' tastes, and because much of both kinds of change can only be allowed for subjectively, comparisons tend to lose meaning when extended over long periods of years.

EXPRESSING ECONOMIC GROWTH AS A RATE

28. The measurement of economic growth requires the choice of a period and the adoption of a statistical means of presentation. For summary purposes, it is usual to employ the average annual rate of increase during the selected period, usually in the form of a compound rate of growth. This does not imply that growth normally takes place at a compound rate from year to year; it is merely a convenient way of expressing an average rate of change. In fact, the year-to-year movements of the selected indicators are usually irregular, being affected both by short-term chance factors, such as the effect of the weather on agricultural production, and by cyclical fluctuations in economic activity. In these circumstances, the choice of a period is important. It is desirable to avoid comparing years which represent different phases of cyclical fluctuation, otherwise the growth rate shown will have been affected by some of the cyclical movement. However, this requires the identification of cyclical phases in the statistical series, which is not easy, especially at the current end of the series. The determination of the trend rate of growth is thus necessarily a partly subjective operation.

29. For certain purposes, it is not sufficient merely to avoid the effects of short-term irregular and cyclical movements of the indicators of economic growth. For the purpose of studying the expansion of economic activity

[1] For some purposes. See Jaszi's paper, *Review of Economics and Statistics*, XLIII, no. 4 (November 1961), 323 and 326.

as it would be in conditions of full employment, the procedure sometimes adopted is to isolate the rate of increase occurring between one peak of full employment and another. This will not necessarily be the same as the trend rate of increase over the period, designed to iron out the short-term irregular and cyclical movements. This concept of 'capacity output' does not seem to have been adopted in many countries in the estimates of the rates of increase in G.N.P. at constant prices prepared for the study of economic growth.

30. Although the effects of short-term fluctuations should be avoided, there is a danger of extending the period of comparison too far. From what has been said earlier about the limitations of the available statistical indicators of growth, it follows that comparisons should not be attempted over too long a period. If the user of the statistics is to supplement them by his own subjective feelings about changes in the quality of consumer goods and the value of public services, and if the statistician is to have any faith in his attempts to match new and old types of goods and services, especially capital equipment, the period of comparison should be reasonably short. Any changes in the pattern of prices which might affect the index numbers used in revaluation can be checked where possible by the use of alternative forms of index number, with start-of-period prices and end-of-period prices as alternative weights. However, this does not get over the fundamental problem: the bill of goods itself changes during the period, not only in quality, but in composition, and the measurement of its growth becomes progressively less meaningful as the movements of the component series become more disparate. Assessing economic growth, like comparing the merits of sportsmen, makes most sense if confined within the span of the assessor's own experience.

31. The choice of a period must be followed by the choice of a method of trend fitting. The simplest method is to calculate the change between the opening and closing years of the selected period and convert it into a compound annual rate of change. Unless care is exercised, however, the results are affected by chance or cyclical factors which may have influenced the values of the opening and closing years. The most satisfactory statistical method is to fit a straight-line trend to the logarithms of the statistics for all of the years in the selected period, by the method of least squares. The gradient of this line, that is, the ratio of its upward movement to its horizontal movement in a given period, is a function[1] of the average compound rate of growth for the period, which is described as the growth rate.

32. In the analysis of the data available for the post-war period in Australia on G.N.P. at constant prices, with and without adjustment for

[1] Log $(1 + \text{growth rate})$.

TABLE 1. *Indicators of economic growth in Australia: 1948–9 to 1962–3*
(£ million)

Period	G.N.P.		G.N.P. adjusted for the terms of trade		Real national income[1] Average 1953–4 purchasing power
	At 1953–4 prices	At 1959–60 prices	At 1953–4 prices	At 1959–60 prices	
1948–9	3,685	(4,291)	3,641	4,396	3,127
1949–50	3,958	(4,609)	3,928	4,751	3,410
1950–1	4,168	(4,854)	4,509	5,436	4,144
1951–2	4,289	(4,994)	4,206	5,134	3,573
1952–3	4,260	(4,961)	4,223	5,085	3,587
1953–4	4,517	5,260	4,517	5,456	3,733
1954–5	4,781	5,586	4,719	5,712	3,973
1955–6	5,033	5,837	4,867	5,867	4,122
1956–7	5,153	5,947	5,046	6,072	4,206
1957–8	5,209	6,049	5,046	6,088	4,097
1958–9	5,657	6,483	5,366	6,410	4,331
1959–60	5,879	6,758	5,640	6,758	4,694
1960–1	(6,130)	7,046	5,839	7,014	4,750
1961–2	(6,177)	7,100	5,919	7,076	4,842
1962–3	(6,515)	7,489	6,286	7,529	5,204

[1] Real national income was estimated in the Secretariat from the Statistician's estimates of national income, divided by the consumer price index, converted to base 1953–4 = 100. The weights of this price index are based approximately on average consumption, 1952–3 to 1956–7.

Notes: Figures in parentheses are estimates made by the Secretariat. Estimates at 1953–4 prices from 1960–1 on are proportional to the Statistician's figures at 1959–60 prices. Estimates at 1959–60 prices for 1952–3 and earlier years are proportional to the Statistician's figures at 1953–4 prices.

G.N.P. adjusted for the terms of trade has been estimated by the Secretariat from G.N.P. estimates and the price index implied in the Statistician's estimate of imports at constant prices.

Sources: Australian National Accounts 1948–49 to 1962–63; National Income and Expenditure 1963–64, and other publications of the Commonwealth Statistician.

changes in the terms of trade, and on real national income, the procedure adopted for this report was to display the data in the form of semi-logarithmic graphs, select a period and fit straight-line trends by the method of least squares. In order to judge the effects of the choice of base years for the index numbers, and to assess the significance of various components of growth, however, attention was then turned to the changes occurring between the beginning and the end of the selected period.

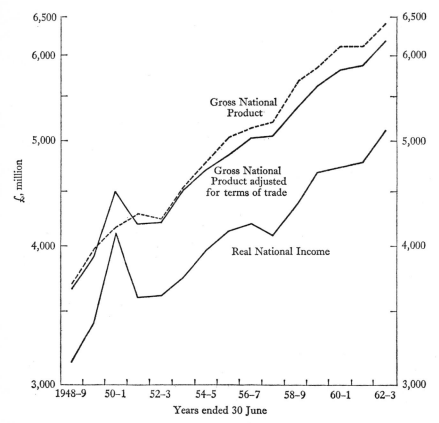

Chart 1. Gross National Product, Gross National Product adjusted for terms of trade at 1953–4 prices* and Real National Income in 1953–4 purchasing power, 1948–9 to 1962–3 (ratio chart). *Source*: Commonwealth Statistician, *Australian National Accounts 1948–49 to 1962–63* and *National Income and Expenditure 1963– 64*. [*Linked with series at 1959–60 prices in the year 1959–60.]

TRENDS IN INDICATORS OF ECONOMIC GROWTH SINCE 1948–9

33. The Commonwealth Statistician has published estimates of G.N.P. at constant prices for Australia for the years 1948–9 to 1962–3, together with an indication of the method of estimation, that is, deducting the value of imports of goods and services at constant prices from the sum of the values of gross national expenditure and exports at constant prices.[1] The

[1] *Australian National Accounts, National Income and Expenditure, 1948–49 to 1962–63*, Tables 10 and 11. Revised estimates appear in the Treasury White Paper *National Income and Expenditure, 1963–64*.

TABLE 2. *Percentage increases from year to year in indicators of economic growth in Australia, and average annual rates of increase: 1948–9 to 1962–3* (percentages)

Year	G.N.P.		G.N.P. adjusted for the terms of trade		Real national income Average
	At 1953–4 prices	At 1959–60 prices	At 1953–4 prices	At 1959–60 prices	1953–4 purchasing power
1949–50	7·4	7·4	7·9	8·1	9·0
1950–1	5·3	5·3	14·8	14·4	21·5
1951–2	2·9	2·9	−6·7	−5·6	−16·0
1952–3	−0·7	−0·7	0·4	−1·0	0·4
1953–4	6·0	6·0	7·0	7·3	4·1
1954–5	5·8	6·2	4·5	4·7	6·4
1955–6	5·3	4·5	3·1	2·7	3·7
1956–7	2·4	1·9	3·7	3·7	2·0
1957–8	1·1	1·7	—	0·3	−2·7
1958–9	8·6	7·2	6·3	5·3	5·7
1959–60	3·9	4·2	5·1	5·4	8·4
1960–1	4·3	4·3	3·5	3·8	1·2
1961–2	0·8	0·8	1·4	0·9	1·9
1962–3	5·5	5·5	6·2	6·4	7·5

(−) Denotes decrease.

Source: Table 1.

Statistician has also published estimates of national income and index numbers of consumer prices, from which real national income can be estimated. For estimating G.N.P. at constant prices adjusted for the terms of trade, indexes of export and import prices published by the Commonwealth Statistician are available, but it was considered more suitable for this purpose to apply the implicit price indicator underlying the Statistician's estimate of the value of imports at constant prices to the value of exports at current prices. The resulting estimates of the three indicators are shown in Table 1 and in the form of semi-logarithmic graphs in Chart 1. In these graphs equal upward or downward movements denote equal percentage changes, not absolute changes.

34. The estimates of G.N.P. at constant prices are available on two bases: for the years 1948–9 to 1959–60, revalued at average prices of the year 1953–4; and for the years 1953–4 to 1962–3, revalued at average prices of the year 1959–60. The graph of the original data reveals a good deal of year-to-year fluctuation. As Table 2 shows, these changes vary from a rise of 8·6 per cent between 1957–8 and 1958–9 to a fall of 0·7 per cent

between 1951–2 and 1952–3. In the period 1953–4 to 1959–60, estimates are available revalued at the prices of both those years. Despite the considerable differences shown for certain years, over the six-year period of overlap as a whole the difference was not great; there was a rise of 30·2 per cent at 1953–4 prices, and 28·1 per cent at 1959–60 prices. This is a difference of 0·28 percentage points in the annual rate of increase.

35. The shape of the graphs indicates three well-marked apparent cycles occurring during the period, with troughs at 1952–3, 1957–8 and 1961–2. Two periods were selected for trend-fitting in order to estimate the rate of growth in the series:

(*a*) The nine-year period from 1953–4 to 1962–3, which appears to cover two cycles (the addition of the recovery period 1961–2 to 1962–3 being balanced by the omission of the recovery period 1952–3 to 1953–4) and would therefore show a trend little affected by short-term fluctuations.

(*b*) The fourteen-year period from 1948–9 to 1962–3, which is the longest period for which the data are available. This appears to cover three cycles. Whether the inclusion of the recent recovery period 1961–2 to 1962–3 should have been matched by the omission of the period 1948–9 to 1949–50 depends on whether this period can be regarded as the beginning of a cycle. There is no evidence to suggest that this period was not merely part of a general post-war recovery movement.

36. For each of the selected periods two series were studied (*a*) G.N.P. at 1953–4 prices, extended forward to 1962–3 in proportion to the changes in the series at 1959–60 prices; and (*b*) G.N.P. at 1959–60 prices, extended backward, in the case of the fourteen-year period, to 1948–9 in proportion to the change in the series at 1953–4 prices. The 'linking' used to extend the series in this way involves assumptions which are considered later.

37. Estimates of G.N.P. adjusted for changes in the terms of trade, at prices of 1953–4 and 1959–60, were made for the same periods, linked in the same way. The adjustment was done by dividing the current value of exports of goods and services by the 'implicit price indicator' underlying the value of imports at constant prices, instead of expressing the value of exports of goods and services at constant export prices. The rates of increase in G.N.P. adjusted and unadjusted, and in real national income, were as shown in Table 3 on p. 368.

The difference of up to one-half per cent per annum between the estimates for G.N.P. adjusted and unadjusted for the terms of trade was due to the declining tendency of the terms of trade from 1950–1 onwards. In other words, because a given value of exports would buy less in imports at the end of the period than at the beginning, the measure of G.N.P. in terms of its purchasing power over the components of gross national ex-

TABLE 3. *Annual rates of increase in indicators of economic growth*
(From trends fitted by least squares)
(Per cent per annum)

Period	G.N.P. at constant prices		G.N.P. at constant prices, adjusted for terms of trade		Real national income Average 1953–4 purchasing power
	At 1953–4 prices[1]	At 1959–60 prices	At 1953–4 prices[1]	At 1959–60 prices	
1948–9 to 1962–3 (fourteen years)	4·0	3·9[2]	{3·6 {4·0[3]	3·5[2] 3·9[2,3]	3·0 3·5[3]
1953–4 to 1962–3 (nine years)	4·1	3·9	3·5	3·5	3·4

[1] Linked at 1959–60.   [2] Linked at 1953–4.   [3] Omitting 1950–1.

penditure rose more slowly during the period than the measure at constant prices of the goods and services produced. To a considerable extent, this was due to the influence of the exceptionally high price of wool in the year 1950–1. If this year is omitted from the series, the annual average rate of increase over the period is raised by 0·4 percentage points. The omission of 1950–1 raises the rate of increase in real national income by about 0·5 percentage points.

38. The differences of about one-half of one per cent between the rates of increase for real national income and the corresponding rates for G.N.P. at constant prices, adjusted for the terms of trade, for the fourteen-year period, and the smaller differences for the nine-year period, appear to be almost entirely due to the rise of depreciation allowances. None of the difference appears to have been due to differences in price movements or to the rise of net income payable overseas.

39. A final adjustment to the figures for the period 1953–4 to 1962–3 may be made, so that the available information may be fully used. This follows up the point made in paragraph 25. In the period 1953–4 to 1959–60, it was pointed out, G.N.P. at 1953–4 prices increased at 0·28 percentage points a year more than G.N.P. at 1959–60 prices (see paragraph 34). For later years, G.N.P. at 1959–60 prices only is available, and the series at 1953–4 prices has been estimated by linking the two series at 1959–60. This linking procedure implies that the divergence does not persist in the years after 1959–60, which seems unlikely. If it is assumed that the same divergence as that disclosed for the period 1953–4 to 1959–60 persisted for the whole period, it will be possible to adjust the rate of increase in G.N.P. at 1959–60 prices to convert it into an estimate of what

would have been shown by a series at 1962–3 prices had one been available. The actual divergence between the rates for G.N.P. at 1959–60 prices and that based on the linked series at 1953–4 prices shown in Table 3 is 0·2 percentage points (more precisely 0·19). The assumption suggested implies that this divergence, which is the result of averaging over nine years a divergence that actually persisted for six, should be raised from 0·2 to 0·3 percentage points. The finally adjusted estimates of the rates of increase of G.N.P. are thus:

	At start-of-period prices	At end-of-period prices
Average annual percentage rate of increase of G.N.P. at constant prices, 1953–4 to 1962–3, least-squares trend	4·1	3·8

The adjusted estimate at 1959–60 prices is called the rate of increase at 'end-of-period' prices rather than at 1962–3 prices, following the terms suggested in paragraph 25. This is to avoid the implication that an actual series at 1962–3 prices had been used. In Appendix N [not reproduced], where projections are made for G.N.P. and other aggregates, the starting-point will be 1962–3 aggregates valued in terms of 1959–60 prices, as shown in the Australian National Accounts, and it is important to be able to project these aggregates forward according to *trends* at start-of-period or end-of-period prices, without making it appear that the aggregates themselves have been *expressed* at prices of either 1953–4 or 1962–3.

CONCLUSIONS*

53. There are a number of other ways in which the approximations which have to be used in national accounting and index-number construction in Australia, as in other countries, may affect the accuracy of the indicators of economic growth available for use. Estimates of exports and imports at constant prices cannot always be exactly matched, in terms of base years, with the corresponding estimates of expenditure at constant prices. Problems in the measurement of depreciation affect the estimation of real national income. The need to change periodically the weighting pattern of the consumer price index to keep it abreast of changing consumer habits introduces unavoidable approximations when the index is used to measure the trend of real national income over a decade or more. Like the other approximations mentioned earlier and the problem of index-number relativity discussed in paragraph 39, these all lead to the same conclusions: that statistical indicators of growth should not be used to measure trends over a long period of years and should not be employed for fine analytical purposes.

* Paragraphs 40–52 (Accuracy of the Australian estimates) and paragraph 54 have been omitted.

24 A note on some aspects of national accounting methodology in eastern Europe and the Soviet Union*

INTRODUCTION

In the eastern European countries and the Soviet Union the range of published national accounts statistics varies from a single index number of national income in the Soviet Union to the very comprehensive 'White Papers' published by the Central Statistical Office of Poland for the years 1954–7.[1] It should be borne in mind that national income and expenditure accounts form—in the planned economies of these countries—only

[1] *Dochód narodowy Polski 1954 i 1955* (Warsaw, 1957); and *Dochód narodowy Polski 1956* (Warsaw, 1958) (including preliminary calculations for 1957). The scope of published methodological discussion in the countries under review is often out of proportion to the volume of published statistics, but it is not always easy to disentangle purely academic discussion from the exposition of methods actually followed by the statistical offices (see, for example, D. Allakhverdyan, *Natsionalny dokhod SSSR*, Moscow, 1958; and P. M. Moskvin, *Voprosy statistiki natsionalnogo dokhoda v SSSR*, Moscow, 1955). In this note, particularly extensive use has been made of the information contained in the two Polish monographs mentioned above, in a recently published book by one of the architects of the Polish national accounts (L. Zienkowski, *Jak oblicza się dochód narodowy*, Warsaw, 1959) and in a Hungarian monograph referring to the year 1956 (*Népgazdasági Mérlegek, Reáljövedelmek, 1956*).

* Since the publication of this 'Note' there have been many attempts at reducing the differences of national accounting practices among East European countries, and between these and the Western countries. To this purpose, meetings of economists and statisticians have been held under the auspices of Comecon, the Council of Mutual Economic Assistance; the United Nations Conference of European Statisticians has also worked on the comparability of national accounts. Proposals have been put forward to draw an accounting structure which would embrace the main elements of both systems, and into which the figures of all countries could be fitted. This 'Note', however, still presents a valuable picture of the methodological problems involved. For a formal comparison of the Western SNA (System of National Accounts) and the Eastern MPS (Material Products System), see R. Stone, *A comparison of the SNA and the MPS*, Symposium on National Accounts and Balances (Warsaw, 1968). The availability of national income statistics of the East European countries and the Soviet Union has greatly improved in the last ten years; see United Nations Economic Commission for Europe, *Incomes in Postwar Europe, a study of policies, growth and distribution* (*Economic Survey of Europe in 1965, Part II*) (Geneva, 1967), chapters 7–12. An attempt at a comparative analysis of growth rates of the income of Western and socialist countries in the period 1950–9, measured following both conventions, is in another ECE study: *Some factors in economic growth in Europe during the 1950s* (*Economic Survey of Europe in 1961, Part II*) (Geneva, 1964), chapter 11, section 1. [Note by D. M. Nuti.]

a part of a wider system of so-called 'national balances of the economy', which includes the balance of individual money incomes and expenditure of the population, the manpower balance[1] and numerous material balances for selected raw materials and semi-finished goods. The published national income and expenditure estimates have been subsidiary in importance to such, more detailed, calculations used as tools for economic planning and policy implementation in these countries.[2] Their construction has therefore been influenced in the past far more by considerations of the needs of the the economic planners in each country than by the desire to construct either indicators of the rates of growth of over-all and sector ouputs and expenditures, or mirrors of the structure of the economy, for their own sake; considerations of international comparability have received still less weight.

The present note is concerned exclusively with national income and expenditure accounts; and it is designed mainly to assist the reader to appreciate the possiblities and limitations, as tools of analysis and comparison of the growth or structure of national economies, of the existing published national accounts in eastern Europe and the Soviet Union. It is by no means certain, however, that the methods and concepts now applied in official national accounts calculations in eastern Europe and the Soviet Union will for long remain unchanged. These are under constant and critical study in the countries concerned, and certain deficiencies—for internal planning as well as for other purposes—are widely acknowledged. At the same time, means are being sought to improve the comparability of national estimates and to unify modes of presentation for all the countries of the area.

I. THE ORIGIN OF NATIONAL PRODUCT OR INCOME

The boundary of production

A basic characteristic of national accounting in eastern Europe and the Soviet Union up to the present time, and a major source of difficulty in comparing trends or structures of national income or expenditure in these countries with those of other economies, has been the definition of the major aggregate—national income or product—as the sum of all 'material production', excluding most services. Such a definition stems naturally from the accepted theoretical basis of official economic analysis and policy in the countries concerned. Its adoption was in keeping with the over-

---

[1] See *Economic Survey of Europe* (1957), chapter VII.
[2] In many countries the operative balances have been evaluated (where evaluation was required) at 'plan' prices instead of at the realized prices used in the national accounts themselves (see below).

whelming emphasis of past economic policy on expanding capacity for material production; and the inconvenience of the concept in relation to other problems of economic policy was until recently slight, both because the volume of consumers' services has been relatively small and because supplementary statistics were developed—both within and outside the system of national accounts—on the generation and expenditure of personal incomes.

In principle, the distinction between 'productive' and 'non-productive' labour, which itself stems from the Marxist theory of value, provides the basis for demarcation of the area of production to be covered in the calculation of national product. Since national income (or net product) is the sum of newly created use values, and value is associated with productive labour, it follows that the delineation of the latter is—in theory at least—equivalent to the setting-up of the boundary of production.[1]

Labour is considered to be productive when it is expended in the process of production proper, or in activities which are a necessary extension of this process for the purpose of bringing the goods to the consumer. Productive labour can therefore be defined and classified as 'labour used in the direct acquisition of goods of nature (agriculture, forestry, extractive industries), in their processing (processing industries, construction) and in their distribution (transport and trade)'.[2]

It follows, therefore, that a wide range of economic activities of a 'non-material' character—such as most communal services, services rendered by the Government (administration, health, education), artistic activities of individuals, passenger transport and the service of housing (i.e. actual or imputed rent)—fall outside the scope of national product as at present calculated in all the economies of eastern Europe[3] and in the Soviet Union. Although the incomes engendered by such services appear in the redistribution phases of national income (see below) in a form somewhat analogous to the treatment of 'transfer payments' in the West, their exclusion from total product (or income) reduces its size and—more important—affects

---

[1] This relationship must not be confused with the breakdown of production itself into 'productive' and 'non-productive'. Thus labour spent on 'non-productive' investment such as housing, schools or hospitals, is naturally considered as productive.

[2] *Dochód narodowy Polski 1956*, p. 7. The treatment of trade workers has, however, been the subject of longstanding controversy. Some attempts have been made to separate such functions as 'sorting, packing and storing', which are considered truly productive, from 'selling, receipt of money, accounting and advertising', which are considered non-productive (see D. Allakhverdyan, *op. cit.* pp. 39–40). But, largely for practical reasons, all activities of trade workers are, in fact, included in national product in all eastern European countries and the Soviet Union.

[3] A partial exception is provided by eastern Germany, where passenger transport and 'personal' communications are included in the area of production, as they were in Poland in the 1947 estimates and are now in Yugoslavia.

both the dynamics and the structure of aggregate income and expenditure. This difference of coverage, as already noted, represents the most important single obstacle to the comparability of national income estimates between 'eastern' and 'western' countries.[1]

The additional condition (not always strictly adhered to) for labour to qualify as 'productive' in the countries under review is that it is 'socially organized'. As in 'western' national accounts, household activities of housewives do not, as a rule, enter the sphere of production; and neither do those of other household members in so far as they relate to non-primary production outside their own trade for their own consumption. However, dwelling construction carried out by households wholly or largely by their own labour is included in production. Moreover, the definition of primary production is everywhere wide enough to accommodate not only agricultural production and food processing (e.g. wine-making) for own consumption, but also—to a varying degree—manufacturing by peasants of industrial goods for their own use, mainly from raw materials of agricultural origin. Indeed where household activities of this kind are excluded, the reason seems frequently to be the difficulty of collecting data, rather than a matter of principle.[2]

The theoretical niceties of the 'productive' and 'non-productive' dichotomy of service activities are likewise not always easy to put into practice. For example, both types of service are often provided by the same enterprise (railway transport or post office), and the separation is to some extent arbitrary; and some services are conventionally treated as non-productive although they have in fact a productive and socially organized character, for example, the services of laundries. Of still more general importance is the drawing of a demarcation line between productive and non-productive workers in a predominantly productive sector. Since this presents insuperable difficulty in the present state of enterprise accounting and statistical reporting, the principle is generally adopted that all personnel constituting the production 'team' are considered to be productive. This means that work performed by an enterprise's salaried employees, guards, messengers, etc., is counted in production, but not, for instance, services provided by medical personnel attached to the enterprise.

In a planned economy there is usually a hierarchy of economic-administrative echelons between the enterprise unit and the central Govern-

---

[1] The treatment of services is by no means uniform in 'western' countries. Notably in the French accounts, public administration (including defence), banking, insurance and domestic services are not included in national income.

[2] For example, in Czechoslovakia, processing of dairy products, wine-making, etc., by private farmers are excluded, but similar activities in collective and State farms are included.

ment; the fixing of the 'horizontal' dividing line between productive and non-productive activities in this field is rather arbitrary, and actual practice varies from country to country. In Hungary and Poland the sphere of material production stops at the level of enterprise management;[1] but in Czechoslovakia, Rumania and the Soviet Union the boundary is placed somewhat higher and includes trade and management personnel at the intermediate level, such as that of associations of enterprises.

Global social product

In all countries under review more than one product aggregate is calculated. The basic magnitude is the 'global social product',[2] which is the sum of the global outputs of all separately enumerated production units; and in computing it the values of inputs from outside each such unit are not deducted. The amount of duplication within this aggregate therefore depends largely on the method of calculation.

The global product of an enterprise represents the production at realized prices within the period considered, and not only the value created within the enterprise. It thus includes the cost of inputs received from outside the enterprise, but normally excludes 'internal turnover' of goods within the enterprise. The global product of an industrial branch (or of all industry) is usually obtained by summing the values of the global products of all industrial enterprises (the so-called 'enterprise method' of calculation). Thus when the basic unit of calculation is the enterprise, the global product of industry differs from what would be called its gross product in 'western' terminology (value added without deduction of capital consumption) not only by the value of inputs derived from outside industry but also by the value of inputs transferred from one industrial enterprise to another within the industrial sector. It is clear, therefore, that the value of global product of industry (and therefore also the value of global social product) is influenced by the industrial structure—the heavier the weight of processing branches and the less significant the vertical integration of industry, the greater is the amount of duplication and the larger the global product.

In eastern Germany the 'enterprise method' of calculation is officially stated to apply, since 1959, to all sectors; and in Poland it is used for all

---

[1] The current Polish definition sets the dividing line 'below the level of central boards or their equivalents'; but in the national income calculations for 1947 central boards were included in the sphere of productive activity.

[2] *Sovokupnyi obshchestvenny produkt* in Russian; *Produkcja globalna* in Polish; *Product social global* in Rumanian. In the Soviet Union, however, the term *valovaya produktsiya* (gross output) is used to describe the global product of an enterprise or economic branch or sector.

sectors except agriculture. In Czechoslovakia, Rumania and the Soviet Union, however, the 'sector method' is used outside industry and agriculture, thus excluding internal turnover within the given sector of activity (such as construction, transport, trade, etc.). In Hungary, Rumania and, since 1956, Poland the global product of agriculture has been calculated by adding separately the values of plant production and of animal production, so that the global product of agriculture includes not only inputs from outside the sector but also a double counting of fodder produced and consumed within the country.[1] In other countries, moreover, services of machine and tractor stations are considered as a third branch of agricultural output, duplicated in the global product.[2]

The values of global products provide bases for the calculation of values of net products. But they also play an important role in their own right. The magnitudes are relatively easy to calculate since they can be derived largely from routine statistical reporting by State enterprises,[3] for which the value of global production still constitutes an important operational target. In the absence of input–output tables, a detailed global product balance throws light on the interconnexions and flows of goods between enterprises, branches and sectors of the economy, and provides a basis for the planning of resource allocation. A growing interest in input–output analysis has, however, been shown in several countries lately, and it is known that at least the statistical offices of Poland, Hungary and the Soviet Union are engaged in the preparation of such tables.[4]

Over short periods of time, trends in global product estimates (agriculture excepted) probably do not diverge greatly from those indicated by the index numbers of net product discussed below.[5] But over longer periods changes in industrial structure can result in substantially different trends in the two aggregates; and inter-country comparisons of trends or structures of total or sector gross products are naturally rendered difficult, not only by the divergences in methods of calculation mentioned above but also by the effects of differences in industrial structure on estimates of global product, even when the method of calculation is common.

[1] In these countries' accounts, therefore, agriculture is treated as though it consisted of two large enterprises, one producing crops and the other animals, the global product being free of internal turnover within each enterprise but gross of turnover between them. This method is sometimes referred to as the 'gross turnover' method.

[2] The recent policy of selling MTS machinery to farms, pursued in most countries of the area, therefore tends to reduce the value of the global product of agriculture outside the three countries mentioned. The CMEA working group mentioned above has recommended that the duplication of MTS services in the accounts be eliminated generally.

[3] Estimates have to be made, however, for private enterprises wherever such exist.

[4] The first Polish input–output table has recently been published (*Biuletyn Statystyczny*, no. 7, 1959).

[5] See the *Economic Survey of Europe* 1958, chapter I, section I.

The identity of net product and national income

The global product of any producing unit or group of units, such as an enterprise, an industrial branch or a whole sector, is always greater than the 'value added' within the production unit or sector at least by the value of material inputs received from outside (i.e. from other parts of the economy or from abroad). The additional margin of difference depends—as was shown above—on the choice of the calculating unit which determines the amount of intra-branch or intra-sector duplication. So far neither the gross product of industry nor that of the whole economy as defined in 'western' national accounts (i.e. the sum of value added in each production unit) has normally been published in most of the countries under review, though its calculation involves no technical problems. However, in Poland for the year 1956 'gross domestic product' thus defined[1] has been calculated, together with the corresponding products of individual sectors. The major aggregate represents the total value of production made available for use at home or abroad during the year, including the provision for domestic capital consumption but excluding any net addition to national resources provided by an import surplus. Similar total and sector gross products can also be derived for a series of years, at current prices only, from the data published in eastern Germany (see below).

The normal statistical practice in the planned economies, however, is to calculate, as the basic national accounting aggregate, the sum of the net products of all separately enumerated enterprises or branches (defined as the value of global product *minus* all material costs including capital depreciation). The value thus derived for the economy as a whole is referred to as 'net product'[2] or 'national income' or, more specifically, as 'national income produced' in Czechoslovakia and Poland, and 'production of national income' in the Soviet Union.

The characteristic feature of methods of calculating national accounting aggregates in the planned economies is the emphasis on the production approach; but official Polish sources indicate that the 'primary incomes' method is also used, particularly, it seems, for building up the net products of each economic sector.[3] Table 1, taken from the Polish 1956 White

---

[1] It is referred to in Poland as 'net global product' (*Produkt globalny netto*). It is conceptually identical with gross domestic product in 'western' national accounts, but the boundaries of production in the two cases are different.

[2] *Chisty produkt* in Russian and Polish; *Netto Produkt* in German.

[3] *Dochód narodowy Polski 1956*. A statement on p. 8 reveals that the product and the income approach are applied 'in parallel'. The description of methods used in calculating the net product of industry (p. 17) suggests that, at least in this sector, the value of material costs is derived by subtracting from the global product of industry the wage

[*Footnote continued on p.* 378

TABLE I. *Derivation of national income and the income elements of net product, Poland, 1956*
(Current prices)

Product	Millions of zlotys	Percentage distribution
Global (social) product	589,573.7	100.0
Production of goods	519,831.8	88.2
[*of which*: Increase in stock of finished output	1,058.1	0.2
Increase in work in progress	1,113.4	0.3]
Services[1]	46,665.9	7.9
Raw materials held for processing and typical semi-manufactures[2]	23,076.0	3.9
Material costs	332,884.8	100.0
of which:		
Materials	259,103.5	77.8
Energy and fuel	7,965.3	2.4
Amortization	19,840.1	6.0
Transport	11,556.3	3.5
Raw materials held for processing and typical semi-manufactures[2]	23,076.0	6.9
Produced national income	256,688.9	—

Elements of primary division of net product	Millions of zlotys	Percentage distribution
Wages and salaries	78,422.4	30.5
Net incomes of individual peasants	60,281.1	23.5
Incomes of production co-operatives (including individual plots)	766.5	0.3
Incomes of state farm workers from individual plots	1,437.3	0.6
Additional incomes of population from subsidiary occupations	5,002.0	1.9
Net profits in private sector (outside agriculture)	6,162.3	2.4
[*of which*: Net incomes of artisans	3,291.9	1.3]
Social insurance	11,809.1	4.6
Balance of budgetary payments	901.6	0.4
Enterprise taxes:		
Total	58,457.9	22.8
State	51,949.7	20.2
Co-operative	1,756.1	0.7
Private	4,752.1	1.9
[*of which*: Individual peasants	3,612.7	1.4]
Balance of profits or losses in socialized enterprises	10,349.5	4.0
Account of price differences in foreign trade	3,800.0	1.5
Produced national income	256,688.9	100.0

Source: Dochód Narodowy Polski 1956.

[1] Mainly the global output of transport, communications and trade, including the 'account of price differences in foreign trade'.

[2] This is the sum of two items separately specified in the more detailed tabulations; and each of them is apparently entered (with immediate direct offset) mainly for accounting convenience. Their coverage is not clear.

Paper, shows the identity of estimates derived by the two methods. Wages, salaries and other incomes refer naturally only to incomes of productive workers within the boundary of production discussed above. The meaning of the last item on the income side ('account of price differences in foreign trade') is explained in the section on foreign trade below.

Similar tabulations, including the break-down of material costs and the main elements of primary income distribution, are shown in Poland for the years 1955 and 1956 for each of the following sectors:[1] industry, agriculture, forestry, building and construction, transport and communications, economic turnover (including foreign trade), other production. Moreover, a summary tabulation of total material cost and of income break-down, including the turnover tax, is given for industrial branches. (For the percentage distribution and incidence of turnover tax, see Tables 2 and 3 below.)

In the Hungarian monograph on national income relating to 1956[2] the presentation of global and net product, and of national income, is somewhat different, and there are important differences in coverage. The basic table relates the global product on one side of the account to 'global expenditure' on the other side, the latter containing the item 'productive consumption' (i.e. the equivalent of 'material costs' in the Polish accounts). Moreover, the production side lists a number of break-downs of the global product: by sector of production, by sector of ownership and by destination (the groups I and II referred to below). Net domestic product by sector of origin is shown in a separate table which—characteristically—bears the title 'national income', although the total of sector ouputs is labelled 'net domestic product'. Primary distribution of incomes by sectors of origin and ownership is shown in still another table. In contrast to Polish accounts, the Hungarian tabulations give no details of material costs and no details for industrial branches. On the other hand, they provide a somewhat finer break-down into branches in the domestic trade sector, which is subdivided into wholesale and retail branches, with foreign trade given the status of a separate sector.

No other country publishes estimates of primary income break-down. In eastern Germany, statistics include series of global and net product (only at current prices) by sectors of origin, with amortization shown as a separate entry. In other countries publication practices with regard to the break-

fund of productive industrial workers, and accumulation. This estimate of total material costs is then broken down into detailed cost categories on the basis of financial reports of central boards (i.e. administrative bodies in charge of various industrial branches) on fulfilment of cost plans. Similarly, in Czechoslovakia, and in eastern Germany since 1958, both the product and the income approach seem now to be followed (*see* J. Kolár and O. Turek in *Wirtschaftswissenschaft*, no. 8, 1957).

[1] And within each economic sector for three ownership categories: state, co-operative and private.   [2] *Népgazdasági Mérlegek, Reáljövedelmek, 1956.*

down of net product by sector of origin vary, but the scope is in general very limited.[1] In the Soviet Union the only available series is a single index number of national income, and annual figures showing the percentage of the national income generated in the socialist sector.

With the scanty information at present available, a more detailed comparative analysis of sector break-downs and coverages is not feasible; but some differences between countries may be noted. The varying treatment of foreign trade from one country to another is a matter of major importance, and is described in the following subsection. Some other divergences in sector coverage are clearly significant: for example, in Czechoslovakia, Hungary, Rumania and the Soviet Union the dwellings built by individuals with their own means are included in 'construction', but in Poland in 'other production'. The latter sector includes in Poland also horse-carriage transport services provided by peasants, which in Hungary appear under 'transport'. In Bulgaria, the value of irrigation and other land melioration schemes is counted as a part of agricultural output. In Czechoslovakia, food processing by peasants and farm workers in the socialist sector is included in agricultural production, and the home processing of agricultural raw materials (such as textile fibres) by peasants appears under 'other production'; but in Poland and Rumania—and, it seems, in other countries—both these types of activity appear under 'other production'. In the Soviet Union the sector break-down (not published) seems to differ from that of other countries of the area in that 'material-technical supply' and 'procurement of agricultural produce' constitute separate sectors rather than a part of 'economic turnover' or 'internal trade'.[2]

The treatment of external trade

In all the countries under review the activities of those employed in foreign trade—as of those engaged in internal trade—are included within the boundary of production. But the treatment of the balance of foreign trade itself (imports and exports of goods and 'productive' services)[3] presents a difficult problem—owing essentially to the special characteristics of the price structures of these economies and the absence of a single exchange-rate effectively relating domestic to foreign trade prices. This problem has not been solved in the same manner in each country.

---

[1] For details see *Yearbook of National Accounts Statistics, 1958* (United Nations, New York, 1959).

[2] Moskvin, *op. cit.*

[3] At least in Czechoslovakia and Poland productive services are, in principle, included and it seems that, for practical reasons, some 'non-productive' services (e.g. passenger transport) may also be included in the balance of invisible trade. The coverage of the external trade balance in other countries is unknown.

In all eastern European countries, except eastern Germany, it is the practice to determine the export or import surplus for purposes of national accounting first of all in foreign exchange prices. The actual export (or import) surplus in foreign exchange prices converted to domestic values, in proportion to the difference between the domestic value and the foreign exchange value of total exports (or imports), is regarded as the appropriate measurement of the margin between 'national income produced' and domestically disposable national income (referred to as 'disposable income', 'distributed income' or 'finally realized income').[1]

But to preserve the identity of aggregate domestic expenditure in domestic prices (on personal and collective consumption and accumulation)[2] with domestic product—or national income produced—*minus* the export surplus (or *plus* the import surplus) it is then necessary that the sum of the net products of the various sectors of domestic output should be adjusted, before calculation of aggregate 'national income produced', so as to take into account the gain or loss of resources, valued at domestic prices, which results from an exact balance of imports and exports at foreign exchange prices (at the actual value of whichever is the lower). This price correction, referred to in the Polish accounts as 'account of price differences in foreign trade', is there shown as a separate entry in the tabulation of produced income by sectors of origin. In other countries, however, this item is included in the product of the foreign trade sector (Hungary) or of 'economic turnover' where foreign trade is not given the status of a separate sector (Czechoslovakia, Soviet Union).

The actual method of calculation of the price-correction factor may be illustrated as follows:[3]

	Exports	Imports	Import surplus
At domestic prices	150	225	75
At foreign trade prices	75	75	—
Ratio of domestic to foreign prices	2	3	
Gain or loss from price differences	−75	+150	

In this case there is no foreign trade surplus or deficit in foreign exchange prices, and there will therefore be no difference on this account between 'national income produced' and 'disposable national income'. The whole

---

[1] That is to say, this margin corresponds (apart from differences of coverage) to net external capital formation, or net foreign disinvestment, in 'western' national accounts.
[2] Measured, of course, in terms of the same material content as is applied in the income or product side of the account.
[3] See also Zienkowski, *op. cit.* and *Statistikai Szemle*, no. 2, 1956; and no. 7, 1957, where Hungarian practices are described in some detail.

difference (75) between the values of imports (225) and of exports (150) in domestic prices is treated as a gain to the economy—or to national product—resulting from the difference between the ratios of domestic to foreign prices for imports and for exports. In the computation of domestic product, 75 will be added either as a separate entry (in Poland) or to the net product of the trade sector (in other countries except eastern Germany).

It is, of course, more usual for foreign trade, in foreign exchange prices, not to balance:

Actual trade

	Exports	Imports	Import surplus
At domestic prices	200	225	25
At foreign trade prices	100	75	−25
Ratio of domestic to foreign prices	2	3	

'Compensating' trade

	Exports	Imports	Import surplus
At domestic prices	150	225	75
At foreign trade prices	75	75	—
Ratio of domestic to foreign prices	2	3	
Gain or loss from price differences	−75	+150	

The third row in each table above shows the ratios of domestic to foreign trade prices, for both exports and imports, which are used as conversion coefficients. At the level at which actual imports would be balanced by exports (both at foreign trade prices) there is a 75 units 'loss' on exports and a 150 units 'gain' on imports from the price differentials, so that the net gain—to be included in national income produced—is 75. There remains an actual export surplus in foreign trade prices of 25 which, converted to domestic values by means of the export price coefficient, becomes 50 in domestic prices; and this is entered in the national accounts as an export surplus of this amount. Thus the actual *import* surplus in domestic prices of 25 has been split into an 'account of price differences' of 75, which enters the accounts as an addition to produced income, and an *export* surplus of 50 to be deducted from that aggregate in arriving at 'distributed', or domestically disposable, income.

It seems that the method described above is followed in all the countries of the area (including the Soviet Union) with the exception of eastern Germany. There the domestic product contains no correction for price differences in foreign trade, and the balance of the values of imports and of exports in domestic prices is considered as the trade surplus and added to (or subtracted from) the domestic product for the evaluation of domestically disposable income.

The introduction of the 'account of price differences' in the accounts of other countries does not correct for the inconsistencies of their domestic price structures. At best it brings the value of foreign trade turnover into line, in some sense, with the internal price structure.[1] The 'gain' or the 'loss' on this account may be entirely illusory, depending on the extent to which internal price relatives reflect real relative costs. Moreover, the apparent gain or loss from foreign trade is a function of its structure, in the sense that the import of goods subject to turnover tax (most consumers' goods) or the export of goods free from this tax (investment goods) tend to increase the gain, and conversely. One consequence of the practice is that the apparent growth of domestic product may be significantly affected by marked changes in the level or structure of foreign trade.

Income and product flows

It was mentioned above that the volume of national accounts data published outside Poland and Hungary is restricted, at best, to the basic aggregates. Consequently, virtually no information is at present available on the magnitudes involved at the various intermediary stages of the process of redistribution of incomes and of product flows, although it is clear from the methodological discussions that such intermediate phases are in fact traced and corresponding accounts set up, at least in some countries such as the Soviet Union and Czechoslovakia.

It is, for example, the general practice to extend the flow of incomes from the primary stage (consisting, in accordance with the concept of boundary of production discussed above, solely of income generated by productive workers) to the final distribution of national income between material consumption and accumulation, so as to reveal the generation and expenditure of 'derivative' personal income (i.e. incomes earned in the non-productive sectors). A simplified scheme of such an extended flow,[2] taken from a Polish publication, is shown in Chart 1.

The first distribution of generated income takes place at the primary stage, a part of the net value of output accruing to the productive workers in the form of the wage fund and the remaining part forming a 'social

---

[1] A negative price differential in foreign trade may be looked upon as the result of un-realistically high net product realized in industry, and conversely (S. Ferge, *Statistikai Szemle*, no. 2, 1956). The introduction of this correction may thus be viewed as an attempt to eliminate partly (i.e. with regard to foreign trade), the distorting effect of a price system divorced from real cost.

[2] It assumes an isolated economy and full public ownership of the means of production.

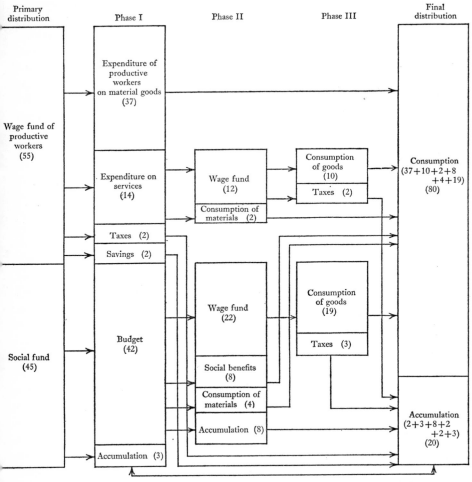

Chart 1. Distribution and redistribution of national income. (The numbers in parentheses are hypothetical.) *Source*: L. Zienkowski, *Jak oblicza się dochód narodowy* (Warsaw, 1959).

fund'.[1] Productive workers spend their incomes largely on consumption of material goods, and this part of their expenditure reappears directly

[1] According to Marxist theory, in a capitalist system of production this part corresponds, broadly speaking, to the concept of 'surplus value'—i.e. that part of the value created by productive workers which is largely appropriated by the owners of means of production. In eastern European countries where a private sector is still in existence, primary distribution includes a third category consisting of non-wage incomes accruing to private producers (mainly peasants) a part of which is then transferred through taxes to the State budget.

within 'consumption' in the final distribution of national income between consumption and accumulation. The remainder of their expenditure—on services—contains some elements of material cost (i.e. cost of materials used in institutions of the non-productive sphere which also reappear directly in aggregate consumption) and also generates a new fund of incomes accruing to non-productive workers. These incomes are spent directly on material consumption and taxes in the simplified scheme illustrated in the chart; but they can of course be subjected to further redistribution in fact.

A relatively small part of the social fund is accumulated at the enterprise level ('retained profits'), but most of it goes into the budget in the form of turnover tax, deductions from profits and other levies, from which payments are made to the employees of non-productive institutions (i.e. in administration, health, education, etc.) and to the beneficiaries of social welfare schemes. These personal incomes may again be either directly consumed or spent on services, thus giving rise to further redistribution. A relatively large part of the budget directly finances investment.

The process of redistribution lasts until all personal incomes are either spent on material goods or saved (accumulated). Since the sum of primary incomes equals by definition the value of net product, it follows that—at least in the absence of foreign trade—the identity of product, income and expenditure aggregates is preserved.

The Polish and Hungarian published tabulations include all the elements of primary distribution and some elements of the redistributive stages (as was noted above); in the Soviet Union, apparently, more systematic efforts are made to construct intermediate accounts corresponding to the various stages of income redistribution.[1]

Similarly, the statistical practices of the Soviet Union and Czechoslovakia include attempts to show commodity (and productive services) flows from the production stage to that of final use, or final distribution of national income. The starting-point is the distribution between 'means of production' (group I) and 'means (or objects) of consumption' (group II), obtained essentially by segregation of enterprises according to the predominant use of their products. Each group consists of two principal subgroups: group I: Goods and services for productive consumption and for

---

[1] The mode of tabulation adopted in the Soviet Union is shown in Moskvin, *op. cit.* p. 110. The separate calculations of 'balances of money incomes and expenditures of the population', which are being made in varying detail in all the countries of the area, make it possible—on the one hand—to assess the over-all volume of purchasing power generated over the year and its distribution among various sectors of the economy and socio-economic groups, and—on the other—to study the structure of consumers' expenditure, including expenditure on services.

productive accumulation; group II: Goods and services for non-productive consumption and for non-productive accumulation. Goods for productive consumption are goods used up in the process of production, whilst those for non-productive consumption are final consumers' goods. The sum of goods for productive and non-productive accumulation should equal gross capital formation, assuming no foreign trade surplus or deficit. The value of the consumption fund is usually obtained as the residual of the total value of goods and services in group II less those destined for non-productive accumulation (again assuming an exact balance of foreign trade).

The Hungarian published statistics also show the break-down of total product into the two large groups but without further subdivision.

2. THE DISTRIBUTION OF NATIONAL EXPENDITURE

In an isolated economy the sum of 'net value added' over a year, within the chosen boundary of production, can be either consumed or invested in the domestic economy. The existence of external trade faces the computer of national accounts with the possibility of calculating two end-use aggregates, one showing the volume of goods and services actually consumed or devoted to domestic investment (or accumulation) over the year, the second including also future claims on or obligations to foreigners acquired during the year. In most eastern European countries there seems to be a tendency to concentrate attention on the aggregate physical resources available for use within the country, this magnitude differing from the value of 'national income produced' by the extent of the foreign trade surplus or deficit and of extraordinary (or unplanned) losses.[1] It is referred to as 'disposable income' in eastern Germany, 'distributed income' in Poland and 'finally realized income' in Czechoslovakia. The same approach seems also to be followed in Rumania and in Bulgaria,[2] but the practice of the Soviet Union is less certain. The Hungarian statistics, on the other hand, present a break-down of end-uses inclusive of the foreign trade surplus or deficit and introduce no separate label for the sum of domestic consumption and accumulation.

[1] Planned losses are generally accounted for on the product side as an element of cost of production.
[2] For the latter country the series of statistics of national expenditure, published in the *Yearbook of National Accounts Statistics, 1958* (United Nations, New York, 1959), consists of two entries only (consumption and accumulation). The sum of these two is there referred to as 'net material product' but seems more likely to be domestically disposable income. An exact check is, however, impossible, since the 1956 statistical yearbook of Bulgaria refers to both the product and the expenditure totals as 'national income' and the value of the former is given in 1952 prices and that of the latter in 1939 prices.

However, the user of published eastern European and Soviet statistics needs to bear in mind, first, that the published trends of loosely defined 'national income' may refer either to 'income produced' or to 'disposable (distributed or realized) income' and, secondly, that references to the shares of consumption or of investment (or accumulation) in national income are likely to refer in some countries to percentages of a total consisting only of domestic consumption and domestic accumulation, in others to shares in national income produced.

Consumption

In all eastern European countries except eastern Germany the definition of consumption (within the chosen 'material' boundary of production) is similar to that adopted in 'western' national accounts in that all durable consumers' goods, except dwellings, are considered to be consumed at the moment of acquisition by the consumer. In eastern Germany, however, the concept of consumption is appreciably wider (and that of accumulation correspondingly narrower) in that it includes the net increment in the value of non-productive construction (dwellings, schools, hospitals, etc.) and capital repairs to such buildings during the year.

The national accounts of all planned economies make a distinction between personal (or individual) and collective (or social) consumption, somewhat analogous to the break-down in 'western' accounts into private and Government consumption. The classification of expenditure incurred by public institutions to satisfy directly the consumption needs of their members or residents (for instance the value of food consumed by members of the armed forces, of milk and meals supplied in schools or of medicaments furnished to hospital patients) is not entirely uniform; but it seems that, outside Czechoslovakia, this type of expenditure is now everywhere counted in personal consumption.[1]

Personal consumption also everywhere includes, in addition to the value of goods and material services consumed by individuals, the depreciation of dwellings.[2] In principle, the latter entry is based on a notional concept of amortization of dwellings, but in some countries—for instance, in Poland—the estimated cost of capital repairs actually incurred during the year is substituted.[3] The exclusion of actual or imputed rent from personal

[1] In the Polish accounts this applies only since 1956; in the Soviet Union there is an additional account of sources of finance, in which such expenditure is shown as collective.
[2] In Czechoslovakia, the depreciation of privately owned dwellings only.
[3] This of course tends to reduce the volume and the share of consumption in times of under-maintenance of the housing stock; the adoption of the notional concept of amortization results in the treatment of the difference between the notional value and actual outlays on repairs as capital loss.

consumption constitutes a major difference between the definitions of this aggregate in the countries under review and elsewhere; combined with the exclusion of other consumers' services, it makes virtually impossible the comparison of indicators of trends of personal consumption, or of its share in national income, in any of these countries with similar indicators in others. The Hungarian accounts list separately, as components of personal consumption, foodstuffs, manufactures, and heat and light, broken down (in the 1956 monograph) by source of purchase. The Polish 1956–7 White Paper distinguishes between food and non-food articles purchased by the consumer and those obtained free. An additional table shows a detailed break-down of personal consumption by articles—the only tabulation of this kind available for any eastern European country.

Collective consumption includes, as a rule,[1] the value of raw materials, fuel, energy and material services used up in enterprises, institutions and organizations outside the productive sphere (passenger transport, health and educational services, administration, defence, etc.) and the depreciation of non-productive fixed assets, other than dwellings. It is usually subdivided into consumption in enterprises and institutions rendering non-material services to the population and that in 'other institutions', mainly public administration and defence.

Accumulation

The accumulation fund is equivalent to that part of 'disposable (distributed or finally realized) income' which is not directly consumed, and thus it normally excludes external investment or disinvestment (i.e. the net surplus or deficit on the current balance of payments).[2] Alternatively, starting with the global social product, accumulation can be derived as follows: global social product *plus* import surplus (or *minus* export surplus) *minus* productive consumption (including amortization) *minus* non-productive consumption *minus* losses.

There has always been a tendency—explicit or implied—in Marxist thinking, to identify accumulation with the concept of 'extended reproduction'. Those goods are accumulated which contribute directly to further production, in contrast to goods consumed which are the result of 'simple reproduction'. A strict observance of these identities would necessitate the exclusion of non-productive investment (dwellings, schools, hospitals, etc.) from the concept of accumulation, since this type of investment has no direct bearing on future production. In fact, as was noted above, only

[1] The different coverages in Czechoslovakia and eastern Germany were noted above.
[2] But as is noted below there seems to be some confusion in the treatment of changes in gold and foreign exchange reserves in some countries.

eastern Germany adheres to this narrow concept of accumulation. All other countries adopt a wider definition, distinguishing at the same time between accumulation of productive and of non-productive fixed assets.[1] The main elements in accumulation are: (*a*) net change in fixed assets; (*b*) change in uncompleted construction; (*c*) change in circulating (working) capital (i.e. stocks and work in progress); and (*d*) change in State reserves. In the Soviet Union, however, the last item appears to constitute a separate fund excluded from the accumulation fund proper.[2]

In the tabulations of eastern Germany and Poland both the first two and the last two categories are combined. In Poland, the sum of (*a*) and (*b*) is referred to as 'net investment' and is subdivided into productive and non-productive investment; in Hungary and the Soviet Union, however, the increase in uncompleted construction is grouped together with changes in stocks. The Hungarian and Polish 1956 accounts show the break-down of net fixed investment by production sectors (but not by branches of industry).

Fixed investment includes the value of capital repairs and the imputed value of activities performed by the population on a 'self-help' basis (e.g. irrigation works carried out by collective farmers). In most countries a distinction is made between breeding livestock and draught animals on the one hand, which are treated as fixed assets, and other livestock which are included under working capital. In the Soviet Union, however, it seems that the total change in livestock is distinguished as a separate item of accumulation. The net growth of forests (i.e. the difference between the annual growth and annual cut less other losses) appears in eastern Germany's accounts together with working capital, but in Czechoslovakia—and it seems in other countries—as an increase in fixed assets.

Changes in State reserves include, *inter alia*, variations in strategic stocks held by the Government.[3] It seems that in Poland at least gold and foreign currency reserves are also included,[4] though this appears inconsistent with the treatment of foreign trade, and the definition of disposable income, described above.

---

[1] The distinction between total productive and non-productive accumulation is more difficult—if not impossible—to make, since the allocation of stocks and State reserves between the two categories must of necessity be arbitrary.

[2] M. Z. Bor, *Balans narodnogo khozyaistva SSSR* (Moscow, 1956), pp. 95–8.

[3] In the Soviet Union (in 1956) 'the reserve fund comprises, first, State material reserves of a long-term character, secondly, reserves of defence goods of a special nature and, thirdly, current operational reserves of the Council of Ministers used in the course of annual plan fulfilment for the satisfaction of current needs as they arise'. (Bor, *op. cit.* p. 97.)

[4] It has been forcefully argued (see for instance L. Zienkowski, *op. cit.* p. 83) that the nature of such reserves is, from the point of view of national accounting, identical with outstanding external credits or debts, and that it is illogical not to treat the two categories in a similar way—i.e. either to include or to exclude changes in both from accumulation.

The value of accumulation and of its constituents is always shown net of amortization, in accordance with the 'net' concept of national income normally used. Linear depreciation rates are applied to the sum of original value of assets and anticipated capital repairs;[1] and the calculation of net fixed investment consists in adding the value of capital repairs to gross investment and then subtracting depreciation charges, fixed according to established norms.[2] The procedure is similar for the calculation of increases in the net value of both productive and non-productive assets. In the case of non-productive assets the amount of amortization allowed is identical with the (positive) entry in the consumption account (see above).

'Investment outlays' and increases in fixed investments

Since amortization for the economy as a whole, and for its parts, is easily available, the calculation of gross national product—and of other magnitudes on a gross basis—need present no accounting difficulties; and it was noted above that such aggregates have been published in Poland. However, the statistics of 'investment outlays'[3] regularly published (in value or at least as an index) in all eastern European and the Soviet statistical yearbooks,[4] do not represent gross capital formation as obtainable from national accounts by adding amortization to the net increment in fixed assets (inclusive of uncompleted construction).

The concept of investment outlays is geared to the planning of investment expenditures and provides an operative indicator, available also on a very short-term basis, of the fulfilment of such plans. For the overwhelming majority of projects the amounts actually spent over a period are reported by enterprises and credit institutions, and in some countries—Bulgaria, Czechoslovakia and Poland—these are supplemented by estimates of expenditure of funds derived from other sources.[5] Outside eastern Germany, investment outlays invariably exclude the cost of capital repairs. They also usually exclude the value of changes in livestock numbers (except

---

[1] The Statistical Office of the United Nations, *Concepts and Definitions of Capital Formation* (Statistical Papers F 3) recommends that 'only those repair costs which materially lengthen the anticipated economic life of the asset or raise its productivity be treated as capital formation' (p. 13). The Soviet definition of capital repair by and large coincides with this—e.g. 'In practice capital repair is usually associated with the process of modernizing equipment, raising its technical level or its capacity' (*Kratky ekonomichesky slovar*, 1958, p. 118).

[2] This method of calculation is very similar to that applied, for example, in Norway.

[3] In Russian, *Kapitalnye vlozheniya*.

[4] In eastern Germany, operational statistics corresponding to investment outlays, and published quarterly, refer to investment in the State sector only and include capital repairs of productive assets. Annual figures, published for the first time in the 1958 statistical yearbook, have the same coverage except that they include all capital repairs. The Soviet data exclude private investment, as do the Albanian.

[5] In practice, mainly expenditure on privately financed dwelling construction.

in Rumania) and of the natural growth of forests, as well as (outside Bulgaria) the value of construction work performed on a voluntary and unpaid basis. On the other hand they include 'wasted' expenditure, such as outlays on projects subsequently abandoned.

For the countries in which investment outlays include private as well as public investment expenditure, the increase in net fixed assets can be derived as follows: Investment outlays *plus* capital repairs *plus* the value of activities on a 'self-help' basis *plus* increase in breeding livestock and draught animals[1] *plus* natural growth of forests[1] *minus* depreciation *minus* capital losses (including abandoned projects and the value of scrapped assets not fully amortized) *minus* uncompleted construction.

One of the advantages of the reporting system in the planned economies is that net fixed investment in the State sector can be determined directly from enterprise accounts. As a rule, enterprises keep inventory cards for each fixed asset, carrying its initial value and subsequent changes in net value due to depreciation and capital repairs up to the point of final disposal. The difference between the aggregate net values of fixed assets at two points of time corresponds to net fixed investment (without uncompleted construction). This identity is, however, true only for the national economy as a whole, since enterprise inventories record transfers of assets between enterprises. Aggregate changes in such inventory values are published everywhere[2] except in eastern Germany and Poland; full capital accounts by economic sectors are regularly published in Hungary.

3. PROBLEMS OF VALUATION AND OF INTERNATIONAL COMPARISON

Some aspects of price formation in planned economies

In national accounting in eastern Europe and the Soviet Union, goods and productive services are valued at the prices at which transactions take place —the so-called 'realized prices'.[3] This approach resembles the market price valuation of 'western' accounting practice, in that realized prices include indirect taxes and subsidies. This conceptual similarity, however, masks the effect of actual valuation methods on the size, structure and dynamics of national income aggregates, stemming essentially from the different nature of price formation in the two types of economic system.

---

[1] In eastern Germany this item appears under working capital.
[2] Either in absolute figures or in index numbers.
[3] Realized prices are different from the 'factory prices' or 'planned prices' which are the normal basis of valuation of current statistics (including index numbers) of industrial output. These current statistics are thus not comparable with the corresponding elements in the global social product in the national accounts.

In the planned economies, where the majority of prices are administratively determined, a distinction is made between the prices of consumers' goods and of producers' materials and equipment. Whereas the prices of goods exchanged among producers are fixed around (or even sometimes below) their labour cost (wage-bill) plus depreciation charge, consumers' goods carry a high turnover tax which constitutes the basic financial source of centrally planned accumulation. Although indirect taxes are imposed on consumers' goods in all countries, and on some articles (particularly tobacco and alcohol) are frequently quite high, the volume of turnover tax in the planned economies is of a different order of magnitude from indirect taxation in most other countries.[1] In 1957, for instance, the ratio of turnover tax receipts to the tax-inclusive value of retail trade (which accounts for an overwhelming share of the total market value of goods subject to turnover tax) varied from around one-third in Poland, to around one-half in Bulgaria, Czechoslovakia, Rumania and the Soviet Union, and as much as two-thirds in Hungary.

Another feature of the price systems in eastern Europe and the Soviet Union is the multiplicity of prices, resulting both from the fact that a particular commodity carries a very different price when sold to the consumer from its price when sold to another producer, and from the varied nature of transactions—each valued at a different price—on the agricultural producers' market.[2] The range of farm prices varies from the low—sometimes below-cost—prices (involving an element of tax) paid by the State for compulsory deliveries, through considerably higher prices for contractual deliveries, to free market prices obtained by the peasants in direct sales to the consumer[3] which, as a rule, are the nearest to those charged by the State retail network.[4] the elimination, or reduction of the volume, of compulsory deliveries and increases in prices paid for them in most countries of the area in recent years, have gone a long way to narrow the range. Nevertheless, the existence of price differentials, and changes in the structure of agricultural sales, have an important impact on the value

[1] This is one reflection of the widely differing methods of tax collection, and of the different roles played by taxation in the financing of investment, in the two main types of economy.

[2] A single price for a given commodity is also rare in free market economies. However, in these economies the spread of prices for a given commodity tends to be a reflection of transport cost differentials and market imperfections. In planned economies multiple prices are built into the system, and the range is frequently so wide that the selection of a representative price offers considerable difficulties.

[3] Still different sets of prices are used in the relations between the State and the State farms.

[4] For instance, in Hungary the following prices were quoted in 1956 for wheat (in forints per quintal): compulsory deliveries, 75; contractual deliveries, 280; free market, 320.

of agricultural production and on its share in national product (see below). Moreover, the diversification of prices gives rise to the problem of valuing goods consumed by their producers (self-consumption). It is now a general rule that self-consumption by peasant households is measured—for the calculation of agricultural output and of personal consumption—at a weighted average price, which takes into account the weights and prices of all types of transaction.[1]

In fixing prices, little or no allowance is made in the planned economies for the scarcity of capital and land, following the principle that the only factor of production is labour (in pricing only 'living' labour is counted since 'embodied' labour is assumed to have been remunerated in the past). Thus the exclusion of turnover taxes would not result in magnitudes corresponding to the 'factor cost' calculations which, in other countries, enable the distorting effects of indirect taxes and subsidies to be eliminated from the values at market prices of the main national accounting aggregates. The deduction of turnover tax would rather correspond to valuation at prime costs.

The impact of price systems on the structure of national income and expenditure

Although it is impossible to determine the precise influence of valuation methods currently applied on the relative weights of the various components of national income and expenditure, certain tendencies—to be borne in mind in any comparative studies—can be identified.

On the product side, the share of agriculture in national product tends to be under-valued for three main reasons: the freedom of the agricultural sector from turnover taxes, and the under-pricing both of compulsory deliveries and of self-consumption.[2] Polish calculations (see Table 2) show that the elimination of turnover and other taxes and subsidies would have increased the apparent share of agriculture in total product in 1956 from around 28 per cent to 33 per cent; and a similar, though less precise, calculation for Hungary indicates an increase from around 32 per cent to 41 per cent. The re-calculation of the value of self-consumption in retail trade prices, mentioned above, was shown in Poland (in 1954) to increase

[1] In Poland, however, the 1956 and 1957 calculations were based on contractual delivery prices. The 1954 and 1955 computations introduced two sets of aggregates: one based on the weighted average concept and the other on urban retail trade prices reduced by the trade margin (see the *Survey* for 1958, chapter IV, p. 5).

[2] It may be noted that whenever a policy of stable retail prices of food is followed, any increase in prices paid to the peasants for compulsory deliveries (or decline in the volume of such deliveries) not only increases the value of agricultural product, but forces a reduction of the value of output of the food industry via a diminution of turnover tax on processed foods.

TABLE 2. Net product and taxes by sectors of origin in Poland and Hungary, 1950
(Percentages)

Sector	Poland			Hungary		
	Share of turnover tax in the net product at realized prices	Share of the sector in net domestic product		Share of taxes in the net product[3]	Share of the sector	
		At realized prices[1]	At conventional prices[2]		In net domestic product at realized prices[1]	In 'total labour cost'[4]
Industry	41·3	49·5	40·1	57·2	45·3	36·4
Building	0·1	8·8	11·6	0·5	6·2	9·9
Agriculture	—	27·9	32·5	} 8·5	31·6	40·6
Forestry	23·1	1·0	1·1	{	3·4	4·7
Freight transport	2·8	2·9	3·7	27·4	13·2	8·0
Trade[5]	12·0	7·8	8·2	40·7	0·3	0·4
Other sectors[6]	—	2·1	2·8	—		
Net domestic product[5]	21·3	100·0	100·0	35·2	100·0	100·0

Note: The net product at 'conventional' prices has been calculated by the Polish Statistical Office, but only the percentage distribution was published in the second White Paper.

It appears that, for all sectors outside agriculture, net product at conventional prices corresponds roughly to total labour cost (including social insurance), and was arrived at by subtracting turnover tax and some other minor taxes from the net values of output at 'realized' prices and by adding subsidies. In agriculture the net income of the producers was considered as the equivalent of the total labour cost. Consequently, the total output (whether marketed, self-consumed or used as intermediate input) was re-priced at the weighted average price paid for marketed output and inputs where then deducted. Since in making this calculation the desire was to eliminate the distorting effects of turnover tax on apparent relative sector outputs, rather than to eliminate turnover tax from the evaluation of original total net domestic product, the second stage of the calculation was the redistribution of original total net domestic product among the different sectors in proportion to their shares in the total resulting from the above calculation. It may be noted that this whole computation is made in domestic prices, making no allowance for the 'gain' or 'loss' to the economy resulting from the foreign trade price differentials.

The figures shown for Hungary, under 'total labour cost', are a rough and ready calculation made by the secretariat on the basis of data published in the monograph (p. 86) mentioned at the beginning of this article, with the intention of adjusting them to the Polish concept. For each sector the figures include the wage cost (plus 10 per cent for social insurance) and the total net income of private producers. Since agricultural production has been already initially calculated at weighted average selling prices, no adjustment was necessary. The output of the foreign trade sector is, however, excluded.

It should be remembered that 1956 was not a typical year for Hungarian national income (but data allowing for a similar calculation are not available for any other year). The share of foreign trade in national product was exceptionally high and that of heavy industries very low. Consequently, turnover taxes had also an exceptionally high share in the national income.

[1] Including turnover taxes and subsidies.
[2] Labour cost plus a small margin of profit (for details of calculation see note above).
[3] Mainly turnover taxes, but including also some 7 per cent direct taxes (almost entirely in the private sector).
[4] Wage cost plus the total net income of private producers (for details see note above).
[5] Including a small allowance for the labour cost of conducting foreign trade in Poland (but not the 'loss' or 'gain' due to the price differential), and excluding both in Hungary.
[6] Some branches classified under this heading in Poland appear in building, freight transport or trade in Hungary.

the share of agriculture from 25·3 per cent to 30 per cent of national product.[1]

The impact of turnover taxes and subsidies in Poland and Hungary on the shares of other sectors is also illustrated in Table 2. Tax-levying practices vary among the countries of planned economies: in Czechoslovakia, turnover taxes are raised exclusively in industry, in the Soviet Union and in Hungary partly in industry and partly in trade, and in eastern Germany before 1955 they were collected almost exclusively in trade but have since been raised in industry. In the last-named country the value in current prices of the net output of trade was virtually the same in 1955 as in 1958, when the change in the method of tax collection occurred, although the value of retail trade in current prices increased over this period by more than 20 per cent.

The incidence of the turnover tax not only increases considerably the share of industry as a whole in national product, but affects the weights of industrial branches, generally exaggerating the importance of the light and food industries as compared with heavy industry. Thus, at 'conventional prices' (see the note to Table 2) the share of food industry in total industrial output in Poland in 1956 becomes only 12·5 per cent, rather than 30·7 per cent at 'realized' prices, whereas that of engineering increases from 15·7 per cent to 24·9 per cent (see Table 3). In relation to a factor cost basis of calculation as applied in 'western' economies this particular bias would be greater, since the capital-intensive branches of industry are relatively under-valued by omission of interest on capital as well as by the present lowness of depreciation rates in all countries except Czechoslovakia.

Finally, the share of the foreign trade sector in the countries where it includes the 'account of price differences' is very senstitive to the composition of exports and imports. The output of this sector will thus be the greater, the higher the share of consumers' goods carrying turnover tax in total imports and the smaller the share of investment goods in exports.

On the expenditure side of the national accounts, the downward bias in the share of accumulation due to the incidence of the turnover tax may be somewhat offset by the under-valuation of self-consumption and by the lowness of depreciation rates. An upward adjustment of amortization rates for productive assets would reduce the value of total net accumulation still further; a similar correction for non-productive assets would have a double effect, not only diminishing the accumulation fund, but increasing

---

[1] In the break-downs of global social product, published in Bulgaria, eastern Germany and Rumania, the share of agriculture is further depressed by the higher incidence of duplication in other sectors. In 1957 in Rumania, for example, the share of agriculture in global product was 31 per cent and in net national product 40 per cent.

TABLE 3. *Turnover taxes in the product of Polish industry in 1956*
(Percentages)

	Share of turn-over tax in the net product at realized prices	Share of the branch in the net product of industry at realized prices	Share of the branch in the net product of industry at conventional prices
Energy	19·2	1·7	2·2
Coal mining	7·2[1]	7·3	15·1
Ferrous metallurgy and mining	15·8	3·9	6·5
Non-ferrous metallurgy and mining	0·0	1·0	1·6
Engineering	4·0	15·7	24·9
Chemical industry	28·6	3·3	3·8
Rubber industry	53·6	1·0	0·8
Mineral extraction	0·0	0·1	0·1
Building materials	2·3[1]	2·4	4·4
Glass and china	6·5	0·8	1·3
Wood products	10·4	3·3	4·8
Paper	11·0	0·8	1·2
Textiles	62·3	18·0	11·2
Ready-made clothing	1·4	2·2	3·6
Leather, furs, shoes	60·3	4·8	3·2
Fats, oils, soap, cosmetics	68·5	1·1	0·6
Food industry	75·3	30·7	12·5
Salt	82·3	0·2	0·1
Printing	16·0	1·2	1·6
Other industries	43·1	0·5	0·5
All industries	42·7	100·0	100·0

Source: Dochód narodowy Polski 1956.
[1] Deficit industries if subsidies are considered.

the consumption fund, since the depreciation of non-productive assets is a positive item in consumption.

The effect of eliminating turnover taxes and subsidies on the structure of expenditure in Poland in 1956 is shown in Table 4. Net accumulation is thus raised from 20·2 per cent to 26·8 per cent, and net investment from 14·6 per cent to 19·4 per cent, of total distributed income. No such calculations exist for other countries; but it was officially stated in Hungary that the share of net fixed investment in national income in the early 1950s was of the order of 35–40 per cent based on labour cost, compared with 25–30 per cent on the basis of realized prices.[1]

[1] *Adatok és Adalékok a népgazdasag fejlödésének tanulmanyorasahoz* (Budapest, 1957), p. 113.

TABLE 4. *Structure of distributed income in realized and*
in conventional prices in Poland in 1956

	At realized prices	At conventional prices
Total distributed income	100·0	100·0
Consumption	79·8	73·2
Personal	74·5	68·5
Collective	5·3	4·7
Accumulation	20·2	26·8
Net investment	14·6	19·4
[*of which:*		
In productive sphere	9·2	12·2
In non-productive sphere	5·4	7·2]
Increase in stocks and reserves	5·6	7·4

Source: As for Table 3.
Note: In calculating net national income for distribution, the computations described in the note to Table 2 were carried a stage further by adjusting net domestic product at conventional prices so as to take into account the foreign trade balance. This (in fact an import surplus) was evaluated by valuing imports at the estimated domestic labour cost of the exports necessary to pay for them in full.

The existence of the biases noted above is generally recognized by statisticians in the countries concerned.[1] Most of them, however, do not propose to introduce into accounting prices charges for other factors than labour; but rather to adjust the relative prices of goods to the relative amounts of socially necessary labour spent on their production. Hence, for instance, the Polish 'conventional price' calculations which, it was hoped, might reveal a basis for a better comparability of the national accounts of the planned economies. Some Polish statisticians have also proposed to give more attention to national income aggregates gross of amortization, since it is obvious that the present widely differing national rates of depreciation reduce the validity of international comparisons.[2]

[1] See, for instance, Kolár and Turek, *op. cit.*; Zienkowski, *op. cit.*; S. Ferge, *Statistikai Szemle*, no. 7, 1957; M. Bor, *Voprosy Ekonomiki*, no. 1, 1958.
[2] See L. Zienkowski, *Przeglad Statystyczny*, no. 1, 1959. V. Nemchinov argues in an article in *Voprosy Ekonomiki*, no. 4, 1959, that the employment of modern electronic equipment could be helpful in recalculating various national accounting magnitudes in prices equivalent to their inputs of socially necessary labour. D. Allakhverdyan (*op. cit.* p. 137) also expresses concern with valuation problems and the lack of attention so far given to them:
  'In recent years the State Planning Commission of the USSR has devoted itself in its operational economic planning primarily to elaborating material production and consumption balances of individual products. There has been considerably less concern with economic balances, the elaboration of which is based upon the application of measurements in value and money. Computation in value (money) permits the com-

The comparability of trends of national income estimates

The exact significance of the impact of the restrictive concept of the area of production in the planned economies on their estimates of the rate of growth of national income at constant prices remains in doubt. Considering the post-war emphasis on rapid industrialization in all countries of the area, it seems highly probable that, at least until recently, the rate of growth of national income recorded in these countries would have been somewhat smaller—in some countries perhaps significantly smaller—had 'non-productive' services been included in the net product. On the other hand, it is not unlikely that the growing attention given to consumers' services in general, and to housing in particular, during the last few years may have changed this situation. It is for this reason, as well as for the sake of comparability with trends in other countries, that suggestions have been made in eastern Europe to extend the current concepts of boundary of production, or at least to allow for alternative tabulations.[1]

Among the effects of valuation practices, the relative under-valuation of agriculture at the time of its relative stagnation and the over-valuation of industry at the time of its rapid growth have undoubtedly contributed to a somewhat exaggerated rate of growth of total product in all countries. Moreover, the addition of new products to estimates of total output (otherwise calculated at constant prices of a fairly distant base year) at the prices at which they first entered significantly into production tended to have a similar effect. On the other hand, the relative under-valuation of heavy vis-à-vis light industry, while the development of heavy industry was accorded priority, probably imparted a downward bias to the rate of growth of industry as a whole.

The distortions of trends of volume which might have been caused by multiple pricing (for example, an increase in the net output of agriculture measured at constant multiple prices could be caused by a decline in the volume of compulsory deliveries or of self-consumption) have been avoided in some countries by applying to each product subject to multiple pricing a single price representing the weighted average of all prices in the chosen base year.[2] Although the choice of the base year has a negligible effect on

mensurability of the material-physical elements of reproduction. However, the scientific investigation of the problems of the balance of accumulation and consumption in the national income still falls short of the needs of the economic life of the country. No global tabular balance of the national economy is drawn up which would embrace all the main aspects of the process of expanding socialist reproduction.'

[1] See, for instance, W. Brus, in *Zycie Gospodarcze*, no. 8, 1959.

[2] Calculations at constant multiple prices are retained, however, for purposes of economic planning because of the need to maintain the links between national income aggregates and other balances of the national economy, such as the balance of money incomes and expenditures.

the dynamics of the output of the given sector, it will affect the weight of that sector in the total and it may also influence the trend in related processing sectors. If, for instance, the base year is one in which the share of low-priced compulsory deliveries and self-consumption in agricultural production was high, subsequent increases in the degree of commercial trading or processing of agricultural produce will give an upward bias to the net output of trade and of the processing industry.

Another factor affecting estimates at constant prices is the periodical revaluation of capital stock which tends to increase total depreciation very substantially on account of past under-valuation,[1] and results in a complete break in the continuity of historical national income series.

It is clear, therefore, that the data referring to trends in national income, or in sectors of income or expenditure, 'indicate correctly only broad tendencies and should be treated as approximate magnitudes only'.[2] This is true, in some degree, of all national accounts; but the biases in the estimates of the countries under review—aggravated by the quick structural shifts and violent changes in price relatives in the post-war period—are of a different order from those in most other countries.

---

[1] In Hungary in 1958, for instance, global coefficients of revaluation were used as a substitute for a complete inventory reassessment, and depreciation totals were raised two to three times.

[2] *Dochód narodowy Polski 1956*, p. 10.

Index

Index

Index